W9-CBX-226

A NOTE FROM THE AUTHOR

Welcome to Advanced Placement (AP) Human Geography. I congratulate you on the purchase of this book, because you are about to embark upon a course that will help you to better understand our world and our place within it.

AP Human Geography is among the fastest growing Advanced Placement subjects, for good reason. It is a truly exciting field of study that provides students with a greater understanding of how humankind's relationship with the Earth has shaped our history and development, as well as how geographers work to help us gain insight into our world. This field of study attracts more and more students each year, and tens of thousands of students seek to test their knowledge on the AP exam. An in-depth understanding of human geography is crucial for achieving success on the exam. This book will give students an edge on test day, with a targeted review of the AP Human Geography course and practical strategies for success on the exam.

You have decided to pursue a course of study that will both challenge you and illuminate your world, and for this you should be commended. Now it's time for you to demonstrate just how much you've learned.

Best of luck,

Kelly Swanson

RELATED TITLES

AP® HUMAN GEOGRAPHY

2016

Kelly Swanson

PUBLISHING

New York

AP® is a registered trademark of the College Board, which was not involved in the production of, and does not endorse, this product.

This publication is designed to provide accurate and authoritative information in regard to the subject matter covered. It is sold with the understanding that the publisher is not engaged in rendering legal, accounting, or other professional service. If legal advice or other expert assistance is required, the services of a competent professional should be sought.

© 2015 Kaplan, Inc.

Published by Kaplan Publishing, a division of Kaplan, Inc.
750 Third Avenue
New York, NY 10017

All rights reserved. The text of this publication, or any part thereof, may not be reproduced in any manner whatsoever without written permission from the publisher.

Material used in this book was adapted from the following:

"German Map Showing Europe in 1940," "Colorado Feedlots," and "Oklahoma Township and Range Land-Use Pattern" reprinted by permission of Westermann, Braunschweig/Germany, Copyright © 2007.

Printed in the United States of America

10 9 8 7 6 5 4 3 2 1

ISBN-13: 978-1-62523-145-1

Kaplan Publishing books are available at special quantity discounts to use for sales promotions, employee premiums, or educational purposes. For more information or to purchase books, please call the Simon & Schuster special sales department at 866-506-1949.

TABLE OF CONTENTS

PART FOUR: PRACTICE TESTS

ABOUT THE AUTHOR

Kelly Swanson has been involved with AP Human Geography since 1997, when 50 teachers from across the United States were brought together to structure the curriculum for the new course. Kelly's course syllabus was published in the first edition of the AP Human Geography Teachers Guide, and he has been active in the Minnesota Alliance for Geographic Education (MAGE) since 1996. Kelly served as a geographic consultant for the Onion's *Our Dumb World* atlas published in 2007. His travels and speaking engagements have taken him around the world. He brings his passion for travel and curriculum writing to the AP Human Geography curriculum. He has been a reader for the AP Human Geography course since 2003, and was a table leader for the 2006, 2007, 2008, and 2014 exams. For the 2009 through 2013 exams, Kelly was selected as a Lead Table Leader. Kelly has taught different geography methods to geography teachers in the United States and around the world, promoting geography as a core academic discipline in any well-rounded education. In addition to teaching the AP Human Geography course, Kelly is also currently a community faculty member at Metropolitan State University in St. Paul, Minnesota teaching the Introduction to Geography courses at the collegiate level.

ACKNOWLEDGMENTS

I would like to thank my wife, Jolaine, and children, Rebecca, Jake, and Zacheriah, for their endless love and support during this entire process. They are my future geographers! Thank you is not enough to say for the time spent writing this book. I could not be more proud of each and every member of my family. I do not deserve such a kind, supportive wife as Jolaine.

I thank the students at Johnson Senior High School in St. Paul, Minnesota, for their hard work in the AP Human Geography course. You have put up with my teaching style, and I know that your hard work will be rewarded.

I would also like to thank Dr. David Lanegran for his assistance in writing this book. Without his support, I would not be where I am today. And a special thanks goes to all of the AP Human Geography reading leadership for their support and kindness over the past decade.

KAPLAN PANEL OF AP EXPERTS

Congratulations—you have chosen Kaplan to help you get a top score on your AP exam.

Kaplan understands your goals, and what you're up against—achieving college credit and conquering a tough test—while participating in everything else that high school has to offer.

You expect realistic practice, authoritative advice, and accurate, up-to-the-minute information on the test. And that's exactly what you'll find in this book, as well as every other in the AP series. To help you (and us!) reach these goals, we have sought out leaders in the AP community. Allow us to introduce our experts:

AP HUMAN GEOGRAPHY EXPERTS

Michael Bolsoni has been teaching AP Human Geography since its inception in 2000, and has been an AP exam reader since 2009. He is a faculty member at the School of Environmental Studies in Apple Valley, Minnesota, where he teaches a variety of social and environmental studies courses.

Rick Gindele is an AP Human Geography consultant conducting workshops and institutes for teachers throughout the United States. He also has served as a reader and table leader for the AP Human Geography exam since 2002. Rick started teaching AP Human Geography in 2000, which was the first year the course was offered.

Part One

THE BASICS

CHAPTER 1: INSIDE THE AP HUMAN GEOGRAPHY EXAM

Human geography is about the interconnections between people and places. Every unit of this book concerns these interconnections. Geography is a constantly changing field of study, yet at the same time, there are foundations to build upon. This book will provide you with some of the building blocks to assist you in your study of human geography.

This book uses a thematic approach in its attempt to cover geography. For example, one cannot discuss a place or region without considering agricultural issues, such as how people produce or obtain their food and how this connects to their population. Agriculture directly affects a country's economic development and how the people use the land. These natural resources need to be allocated by some form of authority in the hierarchy of the society. These resources are usually allocated to meet the needs of the greatest numbers of people, who are congregated in urban centers.

This book explains these interconnections through individual units of geography. Each unit in this book gives a brief description of each section of the Advanced Placement (AP) Human Geography exam. Each chapter in this book encapsulates the overall themes of human geography while providing sufficient detail to give you what you'll need to know to score well on the AP Human Geography exam.

Each of the units of geography covered in this book (**nature and perspectives of geography, population, cultural patterns and processes, political organization of space, agriculture and rural land use, industrialization and economic development,** and **cities and urban land use**) tie in with each other so as to show how the world is a truly interconnected place. Interactions between peoples of different cultures and ethnicities contribute to the ever-changing cultural landscape on our planet, making geography one of the most fascinating subjects to study.

Geographers from around the world developed the AP Human Geography course over a decade ago. Many people perceive geography as the mere memorization of place names and facts. However, rote memorization of place names is only a small portion of what geography really is. **Geography** is the spatial interaction of people and places around the globe.

Memorizing state capitals and world cities builds general knowledge but does little for understanding what the world is like in varied and different locations. The field of human geography tries to get a handle on what the world is like and the influence of humans on their landscapes.

It is important to note that this exam deals solely with the principles of human geography. Physical geography is not included on this exam, and students who take it will not need to know about geology and physical science principles. Although these principles are important in determining the character of a location, they, in and of themselves, are not a part of the course.

OVERVIEW OF THE TEST STRUCTURE

This course is intended to meet the requirements of a college-level course in human geography. The course was structured to meet the guidelines of the National Geography Standards established in 1994 and adjusted in 2012.

The five skills that students will master are as follows:

1. Use and think about maps and spatial data.
2. Understand and interpret the implications of associations among phenomena in places.
3. Recognize and interpret at different scales the relationship among patterns and processes.
4. Define regions and evaluate the regionalization process.
5. Characterize and analyze changing interconnections among places.

The field of human geography for this exam is broken into six main categories of study. **Population, cultural patterns and processes, political organization of space, agriculture and rural land use, industrialization and economic development,** and **cities and urban land use** comprise 90 to 95 percent of the exam. Each of the six main units of study in AP Human Geography comprise anywhere from 13 to 17 percent of the exam. The most notable addition to the course outline since 2011 is the incorporation of natural resources and environmental concerns in the industrialization and economic development unit. The remaining portion of the exam (**Geography: Its Nature and Perspectives**) covers 5 to10 percent of the test and includes geography as a field of inquiry, evolution of geographical concepts and models associated with notable geographers, key concepts underlying the geographical perspective, and geographical skills such as analyzing maps, charts, and graphs.

HUMAN GEOGRAPHY THEMES

The material covered on the AP exam is divided into thematic units. Each of the units has a model(s) associated with it. These models work in an ideal world but rarely work to perfection in the real world. However, to assist in the explanation of spatial patterns, models are necessary in interpreting the world.

FOUNDATIONS OF THE FIELD

The first unit is on the historical foundations of the field of geography itself. The Greeks, Romans, Chinese, and many other peoples have compiled information about the world that we know today. As an academic discipline, the field has grown from its Greek roots to a field of social science studied at hundreds of universities around the world. This history is crucial in determining how we perceive the world at different times. **Maps** are the form of communication for geographers. There are many different types and styles of maps. This points to the fact that studying location is important, as is the fundamental question of *why*? In short, the *why* of where is a primary concern of geographers.

HUMAN POPULATION

The second major unit of the test is the study of human population. This not only looks at the issue of overpopulation, but also at trends and data used in determining demographic principles. Age, sex, race, and ethnicity are examined as well as areas of population growth and decline. Reasons will be analyzed for a region or country's success or failure in controlling population growth. Different models and theories will be examined in relation to place to determine validity. Migration is also included in this unit. **Migration** does not affect world population growth rates, but it does affect the movement and structure of regional populations. Both push and pull factors are important in determining why people move.

AGRICULTURE AND RURAL USE

The third area of the exam is about agriculture and rural use. Nothing uses more land on the planet's surface than agriculture. Food is essential for human existence. The evolution of food production and different styles of farming are addressed. There have been three **agricultural revolutions**, each one instrumental in shaping human history.

LAND USE AND NATURAL RESOURCES

Although it is not a specific section of the exam, the topic of land use and natural resources is covered in the chapters on agriculture and industry. The process of using the four land-use decision-making models is important in determining such things as the value of the land. How a person perceives the value of land determines their willingness to extract the resources that are the raw materials for industry. How these **natural resources** are distributed around the world and who owns them is important in determining world politics, culture, and economic patterns. For example, one cannot mention the Middle East today without oil being an important piece of the conversation. Oil is a key ingredient in the current industrialization process. Also discussed and analyzed are six different **alternative energy sources** and the implications of their use for future energy production.

Questions about environmental issues are becoming more prevalent on the exam. Although this section on Land Use and Natural Resources is not specifically a section on the AP exam, the concepts regarding the environment will be found throughout the other units in this course. Population affects the environment, as does agriculture. Urbanization and Industry have profound impacts on the environment.

INDUSTRIALIZATION AND ECONOMIC DEVELOPMENT

The next unit deals with industrialization and economic development. What factors determine economic success? Why do certain societies make the jump from an agricultural society to an industrial society and then eventually move to a tertiary (service-based) economy? **Globalization** and the spread of products through economic pacts, as well as the world's economic structure, will be discussed. Industry and economic development eventually lead to increased capital. Where there is increased capital, politics comes into play. Authorities allocate the use of the capital to meet the demands of the citizens of a country. The type of political system determines how efficiently demands are met with the capital from either economic development or international donations.

GEOPOLITICS OR POLITICAL GEOGRAPHY

Another unit of the exam covers geopolitics. What determines a state, and who gives sovereignty? What is the difference between a nation, a state, and a nation-state? Colonialism still has a profound effect on the world today. Although colonialism is not as strong as it was 50 years ago, its footprints are found in language and religious patterns as well as architectural styles around the world. The shapes and sizes of different states are important in determining their strength. A **nation** is a group of people with common cultural characteristics. These characteristics may include language and religion as well as other cultural features that tie directly into the next theme, cultural geography.

CULTURAL GEOGRAPHY

This unit examines the impact of language and religion as two predominant aspects of culture. Music and food play an important role in culture as well. When determining regions, culture plays a major role. What are the differences between pop and folk culture? What role does culture play in the physical landscape? Many times, cultures segregate themselves voluntarily based on language and/or religion. This separation and concentration leads to our final unit in this course: urbanization. The congregation of ethnic groups can occur either in urban centers of national prominence or in rural hamlets where agriculture is the dominant form of economic activity. However, ethnicities congregate because of the ease of transition when migrating between cultures.

URBANIZATION

Urbanization pertains to the rise of cities and the influence that they have on the regions around them. Why are some cities more important than others? There are different models of world cities, which will be analyzed based on their location. As the world develops, more people are moving to urban areas for employment as well as the other amenities that cities can offer their inhabitants. This puts strain on the resources of certain cities around the world. Suburbs and edge cities have developed in recent decades, and their impact will also be analyzed.

EXAM FORMAT

The AP Human Geography exam lasts approximately 2 hours and 15 minutes, allocated as follows:

- **First 60 minutes:** 75 multiple-choice questions
- **Ten-minute break**
- **Last 75 minutes:** Three free-response questions

Make sure to pace yourself as you work through the exam. You may write the essays in whatever order you choose; all responses are written in the same booklet.

QUESTION TYPES

There are two types of questions on the exam: multiple choice and free response (essays).

MULTIPLE-CHOICE QUESTIONS

The 75 multiple-choice questions are drawn from the seven thematic areas and cover the entire course. Questions reflect varying levels of difficulty, and the levels are mixed throughout the questions.

Recently, the College Board has begun adding more stimulus-based questions. These are questions with some type of chart, map, graph, or other visual element attached to the question. One or more questions may be asked about a section of the stimulus. This may take the form of a reading section or map interpretation regarding one of the seven sections in the course. Plan your time accordingly with these questions as you will only have 60 minutes to complete your 75 multiple choice questions.

FREE-RESPONSE QUESTIONS

There are three free-response essay questions on the exam. You have 1 hour and 15 minutes to read the essay questions, plan your responses, and write your three essays. Pacing is critical, and it is up to you to budget the time accordingly. Because not all testing rooms have clocks, having a watch (no alarms) is important. Many of the essays involve the interpretation of a map or pictures, which contain information about the place in question. You will need to know your material to score well on this part of the exam.

HOW THE EXAM IS SCORED

The score from the multiple-choice section of the exam counts for 50 percent of your total exam score. The other 50 percent is the combined score from the three essays.

Your "composite" score is converted into a scale of 1 to 5:

> 5 = Extremely well qualified
> 4 = Well qualified
> 3 = Qualified
> 2 = Possibly qualified
> 1 = No recommendation

While some college programs accept a score of 3, the most competitive schools require a composite score of 4 or 5.

MULTIPLE-CHOICE SECTION

Student answer sheets for the multiple-choice section are scored by machine. Scores are based on the number of questions answered correctly. **No points are deducted for wrong answers.** No points are awarded for unanswered questions. Therefore, you should answer every question, even if you have to guess.

FREE-RESPONSE SECTION

The essays are evaluated and scored by hand. Specific rubrics are given to the readers of the free-response questions that students have answered. A student is awarded points based upon how each essay relates to the rubric of the question it answers. Note that wrong answers are not deducted from a student's score. Points can only be added to your essay. That being said, the first essay example will be scored, and subsequent examples are not scored if the question only calls for one example. Therefore, you must be correct on your first example.

The rubrics for the readings are released on the AP central website after the exams. Readers do not see the rubrics until after the official reading has commenced. The rubrics are based on specific point values, assigned by the chief reader at the readings. Some free-response questions may only be worth 6 points, while other free-response questions might have a 12 point value. Those essays are then statistically categorized and incorporated into the bell curve for appropriate scoring, ranging from 0 to 5 on the AP Human Geography exam.

REGISTRATION AND FEES

If you are taking the AP Human Geography course at your high school, registering for the AP exam is easy. Speak with your teacher and your school's counselor or AP coordinator about signing up. Make sure that your name appears on the AP exam order list that your AP coordinator sends out in March.

If you are home schooled or not in a school that offers AP courses, you can still take the exam. Call the Advanced Placement Program at (888) 225-5427 or (212) 632-1780 by March 1 for a list of schools in your area where you can take the exam. Then contact the AP coordinator at one of the schools identified by the College Board to get a place on exam day.

The College Board makes accommodations if you have a documented disability. These may include extended time, large-print exams, use of a word processor, and other necessary accommodations. If you have a need for special accommodations, see your AP coordinator.

At the date of this book's printing, the cost of the exam is $91 within the United States, and $121 at schools and testing centers outside of the United States. For those qualified with acute financial need, the College Board offers a $29 credit. In addition, most states offer exam subsidies to cover all or part of the remaining cost for eligible students. To learn about other sources of financial aid, contact your AP coordinator.

For more information on the AP Program and the Human Geography exam, contact the Advanced Placement Program:

Phone: (888) 225-5427 or (212) 632-1780
Email: apstudents@info.collegeboard.org
Website: apstudent.collegeboard.org/home

ADDITIONAL RESOURCES

TEXTBOOKS

Certainly, no one textbook is perfect, but your selection should be a recognized college text of approximately 400 or more pages. In addition to extensive text written at college level, it should contain good maps, illustrations, art, and documents, and it should be a fairly recent edition. Reading the textbook is a first step to learning the material covered in this course.

The following are the textbooks recommended by College Board, plus a few more we think will be helpful in your studies:

Bjelland, Mark, Daniel Montello, Jerome Fellmann, Arthur Getis, and Judith Getis. 2013. *Human Geography: Landscapes of Human Activities*. New York: Brown and Benchmark.

De Blij, H. J., Alexander B. Murphy, and Erin H. Fouberg. 2010. *Human Geography: People, Place, and Culture*. New York: John Wiley & Sons.

Domosh, Mona, Roderick P. Neumann, Patricia L. Price, and Terry G. Jordan-Bychkov. 2011. *The Human Mosaic: The Cultural Approach to Human Geography*. New York: W.H. Freeman and Company.

Fellmann, Jerome, Mark D. Bjelland, Arthur Getis, and Judith Getis. 2010. *Human Geography: Landscapes of Human Activities*. New York: Brown and Benchmark.

Fouberg, Erin H., and Alexander B. Murphy. 2012. *Human Geography: People, Places, and Culture.* New York: John Wiley & Sons.

Jordan-Bychkov, Terry G. 2104. *Jordan's Fundamentals of The Human Mosaic: A Thematic Approach to Cultural Geography.* New York: W.H. Freeman.

Knox, Paul, and Sally Marston. 2012. *Human Geography: Places and Regions in Global Context.* Upper Sadle River, NJ: Prentice Hall.

Kuby, Michael, John Harner, and Patricia Gober. 2013. *Human Geography in Action.* New York, NY: John Wiley & Sons.

Malinowski, Jon, and David Kaplan. 2013. *Human Geography.* New York: McGraw-Hill.

Norton, William. 2011. *Human Geography.* Don Mills, Ont.: Oxford University Press.

Rubenstein, James. 2013. *The Cultural Landscape: An Introduction to Human Geography.* Upper Saddle River, NJ: Prentice Hall.

Many textbook publishers maintain sites with practice questions and review material, so check your textbook for web support.

WEBSITES

You are also encouraged to explore the official College Board AP website for information about the course and exam: www.apcentral.collegeboard.com.

CHAPTER 2: STRATEGIES FOR SUCCESS

Being prepared is the key to success. Aside from engaging in the course-long practice of reading the textbook, taking good notes, and developing writing skills, you can do specific things before the exam to help you perform your best.

As you work your way through your AP Human Geography course and this book, you should develop a good sense as to what information and skill sets are necessary to do well on the exam. Along with comprehensive review information, this book will provide you with the most effective strategies for tackling each question type as well as tips for managing stress and using your time efficiently during the exam.

In addition, the review questions throughout this book will help you to identify your strengths and weaknesses, provide you with solid test practice, and get you ready for anything on test day.

GENERAL TEST-TAKING STRATEGIES

Following are some test-taking strategies to help you get ready for the exam:

- A thorough review of the material is a necessity; allow four to six weeks for this review. This is an exam on which knowing a large body of information is important.

- Save all your tests throughout the course; these make good review material.

- Forming a study group can be an effective strategy, especially if this approach has proven to be personally helpful in the past. A study group will allow you to benefit from the strengths and wisdom of others. Remember, any study group should have an organized plan that is followed to maximize time use.

- On the day before and the morning of the exam, it's a good idea to lighten up a bit. It may help to briefly look over the visual elements of your text, such

AP EXPERT TIP

Look at the strengths of your group—including your own! Share these with the group so that you know who can take the lead on certain types of review items.

as maps and pictures, and think about them as well as reviewing the guidelines for the essay questions. But take it easy—you want to have enough energy to make it through the exam.

- Do not stay up late the night before the exam. For focus and energy, a good night's sleep is key.

- Eat a healthy meal before the exam and carry a small, nutritious snack with you for the break between the multiple-choice and essay sections (no food or drink is allowed in the exam room). This can really give you a boost of energy when you need it.

- Avoid other students who are excessively anxious or negative—they may affect your concentration and focus. Stay positive and confident that you can conquer the exam!

- Know where the exam will be given (probably not your classroom, and maybe not your school building) and how you will get to it if it isn't at your school.

- Arrive early with everything you'll need for the exam. Take with you the following:
  — A watch (with no alarm)
  — Several #2 pencils with good erasers for the multiple-choice answer sheet
  — Two pens with blue or black ink for the essays.
  — Photo ID
  — Social Security number (or other government-issued ID number)
  — A light sweater or jacket and tissues or a handkerchief—testing rooms are sometimes cold

- Do not bring a cell phone or other specifically banned items with you to the exam.

MULTIPLE-CHOICE QUESTION STRATEGIES

The following are some helpful hints for tackling the multiple-choice section of the exam.

- Mark your answers clearly and neatly on the answer grid.

- Be aware of the time throughout the test—you have 60 minutes. Do not linger over any one question for too long.

- On questions where you aren't sure of your answer, guess quickly if you can eliminate at least two choices or, alternatively, mark the question to return to later.

- Every once in a while, take a second to make sure that the number of the question in the test booklet matches the number of your answer on the bubble sheet. Avoiding mechanical mistakes, such as marking your answers on an incorrect line, can help to avert a test-taking disaster.

- Take the time to read each question carefully. Remember, you're looking for the *best* answer; sometimes one or more wrong answers may sound correct at first, so read all answer choices for each question carefully.

- Ignore other test takers who may finish before you do. Use the entire time allotted to go back to any questions you may have left blank and to make sure your answers are precisely the way you want them to be.

- Answer every question; remember you don't lose any points for wrong answers.

FREE-RESPONSE QUESTION STRATEGIES

WHAT TO EXPECT

There are three free-response questions on the exam. Each question will be distinct and address a different aspect of the course.

Each free-response question on the exam is assigned a rubric, which shows the correct responses to all sections of the question prompt. Although each question carries the same weight on the exam, questions are assigned varying point values based on their complexity for scoring purposes. If you answer a certain portion of the question correctly, you will receive a point for that section based on the rubric. Readers are instructed to look for merit in students' answers and to give credit for responses whenever possible, but that does not mean that you will be given points for wayward answers.

Often, an essay question draws from two or more units in the course. When developing your response, try to give balanced treatment to all aspects of the question, as this will be part of the evaluation criteria.

There is often a map question in the free-response section. This map will have to be read and interpreted using content in any of the seven units for this course. You will also experience some map questions, charts, or other information in the multiple choice section. Geography is the study of spatial interaction, and maps are the form of communication used to relay those ideas. Successful students must be able to interpret maps and infer meaning from the maps' central ideas.

TIPS FOR EARNING POINTS

Not attempting the question is scored as a dash. Attempting to answer the question but receiving no points is scored as a zero. There is a statistical distinction between a dash and a zero. You should *always* try to answer the question, even if you do not know the answer entirely. Often, students who start writing without a clear path will end up thinking their way through the question as they write. It is sometimes possible to score the majority of points for the question in the last part of your essay. Stay positive and give it your best effort.

It is important to note that points cannot be taken away from you. Once you have scored a point, you cannot lose that point. If the point was given to you based on the rubric, the point sticks with you. However, you do not want to contradict yourself in the essay. Get to the point and then move on.

Pace Yourself

Pacing is crucial for writing your essays. You will have 75 minutes for the free-response portion of the exam. You need to get all of your key points down in the test booklet within the allotted time frame. Skipping a question can lead to a low score. You do not have the option, as in other AP exams, to choose the questions that you would like to answer.

When deciding in which order to answer the essay questions, a good approach is to do first the one(s) about which you can present the most concrete information. Remember, all three questions need to be answered. The order in which the free-response questions are answered doesn't matter.

Be sure to label your questions *one*, *two*, and *three*, depending upon which question you are answering. Also, make sure you write neatly; an unintelligible response can prove challenging to score.

You do not need to rewrite the question in your answer. By rewriting the question, you waste valuable time. Use your time to answer the question, not to restate it in your answer. Do not waste the readers' time or your time by restating the question.

Read Carefully and Identify Key Terms

Make sure to read each question carefully to ensure you have a solid grasp of what it is asking and what you are being asked to do when you respond. Identify any key terms, such as *analyze, compare and contrast*, etc. Identifying such key words can help you understand exactly what you are being asked to do so you can develop your answer appropriately.

The following are some commonly used terms:

- To *analyze* is to define components, especially in terms of their relationship to each other and to their meaning and importance.

- To *describe* is often connected to *analyze*; you're expected to give an account of some event or situation and, from the description, produce conclusions regarding its importance, relationships, possible consequences, and so on.

- To *assess* or *evaluate* means to determine a judgment about something, to appraise positives and/or negatives, to take a stand on an issue.

- To *compare* and *contrast* are opposite instructions frequently used in combination; they ask you to show similarities and differences, respectively.

- To *discuss* implies presenting different aspects of something by examining various sides or opinions.

- To *explain* means to give clarification by presenting the details.
- Some questions include the phrase *to what extent*, which calls for a judgment regarding the scope, depth, or limits of the topic.

ORGANIZE YOUR ESSAY

Read each free-response question carefully, and make sure you know precisely what the question is asking *before* you begin to develop your answer. When developing and organizing your responses, remember that a thesis statement is not needed for the exam. This makes geography different from some other AP exams. Students do *not* have to write in paragraph form (meaning an introductory sentence and supporting sentences), nor must they circle or underline vocabulary words.

On the test itself, the answer book mentions that only the first or second examples will be used. They mean it! What this means to you, the test taker, is that if your first example is incorrect but your second example is correct and the question only asked for one example, your second example will *not* be counted. You need to be correct the first time when answering. This is meant to discourage students from guessing in a "laundry list" fashion in the hopes of chancing upon a correct answer.

It is essential to understand that the free-response questions on the test deal with more than one unit of study. Human geography is more about the process of thinking than the memorization of place names or areas. Questions in the past have connected the course units together through some overarching principle. You should link the units to the best of your ability through the common themes of the topic.

The best essays do two things: They address all parts of the question, and they support your answer with specific, accurate examples and information. As you plan the essay, jot down evidence you can use as proof of your claims.

Devote a paragraph to each example and make its connection to some part of the prompt. Organize your evidence in a way that matches the question (e.g., chronologically, by country). An effective essay response should span over a page—ideally at least two pages. If there is time, proofread. It is all right to make additions if you think of any; you can draw an arrow to where the material is to be inserted.

As you read the questions and supporting documents, make notes beside each. Pay attention to sources, especially if it is someone you recognize or if you can connect the source to such topics as religion, politics, or agriculture. Try to tie the sources into the question's topic. For example, if the question is asking about the demographic transition model, tie in the economic development aspects of the model along with the population trends in each of the stages of the model. You may write on your test booklet during the exam. This might be a good place to organize your ideas for the question.

Do a quick rough outline. Then write your response.

POWERFUL BODY PARAGRAPHS

There is no magic number of body paragraphs to include in your response. It is critical to write a strong and concise topic sentence for each body paragraph so that the AP reader knows what the paragraph will specifically address. The most important aspect of a body paragraph is that it illustrates or proves some part of the prompt with specific information. It is essential to elaborate on all parts of the prompt equally well, if possible. Many prompts will ask for at least two tasks. The highest scores go to essays that are balanced between the tasks, so don't say a lot about half the question and very little about the other half. The material (evidence) should be presented in a way that meets the prompt's directive. If you are asked to "analyze," merely describing the material won't earn you a good score.

Essays are ranked by the amount and quality of accurate evidence they present. Essays that don't get beyond very broad, general statements will receive lower scores.

STRONG CONCLUSION

If you have time at the end of your essay, write a short conclusion—three to five sentences are sufficient. A strong conclusion ties together the strands of the essay in a final, compelling way. Do not merely repeat what is stated earlier in the essay—you're better off having no conclusion at all. **You will not lose credit for not having a conclusion, but a strong final paragraph can certainly add to the essay's overall effect and, in some cases, add points.**

BE NEAT AND CLEAR

Be as neat as possible when writing your essay. If nobody can read your essay, it may not be scored accurately. You may produce the most poignant essay ever written, but if nobody can read it, you will not receive points. Every attempt will be made to decipher your writing, but the readers will eventually give up after several people have tried to read your paper.

Have you ever heard the phrase "Say what you mean and mean what you say"? The same principle applies to the AP Human Geography exam. When writing your response, get to the point.

THE SCORING RUBRIC

The essays are usually assigned scores from 6 to 12. Points are determined by the rubric set up by the question leader and chief reader prior to the readings. The rubrics may be tweaked prior to the readings, but once the reading starts, the rubric is always maintained.

As mentioned previously, you do not need to state a thesis in the AP Human Geography exam.

If you quote, which is not a requirement, try to keep the quotations short and few in number. Never quote an entire document; use phrases and sentences to make your point. Never quote without immediately following up with your interpretation of the quoted words.

Keep your personal opinions out of the essay. The pronoun *I* should not appear anywhere in your response. Similarly, don't insert any personal bias or judgment of the sources or the information. This is a presentation of the material and opinions of others, not a personal essay.

Remember, outside information isn't required on the exam. If you do use examples on your exam, use examples that most people will recognize. Although a local example may fit applicably, the readers may not know that particular example and may not offer you points for it. Use examples that are applicable on a state, national, or global scale.

TIME MANAGEMENT

Because there's no way to know if a clock will be in the testing room, it is a good idea to bring a watch and monitor your time appropriately. Read all the material in the essay booklet and estimate how much time it will take you to write your response. In addition, make any notes that will prove helpful.

Remember to observe time limits—this is up to you. The proctor will not tell you when to begin a new essay. Budget your time accordingly to ensure you can complete all parts of the exam. When working on the free-response questions, it is a good idea to leave some blank space after each essay, in case you end up with a few extra minutes and think of something else to add.

STRESS MANAGEMENT

The high school AP program is intended to provide students with the experience and challenges of a college-level course. AP Human Geography demands the level of thinking and analytical skills that college students need to be successful. Although the course work is not always easy, the rewards for successfully completing it are worth the effort. This course can become the foundation for the study and understanding of many other areas of human endeavor. And above all, it helps you understand your world and your place in it.

Talented and motivated students who had the benefit of a solid education can do well on the AP exam. This book is a useful supplement to your textbook, class notes, essays, and tests, and it can help you achieve your desired score.

The key to success is preparation. Students who have prepared thoroughly and diligently for the AP exam should not feel stressed out when test day arrives. If you've taken the steps necessary to achieve success, all that remains is to stay confident and give it your very best effort.

COUNTDOWN TO THE TEST

Although your entire AP course experience is geared toward preparing you for the AP exam, you will want to begin a more intense review about six weeks before the exam.

Prepare an effective study plan by dividing up the course material and allotting a specific amount of time for review. As you move through the course content, refresh your mind on all pertinent people, issues, and events. Some students find it helpful to take notes as they study.

PRIORITIZING WHAT TO STUDY

Prioritizing your study objectives can help you prepare effectively. Making study lists by topic and identifying the areas you need to focus on most can be helpful. About two weeks before the exam, address any gaps in your preparation. For instance, the major reasons why people migrate around the world may be a factor or a question on the exam. If you have trouble recalling the push and pull factors, review accordingly.

Review key terms in conjunction with major concepts of this course along with your textbook. Next, make sure you understand how key terms and concepts relate to specific examples at a variety of scales (local to global).

Remember not to underestimate the importance of taking practice exams. Extensive practice will help you to hone your test-taking skills and develop a solid strategy for tackling the exam. Experience will also help you to gain confidence and learn what your comfortable test-taking pace is, both of which are invaluable on test day.

REVIEW THE MAJOR THEMES THE WEEK OF THE EXAM

Be sure that you are familiar with the major themes of the course. Remember that the essay questions usually tie together at least two of the units. Many of the questions, but not all of them, deal with models of some kind and ask you to apply the model to a real-world situation.

AP EXPERT TIP

If your teacher has had you make a list of the major models and who developed them, use that for review. If not, make your own list. You could also make flash cards out of half sheets of paper, index cards, or presentation software to use in remembering the models, their names, and the geographer who developed the model.

WORLD REGIONS

Although this is a human geography test, and world regions will not be tested per se, it is important to be able to recognize different regions of the world. When looking at the Big Picture view of the world the following regions will need to be known:

- North America
- Central America
- South America
- Europe
- The Russian Federation
- Africa
- Sub-Saharan Africa
- Asia
- Oceania

When looking at the closer view of regions around the world, numerous regions will be used. Some of these include: United States, Brazil, Southern Africa, and Western Africa. These may be questioned using quantitative data relating to individual countries within these specific regions. Having a good atlas handy during your preparation for this course is an excellent way to put these ideas into perspective.

Part Two

DIAGNOSTIC TEST

Diagnostic Test Answer Grid

To score your diagnostic test:

1. Count the number of questions you answered correctly.

2. Number correct ÷ 25 × 100 = diagnostic test score (round scores to the nearest whole number).

Test Score	Result
80–100	Excellent
60–79	Very Good
50–59	Good
40–49	Fair
0–39	Poor

1 Ⓐ Ⓑ Ⓒ Ⓓ Ⓔ   14 Ⓐ Ⓑ Ⓒ Ⓓ Ⓔ

2 Ⓐ Ⓑ Ⓒ Ⓓ Ⓔ   15 Ⓐ Ⓑ Ⓒ Ⓓ Ⓔ

3 Ⓐ Ⓑ Ⓒ Ⓓ Ⓔ   16 Ⓐ Ⓑ Ⓒ Ⓓ Ⓔ

4 Ⓐ Ⓑ Ⓒ Ⓓ Ⓔ   17 Ⓐ Ⓑ Ⓒ Ⓓ Ⓔ

5 Ⓐ Ⓑ Ⓒ Ⓓ Ⓔ   18 Ⓐ Ⓑ Ⓒ Ⓓ Ⓔ

6 Ⓐ Ⓑ Ⓒ Ⓓ Ⓔ   19 Ⓐ Ⓑ Ⓒ Ⓓ Ⓔ

7 Ⓐ Ⓑ Ⓒ Ⓓ Ⓔ   20 Ⓐ Ⓑ Ⓒ Ⓓ Ⓔ

8 Ⓐ Ⓑ Ⓒ Ⓓ Ⓔ   21 Ⓐ Ⓑ Ⓒ Ⓓ Ⓔ

9 Ⓐ Ⓑ Ⓒ Ⓓ Ⓔ   22 Ⓐ Ⓑ Ⓒ Ⓓ Ⓔ

10 Ⓐ Ⓑ Ⓒ Ⓓ Ⓔ   23 Ⓐ Ⓑ Ⓒ Ⓓ Ⓔ

11 Ⓐ Ⓑ Ⓒ Ⓓ Ⓔ   24 Ⓐ Ⓑ Ⓒ Ⓓ Ⓔ

12 Ⓐ Ⓑ Ⓒ Ⓓ Ⓔ   25 Ⓐ Ⓑ Ⓒ Ⓓ Ⓔ

13 Ⓐ Ⓑ Ⓒ Ⓓ Ⓔ

DIAGNOSTIC TEST

MULTIPLE-CHOICE QUESTIONS
Time—20 Minutes
25 Questions

1. In the demographic transition model, which stage would traditionally involve an agricultural society?

   (A) Stage 1
   (B) Stage 2
   (C) Stage 3
   (D) Stage 4
   (E) Stage 5

2. Which of the following is the best example of a primate city?

   (A) Rio de Janeiro
   (B) Paris
   (C) Washington, D.C.
   (D) Shanghai
   (E) Berlin

3. Which form of agriculture is traditionally practiced in drier or more arid climates?

   (A) Shifting cultivation
   (B) Truck farming
   (C) Commercial farming
   (D) Subsistence farming
   (E) Pastoral nomadism

4. Which of the following religions is an ethnic religion?

   (A) Judaism
   (B) Christianity
   (C) Islam
   (D) Buddhism
   (E) Sikhism

5. Which area of the world is experiencing the most rapid population growth?

   (A) East Asia
   (B) Central Europe
   (C) Western United States
   (D) Sub-Saharan Africa
   (E) Eastern Australia

6. Von Thunen's model would best fit which statement?

   (A) Agricultural products need to be close to market to minimize transportation costs.
   (B) Raw materials need to be close to market to minimize transportation costs.
   (C) Lower-income countries are considered periphery locations.
   (D) Farmers practicing subsistence agriculture need to sell their products to market.
   (E) Shepherds practicing pastoral nomadism move their herds to bring them to a commercial market.

7. Which term best describes the movement or tearing down of deteriorated buildings to make way for the building of new ones?

   (A) Primate development
   (B) Urbanization
   (C) Industrialization
   (D) Inner-city development ring
   (E) Gentrification

GO ON TO THE NEXT PAGE

8. Which of the following cities is a holy place to three of the world's main religions?

   (A) Mecca
   (B) Medina
   (C) Jerusalem
   (D) Delhi
   (E) Beijing

9. The U.S. census shows that the population has continued to move in which directions?

   (A) South, then east
   (B) North, then west
   (C) West, then south
   (D) North, then east
   (E) West, then north

10. This theory was adopted by the Germans during World War II and proposed that whoever controlled Eastern Europe and western Asia could control the world.

    (A) Rimland theory
    (B) Heartland theory
    (C) Domino theory
    (D) World systems theory
    (E) Core-periphery theory

11. What would be considered a basic industry for the city of Pittsburgh?

    (A) Automobiles
    (B) Computer processors
    (C) Meat packing
    (D) Iron ore
    (E) Steel production

12. Which alternative energy method is growing due to its base in agriculture?

    (A) Biomass
    (B) Nuclear
    (C) Solar
    (D) Wind
    (E) Hydroelectric

13. The agricultural product that the majority of the world's population depends upon for its survival is

    (A) corn.
    (B) wheat.
    (C) barley.
    (D) soybeans.
    (E) rice.

14. Which area of the world was probably the first to develop cotton, corn, and beans as primary agricultural products?

    (A) Southern India
    (B) Southeast Asia
    (C) Central America
    (D) Eastern Europe
    (E) Eastern Africa

15. Which of the following regions in the United States leads the others in coal production?

    (A) Appalachian Mountains
    (B) Gulf Coast
    (C) Western Pacific
    (D) Upper Midwest
    (E) Southwest Texas

GO ON TO THE NEXT PAGE

16. This approach in geography has been discredited for being racist and discriminatory to certain groups of people.

    (A) Possiblist approach

    (B) Environmental determinist approach

    (C) Cultural ecology approach

    (D) Central place theory

    (E) Weber's least-cost approach

17. The term *nation-state* would best fit which country?

    (A) United States

    (B) Israel

    (C) Brazil

    (D) Japan

    (E) China

18. What do the cities of London and Shanghai have in common with regard to their development zones?

    (A) Both have old, outdated industrial zones.

    (B) Both cities rank one and their development zones rank two in terms of total population.

    (C) Both cities have invested billions into their newly developed industrial zones.

    (D) Their development zones are called "the Dockland."

    (E) Their development zones are not financed by foreign companies.

19. An advantage of a compact state is that

    (A) it allows for greater access to more natural resources.

    (B) it allows for more cultural cohesion.

    (C) it is easier to defend the borders.

    (D) it often is more susceptible to centrifugal forces.

    (E) it is more open to the regionalization process.

20. Which areas of the world have experienced the most devolutionary forces since the early 1990s?

    (A) Western Europe

    (B) North Africa

    (C) Southeast Asia

    (D) Eastern Europe

    (E) South Asia

21. The migration of Muslims to Pakistan and Hindus to India after the Indian partition in 1948 is a good example of what?

    (A) An environmental push factor

    (B) An economic pull factor

    (C) An environmental pull factor

    (D) A political push factor

    (E) An economic push factor

22. Most of the urban areas in the United States follow which urban model?

    (A) Concentric zone model

    (B) Sector model

    (C) Multiple nuclei model

    (D) Central place model

    (E) Von Thunen's model

GO ON TO THE NEXT PAGE ⟩

23. Which statement best describes how European central business districts (CBDs) are different from those of most world cities?

    (A) European cities have their high-rises in the CBD.

    (B) European cities focus their transportation on the CBD.

    (C) European cities have large areas devoted to foreign investment.

    (D) European cities have a colonial center in addition to the CBD.

    (E) European cities have narrow streets and low-rise buildings in the CBD.

24. What do the languages of English, Spanish, and Hindi have in common?

    (A) They are all part of a major religious system.

    (B) They are all spoken in the same countries.

    (C) All three derive from the Afro-Asiatic language family.

    (D) All three are spoken where they are due to colonialism.

    (E) All three are in the Indo-European language family.

25. The fact that there is more interaction and movement between Washington, D.C., and Baltimore than there is between Washington, D.C., and Philadelphia is a function of

    (A) distance decay.

    (B) the gravity model.

    (C) spatial interaction.

    (D) cultural ecology.

    (E) distribution.

IF YOU FINISH BEFORE TIME IS CALLED, YOU MAY CHECK YOUR WORK ON THIS SECTION ONLY. DO NOT TURN TO ANY OTHER SECTION IN THE TEST.

FREE-RESPONSE QUESTION

Time—20 Minutes
1 Question

1. Discuss how the demographic transition model can be used to describe both a country's demographic population and economic development. The statistics for the following three countries should be analyzed and the countries placed in appropriate stages in the model. Describe their economies as well as their demographics. The numbers come from the Population Reference Bureau's 2014 World Population Data Sheet.

	World Averages	Zambia	Argentina	United Kingdom
Birth Rate	20	45	19	12
Death Rate	8	11	7	9

ANSWER KEY

1. B

2. B

3. E

4. A

5. D

6. A

7. E

8. C

9. C

10. B

11. E

12. A

13. E

14. C

15. A

16. B

17. D

18. C

19. C

20. D

21. D

22. C

23. E

24. E

25. A

DIAGNOSTIC TEST: ASSESS YOUR STRENGTHS

Use the following tables to determine which topics (chapters) you need to review most.

Chapter and Topic	Question
Chapter 3: Geography: Its Nature and Perspectives	25
Chapter 4: Population	1, 5, 9, 21
Chapter 5: Cultural Patterns and Processes	4, 8, 16, 24
Chapter 6: Political Organization of Space	10, 17, 19, 20
Chapter 7: Agriculture, Food Production, and Rural Land Use	3, 6, 13, 14
Chapter 8: Industrialization and Economic Development	11, 12, 15, 18
Chapter 9: Cities and Urban Land Use	2, 7, 22, 23

Chapter and Topic	Number of Questions on Test	Number Correct
Chapter 3: Geography: Its Nature and Perspectives	1	
Chapter 4: Population	4	
Chapter 5: Cultural Patterns and Processes	4	
Chapter 6: Political Organization of Space	4	
Chapter 7: Agriculture, Food Production, and Rural Land Use	4	
Chapter 8: Industrialization and Economic Development	4	
Chapter 9: Cities and Urban Land Use	4	

ANSWERS AND EXPLANATIONS

MULTIPLE-CHOICE QUESTIONS

1. B

The demographic transition model is a cornerstone of both the population and the economic development unit. The model is usually broken down into four stages. Stage 1 is characterized by high birth and death rates. Stage 2 has declining death rates yet high birth rates as well; this is the agricultural society. Stage 3 moves into an industrial society, and birth rates begin to fall. Stage 4 is characterized by a tertiary or service-based economy with a country's population eventually reaching zero population growth.

2. B

Paris is the correct answer for this question. A primate city is a city of importance within a country. It must have at least double the population of the second-largest city in that country, and it must be the cultural capital as well as the political capital of the country. Rio de Janeiro would not qualify because São Paulo equals it in population. Washington, D.C., although a political capital, is not the cultural capital or the largest city of the United States. Shanghai is equaled in size and prominence by Beijing; Shanghai is the cultural capital, but Beijing is the political capital of China. Berlin is the largest city in Germany but not by more than double the population of the next-largest city; Munich, Düsseldorf, Hamburg, and Frankfurt, to name a few, rival Berlin in population.

3. E

Pastoral nomadism is traditionally practiced in arid climates and focuses on animals rather than crops.

Nomads sometimes travel great distances for food and shelter for their herds. Shifting cultivation is practiced in wetter areas and involves crops. Truck farming is based on the exchange of commodities, such as fruit. Commercial farming is not concerned so much with climate but with economics. Commercial farmers look to make a profit from their crops or animals, whereas subsistence farmers primarily eat what they grow.

4. A

An ethnic religion is one that you are born into and does not promote conversion of others. The largest ethnic religion in terms of number of followers is Hinduism. Judaism is the correct answer. Christianity, Islam, Buddhism, and Sikhism promote conversion, so they are not ethnic religions.

5. D

Many people confuse high population with high population growth. China, the country with the highest population, has pretty much controlled its population growth through the one-child policy. Growth rates are determined by such statistics as doubling time and natural increase rates. By looking at data from the World Population Reference Bureau, one sees that the highest growth rates are found in sub-Saharan Africa. Total fertility rate, the average number of children that women will bear in their lifetime, is highest in this part of the world. Natural increase rates are approaching 2 and 3 percent of the total population. Central Europe is actually declining in population.

6. A

Von Thunen's model deals with the location of agricultural products relative to a market. Von Thunen's model deals solely with a commercial farming system. The type of product grown or raised by the farmer depends on the cost of the transportation to the market. Heavier, more bulky products are located closer to the market because of their cost to transport. The lighter the product, the farther it can be located from the market, unless it is a perishable product, which needs to be closer to the market. Raw materials are not used in agriculture, and subsistence farmers eat the majority of the products they produce and so do not need a market. Pastoral nomadism is a form of subsistence agriculture.

7. E

Gentrification is the rebuilding of inner-city neighborhoods. The problem with gentrification is that the tax base gets so high that it pushes previous residents out of the neighborhood because they can no longer afford to live there. The positives are that it reduces crime and creates feelings of cohesiveness within communities. Older buildings that are eyesores are torn down to make way for newer buildings that have some value. This value adds to the city in terms of additional property tax revenue.

8. C

Jerusalem contains three separate places that are traditionally holy areas within the city. For Christians, it is where Jesus Christ died on the cross. For Jews, it is the site of the Wailing Wall for atonement. For Muslims, it is the site of the temple from which Mohammed rose when he went to heaven and saw Allah. Mecca is home to the Kabah in Islam, but it is a holy city only to that religion. Medina is the place of Mohammed's birth in Islam. Delhi lies on the Ganges River, which is sacred in the lives of Hindus.

9. C

The center of the United States population has consistently moved west and then south. The census is a detailed counting of the U.S. population every ten years. Since 1790, the census has tracked the geographical center of U.S. population. The population has always moved to the west, and within the last 40 years, has also moved south. As of the 2000 census, the current location of the geographical center of the U.S. population is in southern Missouri.

10. B

The heartland theory, proposed by Hanford Mackinder, was the justification for the Germans to invade Poland and Eastern Europe during World War II. The heartland theory states that whoever controls Eastern Europe and the western section of Asia can control the world. The region focuses on the present-day Ukraine, the world leader in wheat production. Wheat is needed to feed a large population. The region is also home to a large number of natural resources needed as raw materials for industry. Spikeman created the rimland theory. Spikeman believed that the heartland could be contained through alliances. The CIA of the United States put forth the domino theory in the 1960s and 1970s. This theory suggests that when one country falls to communism, many others around it will fall as well because of the political instability created.

11. E

Pittsburgh relies heavily on the steel industry because of its situation. Pittsburgh is ideally located to use the coal from the Appalachian Mountains in its large blast furnaces and get iron ore from the Great Lakes region to produce steel. Automobiles are the basic industry for Detroit. Computer processors are the basic industry for Silicon Valley in California.

12. A

Biomass has been in the news recently as one of the most promising alternative energy sources. Biomass uses agricultural products, such as corn, and produces fuel from them. Ethanol, made from corn, is a key alternative energy source. Many cars and engines now run on ethanol and other biomass fuel products. Nuclear energy relies on nonrenewable uranium to produce energy. Wind, solar, and hydroelectric power would not rely solely on agriculture for raw materials for energy production.

13. E

This question needs to be answered by looking at the world's population. The majority of the world's population, over 58 percent, lives within Asia. Rice, eaten three meals a day, is a high-calorie food that provides energy to millions around the world. Although corn, wheat, soybeans, and barley are important, they are not eaten by as many people on a daily basis as rice. Rice is also an inexpensive crop that millions of people can afford. Subsistence farmers around the world in warmer climates grow rice to sustain themselves.

14. C

Central America first developed cotton, beans, and corn as crops. Domesticated animals there included llamas, alpacas, and turkeys. There are generally believed to be three known hearths of world agriculture: Southeast Asia and Northern India, Southwest Asia and Northeastern Africa, and the Central American isthmus and northwestern South America. Southeast Asia first domesticated dogs, pigs, and chickens. Crops included taro root and rice. Southwest Asia first domesticated cattle, sheep, and goats and first used coffee as well as palm oil.

15. A

The Appalachian Mountains are the leading coal-producing region in the United States. Abundant coal reserves have caused the United States to rely heavily on coal as a power source.

16. B

The environmental determinist approach to geography focuses on the idea that people are the result of their environment. It suggests that people who live in the tropical regions are lazier than those who live in temperate regions because of the climate they live in. According to this theory, those who live in the temperate regions will be the smartest and most hardworking societies in the world because of their latitudinal location. The possiblist approach to geography has replaced the environmental determinist approach.

17. D

A nation is a group of people with common cultural characteristics. A state is an area with a defined, permanently populated territory and sovereign control over its external and foreign affairs. In a nation-state, cultural boundaries and political boundaries overlap almost to perfection. In today's world, there is no perfect example of a nation-state. However, some countries come close. Japan is the closest example to a perfect nation-state in the world today. Of the Japanese population, 99 percent are ethnic Japanese. The total population of Japan is 128 million, and 129 million people in the world speak Japanese as their primary language, and 99 percent of the people in Japan speak Japanese as their primary language. Denmark is another good example of a nation-state.

18. C

Both cities have invested billions into their newly developed industrial zones. The London Dockland area is characterized by newly developed property that is home to commercial and industrial as well as residential properties. It is connected to the subway system in London by the London Dockland Railway. Shanghai has the Pudong development. This development is the largest in the world. Billions of dollars have been invested in its transportation networks as well as infrastructure. Both developments are considered phenomenal success stories. Both areas have attracted foreign investment and gentrified communities around the zones.

19. C

A compact state is a country that is relatively small and circular in shape. The distance from the center to any boundary doesn't vary much. As a result, efficient communication and transportation systems are feasible, making the country easier to defend than other basic shapes of states.

20. D

Since the end of the Cold War in the early 1990s, Eastern Europe has experienced major devolutionary forces (a large political entity breaking into smaller political units).

Examples of this include the Soviet Union devolving into Russia and 14 other states, Czechoslovakia becoming the Czech Republic and Slovakia, and the dissolution of Yugoslavia into Slovenia, Croatia, Bosnia and Herzegovina, Montenegro, Kosovo, Macedonia, and Serbia.

21. D

There are three kinds of push and pull factors: political, economic, and environmental. Environmental moves are often voluntary, such as when people relocate to a more desirable climate. Political factors are often forced upon people: either you move or you will suffer persecution. Economic factors cause people to move to where the jobs are to get employed. The migration of Hindus and Muslims during Gandhi's time was forced upon people. Hindus who were living in present-day Pakistan were forced to move back to India, and Muslims who lived in India were frightened of violence as well. This was an example of a political push factor.

22. C

The concentric zone model is what most people believe exists in American cities today. The poor live next to the central business district, while the wealthy live in the suburbs and exurbs because they can afford the daily commute into the city. This theory does not hold up, however, because of the wealth in many urban neighborhoods. The multiple nuclei model best fits most American cities. This model suggests that most development takes place around areas that are ripe for it. Development may be sporadic at times, but the developers go where they can make the most money. Zoning laws in many suburban areas are trying to curtail development for traffic flow and tax purposes.

23. E

European cities are very distinctive. They have low-rise buildings, usually no higher than five or six stories, in their central business district. These cities were built sometime hundreds of years ago, before the technology of automobiles and high-rise buildings. Most of the other cities in the world have their high-rise buildings in the center of the city because of the high rental rates there, which only commercial properties can afford. Transportation is usually weak in the CBDs of European cities, particularly for automobiles. Streets were built for horses and wagons rather than for automobiles, so European cities usually suffer from more congestion.

24. E

English, Spanish, and Hindi are all languages that fit under the Indo-European language family. The second-largest language family is the Sino-Tibetan language family. Mandarin Chinese is located within this language family. Religious systems do not play a major role in language creation or cessation.

25. A

Distance decay means that there will be more interaction between two things that are closer in distance than things that are farther apart. Because Baltimore is closer to Washington, D.C., than Philadelphia, there is more interaction (movement of people, products, and ideas) between them.

FREE-RESPONSE QUESTION SAMPLE AND ANALYSIS

SAMPLE ESSAY

The demographic transition model is both an indicator of a country's development and its population. It looks at both birth and death rates. The disparity between these two numbers indicates the country's level of economic development.

In stage 1 of the model, there are fluctuations in both the birth and the death rates. This relates to a hunting and gathering society. In this stage, population remains relatively low due to inadequate food sources to supply large populations.

In stage 2 of the model, a society moves from hunting and gathering to a more agricultural basis, as in earth's First Agricultural Revolution. Societies are more dependent upon reliable food sources that are readily available. As long as food sources remain adequate, population continues to grow, and the death rate decreases. Stage 2 is characterized by a high birth rate and a falling, but still relatively high, death rate. Zambia is in stage 2, because the world averages are well below both its birth and death rates. More children are needed in agricultural societies. Children are both a social security system as well as a supply of labor for the farm. In a stage 2 country, the death rate declines due to increased food sources as well as medical advancements and greater availability of health care. Total population in stage 2 increases dramatically due to the gap between high birth rates and declining death rates.

Argentina is a good example of a stage 3 country. In a stage 3 country, the population shifts from being mostly involved in agricultural activities to being mostly engaged in industrial activities. As a society moves into stage 3, the birth rate drops dramatically, but the death rate only drops slightly. Industrial societies tend to have women in the workplace. When more women are in the workplace, they have fewer children, and the birth rate drops dramatically. The death rate continues to fall a little bit due to continued advancements in medical technology. As the country is about to move into stage 4, the total population is high but not growing at a very rapid pace.

The United Kingdom is in stage 4 of the demographic transition model. This stage is characterized by a zero growth rate. A zero growth rate occurs when the crude birth rate is roughly equal to the crude death rate. In stage 4 societies, countries move from being industry based to having more service jobs. More people are selling products than producing them. During stage 4, a country has more elderly people, and the death rate rises. It is possible in a stage 4 country to have a higher death rate than birth rate. Many countries in Eastern Europe are at this point. Children are seen more as an economic liability in this stage due to the increased costs of rearing children. Total population in this stage remains high but will dip when deaths start outpacing births.

ANALYSIS

This free-response question asked you to link the population unit with the unit on economic development. Almost all of the free-response questions on the AP test will link more than one unit together. Questions in the past have linked such themes as population with urbanization, agriculture with industrialization, and culture with population. You must link the pertinent themes in your answer.

When scoring this question, the exam reader would be analyzing your interpretation of both the population data from the three countries as well as your tie-in to the economic development of the countries. Only writing about the demographic data would not score well on this question. To receive full points, you must link the economic development aspects of the demographic transition model with the demographic features of the given countries.

Your essay may receive some points for describing the birth rates and the death rates as well as the total population in each of the four stages of the model. Explanation is needed for stage 1 having fluctuations in both the birth and the death rates. Stage 2 has high birth rates and declining death rates. Stage 3 has declining birth rates and continued falling death rates. Stage 4 has zero population growth, meaning that birth rates and death rates are more or less equal.

Tying in economic development would provide you with additional points. You need to identify that stage 1 societies are hunting and gathering societies, where total population remains low because of unstable food sources. Stage 2 needs to be described as an agricultural society. Total population increases rapidly in agricultural societies because of the need for children as both laborers on the farm and as social security measures. In a stage 3 country, the society is moving from an agricultural base to an industrial base. When this occurs, more women are entering the workforce and delaying childbirth. The total population increase rate decreases. Stage 4 is a tertiary or service-based economy, where societies are more involved in selling items than producing them. Societies may move into the quaternary or even quinary sectors of the economy and remain in stage 4. In quaternary and quinary economies, people are selling intangible items, such as tax services, Internet access, or wireless communication access.

If you answered the question with the aforementioned items, you would score full points or close to it on the test.

Part Three

AP HUMAN GEOGRAPHY REVIEW

CHAPTER 3: GEOGRAPHY: ITS NATURE AND PERSPECTIVES

IF YOU LEARN ONLY FIVE THINGS IN THIS CHAPTER . . .

1. The Greeks were the first society to introduce geography as a subject. Eratosthenes is credited with being the first person to use the word *geography*, *geo* meaning "Earth" and *graphy* "to write."

2. The five themes of geography allow geographers to make each place unique (location) and to tie them together (region). Humans alter the environment to meet their needs (human-environment interaction).

3. Diffusion is the spread or movement of a principle or phenomenon. Relocation, expansion, contagious, stimulus, and hierarchical diffusion are means by which an idea or phenomenon spreads.

4. There are three types of regions: formal, functional, and perceptual or vernacular.

5. There are three main aspects of distribution: density, concentration, and patterns. All are used to assist in determining spatial characteristics on the landscape.

HISTORICAL FOUNDATIONS OF GEOGRAPHY

Geography is the description of the Earth's surface and the people and processes that shape its landscapes. Some have suggested that the study of geography is a complex challenge. It is difficult to define a concept that is ever-changing. Geography is not only a social science but is also a way of thinking. Geographers fight the notion that geography is merely memorization of place names and facts. In actuality, geography is a science that touches upon every aspect of human existence.

It is an innate aspect of human nature to wonder where we are and how we got here. People often feel fear and anxiety from not knowing the answers to these questions. Since their beginning, humans have sought to acquire and define their space. These first crude attempts toward description were the initial building blocks of geography.

Early humans in the Middle East region near present-day Iraq drew the first maps on rocks. Geography is bounded by the physical Earth itself and extends down to the building-level scale. Although architects study building designs, *linking* building designs with other areas is important to geography, specifically in the study of regions, because it helps us to define and organize places. Maps, which are a form of communication, can be drawn to any scale. A map of your school desk drawn to a 1:1 scale would be the size of your school desk. Anything on a scale greater than that of the planet Earth falls under the domain of the science of astronomy.

THE GREEKS

The Greeks first classified geography as a study and a science. Greek philosophers and writers wrote about the Earth being round and established mathematical principles for the world around them. For example, although Homer's *Iliad* and *Odyssey* are both considered classical literature, they are filled with geographic accounts.

Greek explorers sailed around the Mediterranean Sea around 800 BCE and, in many instances, left us fascinating firsthand geographical accounts. These accounts are an invaluable resource; sailors arriving and departing at the port of Miletus, in present-day Turkey, gave the Greeks a practical base for their study of geography as they established three primary continents in the world: Europe, Asia, and Libya (Africa).

Anaximander is the first person credited with making a map of the known world at that time. Anaximander used information from all of the sailors' accounts and produced what is considered to be the first scale map of the world. Although Anaximander's map was fairly accurate on the large-scale map portion of the Mediterranean, it was still inaccurate when considering the small-scale portion of the rest of the world owing to the lack of available information.

Greek explorers had detailed descriptions of areas around the eastern Mediterranean, but information beyond that realm remained a mystery. Details were few, and myths abounded. The rise of mythology led to a multitude of creative ideas as to the whereabouts of the edge of the world and what lay beyond.

AP EXPERT TIP

Notice how this discussion of geography begins with its historical foundations. You will find throughout the human geography course that history—both world and American—are complementary perspectives to geography, just as history is heavily dependent on geography.

The classic Greek philosophers, **Aristotle, Socrates,** and **Plato**, furthered the belief that the Earth was round. Their evidence, along with mathematical and scientific work by Pythagoras, seemed to prove the Earth's roundness.

Eratosthenes is credited with first using the term *geography* to describe this new area of scientific study. Using two points on the Earth's surface, he measured the angle of the sun, and from his calculations, he was able to determine the circumference of the Earth with incredible accuracy. Eratosthenes was 99.5 percent accurate in his calculations.

THE MODERN PERIOD

In 1830, the Royal Geographical Society was founded in London. In 1888, the American counterpart, the National Geographic Society, was formed. In the early 20th century, an important school of thought in geography began to develop. This theory, **environmental determinism**, which proposes that cultures are a direct result of where they exist, was led by geographers such as Carl Ritter, Ellen Churchill Semple, and Ellsworth Huntington. They concluded that warmer climates tend to cause inhabitants to have a more relaxed attitude toward work and progress. This philosophy also led some people to believe that Europeans and those from more temperate climates were more motivated, intelligent, and culturally advanced than those from warmer climates.

During the 1930s, this school of thought was attacked as being prejudicial and undeniably incorrect. Even today, environmental determinism is considered an embarrassment to most in the geographic profession. However, some debate persists regarding the merits and downsides of this controversial theory.

Contemporary geographers favor the **possibilist** approach to geographic study. The possiblist approach to geography suggests that humans are not a product of their environment but possess the skills necessary to modify their environment to fit human needs. In the possiblist approach, people can determine their outcomes.

TODAY AND BEYOND

Today, the field of geography is dominated by two new technologies that are having a profound impact on the study of geography and the Earth. **Global positioning systems (GPS), satellite imagery, remote sensing**, and **Geographic information systems (GIS)** are providing geographers with new means to describe the world. Prior to computer technology, cartographers were limited in the scope and distortion of the maps that they could produce. With current technology, we are seeing more advanced geography entering our daily lives.

AP EXPERT TIP

GPS works through triangulation, so if you understand a bit of geometry, you understand GPS. In geography, you often need to connect with concepts learned in other disciplines. Don't forget to draw on that information even though you may be studying for a different subject.

GPS technology, now found in cars and cell phones, is becoming more and more common. GPS uses latitude and longitude coordinates to determine an exact location on the Earth. GPS technology can be incorporated into handheld devices that pick up signals broadcast by satellites circling the globe. The GPS unit interprets these signals to give you your absolute location.

GIS uses geographic information and layers it into a new map showing specific types of geographic data. Watersheds, population density, highways, and agricultural data are just a few of the geographic features that can be used as layers of data. In many ways, GIS is the new geography, allowing geographers to analyze new data in ways never before imagined.

Aerial photography also allows geographers to see land use changing over time by comparing pictures of places from years past to current photographs. Other technologies, such as Google Earth and other high-tech systems, are revolutionizing the way that we look at the world. Satellite images, remote sensing, and aerial photography are bringing places from around the world onto our computer screens at home, work, and school. Students can see their homes and schools on these websites, and exploration can take place with a click of a mouse. A great website that illustrates the usefulness of these technologies is http://earthshots.usgs.gov. This site, maintained by the United States Geological Survey, uses the latest technologies to document the changes over time with respect to urban growth, agricultural land use, and environmental issues.

MAPS: AN INTRODUCTION

Maps are the basic tools that geographers use to convey information. Although there are many different types and projections of maps, they generally represent the Earth's surface in some fashion. The ability to interpret data from maps is an important skill in determining the meaning of location and place within the study of geography.

A fundamental problem with traditional maps is that when attempting to convey a three-dimensional object, such as the Earth, onto a two-dimensional piece of paper, distortion occurs. The larger the scale, the less distortion, while distortion is greatest on small-scale maps. Maps of cities have very little distortion. Maps of the Earth have plagued cartographers with distortion issues since the time of the Greeks and Babylonians.

SCALE

Scale is the relationship of the size of the map to the amount of area it represents on the planet. Scale is the dimension into which one renders the real world. A map the size of your desk that shows an area the size of your desk is at 1:1 scale. Small-scale maps show more area in less detail. Large-scale maps show a smaller area but in greater detail. An easy way to distinguish between the two items is to think of your house or school. The larger the house or school would look on the map, the larger the scale. A map of a town or city would have a larger scale than a map of a continent. The smallest scale map that one can make is of the world.

There are three ways to write a scale on a map. The first way is to write the scale in words. "One inch equals 100 miles" is an example of a word scale. The next way is to use a line. This line measures the distance on a map. The line may be drawn out to one inch or two inches. The miles or kilometers will then be located along the line to represent the scale of the map. The last way to write a scale on a map is to use a ratio. This ratio is often written as follows: 1:24,000. This means that for every one object on a map, it would take 24,000 of those same objects to cover the same amount of ground in the real world. Thus, 1:24,000 would mean that 1 inch on the map equals 24,000 inches on the planet.

DISTORTION

Cartographers are always concerned with the concept of distortion. When a cartographer tries to put information onto a two-dimensional map, distortion occurs. The further that one goes from the equator, the greater the distortion on the map. Depending upon the type of map being produced, the cartographer can determine the best projection with which to show the information. There are maps that try to space out the distortion equally throughout the map. These maps use an **equal-area projection**. Equal-area projections keep the size or amount of area intact but distort shapes. An example of an equal-area map would be the Goodes-Homsoline projection, which breaks up the globe into continents and separates the oceans. Alternatively, maps that distort area but keep shapes intact are called **conformal maps**. An example of a conformal map would be the Lambert conic projection. On this projection, the distance between latitude lines increases the farther one moves away from the common line of latitude.

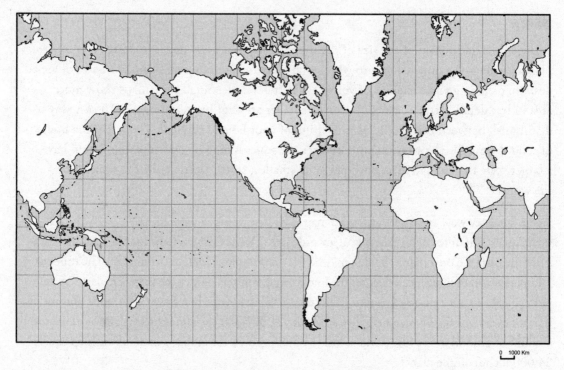

0 1000 Km

Figure 3.1: Mercator Map Projection.

This type of distortion is evident on a Mercator map. Although the Mercator map was and is still useful for determining distance on the surface of the Earth, it greatly exaggerates the land forms around the polar regions. On a Mercator map, all lines of latitude and longitude meet at right angles. These right angles force the top and bottom of the globe to stretch out, creating more distortion of the polar regions. This is why Greenland looks as though it is the size of Africa on a Mercator map projection. The distortion is especially severe on small-scale maps using the Mercator projection. In reality, Greenland is only a fraction of the size of Africa.

MAP CLASSES AND TYPES

Cartographers can use one of four map classes to determine how best to construct their maps. A **cylindrical** map shows true direction but loses distance. The Mercator map projection, shown in Figure 3.1, is an example of a cylindrical class. Another map class is a **planar** projection. Any azimuthal map, which shows true direction and examines the Earth from one point—usually a pole or polar projection—is an example of a planar class. All points go either north from the South Pole point or south from the North Pole point. The third type of map class is a **conic** projection. Conic projection puts a cone over the Earth and tries to keep distance intact but loses directional qualities. The fourth map class is an **oval** projection, which is a combination of the cylindrical and conic projections. The Molleweide projection is an oval projection.

In addition to showing areas, maps may also be used to determine some types of geographic phenomena. **Thematic maps** can be represented in a variety of ways. Area class maps, area symbol maps, cartograms, choropleth maps, digital images, dot maps, flow-line maps, isoline maps, point symbol maps, and proportional symbol maps are all used to determine geographic properties. Geographers and map readers need to be familiar with all different types of maps to determine meaning.

Flow-line maps are good for determining movement, such as migration. **Choropleth maps** put data into a spatial format and are useful for determining demographic data, such as infant mortality rates, by assigning colors or patterns to areas. **Cartograms** chart and assign data by size. World population by country is often shown in a cartogram. Countries with a larger population appear larger on the map. The country with the largest population on Earth is China; therefore, it is the largest country in size on a cartogram map, followed by India, the United States, Indonesia, and Brazil.

THE MISUSE OF MAPS

Maps can also be used to mislead readers. Because maps are a form of communication, maps can intentionally or unintentionally cause confusion or provide misinformation in several ways.

Maps can mislead a reader by intentionally deleting information. By not putting something on a map, the cartographer is making a statement about the importance of the item. For example, some of the maps from the former Soviet Union omitted information, such as military and government buildings, possibly for political or strategic reasons.

Another way a map can be used to mislead a reader is by using colors. Bolder colors usually indicate strength in a factor or a **toponym** (place name) on the map. Conversely, lighter colors often represent weakness. German maps during World War II, such as the one in Figure 3.2, showed Germany in a bold red color while showing the Allied powers in light yellow. These maps were distributed to the German citizens to promote the perception that the Allied powers were weak.

The size of an item on a map usually indicates strength as well. The bigger the item appears, the greater its perceived strength and importance. Conversely, the smaller the item, the less important it seems to be. U.S. military maps that are made public often show U.S. bases with spheres of influence greater than they actually are.

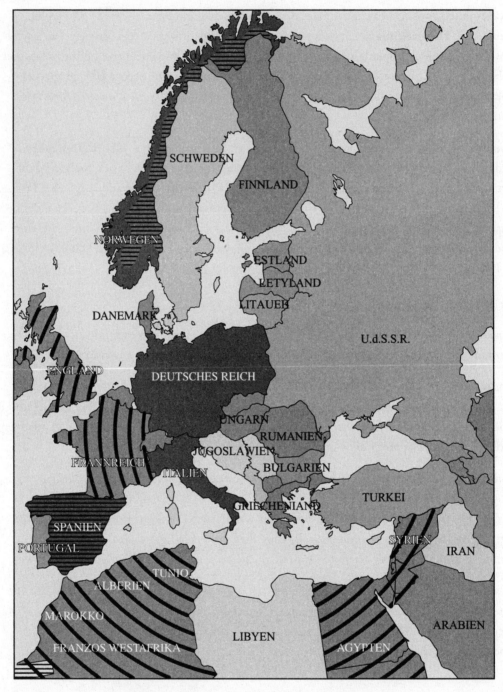

Figure 3.2: German Map Showing Europe in 1940.

FIVE THEMES OF GEOGRAPHY

Geographers have divided the field into two broad areas that are directly related. **Human geography** is the study of human characteristics on the landscape. These include population, agriculture, urbanization, and culture. The other field is **physical geography**, which examines the physical features of the Earth and tries to define how they work. Physical geographers analyze wind, water, and weather patterns. When geographers try to explain a place, they cannot separate the two fields. Physical processes affect human activities, and human activities affect some of the physical processes.

To further define geography, five distinct themes have emerged:

1. Place

2. Region

3. Location

4. Human-environment interaction

5. Spatial interaction or movement

The five themes of geography are a good way to analyze a particular location or region on the surface of the Earth. Geographers from the American Association of Geographers and the National Council for Geographic Education arrived at the five themes in 1981.

PLACE

To classify what we observe on the surface of the Earth, geographers have assigned attributes to assist in the description of one of the major themes of geography—place. Describing the individuality of place can be as simple as showing slides of your latest vacation or as complex as presenting a detailed analysis of agricultural practices in Bangladesh.

DEFINING PLACE

Place is the description of what we see and of how we see and experience a certain aspect of the Earth's surface. Place defines and refines what we are. It is the description of what the location is like. *Hot, cold,* and *busy* can all be used when describing a certain location.

Let's look at some examples that highlight the importance of place as a concept.

AP EXPERT TIP

If Shanghai is one of the fastest-growing cities in the world, what creates that growth and why? What is Shanghai's role within China, for Asia, and the world? See if you can answer those questions now. If not, keep your questions in hand as you read through this study guide. Does the information on page 333 help you answer your question?

It has been said that Shanghai is one of the fastest-growing cities in the world, but what exactly does that mean? What does the phrase *fastest growing* mean? Does it mean the city is the fastest growing in terms of population or in terms of economic growth? More description is needed. This description is at the core of place. Shanghai sits at the junction of the Huangpu River and the Yangtze's delta, making it a major trading port for Asia and the rest of the world. By describing Shanghai's economic growth rate and continued advancement in a worldwide economy, we clarify the phrase *fastest growing*. By giving Shanghai these unique descriptions, we are shaping the view of Shanghai and further refining its characteristics.

New York City is the largest city in the United States. New York City has been called "the city that never sleeps." It has been mentioned as the cultural capital of the United States. It is home to millions of people. The culture of New York is different from the culture of Shanghai. The differences between the two cities help to define the concept of place for both locations and make each city unique.

Minnesota is cold during the winter and warm during the summer. Minneapolis and St. Paul are sometimes called the "Twin Cities" owing to their proximity. However, the two cities are different in both their layout and character. Minneapolis is known for its many nationally regarded theaters and art museums. Minneapolis has more features relating to an entertainment capital, while St. Paul, being the capital of Minnesota, is more of a governmental center. All of these attributes provide greater clarity regarding place.

Descriptions of place are often based upon the cultural attributes or the cultural landscape of the area. By describing the area in this way, we place our subjective attributes on the landscape itself. Office buildings, theaters, places of worship, and so forth can define the cultural landscape, all of which comprise a person's view of a place.

When describing the physical environment of a place, descriptions of natural landscapes are often used. Natural landscapes include mountains, rivers, valleys, or anything within the landscape that is physical. This physical description affects the people of the area greatly.

REGION

Just as all places are unique, common threads in the landscape can be used to pull different places together. The concept of **region** links places together using any parameter the geographer chooses.

The Midwestern portion of the United States is characterized by its dependence on agriculture. The predominant crop in the Midwest is corn. By looking at agricultural productivity and commodity charts at either a state or county level, we can determine the location of corn-growing regions in the United States. These regions are sometimes called "belts." The Corn Belt region in the United States coincides with the Midwest region.

Another example of a region or belt would be the presence of evangelical Christians in the southern portion of the United States. The term Bible Belt is often used to describe the Southern Baptist dominance of the population. Many areas in the South have evangelical churches that take up city blocks. The importance of these churches in the landscape is vital in determining what the South is like, and the attitudes of evangelicals in the South are important in determining the overall culture of the region.

A region can range in size from a single location up to a global area. There are three main types of regions: formal, functional, and perceptual or vernacular regions.

Formal regions are regions where anything and everything inside has the same characteristic or phenomena. This characteristic might include a political zone, language, or other cultural trait.

Germany is a formal region. Germany has a defined political boundary with sovereignty. People who are inside of Germany share the characteristic of being subjected to the laws and regulations of the country of Germany. The people who reside there legally have either been born there or entered the country through a customs office. Whether in Hamburg, Munich, or Berlin, people share the characteristic of being inside the country of Germany. When a person steps outside of the country of Germany into a bordering country, that individual no longer shares the common characteristic of being in the sovereign country of Germany.

The Corn Belt is also defined as a formal region. Even though many of the places within the Corn Belt grow other crops, corn is the predominant crop. Wheat, soybeans, and hay are also grown, but the number-one cash crop and crop of land use is corn. A person may not know that they have stepped out of the Corn Belt unless agricultural commodity data is analyzed.

Functional regions can be defined around a certain point or node. These functional regions are the most intense around the center but lose their characteristics the farther the distance from the focal point. Distance decay, the lessening of a feature as distance is increased from the hearth, is an indication of a functional region.

For example, radio stations use a tower and broadcast on a specific frequency, which a radio picks up. You are listening to your favorite station on the way out of town when the fuzz or static begins to build on the radio. The farther you drive from the city where the tower is located, the fuzzier the signal gets, until eventually you lose it entirely. A functional region could be described as the area in which one is in range of that station.

Shopping mall trade areas are another example of a functional region. Shoppers who live in close proximity to the mall will frequent the mall more often than other shoppers who live farther away. Shoppers who live farther from the mall are likely to live closer to another mall whose influence is greater on them. The trade area is strongest near the mall and decreases with the distance. The sphere of influence is reduced as the distance increases. This process is known as **distance decay**.

The third type of region is known as a **perceptual region** or **vernacular region**. Vernacular regions exist primarily in an individual's perception or feelings. If you were to ask a person from the East Coast of the United States where the Midwest is, you will likely get a different response than from someone who resides in Nebraska. Some people from the East Coast perceive that the Midwest starts in western Pennsylvania and ends around Illinois. While a person from Nebraska may feel strongly that his or her home is located in the Midwest, a person from the East may feel that the person from Nebraska is located in the Great Plains or the North Central region rather than the Midwest.

Another example of a vernacular region within the United States is the concept of *the South*. The South means different things to different people. Where does the South begin? While most can agree that Alabama is located within the Deep South, some may feel that Kentucky may not be Southern enough. Some people may consider all Confederate states in the Civil War to be part of the South. Others may use climate as a criterion. Still others may use the Southern dialect to determine where "Dixie" is.

It is also important to note that a person may be in several regions simultaneously. A person may be in the state of Colorado (formal region), reading a Los Angeles newspaper (functional region), while dreaming of their skiing trip to Utah, which this person perceives as having a large amount of snow in the Rocky Mountains in the West (vernacular region). Regions can overlap depending upon their characteristics.

By using the concept of region, geographers organize data to assist in describing information. Geographers then render this information into maps.

LOCATION

Another theme that geographers use in their analysis of the Earth is location. "Where am I?" is a question often asked. There are two ways to answer that fundamental question. People may use **relative location**, which means giving their location in reference to another feature on the Earth's surface. People may also use **absolute location**, which means using latitude and longitude coordinates.

Site refers to the internal, physical characteristics of a place. For example, New Orleans is a very poor site for human habitation. Being eight feet below sea level

---

AP EXPERT TIP
Make sure you watch for differences in terminology on the exam. Differentiate among city, country, and continent. Failure to do so is a simple mistake that you'll want to avoid.

makes it prone to flooding during times of high precipitation. Its **situation**, however, at the base of the Mississippi River, has enabled its growth. New Orleans is a city with a poor site but an excellent situation. Anchorage, Alaska, is another city with a good situation but a poor site. Located right on fault lines, it is prone to earthquakes, as demonstrated during the Alaskan Earthquake of 1964; registering 9.2 on the Richter scale, it leveled the city.

A person may have a **mental map** of an area when he or she is driving to a familiar location. This mental map is a map that the person believes to exist. It may be very accurate or significantly inaccurate. Mental maps are important because most people possess them, and they can prove useful tools in communication. For example, when we get to our favorite restaurant and want to give directions to a friend so that that person can meet us there, we give directions based on what is inside our head.

When you give directions to your friend to come over to your house, you are probably giving him or her a relative location. Telling your friend to turn left at the gas station and then right at the firehouse is using reference points (gas station and firehouse) to assist in determining the location of a place.

Mexico is located to the south of the United States. When giving this type of data, you are also using relative location. You are assuming that the listener or reader knows where the United States is. Once we know where the United States is, we can determine that it means that Mexico is just to the south of the United States.

Problems can arise when using relative location. You assume that your friend knows where the firehouse or the gas station is, but what if your friend doesn't know these reference points? There needs to be another way to define exactly where you are located. Geographers use latitude and longitude for this.

The grid system that geographers set up uses latitude and longitude, which are the fictional lines that divide the Earth's surface to assist people in determining an exact location. **Latitudes** are parallel lines that run east/west on the surface of the Earth. These are also called **parallels**. The latitude line that runs in the middle of the Earth is the **equator**. This is 0 degrees latitude. Anything to the north of the equator is in the Northern Hemisphere, and anything to the south of the equator is in the Southern Hemisphere. The highest degree of latitude that one can go is 90 degrees. This is the angle where the equator meets the lines of longitude. Ninety degrees north would be the North Pole, whereas 90 degrees south would be the South Pole.

Longitudes, or **meridians**, are the lines that run north and south. The 0 degree longitude line, or **prime meridian** runs through Greenwich, in southeast London, England. Here, visitors can stand with one foot in the Eastern Hemisphere and one foot in the Western Hemisphere. Greenwich was picked for the prime meridian because it is home to the observatory that first set up the system of latitude and longitude.

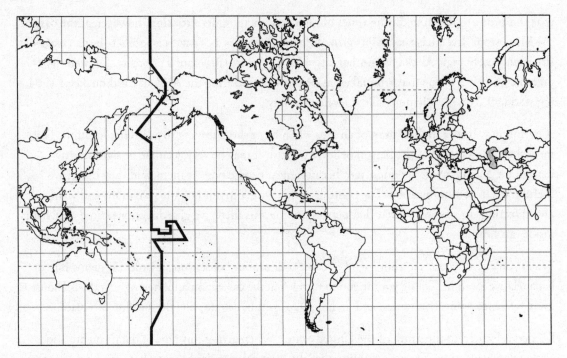

Figure 3.3: International Date Line.

The globe is a sphere made up of circles. All circles possess 360 degrees. A day is 24 hours long. Dividing 360 by 24 equals 15. Therefore, for every 15 degrees longitude traveled east or west, a person will enter a new time zone. Time zones are based largely on that 15-degree principle, although the exact location of the line may vary to take into account other factors, such as political boundaries.

A good example of this is the **International Date Line** (Figure 3.3). The farthest that one can go on the longitude scale is 180 degrees, and that longitude roughly represents the International Date Line. However, the International Date Line zigzags its way through the Pacific Ocean owing to the location of countries there.

HUMAN-ENVIRONMENT INTERACTION

The fourth theme in geography is the concept of **human-environment interaction**. This theme describes how people modify or alter the environment to fit individual or societal needs.

The city of Las Vegas, Nevada, is built in the middle of a desert. Humans have modified the environment around Las Vegas to provide enough water to meet the needs of the city. Water management is a critical issue in areas like Las Vegas. The Hoover Dam creates one of the largest man-made lakes in the world, Lake Mead, and provides electricity to much of the desert Southwest. The flooding of the backwaters directly changed the environment behind the dam and made life suitable in areas such as Las Vegas. The dam's electrical power, recreational opportunities, and water management capability have sustained a large and growing population in the desert.

Humans cannot live in the **five toos**: too hot, too cold, too wet, too dry, and too hilly. Any of these environmental conditions taken to the extreme makes land uninhabitable. However, as human engineering and invention continue to improve, humans can adjust to survive in conditions that they previously could not.

The Ice Hotel in Sweden has made it posh to take a vacation surrounded by frozen water. Guests are welcomed into an igloo and spend their evenings resting within a block of ice. By modifying their environments, humans have enabled habitation of areas that previously were off-limits.

SPATIAL INTERACTION OR MOVEMENT

The last theme of geography is the idea of **spatial interaction** or **movement**. How linked is a place to the outside world? The answer to this question determines much about an area. How well an area is connected to the world determines its importance. Without transportation systems, it is considered a remote area and, hence, less important, regardless of its geographical distance from a destination point. The remote location's spatial interaction is poor owing to its lack of transportation connections.

International airports are a good example of the movement theme. Thanks to international air travel, for example, it is now possible to fly directly from Singapore to New York. New York's John F. Kennedy (JFK) Airport receives direct, daily flights from around the world. Looking at the flight board at JFK, one notices the proximity of New York City to other cities in the world. Within one day, a person can fly from New York City and land almost anywhere in the world. Thus, the spatial interaction of New York City is high owing to its transportation systems, such as the international airport.

In contrast, Devil's Lake, North Dakota, has a small airport. Although it is serviced by daily flights, they must go through a hub in Minneapolis-St. Paul to get anyplace else. This limits transportation into and out of Devil's Lake. The flight board at Devil's Lake looks much different from the flight board at New York's JFK airport.

Many of the cities on the Great Plains in the United States are built 13 miles apart. Railroads determined that this was the distance that farmers could bring their agricultural commodities to town and still make a reasonable profit while limiting the railroads' investment in infrastructure. Towns missed by the railroad line quickly died, while population increased in cities where the railroad was located. Trains brought settlement into areas and agricultural products out of these areas and were the lifeline of these agricultural communities. The spatial interactions of these communities were based on the railroad during their settlement days; today spatial interactions are based on both railroad and highway systems as well as airplane travel.

Spatial interaction often deals with the concept of situation. Situation is how well connected a place is with the outside world. Different places have a better situation than others. As previously mentioned, New Orleans has a wonderful situation. Located at the base of the Mississippi River, all of the goods that come down the river go through ports located around New Orleans. This situation once enabled New Orleans to become one of the richest cities in North America. Chicago's situation is very good because of its position in the central region of the United States, making it a regional hub for transportation. O'Hare airport is one of the busiest in the world, and railroad and interstate systems convene in Chicago. Chicago's situation has enabled it to become the third-largest city in the United States.

By looking through a geographic lens, people can spot the traits of place and begin to describe it. Since human inception, the Earth has been searched, discovered, and defined. By using the five themes of place, region, location, human-environment interaction, and spatial interaction or movement, geographers can identify unique characteristics and define areas with some specificity. These features make each place special. They make each place the center of everywhere and no place the middle of nowhere—quite a mouthful but an accurate assessment of our interconnected world.

SIX ESSENTIAL ELEMENTS IN GEOGRAPHY

About ten years after the five themes of geography were introduced to classrooms around the world, the National Geography Standards were introduced to the classrooms around the United States. These National Geography Standards fall in line with the following six essential elements of geography instruction:

1. The spatial world
2. Places and regions
3. Physical systems
4. Human systems
5. Environment and society
6. Uses of geography in today's society

These elements are essential to understanding what AP Human Geography is about. The fundamental themes of geography are not a part of the curriculum itself but allow us a greater understanding of the themes in the AP Human Geography course.

In other words, as we look at a particular location, such as Seattle, Washington, we can use the five thematic characteristics to define it as a place. The broader picture of Seattle includes the trade on the Puget Sound and the headquarters of Boeing and Microsoft and their vast industrial complexes, all of which assist in describing the city. Likewise, Seattle's agriculture and transportation systems keep it a vibrant city of the U.S. Pacific Northwest region. AP Human Geography focuses on all these elements.

THE SPATIAL WORLD

No place is alone. Some places are lonelier than others, but all places are linked by some factors. These factors can include population, agriculture, or industrial and economic bases. Culture, too, can link locations based on colonialism and other factors. Each of these elements links places or assists in defining places.

PLACES AND REGIONS

By describing places and regions, we assign characteristics to particular locations and link them by means of their commonalities. As previously mentioned, a particular place may be linked by almost any factor one wishes to consider. Level of urban development, language spoken, and religion practiced are just three examples of traits geographers use to define a particular location and link it to other locations.

PHYSICAL SYSTEMS

Physical systems are not among the major five themes of geography, but would most likely overlap with the human-environment interaction theme. The physical systems of the Earth are intricately related to the human systems on the Earth. Physical barriers prevent the movement of people across landscapes, and volcanoes, earthquakes, and floods all prevent people from living in certain locations.

HUMAN SYSTEMS

Human systems are anything that humans have done to modify the Earth's surface. Human systems can include anything from agriculture to hydroelectric construction to homes and office structures, and they affect the natural systems of the Earth in some small or large way. The Earth has limited some of these activities by its topography. The interaction between the physical environment and human systems have had a profound impact on place.

ENVIRONMENT AND SOCIETY

Another of the six essential elements is the relatiionship of the environment and society.
The chapter on Agriculture, Food Production, and Rural Land Use describes four primary ways of using land or perceiving land use: economic, sustainable, environmental, and preservationist. Each of these determines how humans can use the land to their advantage economically or otherwise. In the newly revised AP Human Geography exam, environment and society is a topic that will be gaining importance.

USES OF GEOGRAPHY IN TODAY'S SOCIETY

The last of the six essential elements in geography instruction is how geography is used in today's society. The profession of geographer is often in high demand. Geography allows us to think spatially about the Earth as a whole as well as to think about it on progressively smaller scales, down to levels as small as our interactions with a single person within a particular location. As previously mentioned, technological advancements, including GIS and GPS, have greatly altered business technology, and marketing and distribution patterns across the globe are constantly being affected by the new technology that geography has to offer.

Each of these six essential elements in geography assists geographers in defining place, determining characteristics of a particular space, and describing the surface of the Earth in rich and meaningful detail. Geography is a multidisciplinary approach to studying the world around us. This may involve interpreting data on a variety of scales and avoiding the ecological fallacy. An ecological fallacy is an assumption made at one scale and then applying that assumption to a variety of different scales.

As students interpret information this may come in both qualitative and quantitative forms. You will need to be able to analyze that data and make conclusions based on that data.

DIFFUSION

Diffusion is the movement of any characteristic. Because the world is constantly changing, the Earth can be difficult to examine. Studying movement means tracking a characteristic, such as disease or migration, over time. Diffusion relates to the spatial interaction theme. The more easily accessible something is, the more quickly it can be moved from one culture to another.

The place where the characteristic began is known as a **hearth**, and diffusion is the process by which it is spread. For example, the hearth of the game of basketball is Springfield, Massachusetts. From this point, the game of basketball diffused to become a worldwide phenomenon.

RELOCATION DIFFUSION

Relocation diffusion is the physical spread of cultures, ideas, and diseases through people. When people migrate, they often bring with them various aspects of their culture, such as language. For example, when the Hmong refugees came to the United States from Laos, they brought with them their language, religion, and customs, particularly to California, Minnesota, Wisconsin, and North Carolina. In addition, the physical spread of these people, or their movement from one place to another, is sometimes called **migration diffusion**.

EXPANSION DIFFUSION

Another type of diffusion that takes place is **expansion diffusion**. Expansion diffusion is the spread of a characteristic from a central node or a hearth through various means. Expansion diffusion can be further broken down into three types of diffusion: hierarchical, contagious, and stimulus diffusion.

HIERARCHICAL DIFFUSION

Hierarchical diffusion is the idea that a phenomenon spreads as a result of a group, usually the social elite, spreading ideas or patterns in a society. The social elite may be political leaders, entertainment leaders, or sports stars. For example, elite members of society often start clothing trends. When a political leader wears a particular tie that becomes a fashion, it is an example of hierarchical diffusion. Clothing trends often originate with entertainment stars as well.

Not all trends are started by the social elite. Rap music and the hip-hop culture were started by urban African Americans. This clothing, language, and music culture has moved from urban streets to suburban homes. Much of the language from the urban culture has become part of suburban and rural culture as well, especially among youth.

CONTAGIOUS DIFFUSION

Contagious diffusion is usually associated with the spread of disease. Contagious diseases such as influenza have motivated physicians around the world to find a cure for viral infections. Diseases spread without regard to race, social status, or family status. Contagious diffusion is often rapid.

There are examples of contagious diffusion other than disease. The Internet has led to many ideas spreading through rapid contact. People can observe items on the Internet with relative ease and can get information instantaneously. Live events on the Internet, where people can directly experience something happening, are mediums of contagious diffusion.

STIMULUS DIFFUSION

Stimulus diffusion takes a part of an idea and spreads that idea to create an innovative product. In his book *Human Geography: The Cultural Landscape*, James Rubenstein submits the example of computer operating systems. In the 1980s, two dominant computer systems were being used: Apple's icon-based interface and IBM-based DOS systems. Then IBM used Apple's idea of clicking on an icon to open a program in all its products. Prior to this diffusion, IBM computer users were forced to open programs by typing in the prompt for the program that they wanted to open, a process that was often time-consuming and confusing.

It is also important to note that technology has increased the speed of diffusion. Computers, airplanes, and other forms of transportation allow the rapid transformation and distribution of a diffused feature. Viral videos are a great example of contagious diffusion.

DISTRIBUTION

Everything on the Earth's surface has a physical location and is organized in space in some fashion. This is called **distribution** and may involve anything from buildings, to people, to desks in a classroom. There are three aspects of distribution: density, concentration, and pattern.

DENSITY

Density is how often an object occurs within a given area or space. Density is most often used with respect to **population density**. When calculating arithmetic population density, the number of people is divided by the amount of land of a certain area to arrive at a number of people per square mile/kilometer. Population density can be expressed in other ways as well. **Physiological density** refers to the total number of people divided by the arable (farmable) land. This is a more accurate measure of population density than **arithmetic density**, which calculates the density using all the land in a given area.

A country may have a high density of population yet a low total population. For example, Singapore's population density is far greater than India's population density, even though India has a much greater total population than Singapore. India has much more land than Singapore, making its density much lower. This concept will be further addressed in the chapter on Population.

CONCENTRATION

Concentration refers to the proximity of a particular phenomenon over the area in which it is spread. To rank concentration, a person must count the same number of objects in different areas. In the area of concentration, the objects are considered **clustered** or **agglomerated** if they are close together. If the objects are spread out, they are considered **dispersed** or **scattered**.

PATTERN

Pattern relates to how objects are organized in their space. Patterns may be anything from triangular to linear or even three-dimensional, as with high-rise buildings.

Geometric shapes are used to describe how the phenomena are laid out. If the items are laid out on a singular line, the pattern is **linear**. If they're clustered together, the pattern is **centralized**. The lack of a pattern on the landscape is called a **random distribution**.

These patterns are distributed across the Earth, and geographers interpret them for meaning, working to establish models to explain the patterns. These models are in almost every unit of this book. Models examine behavior and attempt to infer meaning and predict future occurrences. They are important in examining location and other features on the landscape.

During your diagnostic exam, you were asked to predict population growth using the Demographic Transition Model. Using the stages in this model, a person can predict what will happen to population growth as well as to economic structure and dependence. The **Demographic Transition Model** describes human activities in the past and predicts human activities in the future.

APPLYING MATHEMATICAL PRINCIPLES

Geography is a multidisciplinary approach to studying the world around us. This may involve interpreting data on a variety of scales and avoiding the ecological fallacy. An **ecological fallacy** is an assumption made at one scale and then applied to a variety of different scales. Data may come in both qualitative and quantitative forms. You will need to be able to analyze that data and make conclusions based on that data.

REVIEW QUESTIONS

MULTIPLE-CHOICE QUESTIONS

1. Taking photos of Earth from space is also called

   (A) aerial photography.

   (B) satellite imagery.

   (C) geographic information systems.

   (D) geographic positioning systems.

   (E) remote photography.

2. Newspaper delivery areas are an example of which type of region?

   (A) Formal

   (B) Functional

   (C) Statistical

   (D) Graphical

   (E) Vernacular

3. Who first coined the term *geography*?

   (A) Plato

   (B) Aristotle

   (C) Eratosthenes

   (D) Zheng He

   (E) Socrates

4. What geographical feature usually distinguishes time zones?

   (A) 5 degrees of latitude

   (B) 5 degrees of longitude

   (C) 15 degrees of latitude

   (D) 15 degrees of longitude

   (E) 30 degrees of longitude

5. The prime meridian is what degree of longitude?

   (A) 0 degrees

   (B) 45 degrees

   (C) 90 degrees

   (D) 120 degrees

   (E) 180 degrees

6. The linking of places by common traits or characteristics is defined as

   (A) place.

   (B) location.

   (C) region.

   (D) area.

   (E) zone.

7. What type of map has all lines of latitude and longitude meeting at right angles, creating much distortion at both of the polar regions?

   (A) Mercator projection

   (B) Robinson projection

   (C) Molleweide projection

   (D) Azimuthal projection

   (E) Goodes-Homsoline projection

8. What geographical approach suggests that humans possess the ability to dominate their environment rather than that they are defined by the environment?

   (A) Animistic approach

   (B) Temperate approach

   (C) Environmental determinist approach

   (D) Socioecology approach

   (E) Possibilist approach

9. What is the term for the phenomenon that the farther a feature moves from a hearth, the less dominant it is?

   (A) Central place

   (B) Concentric circle

   (C) Regional analysis

   (D) Distance decay

   (E) Sequent occupance

10. If an area has objects in it that are tightly arranged, it is said to be what?

    (A) Dense

    (B) Clustered

    (C) Dispersed

    (D) Scattered

    (E) Regionalized

11. Environmental determinism was replaced by which approach to geography in the late 20th century?

    (A) Distribution approach

    (B) Hierarchical approach

    (C) Stimulus approach

    (D) Vernacular approach

    (E) Possiblist approach

12. Which type of map would have the largest scale?

    (A) World map

    (B) Continent map

    (C) Country map

    (D) Regional map

    (E) City map

13. At what degree of latitude is the North Pole?

    (A) 0 degrees north

    (B) 0 degrees south

    (C) 45 degrees north

    (D) 90 degrees north

    (E) 90 degrees south

14. Which term refers to the physical character of a location?

    (A) Situation

    (B) Site

    (C) Relative location

    (D) Absolute location

    (E) Place

15. What is another name for a meridian?

    (A) Parallel

    (B) Longitude

    (C) Latitude

    (D) Poles (North and South)

    (E) Equator

16. The azimuthal map best reflects what class of map projection?

    (A) Conic

    (B) Cylindrical

    (C) Oval

    (D) Planar

    (E) Mercator

17. 1:100,000 is an example of what type of scale?

    (A) Word

    (B) Line statement

    (C) Fractional

    (D) Small scale

    (E) Large scale

18. Looking at an issue such as total fertility rate from a local to global perspective in geography would be an example of using

    (A) map scale.

    (B) differentiated analysis.

    (C) scale of analysis.

    (D) continuous synthesis.

    (E) regional analysis.

19. What are maps called that keep shapes intact but distort area?

    (A) Conformal

    (B) Equal area

    (C) Azimuthal

    (D) Molleweide

    (E) Relative

20. What is the difference between GPS and GIS?

    (A) GPS uses GIS data.

    (B) GIS uses GPS data to determine location.

    (C) GPS is the layering of data, whereas GIS is the gathering of data.

    (D) GIS is the layering of data, whereas GPS is the gathering of data.

    (E) GPS correlates with GIS, but GIS does not correlate with GPS.

FREE-RESPONSE QUESTION

Directions: While a formal essay is not required, it is not enough to answer the following question by merely listing facts. Your answer should be based upon your critical analysis of the question posed.

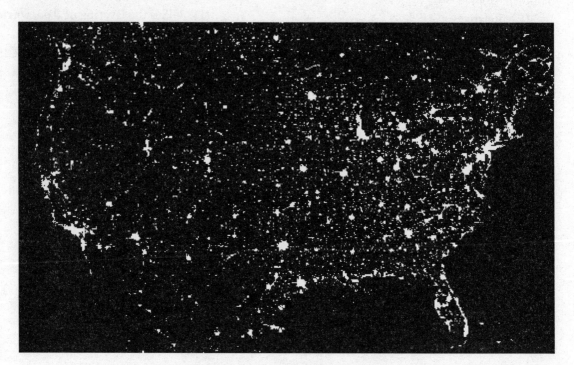

Figure 3.4: The United States at Night
Source: NASA (http://nightglow.gsfc.nasa.gov/states_night.html).

Figure 3.4 is a composite of over 200 images made by satellites orbiting the Earth. The scans were made by the USAF Defense Meteorological Satellite Program (DMSP) Operational Linescan System. The DMSP satellites continue to help in the understanding and prediction of weather phenomena as well as providing key information about population patterns, city light levels, and even rural forest fires.

1. The above composite satellite image of the United States at night reveals electric usage, which is related to population distribution and density. Use this image to answer the following questions.

    (A) Describe the geographic patterns (clustered vs. dispersed) on the image in order to explain the population distribution of the United States.

    (B) Which regions/metropolitan areas of the United States are the most urbanized and densely populated? Which areas of the United States are the least densely populated?

    (C) How will this image change if the current population distribution trends from the last 30 years continue?

ANSWERS AND EXPLANATIONS

MULTIPLE-CHOICE QUESTIONS

1. B

Photographs taken from space are most often referred to as satellite imagery. Satellites orbit anywhere from 5,000 to 30,000 feet above Earth's surface. Aerial photography refers to pictures taken from low-flying planes.

2. B

Newspaper delivery is an example of a functional region, because it is based around a central node, the production site of the newspaper. If one moves outside of the delivery area of the newspaper, one reads a different newspaper.

3. C

Eratosthenes was the first person to coin the term *geography.* He also systematically measured the circumference of the Earth. His measurements were surprisingly accurate, considering that some of his base numbers were incorrect.

4. D

For every 15 degrees of longitude that you move, you enter a new time zone. As you move west, you gain an hour; as you move east, you lose an hour. There are 360 degrees on the Earth, which divided by 24 hours in the day, give 15 degrees of longitude per time zone. You can calculate the time by knowing the longitude of two locations and a time at one of them. By measuring the difference in longitude and dividing it by 15, you arrive at the time of the second location.

5. A

The prime meridian is located at 0 degrees longitude. It was determined that a standard prime meridian was needed, and Greenwich, England, was eventually given the distinction of becoming that location. The primary reason is that this was the location of the observatory that first established the system of longitude. Many different places, including Paris and Philadelphia, have considered themselves to be at 0 degrees longitude at one point.

6. C

Region is the linking of places through their common traits, which may be anything from religion to economic activities. Place is simply the description of one area. Region ties together several places. Location is where the area is.

7. A

A Mercator projection has all lines of latitude and longitude meeting at right angles, causing extreme distortion of both the polar regions. The Robinson and Molleweide projections squish the polar regions together, making the latitude and longitude angles more acute. An azimuthal projection has extreme distortion, because it shows the world from one point of view, generally from one of the polar regions, thus greatly exaggerating the opposite pole.

8. E

The possiblist approach to geography replaced the environmental determinist approach. The environmental determinist approach suggested that owing to their location, specifically in the temperate zones, certain peoples were more likely to succeed than those located in the tropical regions. The possiblist approach refuted the environmental determinist approach by suggesting that people could succeed regardless of their environment. People's ingenuity is a more important factor in their success than the characteristics of their natural environment. An animistic approach does not work in this answer; animism is a belief system. Temperate is a factor in these theories but doesn't work as an answer.

9. D

Distance decay describes the decreasing presence of an item based on distance from its node. Around the node, the presence of the item is strongest. The farther one travels from the node, the less likely the dominance of the nodal feature. This explains the friction of distance.

10. B

If an area has objects in it that are tightly arranged it is clustered. Dense describes the number of objects in the space but not how closely they are arranged to each other. Dispersed and scattered both mean the opposite of clustered.

11. E

This question is similar to question 8. The environmental determinist approach was replaced by the possiblist approach. The environmental determinist approach was considered a discriminatory and racist philosophy that many geographers to this day are ashamed of. On the AP exam, use the questions to assist you in answering other questions. By looking at other questions, you can glean information for the correct answer to the current question.

12. E

The easiest way to think of the answer to a scale question is to consider the size of your house. The larger your house would appear on a map, the larger the scale of the map. In this question, your house would look the largest on the city map. Hence, the city map has the largest scale. Many students get confused because the world map shows a larger area. Don't fall into this trap. Larger area equals a smaller-scale map, and a smaller area equals a larger-scale map.

13. D

The polar regions are always located at 90 degrees. This is because the lines of longitude meet the equator at 0 degrees latitude at a 90-degree angle. It is impossible to go above 90 degrees north or south latitude. One can go 180 degrees on longitude on the surface of the Earth, until one reaches the International Date Line where one enters the opposite hemisphere. The exact points of the poles have all the degrees of longitude. This is where all of the meridians meet. The North Pole is simply located at 90 degrees north because all of the lines of longitude meet there.

14. B

Site refers to the physical character of a location. Situation refers to how well it is connected to other places. A city may have an excellent site and a poor situation or vice versa. A city's location is usually poor due to environmental liabilities. However, if its situation is strong enough to compensate for the negative aspects of the site, the city can survive and even prosper. New Orleans and Chicago are cities that have poor sites but excellent situations, which have enabled them to thrive.

15. B

Longitude is another term for a meridian. Parallels refer to lines of latitude. The junction where lines of parallels and meridians meet defines a person's absolute location.

16. D

A map class is defined by how a cartographer minimizes distortion on a map. Depending upon the type of map they want to produce, cartographers use a certain map class. Within map classes are map projections, which also try to minimize distortion. A planar map is an azimuthal map that looks at the Earth from one particular location, usually a pole. These maps were used during World War II for bombing raids. The location or target was placed in the middle of the map as the focal point to assist bombers in identifying and locating their targets.

17. C

The expression 1:100,000 represents a fractional scale. This is a way of writing a scale to show that for every one of the objects being measured on the map, it takes the second number to cover that distance in the real world. For example, on a 1:100,000 map, 1 inch represents 100,000 inches in the real world. The problem with this type of scale is that expressing distance in terms of measurements we can deal with is difficult. Cartographers often put a word or line statement on maps to show distance in terms such as kilometers or miles.

18. C

In geography, scale of analysis refers to looking at an issue from a variety of scales (local to global). There are many intermediate levels of geographic analysis such as hemisphere, continent, region, country, region within a country, province or state, county, and city level. When you change the scale of analysis, what you are analyzing can quite often change. A problem on the local level might not be an issue on the global scale and vice versa. Map scale in geography refers to the relationship between the space on a map and how much space that represents on Earth's surface.

19. A

A conformal map keeps shapes intact but distorts area. A map that keeps area intact but distorts shapes is an equal-area map. Azimuthal and Molleweide maps are examples of equal-area and conformal maps.

20. D

Global positioning systems (GPS) usually get data in the form of locations. Geographic information systems (GIS) layer data to infer meaning from it. Often, GIS uses the coordinates from GPS as a part of the layering data for maps.

FREE-RESPONSE QUESTION

SAMPLE ESSAY

PART A

The population of the United States is most clustered in the northeast between northern Virginia and Boston. Other areas where there are large population clusters are in the Great Lakes region, the southeast (especially the coasts of Florida), and southern California. Much of the western half of the country is sparsely populated with cities dispersed throughout the region, especially in the Great Plains region.

PART B

From the map provided, it is clear that the most urbanized and densely populated areas are in the area from Boston to Washington, D.C. This region includes the cities of Hartford, Providence, New York City, Philadelphia, and Baltimore. Another densely populated area is in the Midwest where Chicago and Detroit are the biggest urban areas along with Minneapolis/Saint Paul, Cleveland, and Saint Louis. In the southeast, Atlanta, Miami, and Tampa are the big urban areas and in the southwest they are Houston and Dallas. On the west coast, the area between San Diego and Los Angeles, San Francisco, and Seattle are quite evident on the satellite image as the densest cities. One can tell that these areas are densely populated because of the intensity of the lights in these small geographic areas. The least densely populated areas of the United States are in the Great Basin region of Nevada, eastern Oregon and Washington, the Rocky Mountain region, and the Great Plains states from Oklahoma to Montana. These areas are clearly less densely populated because the lights and electricity usage in these areas are not as intense.

PART C

Since the population continues to grow in the south and west, an image of the United States in the future could look quite different. Areas that are now highly populated will continue to be so in the future and show up as bright areas on the map. Areas growing in population, such as the South, will fill in with lights, especially in Florida and Texas (between Houston, Dallas, Austin, and San Antonio). Lights in southern California will cover more land. Finally, areas in the Rocky Mountain West will fill in with more lights and urban areas such as Las Vegas, Phoenix, Salt Lake City, and Denver will get larger. The Great Basin and Great Plains will most likely remain sparsely populated in the future.

RUBRIC FOR FREE-RESPONSE QUESTION

Total point value for question 1 = 6

Part A—Two points possible:

- One point for discussing the clustered areas on the image.
    - Northeast (Boston to northern Virginia)
    - Great Lakes region
    - Coasts of Florida
    - Southern California
- One point for discussing the dispersed areas of the image.
    - Western half of the country
    - Rocky Mountain region
    - Great Plains

Part B—Two points possible:

- One point for identifying specific urban areas associated with population clusters.
    - Boston; New York City; Philadelphia; Baltimore; Washington, D.C.; Atlanta; Miami; Tampa; Dallas–Fort Worth; Houston; Pittsburgh; Cleveland; Detroit; Chicago; Minneapolis/Saint Paul; Denver; Phoenix; Los Angeles; San Diego; San Francisco; Saint Louis; Kansas City; Seattle; etc.
- One point for identifying sparsely populated areas of the United States.
    - Great Basin
    - Western Great Plains
    - Eastern Washington and Oregon
    - Rocky Mountain region

Part C—Two points possible:

- One point for identifying the trend of the Sun Belt gaining in population in the last thirty years.
    - Florida, the Carolinas, Georgia, Houston, Austin, Dallas–Fort Worth, San Antonio, Arizona, and Southern California
- One point for discussing and analyzing the possible shifts in population distribution if the population distribution trends continue.
    - How specific urban areas will expand and even possibly merge into one another, for example Seattle into Portland, Oregon, and so on.

CHAPTER 4:   POPULATION

IF YOU LEARN ONLY SIX THINGS IN THIS CHAPTER . . .

1. The demographic transition model is a tool demographers use to categorize countries' population growth rates and economic structures. The model analyzes crude birth rates, crude death rates, and total population trends in a society at a given point of time. Once a country moves into the next stage of the model, it cannot go back to previous stages, unless afflicted by nuclear war or another horrific calamity.

2. British economist Thomas Malthus coined the term *overpopulation* in the late 1700s. Malthus suggested that the world's population was growing faster than the rate of food production, and as a result, mass starvation would occur. Malthus was correct in his assumption about world population increase but was incorrect in his assessment of agriculture's inability to produce sufficient food. Neo-Malthusians today believe that humanity is ripe for another population calamity.

3. The world's population is growing exponentially. Most of the growth is occurring in less developed countries. More developed countries are either at or near zero population growth. Some Eastern European countries are actually losing some of their population.

4. Population pyramids show the age and sex demographics of a particular country, city, or neighborhood. Inverted pyramids indicate a large percentage of elderly persons in the community. A large base indicates a lot of children in the society and could indicate a less developed country.

5. There are four primary push and pull factors: economic, political, environmental, and social indicators. Each of these reasons has caused millions of people to move.

6. Refugees voluntarily leave an area for fear of death or persecution. Forced migrants are forced by the government to move.

When most people think of human geography, they usually think about population. With a world population of over 7.2 billion people and rising, population and the burden of overpopulation are certainly issues that many areas will be forced to deal with.

Population has been increasing for as long as humans have been on this planet. For the majority of this time, population increase has been slow, but during the past 200 years, population has exploded. Most population growth is taking place in areas, particularly in less developed countries, that are ill-prepared to handle growing numbers of people, leading to a population crisis for the world. This crisis is sometimes called a **population explosion**.

When looking at population, it is important to note that not all areas of the world are overpopulated. Some areas are actually underpopulated due to climatic conditions or other factors.

The study of population characteristics is called **demography**. Demography is the scientific analysis of population trends and it predicts future occurrences based on present statistics. A country's population growth and demographics are important in setting political policy and allocating scarce resources. Two major factors in demographics are the crude birth rate and the crude death rate. **Crude birth rate** refers to the number of births per 1,000 people in the population. The **crude death rate** is the number of deaths per 1,000 people.

Overpopulation is defined as the lack of necessary resources to meet the needs of the population of a defined area. These resources include food, water, and shelter. In a desert, the carrying capacity of the environment is far less than that of an agriculturally productive area.

Carrying capacity is the ability of the land to sustain a certain number of people. The more people inhabit an area, the more likely they will reach the carrying capacity of the environment. Once the carrying capacity is reached, the problems of overpopulation become apparent. People begin to starve, and many deaths occur owing to a lack of resources. Certain factors can alter an environment's carrying capacity, such as technological innovations that can increase food productivity (e.g., the Green Revolution).

As more and more humans inhabit a specific area, the strain on the resources of the environment becomes greater and greater. This causes a form of **environmental degradation** (the harming of the environment). Environmental degradation may take on several forms. Water may become polluted or issues of who gets to use the water become prominent. Watering restrictions are common in most places in the United States during the summer months.

In addition to water use, food supplies may become diminished, a factor which will be discussed in the agriculture unit. The issue is usually less one of food production (unless a natural disaster takes out much of the food source) than one of food distribution.

Other factors impacted by rapid population growth could include a loss of biodiversity. As humans need more land to settle, that often times comes at the expense of losing habitat for plants and animals. Air pollution may also result from the overuse of natural resources due to too many people.

Natural disasters can have a dramatic impact on population growth. Population pyramids become skewed due to natural disasters when a segment of the population dies off due to a catastrophe such as a tornado, flood, or earthquake. For instance, the tsunami that hit coastal areas of Thailand and other parts of Southeast Asia in 2004 wiped out entire populations of children in some communities. When a large segment of the population is lost, a government is hard-pressed to find a taxable income, further straining its ability to provide a community's basic needs.

It is important to note that people cannot live in large populations in five distinct areas: where it is *too hot, too cold, too hilly, too wet,* or *too dry*. Thus, humans are able to thrive on just a small percentage of the planet.

Japan is a good example of a country living on a small percentage of its land. The country of Japan has approximately 127.5 million people in a land about the size of California. However, only 16 percent of the physical layout of Japan can support any population. The rest of the topography of Japan is too hilly. This terrain means that Japan is very densely populated. Space is at a premium in Japan, especially in Japanese urban areas, making property space very expensive in larger cities such as Tokyo, Kyoto, and Osaka.

The term for habitable land is **ecumene**. An ecumene is an area where humans can live. An ecumene includes land with adequate water sources, relatively flat terrain, and available human food sources.

The more than 7 billion people on Earth live on a planet where resources are depleting rapidly. A large majority of them live within 100 miles of an ocean. Most of the Earth is covered in water: The Pacific, Atlantic, Indian, and Arctic Oceans comprise approximately 70 percent of the surface of the Earth.

Other areas of the world are **underpopulated**. The Great Plains of the United States is a good example of an underpopulated region. Although the Great Plains have been called the breadbasket of the United States, this area is sparsely populated and dominated by agriculture. The food availability is good, and the water levels are somewhat sparse but acceptable, yet still very little population is located there.

POPULATION DISTRIBUTION AND DENSITY

Arithmetic density divides the entire population of a country by the total land area to come up with a population density for the country as a whole. Arithmetic density is important when looking at a country's population trends, but it doesn't tell the whole story. **Physiologic density**, on the other hand, is a more accurate way to measure a country's population density. Physiologic density only takes into account the land that is being used by humans, whether as pasture, as an urban center, or in some other way.

Depending on which source or textbook one uses, there are four or five main areas of population density (concentrations) in the world. The four most important areas are East Asia, South Asia, Southeast Asia, and Europe. Sometimes these areas are called population distributions, concentrations, or clusters of the world. The fifth area comprises the northeastern United States and southeastern Canada.

EAST ASIA

The first major area of population density is East Asia. The East Asia region contains the countries of China, South and North Korea, and Japan. This region of the world possesses over 1.5 billion people. China alone has over 1.3 billion people, most of whom live within the eastern third of the country along the Pacific Ocean. This area has favorable climatic conditions for food growth and transportation routes. A high plateau region, known as the Tibetan plateau, dominates the western section of China. The other sections are mountainous, and even today, developing adequate transportation systems within these regions is difficult.

SOUTH ASIA

The second major region of population is the South Asia region. In this region, which includes the countries of India, Pakistan, Sri Lanka, and Bangladesh, population growth is still outpacing policies to reduce growth. Within the next 35 years, India will surpass China as the world's most populated country. Pakistan and Bangladesh are also within the top ten countries in the world in terms of population.

SOUTHEAST ASIA

The third major area of population density is located in Southeast Asia, which includes Vietnam, Phillipines, Malaysia, Indonesia, and Thailand. Vietnam is quickly becoming one of the fastest-growing countries in the world.

WESTERN AND CENTRAL EUROPE

The fourth major area of population density is located in Western and Central Europe and extends eastward into Ukraine. Large cities, such as London, Moscow, and Paris, dominate this section of the world. Europe is mostly urbanized, as opposed to the East Asia and South Asian regions, which are still dominated by agricultural and rural economies.

NORTHEASTERN UNITED STATES AND CANADA

The fifth major area of population density is located in the northeastern section of the United States and southeastern Canada. In the megalopolis of the East Coast of the United

States, the urban area extends all the way from Boston, Massachusetts, to Washington, D.C. This area along Interstate 95 still has a large proportion of the population of the United States, although outward migration in recent decades has diminished its population. The southeastern section of Canada, including the cities of Toronto, Ottawa, and Montreal, contains the majority of Canada's population. This area extends southward into the United States megalopolis region.

Each of these five areas has a high population density that is conducive for economic growth, and climate and access to agriculture are the major factors. If adequate climate conditions no longer existed or food could not be produced fast enough to support the populations, they would eventually die out.

POPULATION AND GROWTH

In the late 1700s, a British reverend by the name of **Thomas Malthus** concluded that the rate of population was growing at a faster rate than agriculture productivity. Malthus coined the term *overpopulation*. It's fitting that an economist coined the term, because economics deals with the scarcity of resources.

Malthus was concerned that the world population was growing at an exponential rate while agricultural productivity was growing only at a linear rate, and that this inequality would eventually lead to a starvation pandemic. Malthus's book, *On Population,* was published in Great Britain and garnered some attention, most of it negative. He predicted that by the late 1800s, Great Britain would be facing a nightmare with a lack of food for its burgeoning population.

Malthus is considered the first person to publicly foresee such a population crisis. He was correct in his assumptions that the world population would grow exponentially (see Figure 4.1), but his theory floundered on the agricultural side. Malthus never could have predicted the inventions that would mechanize farming and modify crops, which have greatly increased productivity.

Today, the world produces enough food to sustain itself, despite the fact that political regimes around the world have halted distribution to some people in need. See the chapter on Agriculture, Food Production, and Rural Land Use for information on productivity and profits across the globe.

Linear growth is simply growth that occurs evenly across each unit of time. For example, a village with 100 people and a linear growth rate of 10 people per year would see an increase of 10 people after the first year, to bring its population to 110. The second year, population would grow by 10 again, to 120, and so on. After 10 years, the population of that village would be about 200 people.

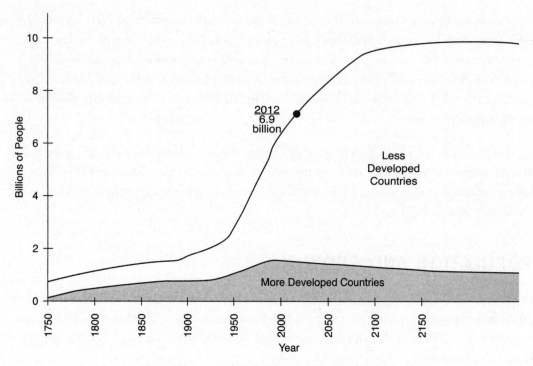

Figure 4.1: World Population Growth Chart.

Exponential growth looks at growth as a percentage of the total population. In the afore-mentioned village, a 10 percent exponential growth rate would mean that the next year there would be 110 people. But then the next year, population would grow by $110 \times 10\% = 11$ new people; the base population of 110 plus the 11 new people equals 121. After 10 years, the population would be 234. The difference between the linear and exponential growth rates within a ten-year span in a village that starts with 100 people is 34. This is how the world's population growth has been expanding since the early 20th century.

As population continues to expand in the 21st century, we can predict which areas of the world will see the greatest growth.

The **neo-Malthusian** viewpoint is theoretical, not necessarily a demographic fact. According to neo-Malthusians, if there are multiple minority groups and no majority group within a population set, the growth rate will eventually resemble the rate of growth of the fastest-growing group within that set. This theory suggests that in a society tending toward the growth of the fastest-growing group, the crude birth rate and fertility rate will continue to inch upwards. Furthermore, the fastest-growing group will eventually become a majority of the population, its larger crude birth rate and fertility rate becoming those of the majority group. Eventually, the trend will continue regardless of the country's economic development. To the neo-Malthusians, the increased fertility and crude birth rates within immigrant communities will eventually cause an increased growth rate in more developed countries.

Going against the demographic transition model, discussed in the next section, the neo-Malthusians believe that the United States is ripe for exponential population growth again because of its immigrant communities. Proponents of this philosophy point out the divide between the crude birth rate of 16 and the crude death rate of 9 in the United States, despite the fact that our economy is well developed in the tertiary (service-based) and quaternary (information-based) sectors.

DEMOGRAPHIC TRANSITION MODEL

The demographic transition model, shown in Figure 4.2, is a good indicator of what will happen to a society or country's population. It is based on three primary factors: the birth rate, the death rate, and the total population. Furthermore, most Demographic Transition Models have four stages. Every society or country must go through these stages, and once a country moves from one stage to another, it does not go backward, unless it suffers a nuclear attack or a cataclysmic event on the landscape.

STAGE 1: HUNTING AND GATHERING SOCIETIES

A hunting and gathering society characterizes stage 1 of the demographic transition model. During this stage, a society has a low total population with fluctuations in both the birth and death rates. When the birth rate is high, the death rate is low, and vice versa.

These variances in the birth and death rates are a natural occurrence and still take place today. When food sources are plentiful and economic times are good, people have more children. When parents are more optimistic about the future, the result is an increase in the birth rate. The reverse is also true. When economic times are poor, parents are more pessimistic about the future and have fewer children. Baby booms and busts are heavily dependent upon economic conditions.

Because food sources are sporadic in hunting and gathering societies (they depend upon herd animals for food), people generally will not have many children for fear of starvation. Thus, population levels during stage 1 remain low.

No countries are in stage 1 of the demographic transition model today. However, some societies, such as the Aborigines of Australia and the Bushmen of Namibia, still practice hunting and gathering. Both of these populations have remained low for centuries owing to their unstable food sources.

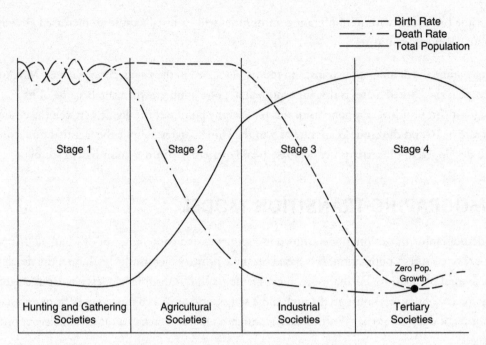

Figure 4.2: Demographic Transition Model.

As humans progressed agriculturally, food sources changed. Instead of relying on animals or seasonal vegetation for food, people began experimenting with farming. This process was known as the First Agricultural Revolution. Although the process took time to begin and accelerate, it was quite significant to the human population. Once people began planting crops and raising animals, they had some consistency in food production. This change helped to stabilize populations, an essential factor in the transition of people from nomadic hunters to sedentary farmers.

STAGE 2: AGRICULTURAL SOCIETIES

Stage 2 of the demographic transition model, agricultural societies, sees unprecedented population growth. Birth rates stay high, but death rates decline sharply in this stage because of more stable food sources and the diffusion of modern medicine. This imbalance between the birth and death rates leads to a sharp increase in the total population of a society.

During stage 2, the S-curve, reflecting the total population number in the demographic transition model, begins to take shape. As you can see from Figure 4.3, total population begins to increase dramatically, eventually stabilizing in stage 4, thus creating an S-shaped curve.

As a country moves into stage 2, the majority of people are involved in farming. These are usually subsistence farmers who are simply trying to feed their families. Stage 2 economies are very basic and use very little technology. Within stage 2 countries, a traditional family structure is valued. Men usually work in the fields, while women stay at home and raise the children. Having many children serves an agricultural society's primary purpose, to possess a sufficient labor force on the farmsteads. In agricultural societies, it is not uncommon for families to have 10 or more children. As the children get older, they become workers on the farm, dramatically increasing productivity.

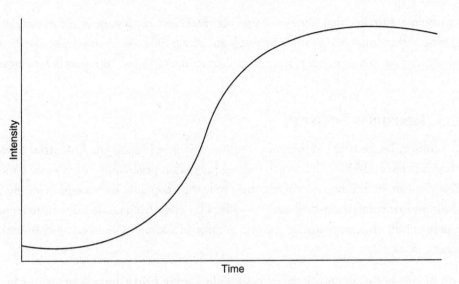

Figure 4.3: World Population Growth: S-Shaphed Curve.

Another reason for having so many children is that they are often seen as a source of security. As people age, they become more dependent upon others, but government structures in stage 2 countries aren't set up to provide public welfare. The elderly often have no form of support outside of individual wealth. Many people work simply to eat.

The overall death rate continues to fall during stage 2. One of the reasons for this has already been mentioned—a more stable food source allows people to live longer. In addition, advances in medical technology as well as the increased effectiveness and availability of medicines allow more people to live healthier and longer. Such advances and medicines cure many of the ailments that devastated populations in prior generations.

Many African countries are still in stage 2 today. You can tell that a country is in stage 2 of the demographic transition model by comparing its birth and death rates with the current world average birth rate (20) and death rate (8). In a stage 2 country, both the birth rate and death rate are higher than the world averages. For example, Angola, located in Central Africa, had a 2013 birth rate of 47 and death rate of 15, both well above the world averages. Liberia is another good example of a stage 2 country with a birth rate of 36 and a death rate of 10.

In both Liberia and Angola, the majority of the population is involved in agriculture. In addition, life expectancy is generally very low in these countries. Only 2 percent of Angola's population is above the age of 65. Sanitation and education are rarely provided, especially in rural areas.

In stage 2 countries, women often have more babies to offset the high infant mortality rate. **Infant mortality rate** is the number of babies per 1,000 that die before their first birthday. **Total fertility rate** is the number of babies that an average woman delivers during her childbearing years. In many developing countries, the total fertility rate is high and may exceed eight children.

It is also important to note that some countries may enter and exit a stage in the model relatively quickly, while other countries get stuck in a stage for a long time. Some countries, like the more developed European countries, stayed in a stage 2 economy for 50 to 100 years before moving into stage 3.

STAGE 3: INDUSTRIAL SOCIETIES

A stage 3 country is characterized by a more industrial society. Initially the **Industrial Revolution**, which began in the mid-1700s in Europe, spurred many European countries to adopt a more mechanized system of farming. As a result, these countries' populations grew dramatically (stage 2) from the improvement in the overall quality of life. This move from an agricultural to an industrial society dramatically changes many aspects of a country, including its demographics (movement from stage 1 to stage 3).

Mass production begins to take shape in factories located in urban areas. Key reasons for declining birth rates in this stage are that the reliance on children for labor decreases and that children become more of a liability than an asset. The assembly line method of production takes form, and children are often not allowed to work owing to government restraints on child labor. In addition, women enter the workforce in greater numbers, gaining career opportunities that often motivate them to delay having children for several years. This reduces the fertility rate of a country.

As a society further develops its economy, more people are involved in the production of goods. The number of factories increases, meaning that more and more people move off the farm and into urban areas for manufacturing jobs. Increased pay for factory jobs and less reliance on the unpredictable whims of nature that affect farmers also support a more stable economy.

During the early 1900s, much of Europe and the United States entered stage 3. Many of the countries in Central and South America are currently in stage 3.

During stage 3, a country's birth rates and death rates will be around the world averages. In a stage 3 country, the birth rate starts out high, persisting from stage 2, but begins to drop sharply. At the same time, the death rate continues to fall. There are several reasons for this, including continuing improvements in medicine and inoculations becoming more common. In addition, the quantity and quality of food increases, as it is now being produced by a more mechanized system of farming. Countries at the end of stage 3 will have average to low birth rates and average to low death rates.

A country like Bolivia, with a birth rate of 24 and a death rate of 7, is at the beginning of stage 3. The high birth rate indicates the country has just entered stage 3. The low to average death rate indicates some development within the country. In comparison, a country like Argentina, with a birth rate of 18 and a death rate of 8, is well established in stage 3. The low birth rate indicates a relatively urbanized and industrialized society, where dependence upon farming for primary employment has become less important.

STAGE 4: TERTIARY SOCIETIES

Conditions permitting, countries will eventually move into stage 4 of the model, which is characterized by a more tertiary or service-based economy. The birth rates and death rates become almost equal in stage 4. When the crude birth rate equals the crude death rate, the phenomenon is called **zero population growth**, or ZPG.

During stage 4, a country moves away from its reliance on industry to a more service-based economy. More people are involved in selling products than in production. For example, more people are selling or fixing automobiles than producing them. Countries in stage 4 do not always have successful economies. There are other factors that determine the success of an economy.

Many European countries have entered into stage 4 in the demographic transition model. Countries like Belarus, for instance, have a birth rate of 11 and a death rate of 14. Poland has zero population growth with both a crude birth rate and a crude death rate of 10. In many Eastern European countries, the crude death rate is relatively high because of the lack of environmental standards established during the communist era in the mid-1900s; pollution on a massive scale led to increased health problems in many areas.

Total fertility rates in a stage 4 country are at or below 2, the natural increase rate (the rate required to replace the two parents). When the total fertility rate is below 2, then the country experiences a loss of population. Several countries in stage 4 are trying to offset this lack of population growth by offering incentives for having children. A toy company in Japan recently offered to pay some of their employees to have children. Without children, the toy company feels that its future is threatened. The Korean government has established several national policies aimed at increasing the fertility rate. These policies include starting kindergarten at the age of 5 instead of age 6 and giving tax breaks to families with more than one child.

During stage 4, children become even more of an economic liability. In addition, women have more access to birth control options, also limiting the number of children being born. Although the population level is high, its growth has flattened out.

POPULATION STRUCTURE

Demography is not only concerned with population growth but also the characteristics of the population itself. How old are the people? What is the gender breakdown of the population? Demographers study all the characteristics of populations all around the world.

One important characteristic of a country's population is its breakdown by age and gender. The **sex ratio** is the number of males compared to females in a population. One of the easiest ways to identify a population's sex ratio is by analyzing a **population pyramid**, a tool that geographers and demographers use. Population pyramids chart populations on a graph. These graphs break down the population based on both gender and age, and it can then be analyzed in terms of the demographic transition model to determine in which stage a society is grouped. Age distribution is also presented in population pyramids, with individual brackets demonstrating age groupings.

Population pyramids are also a good way to analyze population projections. **Population projections** use demographic data to determine future population. By analyzing birth and death rates, one can reliably determine what the population of an area will be 30, 50, or even 100 years into the future, assuming that the governmental structure and cultural customs remain the same.

Population pyramids of less developed countries (LDCs) have a wide base, because the majority of the population of an LDC is under the age of 15. There are also few elderly people owing to the lack of sanitation and medical care.

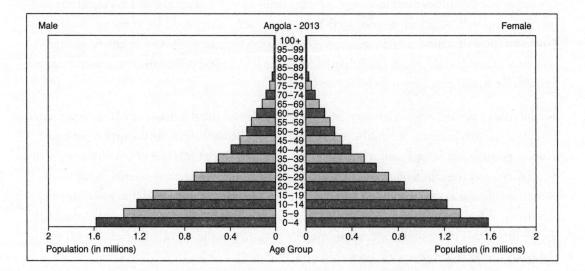

Figure 4.4: Population Pyramid—Angola 2013.

The population pyramid shown in Figure 4.4 is from Angola in 2013. The center numbers are the age groupings of the population. The numbers on the bottom are the population totals of each age group. In a stage 2 country, the base is very wide and the top very narrow. A large part of Angola's population is under 15. These children are dependent upon those older than 15, who can enter the workforce. When the number of people in the workforce, those ages 15 to 64, is low, very few people are available to support the younger population, putting an extra burden on an already strained government. The **dependency ratio** says that those aged 0–14 and over 65 depend on the workforce for support.

Countries that are in stage 2 have what is called demographic momentum. **Demographic momentum** is a continued population increase as a result of a large segment of the population being young. These young people will eventually produce more offspring than their parents' generation, because there are so many of them, thus continuing the demographic momentum. These countries are likely to see monumental population growth for a minimum of 50 years and likely longer.

In a stage 3 country like Argentina, shown in Figure 4.5, there are more adults and elderly in the population and fewer children as compared to a stage 2 country. This makes the pyramid look less bottom heavy, and the population is distributed by age a little more evenly. There are more older people because of improvements in medical care. As the stage 3 society becomes more industrialized, it becomes more urban and offers more access to health care.

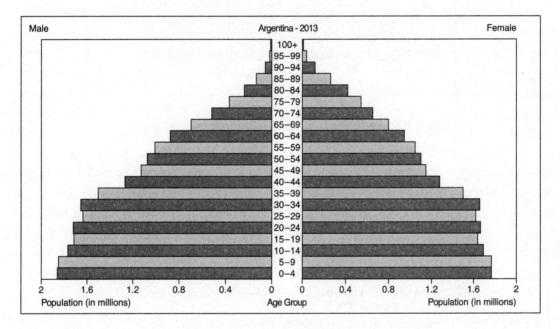

Figure 4.5: Population Pyramid—Argentina 2013.

In a stage 4 country, the percentage of children decreases dramatically, and the workforce segment of the population actually bulges, with 20 to 50 year olds becoming the majority of the population. There are more parents than children. In stage 4, the population begins to see a decrease in total population growth. When the natural increase rate falls below 2, the country begins to lose population, a process called **negative growth**.

A large percentage of the United Kingdom's population, shown in Figure 4.6, is of childbearing years, yet people are choosing not to have many children for various reasons. Children are becoming more and more expensive, and the majority of the population lives in urbanized areas. Furthermore, people are living longer as a result of continued improvements in medical care.

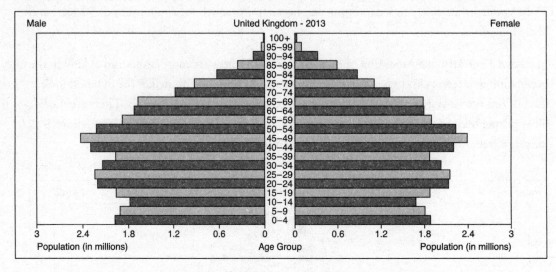

Figure 4.6: Population Pyramid—United Kingdom 2013.

Population pyramids do not only have to be used on a national scale. They can be used to describe cities or even neighborhoods. A population pyramid for a retirement community, which has very few children and a large percentage of residents over the age of 65, would have an upside-down look to it. Mining or fishing villages may have a large percentage of males, due to the job opportunities they offer. Communities where many of the workers are immigrants will often have more males than females. Villages hit hard by war may have an imbalance toward females, because many of the men have been killed in combat.

Assuming that the numbers are correct, population pyramids accurately represent a nation's, city's, or community's demographics in an easy-to-read picture. Having this information allows governments to develop policies and allocate resources to meet the current and future needs of the population. For example, communities with a higher percentage of children ages 0 to 4 will see those children soon move into the educational system. New schools will need to be built and new teachers hired. If the population consists mainly of elderly persons, on the other hand, more health care options will be needed.

BIRTH AND DEATH RATES

The crude birth rate is the number of births per 1,000 people in a population. The crude death rate is the number of deaths per 1,000 people in a population. The average world crude birth rate is 20 per 1,000 people, and the average death rate is 8 per 1,000 people. The **demographic equation** is global births minus global deaths and determines the population growth rate for the world. Currently, the inequity between birth and death rates means the global population is growing by about 80–100 million people per year.

Another statistic that affects a country's population is the **infant mortality rate**. This is the number of babies that die within their first year of life. Like crude birth and death rates, the infant mortality rate is usually given as a rate per 1,000 people. More developed countries have lower infant mortality rates than less developed countries. A more developed country may see an infant mortality rate below 10 per 1,000, while in less developed countries, the infant mortality rate may approach 150 per 1,000. A high infant mortality rate is a huge hindrance to a population. When 15 percent of your population is dying before the age of 1, it is indicative of other social and developmental problems. Women often have more children, uncertain of how many infants will survive and knowing that children will largely determine the family's financial stability as the parents age.

The Gender Inequality Index (GII) is a relatively new measurement to indicate the equality of women in a society. This concept will be discussed further in economic development.

The opposite of the infant mortality rate is the **natality rate** (which is another term for the birth rate). This is the number of live births per 1,000 people in the population. The natality rate and the infant mortality rate always are given per 1,000.

A major population problem in the world is that the crude birth rate in many less developed countries is far outpacing the crude death rate. The result is a world population that has grown extremely fast within less developed countries for the past half century. One of the main reasons is that people in these countries tend to lack adequate birth control often due to low income, religious intolerance, lack of social status, inadequate education, or poor transportation.

Much of the less developed world lives in rural villages, generally the poorest areas of the world, and simply does not have access to birth control measures. Traveling to an urban area may take a week or longer, and to be away from the children and the work that the farm requires is an opportunity cost that families cannot afford. In more developed countries, people have greater access to birth control options and are more likely to use them, reducing the number of births.

AP EXPERT TIP

Take a moment to visualize or to sketch each of these population pyramids so that if you were to see them on the test, you could recognize them immediately.

AP EXPERT TIP

Note how the discussion in the next three paragraphs links gender to population, economic development, politics, and culture. Noticing such patterns allows you to anticipate test questions, see an example of synthesis across topics, and see the importance of the topic of gender in human geography.

Religion also plays a major role in the lack of birth control in some countries. Many religions restrict or even forbid birth control options for their followers as a part of their fundamental beliefs.

Progress is slowly being made. There has been a diffusion of fertility control in recent years. Much of the developed world, which has transitioned into stages 3 and 4, has the access and the resources to purchase birth control and is spreading it to a larger number of women and men across the world. Although there are still many obstacles to overcome, such as distance and money, more people today have access to birth control options than ever before in human history.

In countries where the gender gap (the gap between men and women in terms of status, education, etc.) is high, women are more likely not to have certain rights that men possess. For example, in many countries, women do not have the right to **enfranchisement** or **suffrage**, which means the right to vote. In much of the world, patriarchal societies dominate. In these societies, women are usually subjugated to men, treated as second-class citizens, and have less control over their birth control options. In these societies, the more children that a man sires, the greater his status within the community. This leads to an abundance of children, despite the wishes of the women.

In societies where **dowries** are still present, the woman's family must pay the groom's family for the right to marry the son. Therefore the dowry system puts more value on men and de-emphasizes women. In some extreme cases, infanticide of female babies occurs if a family in poverty cannot afford to pay a future dowry. Many countries, including India, have outlawed the dowry as a means of paying for weddings, but cultural traditions tend to die hard. In some cases, the groom's family will kill the bride because of her inability to pay the dowry, a process referred to as **dowry death**.

Various governments around the world have adopted measures to control the birth and death rates in their countries. Some have been more successful than others. One of the most successful measures of governmental birth control has been enacted in China. In 1979, China adopted its one-child policy to curb its population growth. Since 1979, China has seen a drop in its natural increase rate, total fertility rate, and birth rate. However, despite its successes, a problem with the one-child policy is that it has not been adopted by all minority groups evenly across the country. In western China, where subsistence agriculture is practiced, minority groups are still having more children out of economic necessity. In 2013, China eased its one-child policy for the vast majority of its population for a number of reasons such as labor shortages and skewed sex ratios.

Today in China, it is possible to have more than one child. China is a very proud society where history plays a vital role in the daily lives of its citizens. One of the greatest honors one has is to pass down the family name to one's children. This must be done with a male child. If your first-born child is a female, you are allowed to try to have a second child, but you will be taxed at a much higher rate. Some have suggested that the tax on the second child may be as high as a year's salary for the average worker. If your second child is also a female, you may try for a third, but you are taxed even more. Previously, after three children, the government would not allow you to have any more children. Only the wealthy in China could afford to have more than one child.

Even though these population controls have been enacted, the social and human rights elements have been a concern for many human rights activists, who feel that the treatment of female infants is less than satisfactory. Infanticide and abortions, particularly of female children and fetuses, have risen since the policy was enacted in 1979. China may have controlled its population growth in the meantime, but it may see some other negative demographic factors, such as an imbalance in the sex ratio.

Attempts by other countries to control their populations have not been as successful. Some countries, for example, have attempted the forced sterilization of their citizens, often of their minority groups. Because this has only been done on a small scale, it has had very little impact on the population as a whole. Measures must be applied to an entire country for them to be effective.

Depending upon what stage the country is in within the Demographic Transition Model, it may attempt to impose either pre-natal or anti-natal policies. China's One Child Policy was an example of an anti-natal policy. An anti-natal policy tries to slow down the population growth of a society. Pre-natal policies try to encourage people to have more children.

Often times, population growth is seen as a negative in a society. However, several countries—including Japan, South Korea, and Germany—have implemented policies encouraging their citizens to have more children. Incentives vary from beginning kindergarten at an earlier age to offering tax incentives and early retirement for parents who have more children. During the Cold War, many Warsaw Pact countries gave women medals for having many children.

POPULATION EQUATIONS AND SCIENTIFIC METHODS

Doubling time is the number of years that it takes for a country to double its population. The lower the number, the faster that country will double its population. Countries with a high natural increase rate will double their populations faster than countries with a low natural increase rate.

An equation for approximating doubling time is as follows: doubling time = 70 ÷ growth rate. Thus, if a country has a natural increase rate of 7 percent, its doubling time will be approximately 70 ÷ 7 = 10 years. If a country has a 3.5 percent growth rate, its doubling time is about 20 years, and a 1.75 percent growth rate gives a doubling time of about 40 years. If a country has a 1.75 percent growth rate, it is considered to be increasing its population very rapidly.

If you are given the natural increase rate of any population, you can determine its doubling time to within a couple of years. Morocco, a country located in the northwest of Africa, is 57 percent urbanized. Its birth rate is 19, and its death rate is 5. It is a stage 3 country, in part owing to regulations established by the Islamic religion. Its natural increase rate is 1.4 percent. The doubling time can be figured out as being around 50 years for Morocco.

This can be done for any country that has a natural increase rate. If the country is losing population, like many of the countries in Eastern Europe as well as the country of Japan, there obviously is no doubling time, because a country cannot double its population when the population is declining. Many countries in Europe are experiencing doubling times approaching 700 years with a 0.1 percent natural increase rate. The fastest doubling time in the world in 2013 was the country of Niger. With a natural increase rate of 3.8 percent, its population will double roughly every 18.5 years.

Demographers use the mathematical relationship between doubling time and natural increase rates to calculate growth rates and expected increases in the total population, usually with a high degree of accuracy, assuming that governmental structure and cultural practices of the country do not change. If these factors change, they can dramatically alter the natural increase rates.

To slow down its **demographic momentum**, a country can slow its growth rate in one of three ways. Each of these three methods—imposing government laws, decreasing the birth rate, and increasing the death rate—has its pros and cons.

By decreasing their birth rates, countries can slow down their population growth and natural increase rate. This can be done by law, as in China. It can also be done through the distribution of birth control. The United States has tried making birth control accessible to the masses through free distribution. Also, U.S. high schools teach birth control methods, including abstinence, as a means to reduce the birth rate among teenage girls.

Critics of reducing the birth rate say that making birth control available in this way is not working. Although the pregnancy rate in the United States has been decreasing since its high point in 1990, teenage pregnancy rates are still high. In fact, despite these significant declines, the United States still has the highest teenage pregnancy rate among developed Western countries.

Another means of controlling population is to increase the death rate. By increasing the death rate, population control would be achieved. Increasing the death rate does not mean the killing of innocent civilians. Rather, it suggests that those with terminal diseases not be given the care they need to sustain their lives. This morbid approach goes against many doctors' codes of ethics. Doctors take the Hippocratic oath, vowing "never to do harm to anyone."

However, proponents of this argument suggest that we are spending countless billions on medicines for the clearly terminal that could be used to assist others with manageable diseases, like malaria. Every person is mortal. This mortality principle has led some to this question: If the Earth has a limited number of resources, why are we spending them on people with no hope of survival? Proponents argue that it makes more sense to let one person die today rather than let the natural increase rate continue, see the environment reach its carrying capacity, and experience mass starvation.

Recent studies have suggested that this next generation is the first generation that will live fewer years than their parents. Most can agree that we eat more "junk food" than ever and that obesity is a problem in much of the developed world, especially in the United States.

The bottom line is that the world must find some means of sustainability for the population. **Sustainability** is the saving of resources for future generations to allow them to live at the same or higher standard of living than the population today.

HISTORICAL AND GLOBAL PERSPECTIVES

Until recently, countries have seen an increase in population as a positive event. A greater population means a higher tax base, increased military capability, and more workers for either farming or industrial jobs. Only in recent decades have some areas of the world tried to reduce their overall growth rates.

For much of the world, including today's more developed countries, the population was constant, if not growing minimally, until the mid- to late-1800s. Once many countries in Europe reached stage 3, the population began to settle down. The less developed world is now seeing the highest growth rates and natural increase rates.

By looking at the top 20 countries in the world in terms of total population, shown in Figure 4.7, one notices that Asia contains the greatest number of countries on that list. Southwest Asia and Africa have the highest natural increase rates. One country, in particular, is of concern to demographers. The total population of Nigeria is close to reaching the top of the list in terms of total population. The doubling time of Nigeria as of 2012 was 35 years. This country will see its population of 166 million double within the next 30–40 years.

Countries like Nigeria face the greatest population growth problems. Because the carrying capacity of Nigeria may not be able to support its population, it will either need to increase its agricultural productivity exponentially or begin importing food. In addition, Nigeria will need to increase its boundaries, or it will likely have a refugee crisis due to mass starvation. Its percent natural increase rate, nearly 2 percent, poses a challenge for the countries around Nigeria and the rest of Western Africa.

Bangladesh is another country that is seeing a population crisis. Bangladesh is the size of the state of Iowa. As of 2012, its population was over 152 million.

> **AP EXPERT TIP**
>
> The comparison here between Iowa and Bangladesh compares a known (Iowa) with something that may be unknown (Bangladesh). Try a comparison with other U.S. states and world countries.

In comparison, Iowa's population is around 4 million. Bangladesh's natural increase rate is 1.8 percent. Growing at a rate of 2 percent each year will double its population in 35 years. With more and more countries facing such population crises, the world needs to assess its role in reducing overpopulation.

Why are some countries caught in stage 2 or stage 3 of the demographic transition model, while others are able to move beyond that, to tertiary or even quaternary economies? The answer ties into some of the most fundamental aspects of geography. Some economic systems have allowed for more freedom to assist entrepreneurs in developing products that promote economic success. Most of Europe and the United States fall into this category. When economies change their basic functions, demographics within the country change to correspond with the economic trend.

China is a good example. The 1979 law, which forbade Chinese couples to have more than one child, was enforced by the government. By using government control over family structures, China has seen some success in population control. Also, China's economic policy for the last decade has pumped billions of yuan into the economy to give it a boost. As a result, the Chinese economy is one of the strongest in the world, seeing double-digit annual growth rates. As China has moved into stage 3, the movement from an agricultural to an industrial society has not affected couples' family-planning decisions because, for the most part, they already can only have one child.

Many of the available world demographic statistics are given in terms of *with* and *without China*. Because of heavy government influence, China doesn't really follow the demographic transition model. Several national magazines, including *Newsweek* and *Time*, have focused major news stories on the Chinese economy. Industry is labor intensive, because of the population base that China possesses, and long hours are not uncommon. Because one out of every six persons on Earth is Chinese, including or excluding China can obviously vary the statistical accuracy of any set of world demographic data.

The United States was in stage 2 of the demographic transition model for all of the 19th century. Not until the early 1900s did the United States enter stage 3. This is when the Industrial Revolution and mass industrialization took hold in the United States. Henry Ford's assembly line method of producing automobiles had a ripple effect on almost every other industry in North America, moving people off the farms and toward better and more reliable incomes.

There is a debate about whether the United States is in stage 3 or stage 4 of the model. The U.S. economy is tertiary or service-based, yet the discrepancy between the crude birth rate and the crude death rate leads many demographers to categorize the United States as stage 3.

20 Most Populated Countries

Country	Mid-2014 Populations
1. China	1,364.1 million
2. India	1,296.2 million
3. United States	317.7 million
4. Indonesia	251.5 million
5. Brazil	202.8 million
6. Pakistan	194.0 million
7. Nigeria	177.5 million
8. Bangladesh	158.5 million
9. Russia	143.7 million
10. Japan	127.1 million
11. Mexico	119.7 million
12. Philippines	100.1 million
13. Ethiopia	95.9 million
14. Vietnam	90.7 million
15. Egypt	87.9 million
16. Germany	80.9 million
17. Iran	77.4 million
18. Turkey	77.2 million
19. Democratic Republic of the Congo	71.2 million
20. Thailand	66.4 million

Figure 4.7: The World's 20 Most Populated Countries—2014 (Population Reference Bureau)

The majority of the world's most populous countries come from Asia. Almost 60 percent, or three out of every five persons, on Earth is of Asian decent. The most rapid population growth is occurring in the sub-Saharan African region.

Most demographers can agree that the United Kingdom is in stage 4. The United Kingdom has a very low growth rate, and the majority of its people are working in some type of tertiary or quaternary sector of the economy. Having a low disparity between the crude birth rate (13) and the crude death rate (9) is evidence of being a stage 4 country.

Great Britain entered stage 3 in the 1800s. The Industrial Revolution began in the mid-1700s, and by the 1800s, Great Britain had come into the modern age. After World War II, industry took a backseat to tertiary activities in Great Britain. Even today, some cities in Great Britain are still reeling from the closing of the mega-factories that used to employ thousands of people. Many of these workers have ended up on government assistance due to a lack of industrial jobs. Major urban areas, such as London, have relied more on financial or tertiary economic pursuits than on industrial enterprises.

THE J-CURVE

Ian Bremmer developed what he called the J-curve. The **J-curve** places countries on a scale based on their *openness* and *stability*. The movements of countries on this scale depends largely on their economic progress.

A country can vary between scale elements; it can be relatively free but not very stable. For example, elections may not mean a lot if coup d'états eventually throw the leaders out of office. On the other hand, a country may be tightly controlled but very stable. For example, the former Soviet Union was very stable for most of its history, but its dominating government structure limited the freedom of its inhabitants.

The political stability of a country depends upon its economic success. For instance, countries that depend upon selling their natural resources are successful when the prices of those commodities are high. When prices dip, however, stability decreases, and riots and coups are common.

CAUSES OF POPULATION INCREASE

Five primary factors lead to an increase in population:

1. Medical advances
2. Quantity and quality of food
3. Ethnic and religious issues
4. Economic issues
5. Gender issues

MEDICAL ADVANCES

Medical advances are one of the biggest reasons for an increase in population because they directly affect the death rate. By decreasing the death rate, a country automatically sees its population increase as long as birth rates are constant. Because birth and death rates determine natural increase rates, changing one of the rates affects the overall population growth of a country.

New medicines and inoculations have allowed millions around the world to live longer and healthier lives than ever before in human history. For hundreds of years, explorers were afraid to enter the inner reaches of Africa and South America for fear of malaria. Today, new prevention medication keeps people from catching the disease, and new treatments allow people to live productively for many years after having the disease.

Disease diffusion, which is simply the spread of disease, does not occur as widely as it used to. Although some viruses, such as HIV, SARS, and avian flu, still dominate the news, medicine has eliminated smallpox from the map and made progress against polio, malaria, and the plague.

QUANTITY AND QUALITY OF FOOD

Increased food quantity and quality has had a dramatic effect on the population as well. Advances in agricultural technology have helped to feed billions of people around the world. The advancements in the technology of growing rice, for example, have allowed triple-cropping and increased production in Asia. The importance of rice in the Asian diet cannot be overestimated. Rice is a high-calorie food that provides energy for millions on a daily basis. Rice is eaten in all three meals of the day and is an essential staple crop in the cultures of billions of people around the world.

ETHNIC AND RELIGIOUS ISSUES

Ethnic and religious issues also play a major role in population growth around the world. Many cultures forbid the use of any form of birth control. Some cultures in Africa believe that having relations with a virgin will rid a man of the HIV virus, although it actually risks infecting the young woman with the disease as well as possibly impregnating her.

ECONOMIC ISSUES

Economic issues are a good indicator of a society's population growth rate. If the economy of the country is fundamentally based on agriculture, the odds are high that the country has a high growth rate. If the economy is based on industry or services, chances are high that the population growth is minimal or even nonexistent.

CAUSES OF POPULATION DECLINE

Just as there are reasons for population growth, there are also factors that contribute to population decline. The three major factors that contribute to population decline are:

1. Natural hazards and disasters
2. War or political turmoil
3. Economic issues

NATURAL HAZARDS AND DISASTERS

Natural hazards become disasters when loss of life and property are involved. From a population distribution perspective, millions of people live in areas that are subject to natural hazards. Many earthquake-prone areas, such as California, Japan, Turkey, and Pakistan, have large populations.

Many natural hazards easily become disasters because of population growth, density, and distribution.

Natural disasters can kill thousands of people at a time. Recent earthquakes around the world have killed tens of thousands of people at a time. Many of the deadliest earthquakes occur in less developed countries because of the lack of building codes that would require structures to withstand tremors. Tsunamis, tornadoes, blizzards, and other natural disasters kill thousands more people every year but cause only a small percentage of overall worldwide deaths. Estimates vary, but the Haitian earthquake of 2010 killed anywhere from 100,000 to 200,000 people. Upwards of 19,000 people lost their lives in the Japanese earthquake of 2011 that led to a tsunami, which in turn caused a nuclear disaster at the Fukishima nuclear power plant.

Famines and plagues lead to mass starvation and disease. Famines are usually caused by some type of natural disaster, such as a drought, which affects the food supply. When transportation systems are unable to bring in sufficient food, populations starve. Famine has killed tens of thousands of people in places such as Ethiopia and Sudan. Poverty and lack of health care can lead to plagues, which can also cause the lack of food production in a region.

WAR OR POLITICAL TURMOIL

Another factor that negatively affects population growth is war or political turmoil. In Cambodia during the 1970s, for example, the Khmer Rouge forced millions to leave the country or be killed. This exodus greatly affected Cambodia's population during this time. The Killing Fields of Cambodia have been well documented, and the effects of the political situation of the 1970s are still being felt in that country.

War leads to refugees, who flee for fear of persecution or death if they remain in the country. The ethnic conflict in Rwanda and Uganda resulted in a refugee crisis in central Africa that led to the deaths of millions of people on both sides of the conflict. The battles were so intense that some people say the rivers and creeks ran red with blood.

World War II directly affected the lives of millions of people around the world. Losing a spouse to war affects the entire family structure. In societies where wars have been fought, the male section of many population pyramids has been greatly diminished.

ECONOMIC ISSUES

Various economic issues contribute to population decline as well. The number one reason people move is for economic concerns. If there are no employment opportunities available in your area, you need to go where jobs are available. Such out-migration leads to a decrease in the population of certain areas. Much of the Great Plains region of the United States is experiencing out-migration as a result of a lack of job opportunities. It's important to note, however, that migration does not affect population on a worldwide level.

IMMIGRATION, MIGRATION, AND REFUGEES

Migration is the movement of people. People may move across town or across the world, again for a variety of reasons. As a whole, the percentage of people who move a long way from their place of origin is relatively low.

People who move into a country or region are called **immigrants**. People who leave a region or country are called **emigrants**. Immigration is the influx of people into a particular region or location, whereas emigration is the outflow of people from a particular region or location. **Net migration** is the number of immigrants minus the number of emigrants.

Most people move at least once in their lifetimes. These moves are generally short in distance and rarely involve leaving the country. When migration does involve moving to another country, the destination is usually to one of the major urban centers of the new country. For example, if people move to Egypt, they are probably moving to Cairo. If people are moving to China, they are probably moving to Shanghai, Hong Kong, or Beijing. New York is known for its immigrant neighborhoods.

It is important to note that movement does not affect the world's population. Once the person is alive, their movement on the Earth does not affect the world's population, only a country's population.

THEORIES OF MIGRATION

PUSH AND PULL FACTORS

A **pull factor** is a positive perception about a location that induces a person to move there. A **push factor** is a negative perception about a location that induces a person to move away from that location.

Both push and pull factors are based on an individual's *perceptions* of the area. A pull factor for one person may be a push factor for another. A good example of what could be considered both a push and a pull factor is climate. One person is tired of the cold weather. She doesn't like the major snowstorms that hit her area. She is tired of getting her automobile stuck in the snow. She decides to move to a warmer climate where it does not snow. For this person, the cold weather is an environmental push factor.

For another person, the cold weather is a pull factor. He loves to ice skate and sled with his children down the hills in the winter. He also loves to downhill ski. This

---

AP EXPERT TIP

History, whether world, national, or family, is full of migration stories. Can you tell a migration story using the terms found on the following pages? Storytelling is a powerful tool for cultural survival and for learning and memory.

AP EXPERT TIP

An easy way to distinguish between "immigrant" and "emigrant" is to think about "into" and "exit." An immigrant comes into the country and an emigrant exits it.

person is willing to put up with the inconveniences of the snow so as to enjoy the amenities of the climate. For this individual, the cold weather is a pull factor.

The life course theory, first put forward in the 1960s, posits that people make decisions early on in life that directly affect their life in the future. This theory sees people's lives in a timeline sense but evaluates their lives by looking at their social and cultural perspectives and situations. Marriages/divorces, educational opportunities, and other events occurring or decisions made early in life directly affect people's situations later on their lives. These decisions then may dictate migration preferences and opportunities in the future.

There are four different types of push and pull factors:

1. Economic
2. Political
3. Environmental
4. Social

These three factors are all reasons why people would want to move to a certain location or away from a location, and each can be so strong that people are willing to sacrifice a loss in the short term for monetary, environmental, or political gain in the long term. They are willing to undertake the journey, sometimes thousands of miles, for the opportunity for freedom, employment, safety, or some other positive aspect of another location.

ECONOMIC FACTORS

As previously noted, economic pull factors are the number-one reason people move. Often, they relocate for new employment opportunities. If an area opens a new factory or is in need of more employees, more people may move to the area to fill those available jobs. If the jobs are high paying, people may be willing to relocate at considerable expense.

Economics can also be a push factor. Downturns in the economy frequently lead to business layoffs and shutdowns. Without jobs, people cannot support themselves or their families, so they must go where there are enough jobs. In this case, the economy forces the person to leave an area in search of new employment. Economics has now become a push factor.

Economic factors rely on the idea of **human capital**, the idea that an individual has certain skills that are valuable to a society or a company. Many companies will conduct worldwide searches for top positions and then consequently pay for those employees to move to their location. These people have some skill or experience that makes them of value to the organization; hence the costs that go into the search and moving processes are outweighed by the positives the individual will bring to the organization.

POLITICAL FACTORS

Other push and pull factors are political. Sometimes, people are forced to leave a country for fear of persecution or even death. **Refugees** are people who are forced to flee their homeland for such reasons, to seek some type of asylum in another country. Sometimes refugee movements are on a massive scale, with tens of thousands of people forced to flee their homelands.

The recent migration movement of the Hmong population into the United States is an example of such a refugee movement. The Hmong fought side by side with U.S. soldiers during the Vietnam conflict. When the United States left, the Hmong were forced out of the country for fear of persecution by the new, anti-U.S. government. Thus, the Hmong became a refugee group, and the stories of the Hmong crossing the Mekong River are heroic. Many of the migrations were done in the cover of darkness for fear of being shot by enemy soldiers, and many of the recent immigrants to the United States lost close family members in the move away from their homelands.

An **asylum seeker** is a refugee who is seeking asylum or safety in another country after escaping their home country for fear of their lives. The Hmong were seeking asylum in the United States after the Vietnam War forced them out of their home country of Laos.

The issue of scale is important when discussing the issue of internally displaced people. An **internally displaced** person is a person who has been removed from their home but has not left their country. This has been the case in Columbia, the Democratic Republic of the Congo, and other African countries when the government forced individuals to move from their homes. Often times the innocent (women and children) are the ones who are internally displaced. Rebel movements in many of these countries are the reason for the government movement of its citizens.

Refugees should not be confused with **forced migrants**, who are literally forced out of their homes for either political or environmental reasons. Most of the Native Americans in the United States were forced out of their areas and moved to reservations during the 1800s. The Trail of Tears is an example of a forced migration, when Cherokee Indians from Georgia were forced to move to Oklahoma in one of the largest forced migrations in U.S. history; many died along the way.

The Jews who emigrated during World War II were refugees. Jews from around Europe fled the Nazis for fear of death. Many countries refused to take the Jews. Other countries, like Denmark and Sweden, were havens for Jews as they tried to escape imprisonment and torture. However, Jews whom the Nazis forcibly moved into ghettos, as in Warsaw, Poland, were forced migrants.

There have been dozens of refugee crises around the world during the past 50 years. One of the largest refugee movements occurred in Rwanda and Uganda during the 1990s. The conflict between the Hutus and the Tutsis caused the deaths of hundreds of thousands of people on both sides. Brutal retaliation led to further conflicts. Refugees of this war fled to Congo and other neighboring countries to escape the bloodshed, putting social and economic pressure on these countries and spreading political instability.

The same type of refugee movement occurred in the former Yugoslavia during the 1990s. The breakup of the former Yugoslav Republic led to increased refugee movement into neighboring countries, such as Albania. This type of refugee movement occurs on a daily basis in many locations around the world. People leave their homelands fearing persecution and death. In addition, some people leave to search for freedom, opportunity, and a new life. They want to enter new countries for the opportunity to better their economic situation and to have the political freedom to say and do things that they only dreamed of in their homeland.

ENVIRONMENTAL FACTORS

The last push and pull factors are environmental. This type of migration is usually **voluntary**. In other words, people have the choice to move to a warmer climate or a climate that better suits their lifestyles. Many retirees in the United States have voluntarily moved to Florida for the warmer climate and amenities that Florida can offer them.

The southern portion of the United States has seen a large in-migration during the previous four decades. This area, known as the Sun Belt, shown in Figure 4.8, includes states extending from North Carolina to Southern California. It has seen dramatic growth during the latter half of the 20th century. The invention and mass use of air-conditioning has made warmer areas more livable in the summer. Many new residents are retirees, but many have moved for economic opportunities as well. Many see North Carolina, South Carolina, and areas extending into Georgia as positive places to move. Citizens of these states can participate in summer activities practically year-round. For example, golf in Florida is a year-round industry.

Many job seekers moved from the Rust Belt to the Sun Belt during the 1980s and 1990s. This movement was caused by the closing of many factories in the Northeast and Great Lakes regions. These workers moved to where the new factories were being built. Honda and many other car manufacturers have huge industrial plants in the Sun Belt; Honda builds many of its cars in Alabama, and BMW builds some of its cars in South Carolina.

This Sun Belt phenomenon has skipped several locations. Mississippi, Louisiana, and Alabama have not seen the immense growth of other Southern areas. Other areas that have been skipped in the Sun Belt include sections of western Texas and eastern portions of New Mexico. Part of this is due to poor economic situations. Also, the relative lack of education of the population has negatively impacted these areas' economic growth.

Many communities in the South have offered incentives for people to move to their areas. By offering tax breaks for companies and increased recreational opportunities (parks, sports arenas, etc.), these towns and cities in the Sun Belt have marketed themselves to others areas around the country. This concept is referred to as **place utility**.

Figure 4.8: Sun Belt Areas in the United States.

Several commercials about specific communities have run nationally around the United States. Sioux Falls, South Dakota, has run advertisements throughout the Upper Midwest, presenting itself as the ideal place for your business to be located. This marketing has attracted hundreds of new employment opportunities to a town that is growing already.

Recreational opportunities abound in colder climates as well, but some people are averse to bundling up in winter jackets and wind chills well below zero. Again, an individual's perception of an area determines its attractiveness to them.

Another area in the United States that has seen growth due to its environmental amenities is the mountain state region in the western portion of the country. These areas, including Utah, Colorado, Montana, and New Mexico, have seen population in some of their small towns double over the past several decades. People like the views and the recreational opportunities offered in these areas.

People have left specific areas owing to environmental factors. Hurricane Katrina, which hit the Gulf Coast of the United States, was the costliest natural disaster in the country's history. The storm wiped out communities and forced people out of their homes and into temporary shelters, sometimes located in cities hundreds of miles away. Residents of New Orleans were put on buses and sent to Houston, Texas, as well as other cities around the United States. Many of the people who left New Orleans have decided to make Houston their permanent home. In the Midwest, Americans also face natural disasters, such as tornadoes and floods.

Another example of an environmental push factor was the Dust Bowl, which occurred during the 1930s in the central Plains. At one time, this region was heavily cultivated, and in the 1920s, there was a saying among farmers that "the rain followed the plow." However, when the drought of the 1930s came, many farmers were forced to leave their homesteads and experienced economic ruin. The Dust Bowl resulted in one of the largest migrations in human history. The migration of people from Oklahoma was the backdrop for John Steinbeck's *The Grapes of Wrath*.

Outside the United States, the tsunami that hit the Indian Ocean in late 2005 devastated coastal communities and forced tens of thousands of people out of their homes and into shelters. Natural disasters are one environmental push factor that moves people away from where they live. After the earthquake, tsunami, and nuclear disaster of 2011, tens of thousands of Japanese were forced to move away from their traditional homes. Many of these people cannot move back due to the radiation from the power plant.

SOCIAL FACTORS

The fourth push and pull factor is social. Social factors do not fit into any of the three aforementioned push and pull factors and could include such factors as health care, education, or even religious freedom. Since these can be both push and pull factors, the negatives would be the lack of health care, dearth of opportunities in education, or policies restricting religious practices. The pull factors would be advances in any of these three areas.

Social factors are different from political factors in that a person is not necessarily killed or persecuted for their beliefs but may be imprisoned for religious factors. Because of these factors, people move to attain better education levels that were not available in their previous locations.

RAVENTEIN'S LAWS OF MIGRATION

E. G. Raventein studied migration trends and came up with ten laws of migration in 1885. Many of these generalizations are still valid today; however, women are now migrating internationally in larger numbers than men in some cases. In considering these rules, it is important to think of examples for each law and to determine how valid the trend is now.

1. Most migration is over a short distance.

2. Migration occurs in a series of steps.

3. Long-distance migrants usually move to centers of economic opportunity (urban areas).

4. Each migration produces a movement in the opposite direction, or counter stream (although not necessarily of the same volume).

5. People in rural areas migrate more than people in cities.

6. Men migrate over longer distances than women.

7. Most migrants are young adult males.

8. Cities grow more by migration than by natural increase.

9. Migration increases with economic development.

10. Migration is mostly due to economic causes.

MIGRATION TRANSITION

Wilber Zelinsky put forth the idea that a migration transition occurs in conjunction with a demographic transition. For instance, when a country is in stage 2 (high growth) of the demographic transition, the excessive population growth encourages people to move to another country where there is more economic opportunity. Countries in stage 4 tend to have more economic opportunities because their economies are growing faster than their stable population. When a country is in stage 3 (moderate growth) or 4 (stable growth) people tend to move internally (interregional migration) for job opportunities. Examples of interregional migration include people in the United States moving from the Midwest or northeastern areas to the South for economic and environmental reasons. An example of this would be the Great Migration in the early 20th century wherein African Americans moved from the south to the Midwest, northeast, and west to find jobs in industrial cities and escape racism. Other forms of migration, especially in the United States, include rural to urban, urban to suburban, and suburban to exurban or urban.

HUMAN CAPITAL

The Human Capital model of migration, developed by Larry Sjaastad in 1962, attempts to explain the major reasons why people migrate. This model basically states that people seek to improve their incomes over the course of their lives; therefore, people weigh the costs against the benefits of migrating. William A. V. Clark contributed to the explanation in 1986 with two observations: Migration rates drop as people age since personal wealth is accumulated over time and the potential benefit of moving decreases with increased age. Secondly, Clark observed that psychological and economic costs and benefits are considered before people make a major move—something Sjaastad overlooked in his initial model.

LIFE COURSE

Migration is impacted by major turning points in a person's life such as college, employment, marriage, having children, and retirement. Each of these events helps determine the decision a person makes with respect to migration. For example, the larger the household, the less likely it is the household will relocate. Single people are the most likely to move, followed by couples, families with fewer children, and then families with more children or older dependents. However, larger families can encourage certain types of migration: when couples have children they tend to engage in intraregional migration in order to obtain more space for their growing family. The most frequent example of this in North America is urban-to-suburban migration within the same metropolitan area. Finally, many people in North America move when they retire from work. Warm and sunny states with limited tax burdens on retirees, like Florida and Arizona, have traditionally been favorite spots.

SOCIOECONOMIC CONSEQUENCES OF MIGRATION

Migration impacts both the areas receiving migrants and the areas that the migrants left. Large numbers of migrants can change the socioeconomic nature of an area. Two examples of this in the United States are Miami, Florida, and Dearborn, Michigan. The culture of Miami and the surrounding area of south Florida changed significantly after the Cuban Revolution when many Cuban refugees immigrated to the area. Dearborn, Michigan, is home to one of the largest Muslim populations in the United States, because many immigrants from the Middle East came to the area in the 1920s to work in the automobile industry. As a result, Dearborn and surrounding communities form a unique cultural landscape. On the other hand, large-scale emigration can have a dramatic effect on the area that the migrants leave. For instance, a large percentage of men migrate to the United States for work from many rural Mexican villages, creating a dearth of men in those villages. The effect is a change in the general workforce and culture of the villages with women becoming the heads of households. The long-term consequences have not been well studied; however this situation is a change to the traditional Mexican way of life.

ADDITIONAL TYPES OF MIGRATION

INTERCONTINENTAL MIGRATION

Intercontinental migration is the movement of people across an ocean or continent, such as the movement of the Hmong people from Laos and Thailand to the United States. This type of migration usually involves a large sum of money, including the cost of the trip as well as establishing oneself in the new location.

Intercontinental migration usually involves some type of **distance decay** of the former culture. People begin to assimilate into the culture in which they are presently living. Although they may still hold onto their native language or religion, the influence of their native culture isn't as strong as it was in their original country. This transfer of cultures is called **acculturation**. It usually takes three generations for a culture to lose its native ways. The first generation that comes over speaks very little or none of the new country's language. Their children, however, are educated in the new country's educational system and speak two languages. The native tongue is still spoken in the home, but when the children leave for school, they are immersed in the new country's language. The third generation primarily speaks the new country's language and usually knows very little of the primary language. Most German settlers in the United States were assimilated into U.S. culture through this three-step process. The same process continues today with the Hmong migration.

Churches in the United States first began adopting Hmong families in the 1970s. These churches would welcome a family into the United States and provide them with their basic needs until they could provide for themselves. Once the families had established themselves in the United States, they sent money back home to Laos and Thailand so that other family members could come to the United States. Eventually, cultural mini-centers developed in cities such as Sacramento, California, and Saint Paul, Minnesota. This is an example of a **chain migration**. This type of migration is usually voluntary in nature and functions to reunite families and cultures. It can take many years to bring over a large number of people through chain migration. The first immigrants must establish themselves financially and earn enough money to send back to other family members.

Much of the United States was built on chain migration. Different ethnic groups around the United States, in large and small cities alike, have seen the results of chain migration. Immigrants from countries like Italy and China developed distinctive communities in New York City; Little Italy and Chinatown have become famous among New York City's ethnic neighborhoods. Italians entered the United States at ports in Boston or New York and established themselves in these cultural neighborhoods. Irish settled in Boston, Koreans in Los Angeles. It was easier for immigrants to adjust to the United States in areas where people already spoke their language and practiced their religion. Chain migrations continue today all over the world.

INTERREGIONAL MIGRATION

Another type of migration is interregional migration. **Interregional migration** is just what it sounds like. This type of migration is usually done within a country's borders, from region to region. The snowbirds that migrate from the northeast to the Sun Belt are interregional migrants. This type of migration is usually voluntary as well. Interregional migration should not be confused with **international migration**, which is movement between countries.

INTRAREGIONAL MIGRATION

Intraregional migration is the movement of people within the same region. The most typical example of this form of migration is the move from **rural to urban** areas. This migration is usually done for economic reasons. People move off the farm and into cities in the hope of finding jobs. Rural-to-urban migration usually takes place in less developed countries, where the fastest rate of urbanization is taking place.

Rural-to-urban migration occurred at a great rate in the United States during the second half of the 20th century and still continues today. Farmers who could not make enough to pay their bills were forced to look for employment in urban areas. People were leaving farms in the Midwest and Great Plains in large numbers. According to 2000 Census data, only 2 percent of the population in the United States classifies itself as farmers.

However, there has been an urban-to-rural movement recently within sections of more developed countries due to the high living costs in cities. People are moving away from urban areas into the suburbs and exurbs to avoid the high costs and property taxes associated with the urban lifestyle.

Cyclic Migration

People also move seasonally, usually for agricultural reasons. Societies that practice pastoral nomadism use **cyclic movement**, the seasonal migration of livestock to areas where food is more available. **Transhumance** is the movement of livestock to higher elevations during the summer to escape the heat in the valleys and to lower elevations during the winter to escape the severe cold of the mountains.

Cyclical movement ties in closely with the demographic transition model. As a country moves from an agricultural to an industrial base, urbanization spreads, and reliance on agricultural practices such as transhumance decreases.

Intervening Obstacles

Some **intervening obstacles** can adversely affect trade and migration between areas. An intervening obstacle forces individuals to halt and abort their migration plans due to some negative factor, which can range from cultural to physical.

Physical Obstacles

The first of these factors that limit migration is the **physical environment**. Events such as natural disasters and storms have caused people to alter where they were going. For example, imagine traveling on the Great Plains for the first time. You came from Europe, a place that has thunderstorms but none as severe as the storms that occur on the Great Plains. In addition, tornadoes are heard of in Europe but are not nearly as common as in the Great Plains region. You're in your covered wagon, when ice pellets the size of baseballs begins to pelt your wagon and team of horses or oxen. Even if you survive that, tornadoes spawned by the storm may wipe away everything else. These storms scared off many of the settlers coming to the Great Plains. They left and instead went toward the relatively safe urban areas on the East Coast.

DISTANCE AND COST OF TRAVEL

Another factor that greatly influences migration success is the **distance of travel** and **costs** associated with it. The most expensive trips today are the ones that cross an ocean, and the same was true during the peak migration period in U.S. history. Despite being a wonderful opportunity to achieve success, the transatlantic journey came at a considerable financial expense.

CULTURAL FACTORS

Other factors that can hinder migration are cultural factors, such as **language**. During migration to the United States, Eastern Europeans first traveled to the port cities in Western Europe and encountered many scams. They were often talked into paying for their journey by a person who barely spoke their own language, and after doing so, were taken for a ride and dropped off at a foreign port with promises that they were in the United States. This scam made thousands of dollars illegally and cost many immigrants their opportunity to reach the United States.

GOVERNMENTAL RESTRICTIONS

Not every person who wants to come into a country is allowed access. Many countries around the world have **quotas**. Quotas are limits that governments put on the number of immigrants they allow into their countries. The quota for legal immigrants into the United States is approximately 2 million people per year.

One of the best examples of restriction against entering the United States occurs in southern Florida, particularly Miami. Immigrants from Haiti, the Dominican Republic, and Cuba try to gain entrance, often risking their lives for the opportunity to set foot in the United States.

During the 1980s, Fidel Castro opened up the prisons in Cuba and tried to send the prisoners to the United States. Coast Guard and Immigration and Naturalization Service (INS) officials took them into custody and sent them back to Cuba. (Note that today, the INS is called the U.S. Citizenship and Immigration Services and is a part of the Department of Homeland Security.)

The debate over immigration continues today. The issue of illegal immigration into the United States, particularly across the border with Mexico, has sparked serious debate. A significant number of immigrants, both legal and illegal, come from Mexico. Mexico's struggling economy is a push factor. Citizens from throughout Central America and even South America try to come into the United States, often illegally and with the help of a coyote. A **coyote** is the term used for a person who is hired to help illegal immigrants get into the United States, often at a cost that does not depend upon success of entry.

In the age of terrorism, many consider the porous border of the United States to be a critically important issue. Some feel that **amnesty** is the best way to deal with the millions of illegal immigrants who are in the United States already. Proponents of amnesty suggest that these illegal immigrants are working jobs that Americans simply will not take, typically in the agricultural industry and under less-than-ideal working conditions. These illegal and legal immigrants often send their earnings to their families back in their home country; such transfers are called **remittances**. Opponents of amnesty suggest that these people have broken the law and need to be returned to their country of origin.

INTERVENING OPPORTUNITIES

An **intervening opportunity** is the opposite of an intervening obstacle. An intervening opportunity occurs when a migrant stops and decides to stay at a location along his or her journey because he or she encounters favorable economic opportunities or environmental amenities along the way.

An example of an intervening opportunity would be in the case of a person who is moving from Boston and wants to end up in Miami. Along the journey, he sees the coast of North Carolina and enjoys the area so much that he decides to purchase a home there. Although the opportunities available in Florida are good, this person underestimated his enjoyment of the area around North Carolina. Economic opportunities are also available in North Carolina; thus, he decides to make the stay permanent.

FORCED MIGRATION

SLAVERY

Not all migration is positive. Aside from the negative push factors previously discussed, forced migration has had a dramatic impact on the Western Hemisphere. In the 17th, 18th, and 19th centuries, slaves from West Africa were brought not only to North America, but also to dozens of other countries in the Western Hemisphere to provide labor. Sugar, rice, tobacco, and other crops are very labor intensive and need a lot of workers to meet international demand.

The impact of the slave trade, shown in Figure 4.9, on the demographics and ethnicity of the Caribbean and other countries in the Western Hemisphere cannot be underestimated. Millions of people of African descent are in the United States, the Caribbean, and South America today as a result of slavery.

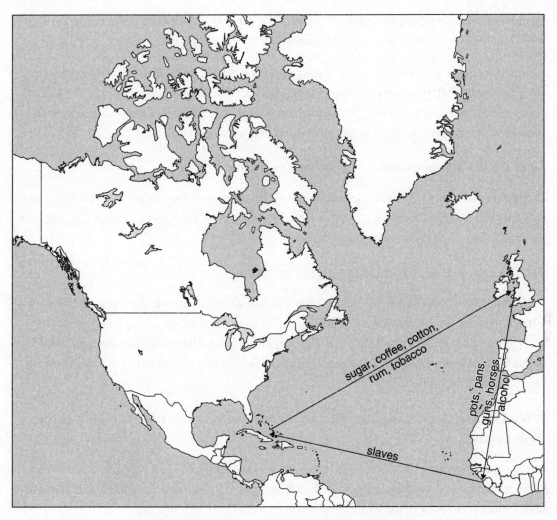

Figure 4.9: Western Hemisphere Slave Trade Map.

TRANSMIGRATION

Transmigration is the removal of people from one place and their relocation somewhere else within a country. This is not always done voluntarily. Indonesia is the fourth most-populated country in the world. A large percentage of the people live on the island of Java. To ease the resource strain on Java, the government of Indonesia put some of its population on other islands. Opponents of the transmigration argued that the government put minority groups in the fringes of the country to quell separatist movements.

U.S. IMMIGRATION: A CASE STUDY

A case study of immigration throughout U.S. history shows distinct patterns. Historically, the two major entry points into the United States were the port of Boston and Ellis Island, which has been turned into a national park in New York Harbor. The primary movement of Americans has been west. However, in the past 50 years, the center of the U.S. population has shifted significantly.

A **census**, which is a detailed counting of the population, has occurred in the United States every ten years since 1790. Census results from 2000 show that the center of population in the United States shifted from Maryland in 1790 to southern Missouri in 2000. This shift is a direct result of the country's international and interregional migration trends.

FIRST ERA OF U.S. IMMIGRATION: 1607 TO EARLY 19TH CENTURY

During the early history of the United States, the primary reasons for coming to this country were religious and economic freedom. After the United States gained independence from Great Britain, more and more immigrants came here.

SECOND ERA OF U.S. IMMIGRATION: 1820S TO 1880S

In the late 1800s, more immigrants came from Europe, and many immigrants, specifically Chinese, arrived on the West Coast of the United States. They took jobs completing the first transcontinental railroad, working in the difficult, mountainous terrain of the western United States. The railroad eventually united the U.S. coasts for the first time (linking in Promontory Summit, Utah, in 1869).

THIRD ERA OF U.S. IMMIGRATION: END OF THE 19TH CENTURY TO THE BEGINNING OF THE 20TH CENTURY

Immigration into the United States saw one of its peaks during 1900 to 1920. These immigrants came primarily from southern Europe, including Italy, Spain, and Greece, which saw millions of their residents emigrate to the United States.

A major migration within the United States, which often goes unmentioned, is the migration of African Americans from the South to major urban centers in the North during the 1900s. Tens of thousands of African Americans moved into northern cities, such as Chicago and Cleveland. They also moved to the northeast for employment opportunities in industrial centers.

During the 1930s, immigration declined dramatically, going from almost 1 million people per year to less than 50,000. During World War II, immigration into the United States almost ceased. However, some Jews escaped Europe and came to the United States.

FOURTH ERA OF U.S. IMMIGRATION: 1950S TO PRESENT

Since the 1950s, immigration into the United States has continued to rise. Whereas during the 1800s, the majority of immigrants came from countries, such as Denmark, Sweden, and Norway, in northern Europe, now immigrants come primarily from Latin America and, increasingly, from Asia.

Immigration rises during periods of economic prosperity in the destination country. Today, immigration rates in the United States exceed the top rates of the 1920s. The second peak in immigration occurred at the end of the last century. The greatest number of international immigrants into the United States came from 1980 to 2000.

Future trends in immigration will depend heavily upon the policies of the U.S. government. Meanwhile, the issue of illegal immigration continues to be debated and becomes an issue during every major national election.

The H-1B visa is a special permission from the United States government to extend stays or permit allowances for more immigrants with "special occupations." These special occupations are usually highly skilled labor that cannot be met with United States employees. These H-1B visa participants are highly skilled, highly educated labor drawn from other countries for the high wages and opportunities available in the United States. This has come under criticism from labor unions who feel that the United States should instead employ and train its own citizens for this type of work.

REVIEW QUESTIONS

Multiple-Choice Questions

1. What stage of the demographic transition model do most demographers agree the United Kingdom is in?

    (A) Stage 1
    (B) Stage 2
    (C) Stage 3
    (D) Stage 4
    (E) Stage 5

2. What is the main difference between population clusters in Asia and Europe?

    (A) In Asia, most people live in urban areas.
    (B) In Europe, most people live in urban areas.
    (C) In Asia, most people make their living in the secondary sector of the economy.
    (D) In Europe, most people make their living in the primary sector of the economy.
    (E) In Asia, the tertiary sector of the economy is stagnant.

3. Which of following regions is considered to be in the five primary areas of population density in the world?

    (A) South Asia, including India, Pakistan, and Bangladesh
    (B) Eastern South America, including Argentina and Uruguay
    (C) Sub-Saharan Africa
    (D) Northern Europe, including Finland
    (E) Central Asia, including western China and Mongolia

4. What reason best explains why the rate of natural increase is greater in less developed countries than in more developed countries?

    (A) In less developed countries, people have fewer children due to having an industrial society.
    (B) In more developed countries, people have more children due to having an agricultural society.
    (C) In less developed countries, people have more children due to having an agricultural society.
    (D) In more developed countries, people have fewer children because children are economic assets.
    (E) In less developed countries, people have fewer children due to having a tertiary society.

5. The Dust Bowl in the Great Plains is the best example of which push or pull factor?

    (A) Political pull factor
    (B) Economic push factor
    (C) Environmental pull factor
    (D) Environmental push factor
    (E) Economic pull factor

6. What is the seasonal migration of livestock to pasture lands where food is more plentiful called?

    (A) Transhumance
    (B) Natality
    (C) Sustainability
    (D) Step migration
    (E) Interval migration

7. Country Populationville has a crude birth rate of 25 and a crude death rate of 13, while the country of Demograville has a crude birth rate of 40 and a crude death rate of 25. Which country will experience the fastest natural increase rate?

   (A) Neither of them will, because Population-ville has a natural increase rate above 2.

   (B) Populationville will, because its crude birth rate is higher.

   (C) Demograville will, because its crude birth rate is higher.

   (D) Populationville will, because its crude death rate is lower.

   (E) Demograville will, because the naturual increase rate is higher.

8. What revolution coincided with the world's population explosion?

   (A) First Agricultural Revolution

   (B) Second Agricultural Revolution

   (C) Third Agricultural Revolution

   (D) Scientific Revolution

   (E) Demographic Revolution

9. The *five toos*—too hot, too cold, too wet, too dry, and too hilly—refer to which term?

   (A) Cohort

   (B) Distance decay

   (C) Ecumene

   (D) Transmigration

   (E) Intervening opportunity

10. Stage 2 of the demographic transition is characterized by

    (A) high growth.

    (B) low growth.

    (C) moderate growth.

    (D) zero growth.

    (E) arithmetic growth.

11. A person is trying to move from Miami to San Diego but decides to stop and stay in Dallas. This is an example of what?

    (A) Intervening obstacle

    (B) Intervening opportunity

    (C) Voluntary migration

    (D) Environmental pull factor

    (E) Distance decay

12. During what 20-year period has the United States seen the greatest immigration in terms of raw numbers?

    (A) 1850–1870

    (B) 1900–1920

    (C) 1920–1940

    (D) 1960–1980

    (E) 1980–2000

13. The idea that once a culture locates in another area, the original customs and traditions eventually die out or are less strong, is best characterized by which term?

    (A) Place utility

    (B) Acculturation

    (C) Distance decay

    (D) Transhumance

    (E) Gravity model

14. The S-curve is best used to illustrate which geographic principle?

    (A) The tendency for cities to be associated with each other based on their population sizes

    (B) The graph that demonstrates the migration route for migrants in World War II

    (C) The exponential growth of human population over time

    (D) The openness and stability of countries over time

    (E) The model that describes the decline of population growth as countries industrialize

15. The movement of persons from the Rust Belt to the Sun Belt is an example of which type of migration?

    (A) Intercontinental

    (B) International

    (C) Interregional

    (D) Interurban

    (E) Intercoastal

16. The population explosion began in which century?

    (A) 17th century

    (B) 18th century

    (C) 19th century

    (D) 20th century

    (E) 21st century

17. Which statement would best fit the Gravity Model in relation to migration?

    (A) New York and Los Angeles are closely linked based on their distance.

    (B) New York and Los Angeles are not linked at all because of their distance.

    (C) New York and Los Angeles are linked due to their populations.

    (D) New York and Los Angeles are not linked due to their populations.

    (E) New York and Los Angeles are linked due their proximity to ports.

18. Which of the following means of population growth deterrence has been the most successful?

    (A) Increasing the death rate as in the Sudan

    (B) Decreasing the birth rate as in the United States

    (C) Increasing government laws as in China

    (D) Decreasing government laws as in the United States

    (E) Decreasing the death rate as in India

19. Which of the following countries can you assume has the greatest demographic momentum based on its crude birth rate and crude death rate?

    (A) Mozambique: 44 birth rate and 15 death rate

    (B) Tanzania: 40 birth rate and 9 death rate

    (C) Ethiopia: 34 birth rate and 8 death rate

    (D) Zimbabwe: 33 birth rate and 11 death rate

    (E) Reunion: 17 birth rate and 5 death rate

20. Which group of people believes that the world is ripe for a population explosion?

    (A) Neo-Malthusians

    (B) Bressnerians

    (C) Malthusians

    (D) Demographers

    (E) Neo-Bressnerians

FREE-RESPONSE QUESTION

> **Directions:** While a formal essay is not required, it is not enough to answer the following question by merely listing facts. Your answer should be based upon your critical analysis of the question posed.

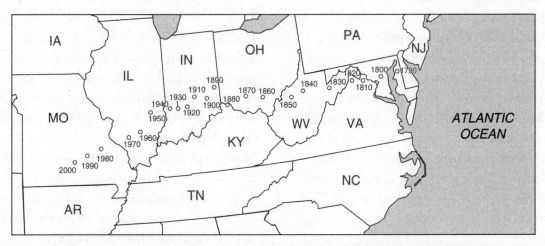

Figure 4.10: Geographic Population Center of the United States (1790–2000).

1. Figure 4.10 shows the geographical centers of population in the United States from the 1790 to the 2000 census.

   (A) Describe the geographic patterns of migration in the United States on the map.

   (B) Discuss the reasons for these migrations in the context of the second era (late 1800s) and the third era (early 1900s). Make sure to discuss pull factors in your response.

   (C) Discuss the reasons for the movement of the Geographic Population Center of the United States from 1970 till the present, using international and interregional migration patterns.

ANSWERS AND EXPLANATIONS

MULTIPLE-CHOICE QUESTIONS

1. D

Most demographers believe that the United Kingdom is in stage 4 of the Demographic Transition Model. With a birth rate of 13 and a death rate of 9, the United Kingdom has not gone past zero population growth to enter what some demographers believe is the transition into stage 5, (E). There are no countries in stage 1, eliminating A as a possible answer. Stage 2 is characterized by a high birth rate and high death rate. The United Kingdom's birth rate is not high, which eliminates stage 2 (B) and stage 3 (C) a possibly answers. This makes (D), stage 4, the correct answer.

2. B

In East, South, and Southeast Asia the majority of the population still lives in rural clustered settlements. Conversely, in Europe the majority of people live in urban areas. This is primarily a function of the fact that Europe is an industrial/post industrial society whereas most people in Asia engage in agriculture, even though that is changing rapidly.

3. A

The five primary areas of population density in the world are East Asia, South Asia (including India, Pakistan, and Bangladesh), Southeast Asia, Western and Central Europe (including Ukraine), and the northeast corridor of North America and Canada. Sub-Saharan Africa can be a tricky choice. Sub-Saharan Africa is one of the fastest-growing regions in the world but still does not have a high population density. Because sub-Saharan Africa is predominately agricultural, many of its people are spread out in the farming provinces or states of the countries.

4. C

In the Demographic Transition Model, population growth takes place in stage 2. This stage is dominated by agriculture, and children are economic assets because they help on the farms, and they are a form of social security for parents. In the industrial and tertiary societies, children become an economic liability, and people begin to have fewer children.

5. D

The Dust Bowl was part of one of the most difficult times in United States history for farmers, specifically in the Great Plains region. Abnormally arid conditions shriveled crops and starved hundreds of thousands of head of cattle in the region. This forced farmers off their land. Economic push factor is a plausible answer to this question, but the economic push factor was caused by the environmental push factor. You should have been able to eliminate political pull as a factor. The Dust Bowl was not a reason for anybody to move to the area, eliminating the pull factors.

6. A

Transhumance is the seasonal migration of livestock. The remainder of the answers tie in with migration except for sustainability. Choices (B) and (C) can be eliminated right away, because they deal with population issues, leaving you with three potential answers. Step migration is the movement of people with different stops along the way. These stops may last months or years, but they are temporary; the migrants ultimately continue their journey to reach their intended destination.

7. E

These types of questions ask you to do some simple math based on the assumption that you know how natural increase is measured. Natural increase is simply the difference between the crude birth rate and the crude death rate. The difference between Populationville's crude birth rate and crude death rate is 12 (25 minus 13). Demograville's difference is 15 (40 minus 25). Both numbers must be included in calculating the natural increase rate.

8. B

This one can be a tricky question. World population began to increase exponentially in the 20th century. The Second Agricultural Revolution caused a decrease in overall death rates, thus causing population to grow. This is the correct answer. The Industrial Revolution began in the 1750s in Great Britain and diffused into the United States in the 1800s. The First Agricultural Revolution was the transfer process from hunting and gathering to planting and sustaining. This process began thousands of years ago. The Second Agricultural Revolution coincided with the Industrial Revolution. The mechanization of farming allowed farmers to produce many more products, growing the population's food supply. The Third Agricultural Revolution, sometimes called the Green Revolution, involved the genetic engineering of agricultural products to sustain crops in environments where they would not grow naturally. This revolution started in the 1950s, and debate occurs today as to whether it is still occurring; some say that it ended in the 1980s.

9. C

An ecumene is an area that is conducive to human populations. This is the correct answer. A cohort is a group of people who are in a similar circumstance. Distance decay refers to migrants losing their home culture the farther they move from their hearth. Transmigration is the forced removal of citizens into other areas of the country by the government. An intervening opportunity motivates migrants to stay in a location along their original, planned route.

10. A

In stage 2 of the demographic transition, death rates dramatically drop while birth rates remain at the same high level or drop slightly. The difference between the crude birth rate and the crude death rate becomes dramatic, and as a result the population is characterized by high growth.

11. B

Question 11 gives an example of an intervening opportunity. An intervening opportunity occurs when a person or family likes the amenities in an area and stops to reside there permanently, although they did not intend it to be their final destination. An intervening obstacle forces a stop in migration. Intervening obstacles affect migrants negatively, while intervening opportunities affect them positively.

12. E

The greatest number of international immigrants into the United States came from 1980 to 2000. This number is almost matched by those who came from 1900 to 1920. More immigrants arrive during periods of economic prosperity in the destination country. Both the 1980–2000 time span and the 1900–1920 time span saw economic growth. The answers referring to 1850–1870 and 1920–1940 are incorrect. These periods saw some of the least immigration into the United States owing to wars.

13. C

Distance decay is the principle that the farther one moves from a cultural hearth, the less present that culture is on the landscape. The farther that one moves from one's homeland, the less likely one is to hold onto one's cultural ways; eventually one will be assimilated into the new country's culture. Acculturation is an interesting alternative for this question, but acculturation is the process of assimilation into the new culture, not the loss of the home culture. Distance decay is the correct answer.

14. B

The S-curve shows the world's population levels during the four stages of the demographic transition model. Population growth starts out slow to moderate, then becomes exponential. After a period of exponential growth, population increase eventually slows owing to lack of resources and population may even decline. This resulting graph line resembles the letter *S*. Choice (A) describes the gravity model. Choice (D) describes the J-curve model.

15. C

The movement from the Rust Belt to the Sun Belt is an example of interregional migration. Interregional migration occurs within the same country. Intercontinental migration usually involves crossing oceans but always means moving from one continent to another and traveling a long distance. International migration, a move from one country to another, can be intercontinental migration. Interurban migration is the movement of people into a new urban area.

16. D

World population started to grow exponentially in the 20th century. Many of the world's more developed countries transitioned out of the population growth cycle in the mid-1900s. However, many of the less developed countries are still in a period of immense growth. Most of the population growth in the world is taking place in the less developed countries.

17. C

The gravity model suggests that areas are linked together based more on their populations and their importance based on those population levels. Distance is not really a factor in linkage if the population is high in both of the cities being compared. The Gravity Model multiplies the populations of the two cities and divides the product by the distance between the two cities squared. Therefore, distance is relevant but population difference more so. World cities such as New York and Los Angeles are closely linked because of their populations, which affect trade routes, airline routes, etc.

18. C

Most would agree that the most successful means of population deterrence has been China's one-child policy, enacted in 1979. This policy has put China's total fertility rate at 1.5, below the rate of renewal. The United States has not been successful at controlling population growth by decreasing the birth rate.

19. B

According to the information, Tanzania has the greatest demographic momentum. The difference between its crude birth rate and crude death rate is an astonishing 31 points. These children will have children when they reach childbearing age, creating demographic momentum. This means a large number of children will be born in Tanzania within the next 50 years. The greater the difference between crude birth and death rates, the greater the rate of natural increase. The greater its rate of natural increase, the more demographic momentum a country possesses.

20. A

Neo-Malthusians believe that the world is ripe for another population explosion that the world simply cannot handle. Even with the agricultural production occurring with the Green Revolution, population growth is outpacing the ability of the world to feed itself and this will result in a worldwide food shortage and mass starvation and wars.

FREE-RESPONSE QUESTION

SAMPLE ESSAY

PART A

Since the first census in 1790, the population center of the United States has moved west and slightly south; the population center was in eastern Maryland in 1790 and was in south central Missouri in 2000. In every census since 1790, the population center showed westward movement, and in every census since 1950, it has moved southward, too.

PART B

From 1880 to 1890 the population center of the United States moved significantly northward and slightly westward. This era saw many people migrating to the United States from Scandinavian countries, especially Norway, Sweden, and Finland. The pull of inexpensive farmland in a climate similar to that of their homeland attracted millions of these immigrants to the upper Midwest (Minnesota, North and South Dakota). As a result, the center of the U.S. population shifted northward. The third era of migration started in 1900 and lasted until the early 1920s. This era saw many immigrants coming to the United States from Eastern and Southern Europe. Large numbers of Italian and Greek immigrants first settled in the northeast, and many Eastern European immigrants tended to move to cities in the Midwest such as Chicago and Cleveland. The pull of factory jobs and economic opportunities in these northeastern and Midwestern cities attracted millions of immigrants. As a result, the center of the U.S. population didn't move very far west or south during these decades.

PART C

The center of the U.S. population has significantly moved to the south and west since 1950 because of international and interregional migration trends. Internationally, most immigrants since 1970 have come from Latin America and Asia. A large percentage of Asian immigrants first settled on the west coast in large cities such as Los Angeles, San Francisco, and Seattle. Many Latin American immigrants, especially from Mexico, established themselves in the southwest in areas such as southern California, Arizona, New Mexico, and Texas. Next, interregional migration from the Midwest and northeast to the West and South helped shift the center of the U.S. population to the south and west. The pull of better weather, more job opportunities, and lower taxes for retirees has attracted millions of people to the Sun Belt, which stretches from the southeast to the southwest. The combination of international and interregional migration has significantly shifted the center of United States population from central eastern Illinois in 1950 to southern central Missouri by the year 2000.

RUBRIC FOR FREE-RESPONSE QUESTION

Total point value for question 1 = 10

Part A—Two points possible:

- One point for identifying that the population center has moved westward.

- One point for identifying that the population center has moved southward.

Part B—Four points possible:

- Two points for identifying the second era of migration with discussion of accurate pull factor(s).

  — Late 1800s from Western and Northern Europe (Scandinavia and Germany)

  — Pull factor of inexpensive land and familiar climate in the upper Midwest

- Two points for identifying the third era of migration with discussion of accurate pull factor(s).

  — Early 20th century from parts of Southern and Eastern Europe

  — Pull factors of economic opportunities in Northeastern and Midwestern cities

Part C—Four points possible:

- Two points for identifying sources of international migrants and where they are moving to within the United States and how this is changing the center of the U.S. population.

  — Asian and Latin American immigrants moving to the West Coast and southwest

  — Chain migration from Asia and Latin American has meant a large number of immigrants who are realted to previous immigrants coming to the United States.

- Two points for identifying the dynamics of interregional migration with the United States and how it is changing the center of U.S. population.

  — People moving from the northeast and Midwest to the southeast and west for economic and environmental reasons

CHAPTER 5: CULTURAL PATTERNS AND PROCESSES

IF YOU LEARN ONLY EIGHT THINGS IN THIS CHAPTER . . .

1. Language is the means of mutually comprehensible communication among people. There are thousands of languages around the world, but many of them are dying out.

2. Folk culture is practiced by a relatively small number of people in a particular area. Popular culture is diffused rapidly around the world through mass communication.

3. The largest language family is the Indo-European family of which there are many branches, including the Romance and the Germanic languages. The second-largest language family is the Sino-Tibetan family, which includes the most spoken language in the world—Mandarin Chinese.

4. Dialects are forms of a language that differ based on vocabulary, syntax, and speed.

5. There are five primary religions in the world today: Christianity, Islam, and Judaism (the Western religions) and Hinduism and Buddhism (the Eastern religions). Christianity is the largest religion in the world with just over 2 billion followers. Islam is the fastest-growing religion in the world.

6. Religions are defined as monotheistic or polytheistic (worshipping one god or more gods) and ethnic or universalizing (people must be born into or can be converted to the religion).

7. There are architectural differences in religious structures around the world. Christians use churches, Jews use synagogues, Muslims use mosques, Hindus use temples, and Buddhists use pagodas.

8. According to Carl Sauer, cultural landscapes can be read and interpreted based on cultural features such as murals, language of signs, religious architecture, and even food preferences.

THE MEANING OF CULTURE

Culture is often defined as the way of life of a particular people. In many ways, culture is what defines us. Language, religion, food, and music are all aspects of culture. Although no two cultures are exactly alike, geographers can establish links between cultures and combine them into regions.

Trying to define the culture of a group of people can be difficult. Broad generalizations about a group are required to discuss their culture, but not everybody in the culture has the same values. Ethnicity and culture are intertwined; much of a particular group's culture is defined by ethnicity, and much of ethnicity embodies the main attributes of a culture. The term *culture*, in and of itself, can take on different meanings. Often, when somebody suggests that another person is "cultured," they are not referring to their cultural identity but rather to their appreciation of the arts and sciences. Thus, a cultured person may attend symphonies and art festivals. Another use of the term *culture* is to identify a particular group of people defined by demographics (e.g., "teen culture" and "retirement culture").

The Advanced Placement Human Geography course deals with culture in terms of language and religion among other items. Another subset of culture relates to folk and popular culture. This chapter will assess the foundations of culture in the context of individual cultures and will also compare and contrast these individual cultures from a geographer's perspective. In the same way cultural geographers do, this chapter will also look at trends over time to analyze the distinctiveness (stability or change) of cultures and whether cultures are dying out, perhaps owing to globalization.

Material culture encompasses anything that can be seen on the landscape, including such things as houses, furniture, and musical instruments. The material culture produces what is called the built environment. The **built environment** is the tangible impact of human beings on the landscape.

Nonmaterial culture is anything that makes up culture that cannot be touched, such as language and religion, as well as folklore, philosophies, and superstitions.

Folk culture is the practice of a particular custom by a relatively small group of people in a focused area. The practice of folk customs is part of what makes each area unique and distinguishes peoples. Most folk culture is passed from generation to generation by means of oral history. In some cultures, fathers teach their sons how to harvest crops the way it has been done for hundreds of years, and mothers teach their daughters how to sew as their mothers taught them.

Stories that are passed from generation to generation are known as **folklore**. These stories are an important part of the overall culture of a group. They pass on a people's values and the legends from generation to generation. They can maintain feelings of nationalism within a group. Bedtime stories are good examples of folklore. They usually involve a theme of good versus evil.

Sometimes, folklore takes on a life of its own, creating heroes. William Wallace was a heroic figure to the Scottish people. His resistance against the King of England was legendary. His story is told in the movie *Braveheart*, with Mel Gibson portraying William Wallace. Today, William Wallace is memorialized by a statue in Stirling, Scotland. Although he died in 1305, he is still known as one of the greatest patriots of Scottish history, and his legend has passed on from generation to generation for over 700 years.

In the Appalachian Mountain regions of Kentucky and West Virginia, "Jack tales" are often passed from older to younger generations. **Jack tales** are stories that involve the character Jack and his adventures. One of the most famous Jack tales is "Jack and the Beanstalk."

The opposite of folk culture is popular culture. **Popular culture** is the practice of customs that span several different cultures and may even have a global focus. A folk culture may become part of the popular culture through its own popularity. For example, as Tex-Mex music, also called Tejano music, becomes more common in the United States, it eventually will no longer be considered folk music but become part of popular culture.

Much of the difference between folk culture and popular culture is determined by the areas in which they have influence. Folk culture is practiced in a relatively small area, whereas popular culture may be practiced by a wider area. Cajun people in southwestern Louisiana listening to Cajun music is an example of folk culture. This particular style of music is heard in many areas of the country, yet it is not as prevalent in those areas as in southwestern Louisiana. On the other hand, the continued trend toward a global culture of business attire, involving the wearing of Western-style business suits, is an example of popular culture.

Likewise, the consumption of blowfish in Japan is an example of folk culture. Blowfish are consumed primarily in Japan but also in China and other small regions in Asia. The diffusion of American fast food, however, is an example of popular culture. Big Macs can be purchased from Moscow to Buenos Aires, and McDonald's, a transnational corporation, has expanded to dozens of countries. In Poland, China, and other countries, the opportunity to eat at McDonald's is a status symbol.

When cultures mingle together, a **multicultural society** develops. The United States is a multicultural society due to the influence of migration on the country. Nowhere is this more evident than in certain neighborhoods in urban areas. Transportation innovations and technology have allowed products to be shipped to areas around the globe within hours, not weeks. This technology has increased the cultural opportunities for millions worldwide.

THE CULTURAL LANDSCAPE

The evidence of culture on the space around us is in the cultural landscape. The term was coined by Carl Sauer, one of the preeminent cultural geographers in the late 1900s. **Cultural landscape** refers to the interactions of a group in relation to their own cultural practices as well as to the values of a society as reflected through artifacts and architecture. This is different from the **natural landscape**, which deals with the physical Earth and is often associated with the field of physical geography.

Culture is one of the most fascinating units in geography. People travel around the world to see other cultures. Such journeys can be both invigorating and anxious. Unfamiliar surroundings can lead to uneasiness. As one becomes more immersed into a particular culture, however, one becomes more comfortable.

People move for economic, environmental, and political reasons and find themselves in new locations, which have different cultures. How a person adapts to a new culture is called an **adaptive strategy**.

For example, imagine a person has just moved from southern Florida to Michigan because of a job transfer. She has never experienced snow before. Wearing a heavy jacket may be a foreign concept to this person. She may have to learn how to drive on snow and ice. This learning process is her adaptive strategy.

MUSIC AND CULTURE

One of the most fun ways to analyze culture is through music. By analyzing musical styles and lyrics, one can pick up on the characteristics of particular cultures. Religion also plays a role in the expression of ideas through music. For example, the culture of the U.S. South and the values of the Bible Belt are often expressed in country music, centered in Nashville, Tennessee.

What is folk music? Most geographers can agree that folk music or **folk songs** describe a group of people. Woody Guthrie and Pete Seeger are two examples of artists who sing American folk songs.

One of the best ways to quantify the listening habits of a particular group of people is to analyze the radio stations that they listen to. Radio stations often play a particular format of music, anything from hip-hop to country to jazz, and a researcher can describe regions based on the number of stations of each type in each region. Because radio stations are private enterprises, they need to play a style of music that people will listen to. If nobody is listening, the radio station will not be able to sell advertising and will quickly go out of business.

COUNTRY MUSIC

Country music has its roots in the southern portions of the United States. The pioneers of country music include such folk heroes as Hank Williams and Marty Robbins. This style of music has had a dramatic impact on several different regions in the United States.

Country music has its roots in the 1920s. The foundations of country music come from the spiritual songs sung in many churches in the South. Kentucky, Tennessee, West Virginia, and Texas are believed to be the hearths of country music; hence the location of the Grand Ole Opry in Nashville, Tennessee. Country music uses guitars and violins, instruments that were brought over from other countries, but the style of music is distinctly American.

The term *hillbilly* was first used to describe this new style of music. Because it came from Appalachia, where a large percentage of the people lived in poverty, this term quickly generated a negative connotation. The term *hillbilly music* was replaced with *country music* in the 1940s.

Hank Williams put country music on the map nationally. Hank Williams was credited with the movement of country music from the South to more national prominence.

The Grand Ole Opry, a legendary country music hall, has seen the greats—even Elvis Presley—play. WSM, one of the pioneering music stations of country music, first broadcast the Grand Ole Opry in 1927. On clear evenings, WSM can be heard in many parts of the United States.

The Country Music Hall of Fame is located in Nashville, Tennessee, in part because the Grand Ole Opry is located there. The Southern states, especially the Deep South, have an affinity for country music. The fundamental aspect of the Baptist religion, that of being saved, is prevalent in many of the old country songs. Deep religious values are often expressed in the old-time country songs and even in many current songs.

Listening to the legends of country music, one begins to appreciate the complexity of the music and its reflection of Southern culture. Don Williams, Hank Williams, Johnny Cash, Merle Haggard, and Waylon Jennings all contributed richly to country music. These artists diffused country music to all parts of the world. Huge stars, such as Johnny Cash and Willie Nelson, sold out shows frequently throughout Europe and in other regions.

BLUEGRASS MUSIC

A style of music that is closely related to country music is bluegrass. Bluegrass music originated in the Appalachian highland regions extending westwards to the Ozark Mountains located in southern Missouri and northern Arkansas.

Bluegrass music is characterized by such musical instruments as washboards, fiddles, banjos, and even spoons. The style of music has Irish and Scottish roots, as well as African-American influences. It was started in Kentucky by Bill Monroe and his band, the Blue Grass Boys, in the 1940s. Kentucky is credited with being one of the hearths of bluegrass music.

Two of the most important bluegrass music players are the banjo players Lester Flatt and Earl Scruggs. Both Flatt and Scruggs have made numerous recordings of bluegrass music.

Figure 5.1: Bluegrass Stations in the United States.

Figure 5.1 shows a map of the radio stations that play bluegrass music in the United States. Although radio stations that play this particular style of music are located throughout the United States, they are concentrated in the Appalachian and Ozark Mountains.

For some, bluegrass music has a negative connotation; it has sometimes been labeled a poor brand of country music. However, it has a rich tradition that's all its own. Barbeque and bluegrass festivals are common around the South in the summer. In addition, numerous websites are devoted to bluegrass music. Concerts around the United States play to thousands of fans of this particular style of music.

BLUES MUSIC

Another brand of music that is distinctly American is the blues. The blues developed from African-American music. It can be traced back to West Africa but has been modified by American musicians specializing in different forms of American blues music.

The origins of American blues can be traced to the Mississippi Delta region, where spirituals and working chants were sung in the cotton fields by sharecroppers. In the 1940s and 1950s, this style of music began to come into its own in the region.

The king of the delta blues is Robert Johnson. Robert Johnson was a recluse, and very little is known about him. Robert Johnson was inducted into the Rock-and-Roll Hall of Fame in Cleveland, Ohio, and many musicians consider him to be the grandfather of rock-and-roll music. Johnson recorded several different records before dying in 1938 at the age of 27.

TEJANO MUSIC

Yet another style of music heard around the country today is called Tex-Mex or Tejano music. Tex-Mex music is found in the Southwest. (*Tejano* is Spanish for Texan.) The Tex-Mex culture has a distinctive style of music and food; it is neither American nor Mexican, but instead a blend of both.

The increase of Spanish-speaking Americans has led to a surge of interest in the Latino culture in many areas. The Spanish-speaking regions include the Cuban settlements in the Little Havana community in southern Miami, the Mexican neighborhoods in southern California, and many communities in between. *Time* magazine felt that this "region" was so important, it devoted almost an entire issue to "Amexica."

Tejano music has gone mainstream in the past two decades owing in part to the popularity of Selena Quintanilla-Perez. Known as Selena, she modernized and captured Tejano music and put it on the cultural map.

One of the greatest legends in Tex-Mex music is Flaco Jimenez. Flaco Jimenez, originally from San Antonio, Texas, learned to play the accordion from his father. Flaco Jimenez has appeared on both stage and screen.

In Tex-Mex music, guitars and mariachi-style bands play upbeat tunes. The result is high-energy music that has many fans stomping their feet all across the United States.

As the demographics of the United States continue to change and Latinos continue to increase in numbers, so will the popularity of Tex-Mex or Tejano music.

CAJUN MUSIC

Cajun music, sometimes referred to as Creole music, stems from south-central Louisiana, where the Acadians (French Canadians) migrated from southeastern Canada. Baton Rouge, Lafayette, and other towns in Louisiana are famous for their French heritage. Cajun music is often sung by the Cajuns and the Francophone Creole people living in Louisiana. Cajun has had an influence on the closely related zydeco style of music.

Cajun music includes the accordion as well, but Tex-Mex music is sung in Spanish while Cajun music is sung in Cajun, which is a French dialect all its own. The instruments used in Cajun music include the accordion, fiddle, and even the washboard. The music is usually upbeat and danceable.

Dewey Balfa is credited with the resurgence of popularity of Cajun music. Balfa plays his music in Cajun music festivals around the country. His music brought attention to the Cajun people and their culture in southern Louisiana. Along with Dewey Balfa is the group called BeauSoleil. BeauSoleil comprises five artists who have been playing together for more than 30 years and have many hit songs.

POLKA MUSIC

Another style of music that has a distinct culture associated with it is polka music, found in the upper Midwest—especially North Dakota, South Dakota, Minnesota, Wisconsin, and Michigan. This style of music was brought here by immigrants from Scandinavia, Poland, and Germany. A form of dance is associated with polka music. The dance usually involves a two-step pattern that accompanies the upbeat music.

There are different styles of polka music. Traditional polka music began in what is now the Czech Republic, but different versions of it originated in other areas, including Poland and Sweden. Then in the United States, the style was changed, especially in Chicago by Polish immigrants. This music has been called the Chicago push style of polka. The Polka Hall of Fame is located in Chicago, Illinois.

Cleveland, Ohio, is also known for its polka roots. Joey Miskulin is one of the most famous conductors of polka music today. One of the all-time great polka music kings was Frank Yankovic, who played Slovenian-style polka and earned the first ever Grammy award for polka music in 1985.

Radio stations tend not to play polka music as their primary format but rather in addition to their usual play lists. Figure 5.2 shows the radio stations in the United States that play polka music for at least one hour during each week. This map shows that most polka music stations are in the north-central United States, correlating with the immigration patterns of eastern and northern Europeans. Another major region of polka music is in southern Texas, correlating to German settlement in areas around New Braunfels just north of San Antonio.

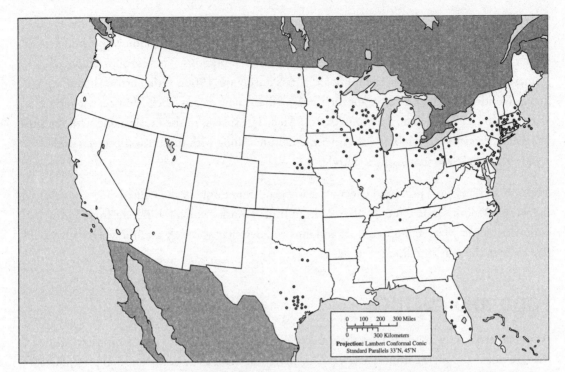

Figure 5.2: Radio Stations in the United States that Play Polka.

Some church services in the upper Midwest include polka music. The polka music culture is more popular with the older generation than younger people, leaving many wondering about its future. Many young musicians are choosing to play instruments other than the accordion, which is fundamental to polka music.

MOTOWN MUSIC

Motown is a style of music named after the city in which it originated. Detroit is often called the "motor city." *Motor city* shortened became Motown. This forerunner of modern rock-and-roll has been credited with a revitalization of urban music in the 1950s and 1960s.

Motown is not only the name for a style of music but also the name for the Detroit-based record label that recorded many musicians. Berry Gordy, Jr., established the record label in 1959, and it was an instant success. Gordy later sold the Motown record label to Universal Music in 1988.

Motown has been associated not only with music but also with the integration of cultures in the United States. During the 1950s and early 1960s, the United States was engaged in the Civil Rights struggle. The music played by African Americans in Detroit caught on in many neighborhoods that were not African American. The appeal of Motown music to all types of people encouraged racial integration.

Gordy's first superstar act was a group called the Matadors, who later changed their name to the Miracles. Their lead singer was Smokey Robinson. The Miracles were soon joined by groups like Diana Ross and the Supremes, The Jackson 5, and The Temptations. These groups produced numerous number one hits on the Billboard charts during the 1960s. Other artists, including Stevie Wonder and Marvin Gaye, got their start with the new record label. More recent additions to the Motown label include the group Boys II Men. The success of the music along with the label has made *Motown* synonymous with American culture. Along with the antiwar protests of the 1960s, this music was iconic of the decade.

Music of all types has a profound effect on many people, not only in the United States but around the world. African music is much different from Indian music, which is different from South American music. Many cultures use art and music to describe who they are and where they would like to be in the near and distant future.

FOOD AND CULTURE

Food is a terrific way to understand the concept of folk culture because certain areas have dishes that are distinct to their cuisine. *National Geographic Magazine* did a study on food preferences around the world. Many different foods from the United States ranked high on the food preference list that was compiled for this study. Hamburgers, hot dogs, fried chicken, french fries, and pizza scored the highest on the food preference list. Just as important as the foods that were selected were the foods that were not selected. The least popular foods included such delicacies as smoked black whale meat, rappie pie, pinchberry tart jelly, and fried cod tongues. Very few people who took the survey had tried these foods before, nor were they even willing to. Other foods from around the world that tend not to appeal to the masses are sheep's eye from Kyrgyzstan, kangaroo tail from Australia, and marmot from Mongolia.

INTERNATIONAL FOOD CULTURES

Different food preferences from around the world say a lot about a particular culture. The location of a restaurant relative to a food source may determine the dishes on its menu. For example, China has a "noodle line." North of the noodle line, where more wheat products are grown, noodles are produced and are a daily part of the diet. To the south of the noodle line, where the climate is warmer, rice is grown. In these areas of China, rice served with a sauce and vegetables is the daily diet.

Szechwan food comes from the Sichuan region in south-central China. Szechwan food is known for its spiciness, due to the Szechwan peppercorn plant. One of the most famous Szechwan dishes in the United States is kung pao chicken.

Much of the world's diet depends upon the agricultural products grown in a certain region. Rice is a staple crop in Asia. Millet is a staple crop in many parts of Africa. Manioc is grown in South America and is used in many dishes in Brazil.

The United Kingdom recently made fish and chips its national dish. In the United Kingdom, *chips* refers to fried potatoes. In the United States, fried potatoes are called french fries, and *chips* are potato chips.

In Denmark, sandwiches called smørrebrød are eaten open-faced on one slice of bread. Sandwiches are eaten with forks and knives in Denmark. It is often considered rude to eat a sandwich with your hands.

Iceland has many distinctive delicacies, due in part to its location. Fishing is a major industry, and shark is eaten on special occasions. The shark is kept outside to rot. Once the shark is "ripe" enough, it is cut down and served to the waiting consumers who love the taste.

In many parts of East Asia, including China, snake is eaten. The consumption of snake is said to give the human body spirit and energy as well as warming the heart.

The blowfish, or *fugu*, is a high-priced delicacy in Japan. Chefs need to take a special course in how to prepare the deadly fish. If cut the wrong way, its toxins will be released into the flesh, killing the eater. The cost of a fugu dish can run as high as U.S. $200 per plate.

In the Andes of South America, guinea pigs are considered a delicacy. The guinea pig, called a *cuy*, is fried whole and brought to the consumer in a lifelike stance. *Cuy* is usually consumed for special celebrations, such as anniversaries or birthday parties.

In parts of Tanzania, mopane worms are mixed with peanut butter to provide a nutritious, tasty snack. Ants are eaten in Brazil in the Amazonian rain forest. In Australia, many Aborigines eat raw worms for their liquid content in arid regions.

In Scandinavian countries, fish is a primary food source. Lutefisk is dried codfish soaked in lye and then baked. Many Scandinavians love lutefisk with mashed potatoes and white gravy. Many towns in North Dakota, Minnesota, and Wisconsin still have lutefisk bakes in country churches, and the fish is still served on holidays in the region.

FOLK FOOD

All of the aforementioned dishes are part of folk food. A **folk food** is attributed to a particular people or a culture. Each of these folk foods is concentrated around a particular hearth or a nodal region. Popular culture as expressed by food does not necessarily have a hearth, or it has become so common that the hearth has either been forgotten or become relatively unimportant. For example,

McDonald's hearth is in Des Plaines, Illinois, but the widespread diffusion of McDonald's has minimized the importance of its hearth.

U.S. fast-food chains, such as McDonald's, KFC, and Burger King, are beginning to dot the landscapes in areas of the world that had never experienced fast-food culture. China, for example, now has thousands of KFCs.

U.S. FOOD CULTURES

In the United States, there are distinct food regions. New England is known for clam chowder. Lobster from Maine southward to Cape Cod is another delicacy of this region of the country. Southern food has come under criticism in the past decade for being unhealthy. However, the traditional fried chicken along with collard greens and peach or cherry cobbler is a treat for many.

BARBECUE

One cannot talk about Southern food without mentioning barbecue. Barbecue in the South is considered an art form. Barbecue can be mustard-based, ketchup- or tomato-based, or vinegar-based. How the barbecue is served ranges from wet to dry. Wet barbecue puts the sauce directly onto the meat after the meat has been cooked. Dry barbecue has the sauce cooked right into the meat. People swear by one or the other method, and loyalties to a particular style run deep. Also, some places specialize in pork while others specialize in beef barbecue. Smoked barbeque smokes the meat in cooking houses for upward of 24 hours.

Some cities have become synonymous with their barbeque styles. Memphis and Kansas City are both known for their distinctive styles of barbecue. In Kansas City, molasses is added to the barbeque sauce. Today in Kansas City, there are over 100 barbecue establishments located within the metropolitan area. Like Kansas City, Memphis has over 100 barbecue establishments within the metropolitan area.

To suggest that only these two areas have great barbecue would be blasphemy to many barbeque connoisseurs. North Carolina and South Carolina each claim to have the best barbecue of any region in the United States. South Carolina uses the four separate styles of barbecue. Mustard-based barbecue uses a light yellowish paste, and its sweet taste has many followers. Ketchup- or tomato-based barbecue (both light and heavy) as well as vinegar-based barbecue are also found in South Carolina.

In Texas, barbecue has almost become synonymous with the state. People will drive for miles to get the taste of specific styles of barbeque in the Hill Country, Dallas, and western sections of the state. The upper Midwestern regions also have barbecue establishments. Many of these establishments were started by immigrants from the South.

Barbecue festivals are held around the United States throughout the year. During these festivals, many establishments enter their barbecue sauces for prizes and compete for buyers. The secret recipes of barbecue sauces are jealously protected.

Barbecue varies around the world from Mongolia to Australia to South Africa to the United Kingdom. Each area has its own methods of preparing the meat, and the types of meat vary greatly. In Central Asia, sheep, or mutton, is often used. Many regions around the world even barbecue seafood products.

SPORTS AND CULTURE

The spread of baseball and basketball around the world from the United States is a form of hierarchical diffusion. Many Americans have become dismayed at the lack of success of U.S. teams in international play. Some suggest that the play of the United States has not gotten worse; rather, the play of the rest of the world has improved. The Dominican Republic and Venezuela have a proud tradition of producing many Major League Baseball players. Children in these regions grow up playing the sport from a very young age. Japan also has created a culture of baseball. In fact, while many Japanese players have come to the United States to play, many major league players have left the United States to play professional baseball in Japan.

The world's most popular sport is soccer. Called *football* in most areas of the world, it attracts the fervent loyalty of its fans. The history of football dates back over 2,000 years in China and Europe, when people began to play games that involved kicking a sphere with their feet. Football diffused from the United Kingdom eastward into mainland Europe as far as Russia. Most historians credit the British with the modern rules of the game. The size of the field as we know it today with the two goals on each side was established in the 16th century.

Football in the United States still has not caught on as it has in other regions of the world. Major League Soccer (MLS) has national television coverage, but ratings continue to remain low, despite the popularity of the sport among youth. More young children play organized soccer than any other sport. However, many Americans feel that the game is simply too boring to watch.

Today, one of the governing bodies of football is FIFA (Federation Internationale de Football Association), which governs the World Cup. The World Cup is played every four years in a different part of the world. The tournament brings together countries in one of the most watched televised sporting events on the planet. Figure 5.3 shows the cities that have hosted the World Cup and the World Cup champions. In the 1994 World Cup, when Colombia lost to the United States, a Colombian defender, Andres Escobar, was shot and killed upon his return home. He had accidentally scored a goal against his own team, causing his team to lose. Some suggest that his death was caused by drug lords, who lost a lot of money gambling on the game.

World Cup Winners (Men)		
Year	Location	Champion
1930	Uruguay	Uruguay
1934	Italy	Italy
1938	France	Italy
1950	Brazil	Uruguay
1954	Switzerland	West Germany
1958	Sweden	Brazil
1962	Chile	Brazil
1966	England	England
1970	Mexico	Brazil
1974	Germany	West Germany
1978	Argentina	Argentina
1982	Spain	Italy
1986	Mexico	Argentina
1990	Italy	West Germany
1994	U.S.A.	Brazil
1998	France	France
2002	South Korea/Japan	Brazil
2006	Germany	Italy
2010	South Africa	Spain
2014	Brazil	Germany

Figure 5.3: Men's World Cup Winners, 1930–2014.

Hooligans are fans who incite violence at football matches, often through hurling racial or religious epithets against opposing players and fans. FIFA has forced games to be played in empty stadiums as a punishment for hooliganism.

The fans' devotion to football cannot be overestimated. Some people live, breathe, and die with the results of their local club teams as well as their national teams. The emotional state of England was depressed for days after the 2010 loss in World Cup play. Some stadiums in Latin America can seat over 100,000 screaming fans. Fights and fires have broken out in the crowds, causing deaths in stadiums around the world.

ARCHITECTURE AND CULTURE

The architecture of residential, commercial, and spiritual structures varies greatly around the world. Houses are the dominant structures in many areas of the world. Houses are the primary structure for the family unit on which societies are based, and the home can be considered the foundation of culture. Homes are built in many different shapes and sizes.

Most folk housing is constructed with the materials that are nearby, in large part determined by the climate of the area. Many traditional huts in Africa are constructed with the grasses and the wood that are nearby. Adobe, bricks made out of mud, is used in many Latin American countries where lumber-quality wood is scarce. Many houses in the United States are built with wood, which is abundantly available.

In Mongolia, gers (also called yurts) are the primary form of housing for nomadic hunters. Gers are easily mobile. Gers are frequently round and measure 20 to 30 feet in diameter. Camels and other pack animals haul the gers from location to location as the nomads move their herds across the plains.

In Native American cultures of the Great Plains, the teepee was the predominant style of housing. Because these tribes had a mobile culture, they needed a housing style that could be moved readily. A frame of sticks was used to support the covering, which was made of stitched hides. An opening at the top of the teepee allows for smoke from a fire to escape. Early settlers on the Great Plains built houses from sod because of a lack of wood. Many of these structures were under the surface of the earth. Dirt would be piled into a mound and grass planted or sod placed on top of the mound to protect the structure from erosion and to prevent leaks.

The **indigenous architecture** of the United States includes the architecture of Native Americans as well as of the first settlers, such as log cabins. Any structure on the landscape that is not built by a professional craftsperson or artist would be considered indigenous architecture.

Different regions emphasize different parts of the house. In Islamic households, Muslims have a special wall that faces Mecca. Islam requires them to pray facing Mecca five times a day. In many other cultures, doors into the house must face certain directions for either religious or other cultural reasons. In many homes in China, feng shui properties are extremely important. This includes a front door facing the east, a curved walkway leading up to the house, and a backyard larger than the front yard, among other factors.

Noted geographer Fred Kniffen has identified three distinct regions of folk housing types in the United States today. The three styles include the New England–style house, the Middle Atlantic–style house, and the Lower Chesapeake–style house.

Within the New England style, Kniffen identified four major housing types: the saltbox, the two-chimney, the Cape Cod, and the front gable and wing styles. All four of these homes can be seen in New England today as well as in the north-central United States owing to migration.

The Middle Atlantic housing style is characterized by what is called an "I" house. The I house is characterized by a two-story structure with gables on either end. From the Middle Atlantic region, this housing style moved southward along the Appalachian Mountains and then westward into the south-central states.

The Lower Chesapeake style of house usually has two stories with chimneys located on both sides. From Lower Chesapeake Bay, this housing type diffused south along the Atlantic coast.

Today, housing styles are very similar around the United States. The increase of housing developments means that construction companies usually build similar types and styles of houses. Consumers simply make minor choices about the room structure and finishing touches of new homes but not in the overall type of the house.

The township and range patterns established by early settlers dominate the landscape in the Midwest and Great Plains regions. The township and range system is still evident when one flies over the United States. Long rows of roads are laid out on the flat landscape in square or rectangular patterns. This is called the **Anglo-American landscape**, a folk landscape.

The **folk landscape** is what people perceive the landscape to be based on their cultural notions of an area. One of the great folk landscapes in the United States is the Wild West, perceived as a rugged environment where settlers took the law into their own hands. The image of cowboys herding cattle and sleeping beneath the stars has a quality of Americana to it. In reality, the landscape of the Western frontier was anything but romantic, requiring long hours of hard work every single day. When reality clashed with perception, many settlers turned around and went back to the urban areas on the East Coast.

In much of the United States, architecture is relatively new in comparison to that of the rest of the world. Part of the U.S. culture is to replace the old with the new. In European culture, on the other hand, tradition is prized and buildings are on average much older. In areas of Copenhagen, some houses are over 500 years old. The **traditional architecture** of an area are the structures built as it was being established. For example, the traditional architecture of a city would be the original industrial plants established as the city was founded.

What does the United States look like today? The United States has a somewhat uniform appearance due to the popular culture of fast food. When one travels across the United States, it is not uncommon to see several McDonald's and other fast-food restaurants by the interstates. These restaurants bring some continuity and uniformity to the landscape, and erase the distinctiveness of place, replacing traditional mom-and-pop restaurants. Modern U.S. architecture varies but is largely dependent upon global popular culture. New home construction is cyclical: When interest rates are higher, new home construction decreases; when interest rates are low, new home construction increases.

LANGUAGE AND CULTURE

Language is one of the most important aspects of culture. Very few things tie a group together quite like a common language. **Language** is the ability to communicate with others orally and/or in writing. Language is both a unifying and dividing factor in nations.

There is a saying that language is a dialect with an army behind it. In some cases, this is true. The majority of a country's population can wield its political power to ensure the widespread adoption of its language. The imposition of a dominant language has been used to enforce political unity. However, many independence movements have been fueled by a nation's desire to use its own language.

Language makes traveling internationally a lot of fun—and sometimes frustrating. It is challenging to communicate with somebody who does not speak your language, but it can be exhilarating. The United States is notorious for teaching students only one language in school. In contrast, European countries sometimes teach students four or more languages. A **monolingual country** only has one official language in which all government business is conducted. A **multilingual country** has more than one official language. Switzerland is an example of a multilingual country with four official languages: German, French, Italian, and Romansh. Current estimates are that over 6,000 languages are spoken in the world today. Most of these are spoken by remote tribes and many by only a few dozen people.

Lingua Francas

Although the United States does not have an official language, the overwhelming majority of its citizens speak English. English has become the most widespread lingua franca in the world. A **lingua franca** is a language used as a common tongue among people who speak diverse languages, often to conduct business. For example, all airline pilots in the world must communicate in English. If an Angolan pilot is flying into a Bangladesh airport, that pilot must communicate in English, as must the control tower staff. In addition, many international industries prefer to use English as the language of business, publishing their professional brochures in English and insisting that their employees speak English.

The more developed a country, the more its language is used in worldwide commerce. As the Chinese are gaining more of a foothold in the global economy, the importance of learning Mandarin Chinese has increased. In many parts of Southeast Asia, Mandarin Chinese is becoming a lingua franca. In many areas of eastern Africa, English is not the lingua franca but rather Swahili. Spanish and, increasingly, Mandarin Chinese are commonly taught in U.S. schools today. Because business culture is becoming more global, the ability to communicate in another language is gaining increasing status and importance. Learning a new language is an important step in what is called an adaptive strategy. Learning another language makes the communication process much easier when entering another language region.

LEARNING LANGUAGES

The acquisition of a language involves several different skills. The first skill is the ability to speak and sound out the words. For many Westerners, the acquisition of Asian languages is difficult. For example, in Mandarin Chinese, the sound intonations are different than in English, and many sounds are completely different. The second skill is the ability to write the symbols that are associated with each sound or meaning. The third major skill is comprehension, mostly through vocabulary acquisition. As you are reading this book you are, hopefully, inferring meaning from the symbols that constitute the English alphabet. Much of the culture of a non-oral society is expressed in its literature, which plays an important part in the transfer of culture to future generations.

LINGUISTIC DIVISIONS WITHIN STATES

Several countries are divided by language barriers. Belgium is less united than it might be, because people in the Flanders region in the north speak Flemish while people in the south speak French. The demarcation lies on an east-west axis near the capital of Brussels. India has over 800 languages spoken within its borders, posing a barrier to developing loyalty to the state over one's nation. The island of Papua New Guinea is said to have over 1,000 languages. Many of these languages are spoken by indigenous groups who have rarely, if ever, seen people from outside their villages.

A country that has seen conflict over linguistic identity is Canada, where French-speaking Québec has several times tried to secede. Canada is officially bilingual; both French and English are languages of business and government. French Canadians have an accent that is different from that of people in France. By law, products sold in Canada must include directions or instructions in both English and French.

DIALECTS

A **dialect** is a form of a language that is unique in sound, speed, **syntax** (the grammatical arrangement of a language), and vocabulary. Dialects can often be difficult to understand, depending on how far they've diverged from the listener's speech. Dialects in the United States include the northeastern accent, the Southern accent, the Midwestern accent, the Cajun accent, and accents that are based on age.

An **isogloss** is the boundary of a dialect. Isoglosses can be difficult to determine, because patterns of speech vary among members of the same groups of people. Geographers or linguistic experts interview people of different regions to determine speech patterns. They will have people pronounce different words. In the North, *you guys* is often used to mean "a group of people." In Appalachia, *you'uns* is used in the same way; in the South, the word is *y'all*. The boundary lines for each of these units of speech are established through an isogloss.

The Northeastern dialect is evident in the city of Boston, as well as other parts of New England. One of its major characteristics is the elimination of the sound of the letter *r* when a short *a* precedes it. The letter *a* is held out with an "aaah" sound, so for example, *party* becomes "*pahty.*"

The Southern dialect involves sustaining vowels. It can be broken down further by different regions of the South; it is different in Mississippi, Texas, and North and South Carolina.

The Upper Midwestern accent or dialect seems to love the letter *o*. The long *o* sound is sustained in many words and pronounced very distinctly. Some Minnesotans pronounce their state with a *d* instead of a *t*: *Minnesoda*. Also, the *o* syllable is held longer and stressed more than any other part of the word.

Dialects can also be computer generated. New technology, such as global positioning systems in automobiles, have the ability to talk, taking the driver to a destination one turn at a time. The programming of these voices has a lot of research behind it. The voice needs to be clear, and its inflection and tone need to be soothing, not irritating. These computer-generated dialects have their speed, vocabulary, spelling, pronunciation, and syntax programmed for the ease of the listener.

There are also different dialects of English around the world. "BBC British" pronunciation (spoken by announcers on British Broadcasting Corporation television and radio news programs) is the most recognized in the world. Many Europeans, Africans, and Asians who study English are taught the British style of English. However, Australia and South Africa have distinct dialects of English, as does the United States.

There are several reasons for the differences between the American and the British versions of the language. One of the main reasons is the distance between the two countries, which caused the two versions of the language to evolve separately. New words were created in the new location to describe things not encountered in the old area (e.g., *canoe* and *chipmunk*). Also, an important event in regards to the development of American English came with the creation of an American dictionary by Noah Webster in 1828. In Great Britain, the word *mom* is spelled *mum*. A *loo* refers to a bathroom. You wait in a *queue*, not a line. You would take the *lift* to your hotel room instead of the elevator. *Pants* refers to underwear in many parts of the United Kingdom, whereas in the United States, it simply refers to clothes that you wear on your legs.

Even within the United Kingdom, there are different dialects. For example, in George Bernard Shaw's *Pygmalion* (filmed as *My Fair Lady*), Eliza Doolittle demonstrates the Cockney accent of eastern London. This section of London has long been considered one of the poorer areas of the city, and thus the accent has a low-status connotation. There are also Scottish and Irish dialects.

English has changed over the centuries. Shakespeare's plays and the King James Bible, written in 1611, may be difficult for modern readers to decipher. The language continues to evolve as well. New words are constantly being added because of new inventions and innovations. A decade ago, the term *text messaging* was known by very few. Now, many of us *text message* several times a day. The French have an institution, the Académie française, that determines how and whether different words from around the world will be translated into French. The French feel that to keep the purity of their language, they need to regulate the inclusion of new words. Recently, the Oxford Dictionary selected "selfie" as the word of the year.

PIDGIN, TRADE, AND CREOLE LANGUAGES

In many cases, when cultures collide, languages mix. A mixture of languages is known as a **pidgin language**. Pidgin languages are often very elementary in grammar and vocabulary but are nonetheless useful, allowing trade to occur. Sometimes a pidgin language becomes a new language altogether.

When the first European settlers came to North America, they encountered Native American societies, and the result was the creation of a **trade language**. A trade language is a made-up language that is used by people who want to trade. Each party learns the modified language to communicate with the other and conduct trade. Instead of learning the dialects of the six main Native American languages, the Europeans could learn the modified trade language. Likewise, Native Americans did not have to learn English, French, Spanish, and Portuguese.

The Cajun language was created by mixing English and French. The traditional Cajun dialect may be incomprehensible to either an English speaker or a French speaker. Likewise, Spanglish often uses Spanish and English words within the same sentence.

A **creole language** is a stable language resulting from the blend of two or more languages that often does not include features of either. In Haiti, people speak a creole language that is a blend of African languages with French. The result is a broader choice of vocabulary as well as a language that is native to Haiti. (NOTE: Do not be confused by the other use of the word *creole*. A Creole is a person of European descent who was born in a European colonial area, particularly in Latin America or the Caribbean.)

OFFICIAL LANGUAGES

As aforementioned, an **official language** is a language in which all government business is conducted. Some countries have more than one official language. Official languages are hotly debated in many countries. If your language is not one of your country's official languages, you may fear that your language will die out, meaning that you will lose an irreplaceable part of your cultural heritage.

There has been a lot of talk in the United States about making English the official language. Proponents suggest that having an official language will save money, because government forms, ballots, and so on will need to be printed in only one language instead of the dozens of languages currently used. Proponents also say that they are trying to preserve the American culture. The proponents of having an official language argue that anybody has the right to speak any language they want at home, but when dealing with federal, state, and local governments, communication should be done in English. Some individual states in the United States have adopted English as their official language.

Opponents of establishing an official language suggest that by having an official language, the United States would lose an integral part of its culture. They argue that the United States was built upon diversity of language and culture. Also, by mandating the use of a particular language, opponents suggest that we are discriminating against those who cannot speak English. Over 80 percent of the U.S. population speaks English, but not necessarily as a first language or at home.

In the 2001 Supreme Court case of *Sandoval v. Alabama*, Sandoval sued the state of Alabama, insisting that she had the right to take her driver's license test in Spanish. The court, by a five-to-four margin, voted that Sandoval did not have the right to take the test in Spanish. Even though the United States does not have an official language, this court case set a precedent for enforcing homogeneity of language and, hence, culture.

The debate over having an official language will get more heated as more Americans speak English as a second language. Eventually, the United States will have to decide its future in regard to the use of one or even multiple official languages. The issue will eventually come up before the Supreme Court again, as several states have declared official languages.

This type of debate over issues such as an official language can cause cultural conflicts within a community. While some people see a policy as preserving culture, others see it as stifling diversity within a region. Regions such as Quebec have seen divisive debates over whether the official language should be English or French.

LINGUISTIC DIVERSITY AND EXTINCTION

Having everyone speak the same language is important to maintaining a unified identity within a state's borders. However, learning more than one language gives an individual more opportunity for cultural and economic success. The learning of more languages is known as **linguistic diversity**. Linguistic diversity can operate on both a large and a small scale. When a person speaks more than one language, she has linguistic diversity, making her more marketable in the global economy. When a society speaks more than one language, linguistic diversity can be seen as a problem because it can hinder unification.

On a global scale, there is a gradual decline of linguistic diversity. Within the next century, the number of languages, currently about 6,000, is expected to decrease by over 90 percent to just over 600 as less dominant languages die out. Young people usually leave isolated villages to obtain work in urban areas, where the dominant language is spoken. Eventually, only the elderly speak a language, and when they die, they take the language with them. This process is called **language extinction**. The result will be a world that is dominated by megalanguages, such as Mandarin Chinese, English, Spanish, and Hindi.

LANGUAGE FAMILIES

Language families are groups of languages organized by their common heritage. The result is the language tree, which demonstrates how different languages and linguistic groups are related to each other. **Language subfamilies** are smaller groups of languages within a language family.

The subfamily of West Germanic languages includes present-day German as well as English. The Northern Germanic language subfamily includes the Scandinavian languages of Danish, Swedish, Norwegian, and Icelandic. It also includes the Gothic language, now extinct, spoken by the Goths in Germany during the fourth through sixth centuries.

The term *Romance language* comes from the word *Roman*. These languages descended from the Latin spoken in the Roman Empire and spread by Roman soldiers across much of southern Europe. Italian, Spanish, French, Catalan, Romanian, and Portuguese are all Romance languages spoken today.

Language groups are people whose languages are descended from a common tongue. For example, most people in France and Spain belong to the same language group, because both French and Spanish are Romance languages. In Scandinavia, the populations can understand each other with relative ease because their languages are all part of the Northern Germanic subfamily. Swedish, Danish, Norwegians, and to a lesser extent, Icelanders can comprehend each other relatively well. The word structure, vocabulary, and pronunciation are similar enough to decipher meaning from ordinary sentences.

Studying language is one of the easiest ways to detect diversity on the landscape. Something very familiar, such as a bag of potato chips, can seem foreign when packaged in another language.

THE INDO-EUROPEAN LANGUAGE FAMILY

The Indo-European language family, which includes English, is the largest language family in the world. The languages spoken in the Indo-European family extend not only throughout Europe but also throughout most of the Western Hemisphere owing to colonization in Australia and South Africa. Indo-European languages are also used in India and southwestern Asia. The Indo-European language family includes the Greek languages of Aeolic, Ionic, and Doric, as well as the Asian languages of Farsi, Bengali, and Hindi. Farsi is spoken primarily in Iran, Hindi is the dominant language of India, and Bengali is the language of Bangladesh. Of the top ten languages spoken in the world today, seven are descendents of the Indo-European language family.

THE SINO-TIBETAN LANGUAGE FAMILY

One of the other major language families is the Sino-Tibetan language family. Upward of 20 percent of the world's population speaks a Sino-Tibetan language. The Sino-Tibetan language family includes the most widely spoken language in the world—Mandarin Chinese. Mandarin

Chinese, sometimes called Han Chinese, is spoken by just over 1 billion people. Although the majority of the people who speak Mandarin Chinese are located in mainland China, Taiwan and Singapore each have large areas where Mandarin Chinese is spoken. Other languages in the Sino-Tibetan language family include Thai, Cantonese, and Burmese.

Like the United States, China possesses numerous dialects. About 75 percent of Chinese people speak Mandarin Chinese. Cantonese is another form of Chinese. Cantonese and Mandarin Chinese are like the Scandinavian languages: Speakers of one can sometimes understand speakers of the other, but different words and sounds make comprehension difficult.

There are even different dialects within the urban areas of China. For example, people in Shanghai speak a unique dialect. Many minority groups in the western sections of the country speak other Sino-Tibetan languages, such as Hakka, Min, Wu, and Xiang. Most of these minority groups are nomadic herders, and their populations are relatively small. Some of the Muslim traders in the remote western regions speak Arabic, which is not a Sino-Tibetan language. The national government of China is now embracing Mandarin as the official language to unify the country.

THE AFRO-ASIATIC LANGUAGE FAMILY

Another language family with many language groups is the Afro-Asiatic family. Many of these languages are spoken in northern Africa. The language most often spoken is Arabic; it is spoken in northern Africa and the Middle East. Arabic is part of the Semitic language subgroup. Other languages within the Afro-Asiatic language family are Hebrew, Somali, and Berber. The Berber languages are spoken primarily in Morocco and Algeria.

THE NIGER-CONGO LANGUAGE FAMILY

The Niger-Congo language family consists of the languages found in southern Africa, including one of the dominant languages in the area, Swahili. Zulu, spoken in South Africa, is also a part of the Niger-Congo language family. Many of the Niger-Congo languages are spoken by only a small part of the country's population. Over 9 million people speak Zulu as their primary language, and 5 million people speak Swahili as their primary language. However, Swahili is a lingua franca in the East Africa region. The majority of these languages diffused through colonization or relocation diffusion. Another way in which these languages were diffused was through trade.

ORIGINS OF LANGUAGE FAMILIES

Most historians and geographers agree that the hearth of human settlement was in present-day Iraq. The Babylonian Empire began in the Middle East and moved outward. Today's language families originated from prehistoric language families, including the Sino-Caucasian, Nostratic, and Austric language families. The Sino-Caucasian language family was the forerunner to today's Sino-Tibetan language family. From the Nostratic language family come today's Dravidian, Altaic, Uralic, Afro-Asiatic, and Indo-European families. From the Austric language family came the

Austronesian language family, spoken today on many islands in the South Pacific. Also, the Austro-Asiatic languages, of which the largest is Vietnamese, descended from the Austric language family.

LANGUAGES AND THE LANDSCAPE

Languages are a distinguishing feature on the landscape. Different place names, **toponyms**, are often indicative of the people or cultures that live there. When looking at a map of Québec, one immediately sees the impact of French colonization in the toponyms. The same holds true of areas around the border between the United States and Mexico and throughout California, which reflect Spanish influence. For example, *Los Angeles* means "the angels."

In Tennessee, the term *knob* is used to refer to a hill. Several towns, such as Pilot Knob and Orchard Knob, are named after hills. *Hollow* is another regional topographic term. A hollow is a small valley. Sleepy Hollow in New York was made famous by Washington Irving's 1819 short story, "The Legend of Sleepy Hollow." The word *bayou* refers to swamp-like wetlands in Louisiana and Texas. Phelps Bayou and Routh Bayou are just two place names that include this term.

In northern areas of the United States, there is a tendency, inherited from New England migrants, to name places relative to a previous settlement point. The four cardinal directions (east, north, west, and south) are put in front of town names to describe their location with respect to a larger urban area. South Saint Paul and West Saint Paul are two suburbs of Saint Paul, Minnesota. Interestingly enough, West Saint Paul is located south of Saint Paul. The term *west* was given to describe the river traffic on the Mississippi River. Anything on the left of a boat traveling northward was "west," and anything to the right of the boat was "east." In Saint Paul, the river turns, and the left side of the river is to the south; however, the term *west* stuck.

Many U.S. places are named after the Native American tribes that were located in the area prior to European settlement. Almost half of the 50 states have names derived from Native American words. For example, Kentucky is named after the Iroquois word for "land of tomorrow." Minnesota comes from Lakota and means "sky-tinted water." Utah is named after the Ute tribe, with *Ute* meaning "people of the mountains."

RELIGION AND CULTURE

Religion is the value system that people place on themselves and others based on a spiritual or divine aspect of the world. The variety of religions and religious practices across the globe is a major aspect of cultural geography. Geographers have a particular interest in religion in terms of people's attitudes and actions and in the distribution of different religions around the world throughout history. Major religions have a daily impact of the lives of billions of people. For example, religious architecture impacts the world's landscape, and ceremonies are important aspects of every culture.

Religion often determines behavior constraints in a society, and it offers humans parameters for forming their characters, and hence behavior. Most countries, however, have a cultural set of morals that people agree to, regardless of religion, which determine acceptable behavior. Societies set up laws and courts that may have historical connections to religion but may or may not be separate from any established faith.

Religion is often a cultural aspect that a person is unwilling to compromise on. Because of an unwillingness to bend the foundations of faith, people and states get into disagreements and even wars.

In all religions, an object of faith is present. **Faith** is the belief in things not seen or the things that cannot be proven.

Two main characteristics are used to classify religions. The first is whether the religion is monotheistic or polytheistic. **Monotheistic religions** believe in only one god. **Polytheistic religions** believe in multiple gods. The second characteristic concerns how worshipers enter the faith. In **ethnic religions**, a person is born into the faith, and little to no effort is put forth to convert others to the religion. This is the opposite of a **universalizing religion**, where members actively try to convert others. Another name for a universalizing religion is a **proselytic faith**.

Usually, but not always, universalizing religions are larger than ethnic religions because of their proselytizing activity. The largest ethnic religions in the world are Hinduism and Judaism. The largest universalizing religions include Christianity, the largest religion in the world with over 2 billion followers, and Islam, the fastest-growing religion with close to 2 billion followers. Buddhism is another religion found in many parts of East Asia.

People who do not believe in any god or god-like figure are called **atheists**. Many of these people like to go by the term *secularists*. A **secularist** is a person who wants to separate religion from all other aspects of society, including government and other social institutions such as marriage. A secularist has concluded that there is no god or simply doesn't care if one does exist. **Jainism** is a religion that is based on nonmaterialism but at its core is considered a form of atheism.

There are five primary religions in the world today. These religions have their foundations in one of two places. Both Buddhism and Hinduism began in India, whereas the other three primary religions—Christianity, Islam, and Judaism—began in Southwest Asia.

CHRISTIANITY

As aforementioned, **Christianity** is the world's largest religion, with just over 2 billion followers. The variety in the Christian religion is immense, from the Russian and Greek Orthodox Churches to the Protestant Churches found in Northern Europe and in many portions of the United States. There are three main branches of Christianity: Roman Catholic, Protestant, and Orthodox.

ARCHITECTURE

The religious architecture of Christianity is focused around the cross, which is usually located somewhere within the primary structure of worship, the church. The steeple of the church extends to the heavens to symbolize a reaching toward God. The cross is often located at the top of the steeple to signify God in the heavens. (See Figure 5.4.)

In the Middle Ages in Europe, churches were built with great splendor but also at great expense. Many of these churches are still standing today; Notre Dame in Paris and the Canterbury Cathedral in England are just two. In many European towns, the church was built in the center of towns and homes were built around it; this is because the church was seen as not only the religious center but also the social center of the community. Likewise, in many communities today in the United States, churches are just as much a social space as they are a place of religious significance.

Figure 5.4: Church.

Foundational Beliefs

The foundation of the Christian religion is the life of **Jesus Christ**, who, according to the Bible, lived on Earth and died on a cross. After death, he was resurrected, and his transcendence of death means that followers of the Christian faith can be saved. Jesus Christ took on the sins of humanity (or all Christians, or Christians who meet certain criteria—different denominations offer different interpretations) when He died. In some denominations, all humans are created evil and their only hope of salvation is a belief in Jesus Christ; other denominations believe that newborn babies are without sin and offer hope of salvation through good works and repentance in this life.

The holy book of Christianity is the Bible. **The Bible** is composed of two distinct sections: the **Old Testament** and the **New Testament**. The Old Testament is based on the lives of the Israelites and follows the lives of Moses, Abraham, David, and other leaders prophesying about the coming of the Savior, whom Christians believe to be Jesus Christ. The New Testament describes the life of Jesus Christ and the foundations of the new faith. Most Christians believe in the existence of the Holy Trinity: God, the Son, and the Holy Spirit. These three combine to form one God.

Structure

Who leads the church varies by denomination. The head of the Roman Catholic Church is the pope; the hierarchy also includes cardinals, bishops, and priests. For Protestants, the head of the Church is a pastor or minister. For the Orthodox Church, the head is a patriarch.

Distribution and Diffusion

One justification for colonization was the opportunity to convert "unsaved" populations outside of Europe. To almost all of the areas that Europeans colonized, they brought their religion with them. Christian missionaries from a variety of denominations are found all over the world today in both urban and remote areas. Because of these missionaries, Christianity is now growing fastest in Africa and Asia.

In the first century CE many evangelists migrated (relocation diffusion) throughout the Roman Empire spreading the teachings of Christ. During early Christian times, people would often spread the teachings from neighbor to neighbor (contagious diffusion). In the early 4th century CE the Roman Emperor Constantine supposedly converted to Christianity on his deathbed. This allowed for the hierarchical diffusion of the religion throughout the empire (hierarchical diffusion). During the age of exploration (early 1400s through 1600s), many Christian missionaries spread the religion and converted indigenous populations all over the world. Through the combination of these different forms of diffusion, Christianity has become the most widely distributed religion on Earth.

DENOMINATIONS

Denominations are branches of a religion that differ on specific aspects of the principles of the religion. The largest denomination of Christianity is the Roman Catholic Church. Over 1 billion people are professed Roman Catholics, making this the largest denomination of any religion in the world. The Roman Catholic religion is based in Vatican City, where the Pope resides. The Roman Catholic Church is the oldest denomination in the Christian religion. It was started by the Apostle Paul in the first century BCE in Rome.

During the Protestant Reformation, Martin Luther developed the idea of a personal relationship with Jesus Christ, instead of talking to God through priests and the hierarchy of the Roman Catholic Church. He posted his *95 Theses* upon a church door in Germany in 1517, launching the Protestant movement (named after the "protesting" against the Catholic Church). Luther created the Lutheran Church in northern Europe. Other Protestant denominations have branched off, creating the Baptists, Presbyterians, Methodists, and many more. Today, just over 400 million people are professed Protestants.

The results are indelible on the landscape of the United States. The South is dominated by one of the largest branches of Christianity in the United States, the Southern Baptists. Fundamentalist Baptists generally do not believe in drinking, premarital sex, or dancing. Methodists dominate the midsections of the country, whereas Lutherans still dominate the northern sections. The Roman Catholic Church has a strong foothold in New England, Southern Louisiana, and the Latino Southwest.

ISLAM

The second largest religion in the world today is **Islam**. The followers of Islam are called **Muslims**. The Muslim population is approaching 2 billion people. The majority of Muslims live in the Middle East, Northern Africa, and Southeast Asia.

Islam is a universalizing, monotheistic religion. Some of the same prophets exist in Islam as in the Jewish and Christian religions. For Muslims, prophets like Abraham hold spiritual significance, and Jesus Christ was one of the prophets but not the main prophet. The primary prophet is Muhammad, who lived in the sixth century CE. According to traditionalist theory, he received divine revelations from Allah (God) and wrote them down into what is today known as the **Koran** (Quran).

ARCHITECTURE

The religious architecture of Islam is centered around the **mosque**. The mosque is also a focal point of any Islamic community. Many mosques have several **minarets**, which extend from the sides of the mosque and reach up to Allah. The minaret is usually one of the tallest structures in an Islamic community. The verticality of the minaret signifies the relationship between Heaven and Earth. (See Figure 5.5.)

FOUNDATIONAL BELIEFS

There are five fundamental principles in Islam, sometimes called the **five pillars of Islam**. Each Muslim needs to strive to achieve the five pillars. The five pillars, listed in no particular order, are:

1. There is only one God, Allah (Shahadah).

2. Prayer must be done five times daily facing the city of Mecca (Salah).

3. Taxes must be paid directly to the poor and needy or the mosque (zakat).

4. One must fast during Ramadan (sawm).

5. One must make a pilgrimage to Mecca once during one's life (hajj).

The profession of Allah as being the one and true god is taken by all Muslims upon acceptance of the faith. It means more to Muslims than anything else in life. A Muslim's passion for religion should dominate every aspect of life. When one accepts the creed of Allah, or the **Shahadah**, one has officially become a Muslim and then needs to follow the other four pillars of Islam.

Figure 5.5: Mosque.

The **Salah** must be prayed five times daily: at dawn, in the early afternoon, in the late afternoon, just after the sun has set, and during the nighttime hours. These prayers must face the **Kabah**, which is the stone in the center of the primary mosque in Mecca. Praying five times a day helps Muslims focus on Allah throughout the day, no matter how busy their lives may be.

The **zakat** is the giving of alms to the poor or needy. It is given to the mosque once a year. In Christianity, the traditional tithing amount is 10 percent. In the Islamic religion, the amount varies depending upon one's income and savings. The zakat is not a tax nor is it a tithe. It is a form of worship that is required of all Muslims. Through the giving of money, one purifies one's own heart and maintains the purity and holiness of one's family. The recipients of the zakat are the poor, the needy, and the converts to Islam. Travelers may also receive some of the zakat funds to assist them in their hajj to Mecca.

Muslims must fast, or perform the **sawm**, during the holy month of **Ramadan**. Ramadan, the ninth month of the Islamic calendar, usually occurs during the late fall in the United States. (In the Islamic world, calendars are based upon the lunar cycle, while in the Western calendar, months are based on the solar cycle.) Muslims fast during the day. Once the sun sets, they are allowed to eat. It is thought that fasting focuses one's thoughts on Allah as well as focusing the attention of Muslims on the poor.

The pilgrimage to Mecca is called a **hajj**. Sometimes the hajj is called the "Muslim pilgrimage." If one can afford the journey, one should make a trip to Mecca and attend the ceremonies around the Kabah. **Mecca** is the holiest city in Islam. Medina and Jerusalem also have religious significance to Muslims.

STRUCTURE

The leader of the mosque is called an **imam**. The imam leads prayers at the different times of the day and is in charge of an individual mosque.

DISTRIBUTION AND DIFFUSION

Islam began in present-day Saudi Arabia and extended its borders rather quickly along trade routes, reaching Southeast Asia in the Middle Ages. Islam even extends to western China, and most of Central Asia is Islamic. In addition to its spread eastward into Asia, it spread westward throughout northern Africa. Today, Indonesia is the country with the largest population of Muslims.

Islam diffused in a matter of centuries throughout North Africa, the Middle East, Central Asia, and northern India from its heart in the Saudi Arabian peninsula. The religion spread by a combination of the expansion and conquest of invading armies (relocation and hierarchical diffusion). Later Islam spread to various ports throughout the Indian Ocean region to parts of East Africa and Southeast Asia via trade networks (relocation and contagious diffusion).

Today Islam is also spreading, in small numbers, to Europe and North America via migration (relocation diffusion).

DENOMINATIONS

There are two fundamental branches of Islam in the world. The **Shiites,** or **Shiahs,** comprise about 15 to 20 percent of all of Muslims. The largest percentage of Muslims are **Sunnis**. On the whole, the Shiites are the more conservative branch of Muslims, interpreting the Koran literally. The Sunnis are more liberal in their interpretation of the Koran and have made exceptions to traditional beliefs in response to modern times.

Shiite Muslims live predominately in Iraq and Iran, whereas Sunni Muslims live in the rest of the Middle East, Northern Africa, and Southeast Asia. Many of the governments in these areas are theocracies. A **theocracy** is a state that is ruled by religious leaders, where religion plays an integral part in the administration of the country. The laws and principles outlined in the Koran play a vital role in the institutional laws of the society. Islamic theocracies are ruled by **Sharia Law**. Sharia Law does not separate church and state. It based on the Koran and the teachings of Muhammad.

Fundamentalism is based on a literal interpretation of a holy book and urges strict behavioral guidelines to comply with the basic principles of a religion. Failure to follow those basic rules means less likelihood one will enjoy the benefits of the afterlife.

JUDAISM

One of the oldest religions in the world is **Judaism**. It's important to note that Jews may follow the Jewish religion, but the Jewish population also includes people who are born into Jewish families or have Jewish ancestry but are not religious. Most geographers would agree that the Jewish people are a nation. In 1980, the Supreme Court ruled in a discrimination case that being Jewish could be classified as a "race." However, the idea of race frightens many Jewish people, owing to the devastating application of that term to them during the Holocaust. Most would agree then that the Jewish population is an ethnicity.

ARCHITECTURE

The Jewish symbol is the **Star of David** (see Figure 5.6). The Star of David is displayed on synagogues. The Star of David is significant because David was one of the patriarchs of the Jewish religion. The Star of David is even incorporated into the Israeli flag. Some scholars suggest that the six sides of the star represent the days of the week. Other scholars suggest that the six sides of the star represent the astrological chart at the time of David's anointment as king.

Figure 5.6: Star of David.

FOUNDATIONAL BELIEFS

Judaism is an ethnic religion and a monotheistic religion. The god figure is called **Yahweh** in Hebrew. The Jewish holy book is called the **Tanakh** or, more commonly, the **Hebrew Bible** and consists of three separate items: The Torah, The Nev'im, and Ketuvim. **The Torah** consists of the five books written by Moses. **The Nev'im** is composed of the writings of the prophets of the Jewish religion. **The Ketuvim** consists of eleven different books. Jewish worship is led by a rabbi in the synagogue on Saturday, the holy day in the Jewish faith.

The foundations of the Jewish faith are also fundamental tenets of Christianity and Islam, as well as the Bahai faith. Religious Jews believe that Yahweh is an omnipotent yet loving God. In the Jewish tradition, the faith began when Yahweh made a covenant with Abraham, who is considered the patriarch of the Jewish religion. The tenets of the faith are embodied through Moses in the Ten Commandments, which are written in the Talmud.

DISTRIBUTION AND DIFFUSION

The majority of the world's Jewish population lives in the United States, and the majority of Jews in the United States live in larger urban areas on the East Coast, such as New York City. The place most associated with Judaism is Israel. Israel was founed in 1948 as a homeland for Jewish populations after World War II. Because of this establishment of a state in an area formerly occupied by Palestine, tensions have been high between the Jewish population and the Palestinians now living in the occupied areas (Golan Heights, Gaza Strip, and the West Bank). When Israel was created, 7 million Jews occupied the state of Israel. There are over 14 million Jews today. They are dispersed around the globe, but most live in the United States and Israel.

DENOMINATIONS

Like Christianity and Islam, Judaism has different branches. The most traditional, ultra-Orthodox branch is one of the most widely known. Sometimes known as Haredi Judaism, this ultra-Orthodox branch considers all other branches of the Jewish religion to be unreal, because they do not follow the patterns and traditions of the ancestors.

Orthodox Jews are similar to Haredi Jews in that they believe that Yahweh gave the Ten Commandments to Moses and these laws must be accepted and practiced. However, Orthodox Jews can live within modern society, whereas the ultra-Orthodox see modern society as sinful and try to avoid its temptations. The Orthodox branch feels that the Torah came from Yahweh but that humans have had a profound impact on it. They believe it is open to interpretation and can change with the times. Religious practices can accommodate modern culture if adaptation is deemed necessary. However, even modified traditions cannot depart from the fundamental tenets of the religion.

Another branch is Reform Judaism. Reformists also believe in the fundamental tenets of the religion, such as the Torah. However, they believe strongly that the Torah is open to continuous interpretation. They believe in demonstrating their faith through action.

The American-based Reconstructionist branch of Judaism is fundamentally different from some of the other branches. Reconstructionists believe that the religious community must evolve if change is to assist the Jewish religion as a whole; still they believe that traditions should be kept intact. They emphasize personal autonomy over religious custom.

The Humanistic form is one of the newest branches of the faith; it was founded by Rabbi Sherwin T. Wine in 1963. Humanists believe in a humanistic approach to Judaism, meaning a reliance on a nontheistic approach to the faith. They emphasize their Jewish roots, not a belief in Yahweh as a supernatural figure. Rational thought is of vital importance.

Another branch of Judaism is the Flexidox version. Flexidox Judaism was started in 2003 by Rabbi Gershon Winkler and is considered by some to be the most liberal of all of the branches of the faith, though it remains conservative on such practices as eating kosher foods and keeping the Sabbath on Saturday.

HOLIDAYS

The Jewish calendar has a lot of significance in the faith. One of the most widely known holidays is **Passover**. Passover always occurs on the 15th day of the Jewish month of Nissan. Over 80 percent of all Jews have attended a Passover seder, or holy service.

Rosh Hashanah is the Jewish new year celebration that occurs in the month of Tishri in the Jewish calendar. During Rosh Hashanah, Jewish people look back at the previous year, analyze their sins or mistakes, and try to amend those sins by resolving to live a better life during the upcoming year. During Rosh Hashanah, no work is done for 24 hours. Worshippers spend most of the day at the synagogue in introspective thought.

One of the most important holidays of the year is Yom Kippur. **Yom Kippur** is the holiday of atonement in the Jewish faith. It occurs on the tenth day of Tishri in the Jewish calendar. Jewish followers follow a true fast, with no food or water, and try to make up for the sins between man and Yahweh. The only people who are exempt from fasting are children under the age of nine and pregnant women. Fasting may also be lifted when someone is at risk of death. This Day of Atonement is a special time, because once sins are made known, they are sealed in a book forever until the Day of Judgment.

RELIGIOUS CONFLICT IN THE MIDDLE EAST

Each of these three religions—Christianity, Islam, and Judaism—has its roots in modern-day Israel. Jerusalem is the holiest city in the Christian faith, because it is where Jesus Christ was crucified. It is also one of the holiest places in the Jewish religion, because the temple was located there. Currently, the **Wailing Wall**, now called the **Western Wall**, is what is left to remember the site of the temple. The Western Wall is located on the Temple Mount, which is the most holy site in the Jewish religion. The second temple in Israel stood from 516 BCE to 70 CE, when the Romans destroyed the city of Jerusalem.

For Muslims, Jerusalem is the third-holiest city, behind Mecca and Medina, both in Saudi Arabia. The Al-Haram al-Qudsi al-Sharif, or the Noble Sanctuary, is located in Jerusalem. It is the site where Muhammad had a dream in which he went to heaven on a horse with a woman's face and saw Allah. One of the most famous sights in Jerusalem is the Dome of the Rock, which stands high above the city's skyline.

Because Jerusalem is the base of three of the world's major religions, numerous conflicts have occurred during the past two millennia. During the Crusades, Christians wanted to take back the Holy Land from the Muslims, who had taken it over in the 11th century. The Christian kings and queens of Europe sent thousands of soldiers but only took control of the land for a short period.

Jews and Muslims have been in conflict in recent years with the establishment of Israel as a state in 1948. Many Palestinians feel that they were treated unfairly when the boundaries were established.

This tension has led to more than a half century of conflict involving suicide bombings, cluster bombs, and thousands of dead soldiers and civilians on both sides.

The issue of ownership of the Holy Land is a tense one. Jewish citizens of Israel point out the high standard of living of the Jewish people and the poverty of the Palestinians living in the occupied territories: the West Bank, Golan Heights, and Gaza Strip. The Palestinians object to the Israeli state's claim on property that they had legitimately owned for over 1,000 years. The result is a 50-year reign of terror in one of the world's most important cultural areas.

MONOTHEISM AND POLYTHEISM: WEST AND EAST

Christianity, Islam, and Judaism are all **monotheistic**, believing that there is an almighty, omnipotent god that reigns over humans. This god figure (God, Yahweh, or Allah) can be loving yet judgmental. Nonbelievers will find themselves in hell after they die, while the faithful will go to heaven.

Many scholars trace these three religions' roots back to Zoroastrianism. **Zoroastrianism** is the belief in Zarathustra as the father of religion and in the concept of both good and evil. These principles are at the heart of all three Western faiths. However, Zoroastrianism is dying out. Today the religion is primarily practiced in Iran and India.

As opposed to the Western religions, whose hearths are in the Middle East, the two major religions of Asia have their hearths in India. Although India today is primarily Hindu, the foundations of Buddhism began there. From India, it spread into Eastern Asia and is now one of the main religions of East and Southeast Asia.

Both Hinduism and Buddhism are nearly the antitheses of the Western religions. Instead of having one god (monotheism), eastern religions practice **polytheism** (belief in many gods). Eastern religions focus on meditation to achieve release from desires. Forgiveness comes from the gods but can also be earned through good works. In Western religions, forgiveness for sins comes only from the god figure.

HINDUISM

Many geographers consider **Hinduism** to be the oldest religion on Earth, with origins dating back over 3,000 years. It is an ethnic religion: One can practice the religion, but you cannot become a Hindu unless you are born to Hindu parents.

ARCHITECTURE

The majority of the world's Hindus live in India. Hinduism is the world's third-largest religion, in part because India's population is so large. Over 80 percent of the population of India professes to be Hindu. Also, over 90 percent of the population of Nepal professes to be Hindu. As with Judaism, the diffusion of Hinduism is almost nonexistent except for cases of relocation diffusion, when Hindus migrate to other parts of the world. However, more Hindu temples are being built in the United States with the immigration of more people from India.

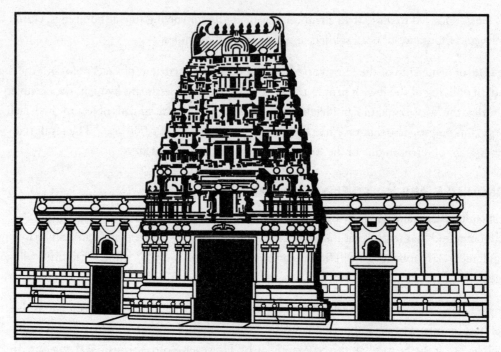

Figure 5.7: Hindu Temple.

FOUNDATIONAL BELIEFS

The foundations of the faith are built on a legal code of behavior in addition to the principles of the deities themselves. There are three primary deities in the Hindu faith: Brahma, Shiva, and Vishnu. **Brahma** created the universe. **Shiva** destroys the universe, and **Vishnu** is the preserver of not only the Earth but also the universe. These three gods keep the balance in the universe. These three primary deities are called the **triumvirate**.

In India, thousands of temples (see Figure 5.7) are devoted to the worship of Shiva and Vishnu, while only two temples are devoted to Brahma. Vishnu and Shiva each have their different sects of the religion. Over 70 percent of all Hindus worship Vishnu, and 25 percent worship Shiva. The third sect of the religion belongs to the mother goddess called **Shakti**. Shakti is the female personification of God and the word means energy. Shakti also represents the power of femininity.

SECTS

Vishnu worshipers are called **Vaishnava**. They believe that Vishnu is the true god in the religion and that the other gods exist but are not as powerful as Vishnu. Vishnu has been reincarnated nine times in the history of the world. Believers of Vishnu feel that when he is reincarnated again, the end of the world will be near. **Reincarnation** is the belief that one has lived a previous life and will continue to live another life after death. Most Hindus believe that Vishnu is represented by a human-looking figure with blue skin and four arms extending from the main body.

Shiva is the destroyer of the universe. However, Shiva is not necessarily seen as a negative deity. For something to be rebuilt, it must be destroyed first. The role of Shiva is to destroy what is wrong with the world to create something new. However, Shiva can be conceived of as evil, too. Therefore, Shiva is in constant conflict between good and evil. Shiva is married to **Parvati**, who keeps Shiva in balance. When Shiva is represented as a person, his face and throat are blue.

The last of the triumvirate is Brahma. Brahma is the creator of the world and the universe. Because Brahma created the universe, he is considered the first god in the triumvirate. Brahma consists of four heads facing in all the directions. These four heads are thought to represent the **Vedas**, which are holy texts in Hinduism. There are also four caste systems in India, which are also thought to have originated from Brahma.

There are also thousands of other gods, which may be represented by different symbols of the life cycle. The worship of these gods can be done in many different ways.

REINCARNATION

Hinduism deals with the individual's spiritual placement in life as well as in previous lives. The good deeds that one does in this life count toward a higher standing in a future life. Conversely, negative deeds count against a person, causing him or her to lose standing in the hierarchy of the afterlife.

One of the highest forms one can achieve is that of a cow. Cows are seen as life builders. They provide milk for the sustenance of people, and dairy products are staples in the Indian diet. Their droppings are often used as insulation in houses in India. The killing of a cow is a terrible crime in the Hindu religion, because Vishnu was a cattle herder. To upset a cow would bring the wrath of Vishnu on you or your family. Because of this belief, cows roam the country. Traffic may come to a standstill in huge cities such as Calcutta, Mumbai, and Delhi when a cow crosses the road.

BUDDHISM

Another of the Eastern religions, Buddhism focuses of the elimination of unwanted desires from the human soul through meditation. Therefore, the worship of a god is not a part of the Buddhist religion. Instead, the religion focuses on the personal devotion of the individual follower. The majority of the world's Buddhists live in East Asia, and the Buddhist religion extends from Northeast to Southeast Asia.

Buddhism is a universalizing religion. However, one can be a Buddhist as well as an animist or a follower of any other faith, as long as that other faith allows it. When a person combines two or more faiths into one belief system, the result is known as a **syncretic religion**. In many cases, followers of Buddhism also follow Shintoism or Confucianism.

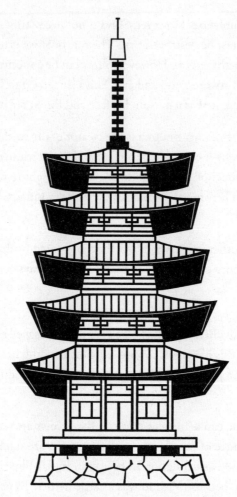

Figure 5.8: Pagoda.

ARCHITECTURE

Buddhists do not have churches or mosques but rather **pagodas** (see Figure 5.8). Pagodas are tall buildings of ornate design. They often extend high into the sky and are the focal point of many Asian communities. Pagodas are made more for individual worship than congregational worship and, unlike many Western places of worship, do not serve as a social space. Individuals will enter a pagoda and burn incense to release the spirits of their ancestors and contemplate or meditate on the principles of becoming a better person.

FOUNDATIONAL BELIEFS

The foundation of the Buddhist religion focuses on **Siddhartha Gautama**. Siddhartha was a prince who lived in Nepal during the fifth century BCE. His father was the king of a large empire and tried to shield his son from the religious teachings of the day as well as the poverty of the time. The prince lived a life of luxury until his teen years. He left the confines of his palace and saw abject poverty. He felt this was unjust, and from that moment on, he began living a life focused on getting rid of material possessions to obtain a state of Nirvana. It is thought that Siddhartha received his enlightenment at the Bodhi tree in northeastern India, still a holy site in the Buddhist religion.

There are four universal or noble truths in the Buddhist religion. These truths are the cornerstone of the faith.

1. All living beings should experience and endure suffering.
2. Suffering leads to the desire to live, which leads to reincarnation.
3. The goal is to leave the suffering of this Earth perpetuated by reincarnation.
4. Nirvana can be achieved through practicing the following eight steps: rightness of belief, resolve, speech, action, livelihood, effort, thought, and meditation.

STRUCTURE

Buddhist monks live in monasteries, usually separated from urban areas so the monks can focus on meditation. They often leave their monasteries only to beg for food. The villagers in the surrounding region will donate food to the monks as they travel.

DISTRIBUTION AND DIFFUSION

Since its founding, Buddhism has spread from Nepal and India across East Asia. Like Islam, Buddhism was spread along trade routes. Most of East Asia professes to be Buddhist. Many Chinese claim to be Confucian and Buddhist; likewise, many Japanese claim to be Shintoists yet follow Buddhism as well. Today, few remnants of Buddhism are left in India, the religion's birthplace.

Asoka, emperor of the Mauryan dynasty in India, converted to Buddhism around 257 BCE. He sent missionaries (relocation, hierarchical, and contagious diffusion) to Sri Lanka, to Myanmar (Burma), to Tibet, and throughout India. A few hundred years later, missionaries traveling on the Silk Roads spread Buddhism to China and eventually the religion spread to Korea and Japan. Today Buddhism is well represented throughout most of East and Southeast Asia and Sri Lanka.

SECTS

As with other religions, there are different branches of Buddhism. The largest is the Mahayanist, the northern branch, which includes approximately 56 percent of all Buddhists. China, Japan, and Korea for the most part practice the Mahayanist branch of Buddhism. The Theravadas, the southern branch, is the second-largest branch of Buddhists. Southeast Asia is the home of the Theravadist branch. The last branch is the Tantrayanists, located in the Tibet region of China and in Mongolia.

OTHER UNIVERSALIZING RELIGIONS

The world's five main religions do not encompass all the belief systems of the world. Many smaller religions are practiced by millions of people, and some play major roles in the regions where they dominate.

SIKHISM

Sikhism is a belief in one god formed as a rejection of India's caste system. Founded by Guru Nanak, Sikhists believe that all people are created equal. Therefore, different communities are established where people of different caste systems can congregate and eat together. Individual responsibility is crucial in this faith. Sikhs are located primarily in the Punjab region of India as well as in Pakistan; Sikhism has approximately 24 million followers. Sikhs are best known for the turbans they wear on their heads. Also, men are not meant to cut their facial hair.

BAHAI

Another universalizing religion is the **Bahai** faith, which is practiced in many parts of Africa and Asia. Founded in Iran in the mid-1800s by Siyyid 'Ali Muhammad, the Bahai faith is similar to the Sikh faith in that Bahai followers believe that there should be no class distinctions. The Bahai faith extends this philosophy to race and religious differences as well.

MORMONISM

Mormonism, another universalizing faith, is centered around Utah in the United States. This Church is also known as the Church of Jesus Christ of Latter Day Saints. Founded by Joseph Smith, who was proclaimed a prophet of God, and later continued by Brigham Young, Mormonism has established itself as the dominant religion in Utah. The Book of Mormon is the fundamental book in the religion, and Mormons believe that it, in addition to the Old and New Testaments, contains the teachings of God.

Although Mormonism is often classified as a Christian religion, there are distinct differences between Mormons and other Christians. Other Christian denominations do not believe that Joseph Smith was a prophet of God. The Book of Mormon is considered sacred to Mormons but not to other Christians. When most people think of Mormons, they think of polygamy, which was practiced by the church's founders. **Polygamy** is the marriage of one man to more than one wife and is illegal in the United States. In 1890, the church outlawed the practice of polygamy and today even excommunicates (removes from the Church) those who follow the practice. Today, very conservative or fundamentalist Mormons still believe in the practice and are sometimes prosecuted for it.

ETHNIC RELIGIONS

There are many different ethnic religions around the world. Anthropologists agree that almost every society needs some supernatural worship figure in its culture. This need can be met in a variety of ways. Each of the following religions is strict in its adherence to its fundamental principles.

ANIMISM

Animism is a belief in luck and spirits. Spirits inhabit natural objects and can be either positive or negative. When one of the negative spirits enters your house, field, or animals, it must be removed by a shaman. A **shaman** has the ability to intermediate between the supernatural and real worlds. The shaman can remove evil spirits by performing ceremonies. In a basic definition, animists believe in the existence of souls and good versus evil.

Animism exists in many locations in the remote sections of Southeast Asia, including the islands of Indonesia and Papua New Guinea. Other areas where animism is widely practiced are rural Africa and the Amazon Basin of South America. Also, many Native Americans hold animistic beliefs.

Animism takes on many different forms, and although the names of the gods and the practices may be different, the same themes are consistent across societies that practice animism. There are souls and spiritual beings on Earth. These spirits can be both positive and evil and are in a constant battle.

CONFUCIANISM

Confucianism is based on the teachings of Confucius, who lived in China about the same time as Siddhartha Gautama lived in Nepal—during the fifth century BCE. Confucianism focuses on relationships. Much of the teachings of Confucius are still fundamental to Chinese society and can be linked with the philosophy of feng shui. This **geomancy (feng shui)** concerns maintaining proper relationships in life through the positioning of items to keep the flow of energy in harmony. The principles of yin and yang come from Confucianism. For every good there is an evil; for every positive there is a negative.

TAOISM

Taoism, or **Daoism**, like Confucianism, is based on the release of personal desires. Whereas Confucius believed in public service, however, Taoism is based on a mystical understanding of the harmony of life. Started by Lao Tzu, a Chinese philosopher who was a contemporary of Confucius, Taoism is based on the philosophy that things happen that cannot be explained by rational thought.

SHINTOISM

Shintoism, practiced primarily in Japan, has characteristics of both polytheism and monotheism. Shintoists believe that nature is divine. The forces of nature, including rivers, mountains, and other natural features, have spirits associated with them. A person's ancestors play a vital role in preserving the spirits associated with each item. Shintoism became the official religion in Japan in the early 1900s. The religion stresses the battle between good and evil.

SACRED PLACES AND SPACES IN RELIGIONS

In many religions, certain locations hold spiritual significance for the faithful. These places, called **sacred spaces**, are reserved and preserved for their holiness. In many cases, these sites attract millions of visitors and much-needed tourist dollars in economies that need the income.

What is interesting about the sacred places in various religions is how they are used. During the hajj, millions of pilgrims follow the path to the Kabah in Mecca; it has become part of the culture and economy there. Other places are feared and are not visited by the followers of the religion. Many of the sacred burial sites in Native American religions are treated this way. To walk in these sacred places will bring followers bad luck.

One of the largest religious structures in the world is the **Taj Mahal** in Agra, India. The Taj Mahal was built by a Muslim prince as a mausoleum for his deceased wife. It is one of the great structures of the world.

For Hindus, the **Ganges River** is the holiest river in the world. Upon one's death, Hindus burn the body and scatter the ashes in the Ganges. Scattering the ashes there brings forth the hair of Shiva, one of the main deities of the Hindu faith.

Many faiths consider the death of an individual a sacred occurrence. Because of this, the process of handling the physical body is an important custom for faiths around the world. In many cases, how the body is handled after death determines the fate of the individual in the afterlife.

The Christian tradition usually involves the burial of a dead body in a cemetery. Large areas of land in the middle of urban centers are used for this purpose. These areas could be developed very profitably. However, the treatment of the dead is important in Christianity. In many areas of the United States, laws stipulate that land that was once a cemetery cannot be used for any other purpose for upward of 50 or even 100 years after the cemetery has shut its doors. Muslims and Jews also bury their dead in cemeteries.

In the Hindu religion, the dead are not buried but rather are cremated on a pyre to purify the soul before reincarnation can occur. As previously mentioned, the ashes are often scattered in the Ganges River to ensure the deceased has a better next life.

Some religions, such as the Zoroastrian faith, simply leave the body in the open air. Burying the dead would upset the balance of the Earth. Buddhists often use this method as well.

The impact of religion on the landscape is profound. Religious toponyms (place names) mark many landscapes. Québec is renowned for its Catholic toponyms. Many areas in California and the Southwest are dotted with cities named after Catholic missions. For example, Mission Viejo, California, was named after the mission started by Spanish priests hundreds of years ago.

RELIGION AND CONFLICT

Many battles have been fought and much blood has been shed in the name of religion. **Religious conflicts** are occurring throughout the world as you read this book.

Almost all religions have fought with another culture for control of **interfaith boundaries**, the boundaries between people of different faiths.

Christians fought against Muslims, and sometimes other Christians, over several centuries in a series of Crusades.

The conflict between India and Pakistan is still ongoing. Pakistan is a Muslim country, whereas India is predominantly Hindu. Both of these countries have nuclear weapons. Much of the rhetoric is about control of the land in northern Kashmir, but the fundamental disagreement is over religion. In the name of religion, terrorists have bombed trains and buildings, killing hundreds of innocent civilians.

In Sri Lanka, Buddhists and Hindus have been in conflict for the past 25 years. The Tamil Tigers are trying to lead a separatist movement against the formal government of Sri Lanka. The Tamils, primarily Hindu, have forced Muslims out of their region and have led attacks against Buddhist monasteries.

In Northern Ireland, the Irish Republican Army led a revolt against the Protestant government of Great Britain. Northern Ireland has a large Catholic minority, and many of its citizens would rather be ruled by a Catholic Irish government than a Protestant British government.

As in political geography, many religious enclaves and exclaves exist. An **enclave** is a group of people with a particular religion surrounded by people of a different religion. In some cases, this can cause turmoil. An **exclave** is a group of people who are physically separated from their religious hearth. For example, many missionaries practice in exclave environments in the remote areas of the South Pacific or Asia. If the community has an outlet to an ocean, then it is not considered an exclave.

CULTURAL DIFFUSION

Hierarchical diffusion is defined as the diffusion of something from a minority to the majority. Rap music is an example of this. It spread from the inner city to the suburbs and eventually to rural areas in the United States and now has become popular around the world. Even though the diffusion didn't come from somebody in political power, it came from people with cultural power. Superstars in sports and music have a powerful influence on the clothing lines and behaviors of many of today's youth.

Usually, the term *contagious diffusion* is used to describe the spread of a disease, but the same principle can be used when discussing the spread of cultural principles. **Contagious diffusion** is the rapid spread of an idea. This may occur through the Internet or some other type of mass communication system. Contagious diffusion can be used for marketing purposes. Marketers dream of their product going "viral" on the Internet. Going viral means that their product will be seen by many people in a short amount of time, gaining even more exposure for their product.

The broadcasting of the Super Bowl is a type of contagious diffusion, leading to sales of National Football League (NFL) merchandise around the world. Minnesota Vikings baseball caps can be purchased on the island of Tenerife in the Canary Islands, located just off of the coast of Morocco. This rapid spread of the idea and the game itself has led to millions of dollars in additional revenue for the NFL.

Stimulus diffusion is the application of a concept to another product. The American pizza is an example of stimulus diffusion. Americans borrowed the idea from Italian food culture. Pizza can now be ordered almost anywhere in the world. Pizza chains, such as Domino's and Pizza Hut, have established offices in many countries. These transnational corporations are assisting in the spread of American-style pizza.

Relocation diffusion is the spread of a cultural aspect through migration. Language is often spread via relocation diffusion. When Italians came to the United States, for example, they brought with them their language. Even though the heritage of Italian culture has stayed strong, the use of the language usually fades away within three generations. This is the process of **acculturation**. As people become more American in their customs and cultures, they are assimilating into the new culture. **Assimilation** is the gradual dying out of the old culture and its replacement with the new culture.

OBSERVING THE CULTURAL LANDSCAPE

One of the best places to observe the cultural landscape is in a city park. City parks exhibit traits of the surrounding landscape and culture. By looking at parks, a person can assess the cultural values of the society.

When analyzing a park, observe the different statues. Whom are the statues representing? What are they made of? Usually, the statues provide a look into the history and geography of the area, indicating the past heroes of the community.

In many larger cities, the ethnicity of the area will be evident through the public artwork on display in the park. Also, the area around a park will have commercial activities that cater to a specific ethnicity. For example, in the Southwestern United States, many Latino-owned grocery stores sell items familiar to most Latin American immigrants, and the parks showcase Latino artwork.

How the land is being used is important as well. Are there large areas for socializing? How many park benches are there? How many trails are located within the park, and are they walkways, bike paths, or horse trails? Some parks allow motorized vehicle access, while others ban all vehicles from the property.

No place is inherently boring. Each place is distinct and interesting in its own way. A geographer has the ability to see the differences between places and the uniqueness of each. You may live in an area that seems bland, and as you travel by different landscapes every day, you may take them for granted. Instead of taking them for granted, evaluate them as a human geographer would. You may have walked down your street daily for the past decade or more. But somebody from a different region of the world might see it from a very different perspective. This is what makes geography so much fun!

REVIEW QUESTIONS

MULTIPLE-CHOICE QUESTIONS

1. What is the world's fastest-growing religion?

   (A) Christianity

   (B) Hinduism

   (C) Islam

   (D) Buddhism

   (E) Judaism

2. Which language has become the world's primary lingua franca?

   (A) Mandarin Chinese

   (B) Hindi

   (C) German

   (D) Spanish

   (E) English

3. The following structure would most likely be found in which country?

   (A) Ecuador

   (B) Germany

   (C) India

   (D) Thailand

   (E) Israel

4. Which of the following is the largest proselytizing religion?

   (A) Hinduism

   (B) Christianity

   (C) Islam

   (D) Buddhism

   (E) Shintoism

5. Regionalization would best explain the characteristics of the study of

   (A) popular culture.

   (B) adaptive strategies.

   (C) built environment.

   (D) material culture.

   (E) folk culture.

6. Which of the following best exemplifies folk culture?

   (A) A dialect that is similar in two different regions of the country

   (B) The purchasing of rap music by white suburban youth

   (C) Cajun music

   (D) Eating Chinese food in New York City

   (E) The burial of the dead

7. Where is one of the hearths of country music?

   (A) Galveston, Texas

   (B) Montgomery, Alabama

   (C) Atlanta, Georgia

   (D) Nashville, Tennessee

   (E) Charlotte, North Carolina

8. A good example of a monolingual country would be

   (A) Japan.

   (B) Canada.

   (C) Switzerland.

   (D) South Africa.

   (E) Turkey.

9. When European settlers established relations with Native Americans, a new language was created to ease translation for both groups. What is that language called?

   (A) Constitutional language

   (B) Trade language

   (C) Creole language

   (D) Official language

   (E) Indigenous language

10. Which of the following religions is the best example of a polytheistic religion?

    (A) Shintoism

    (B) Judaism

    (C) Atheism

    (D) Christianity

    (E) Islam

11. Which of the following statements best explains the diffusion of Muslims?

    (A) The country with the largest amount of Muslims is India because they were born there.

    (B) The country with the largest amount of Muslims is Saudi Arabia since it is the hearth of the religion.

    (C) The country with the largest amount of Muslims is the United States due to immigration patterns.

    (D) The country with the largest amount of Muslims is Indonesia due to trade routes.

    (E) The country with the largest amount of Muslims is Iran due to the presence of the Shiite branch.

12. Where in the United States does Roman Catholicism dominate?

    (A) southern New England

    (B) Southwest

    (C) Pacific Northwest

    (D) Southeast

    (E) Midwest

13. Many Islamic states in the Middle East region combine religion and state and don't separate them. This is an example of what?

    (A) Monotheism

    (B) Plural society

    (C) Democracy

    (D) Theocracy

    (E) Multilingual society

14. The two primary Eastern religions of Hinduism and Buddhism each have their hearths located where?

    (A) Jerusalem, Israel

    (B) Western Saudi Arabia

    (C) Eastern China

    (D) Southeast Asia

    (E) Northern India

15. What is the largest polytheistic religion in the world?

    (A) Christianity

    (B) Islam

    (C) Hinduism

    (D) Shintoism

    (E) Animism

16. What language is known as the lingua franca of Eastern Africa?

    (A) Hindi

    (B) English

    (C) French

    (D) Swahili

    (E) Zulu

17. What percentage of the world's languages are expected to die out within the next century?

    (A) 90 Percent

    (B) 75 Percent

    (C) 50 Percent

    (D) 25 Percent

    (E) 10 Percent

18. Which distinctive cultural region in the United States has its own food, music, and language along the border with Mexico?

    (A) Italian-American

    (B) Swedish-American

    (C) Cajun

    (D) Creole

    (E) Tejano

19. Which of the following is the best example of folk food?

    (A) Hamburgers in the United States

    (B) Pizza in the United States

    (C) McDonald's french fries in Germany

    (D) KFC in China

    (E) Blowfish in Japan

20. The modern game of soccer (football) spread to many parts of the world because of British colonization. This is an example of what type of diffusion?

    (A) Expansion

    (B) Hierarchical

    (C) Relocation

    (D) Stimulus

    (E) Contagious

FREE-RESPONSE QUESTION

Directions: While a formal essay is not required, it is not enough to answer the following question by merely listing facts. Your answer should be based upon your critical analysis of the question posed.

1. Explain how English has become the most dispersed language on Earth by answering the following questions.

   (A) Explain in detail how the English language is a product of relocation diffusion and cultural convergence.

   (B) Discuss the global distribution of English starting with colonization and ending with globalization.

   (C) Explain why English is spoken so differently around the world and even in different regions of the same country (for example, the United States). Give examples of different English dialects and the geographic factors that contribute to them.

ANSWERS AND EXPLANATIONS

MULTIPLE-CHOICE QUESTIONS

1. C

Islam is the world's fastest-growing religion owing to population growth in many of the countries where the religion is practiced. The Middle East, which is predominantly Muslim, is one of the fastest-growing regions of the world demographically. Christianity is the world's largest religion with just over 2 billion followers. Hinduism and Judaism are ethnic religions, so their growth is not augmented to a great degree by conversion. Universalizing religions tend to have more people because of their drive to convert others.

2. E

English has become the world's primary lingua franca because of the dominance of the economies of English-speaking countries, including the United States and Great Britain. People in many countries have an incentive to be able to conduct business in English. However, as more citizens of developing countries obtain higher levels of education, they can translate some industry-specific literature, minimizing the role of English as a lingua franca. Mandarin Chinese is quickly gaining ground owing to China's importance in the world economy. Hindi is spoken by a lot of people, but because India's economy is relatively weak in global terms, it is not a lingua franca.

3. D

The picture shows a pagoda, which is common in Buddhist countries. Buddhism is the primary religion in East and Southeast Asia. Ecuador and Germany are both Christian countries. India is a Hindu country, and Israel is a Jewish state.

4. B

A proselytizing religion tries to convert people to its ranks. Another name for a proselytizing religion is a universalizing religion. Because Hinduism and Shintoism are both ethnic religions, neither can be the answer. Islam is a close second to Christianity in terms of total numbers of followers, but Christianity is still the largest religion in the world with over two billion followers.

5. E

Regionalization describes the uniqueness of a certain place by using characteristics that distinguish it from other places near it. Folk culture involves these regional characteristics, such as country music, Cajun music, or polka music. Popular culture does not describe regionalization but rather globalization. Adaptive strategies are simply ways in which people learn a new culture. The built environment is the structures that humans have constructed upon the landscape.

6. C

Folk culture is the unique traits of a specific culture or area. This can involve storytelling, dialect, music, food, and numerous other distinguishing characteristics—all aspects of Cajun music. Dialects that are similar to each other yet are separated by a considerable distance would be hard to find. Rap music is an aspect of popular culture. Chinese food in New York City is an example of an ethnic neighborhood, if the Chinese restaurant is located within Chinatown. The burial of the dead is not an example of folk culture because people around the world with the same religion usually treat the dead the same way.

7. D

The hearth or node of country music is located in Nashville, Tennessee. The Grand Ole Opry started in Nashville over 50 years ago and is still going strong.

The Country Music Hall of Fame is located within Nashville, and fans from all over the world come to visit it and other attractions associated with country music.

8. A

A monolingual country is a country that speaks only one language. Japan and Denmark are the two best examples of nation-states, where almost everyone in the state speaks the same language. Canada is a bilingual country, with both French and English being official languages. Switzerland has four official languages. South Africa includes speakers of Afrikaans, English, and Zulu within its borders. In Turkey, the Kurds speak Kurdish while the Turks speak Turkish.

9. B

A trade language is a made-up language that uses vocabulary from two or more languages. A trade language was developed for the ease of both Native Americans and Europeans. A creole language is similar to a trade language but has become so common that the majority of people in an area speak it. An example of an indigenous language is one that Native Americans spoke before contact with the Europeans. An official language is established by a government that mandates all government business be conducted in that language.

10. A

A polytheistic religion is one where more than one god is worshipped. Judaism, Christianity, and Islam are monotheistic religions. Atheism is the absence of a godlike figure. Shintoism is a polytheistic belief in the spirits of nature and one's ancestors, who provide the positive imprints of life on those who are still living a physical life.

11. E

The country with the largest amount of Muslims is Indonesia. This is because of early trade routes and then the population growth seen in Indonesia since. India has the second largest number of Muslims, but they are still outnumbered by Hindus in that country. Even though Saudi Arabia is the hearth of the religion, the physical geography of the landscape does not allow for a large population base.

12. B

Roman Catholicism dominates in areas that experienced high levels of immigration from countries where Roman Catholicism is strong. For instance, southern New England (Massachusetts, Rhode Island, and Connecticut) experienced large numbers of immigrants from Ireland in the 1840s and 1850s and Italian immigrants in the early 1900s. Many of these immigrants stayed in the area, thus increasing the percentage of the overall population that is Catholic. In the American southwest, many people are Roman Catholic because the area was settled by colonizers from Spain, a predominantly Catholic country, and because of recent immigration from Mexico and other Catholic Latin American countries. The Pacific Northwest is the least religious region of the United States, whereas Baptists dominate the southeast.

13. D

A theocracy does not separate religious laws and governmental laws. Many of the religious laws are incorporated into the social and political structure of the society. Iran and Saudi Arabia are good examples of theocracies. Both are ruled in large part by Muslim clerics. The Vatican City is an example of a Christian theocracy. The Roman Catholic Church's laws govern the papal state.

14. E

Northern India is the home of both Hinduism and Buddhism. Many believe Hinduism is the oldest religion in the world, dating back over 3,000 years. Buddhism began with the Nepalese prince Siddhartha Gautama in northern India. The Western religions had their beginnings in the Middle East.

15. C

The largest polytheistic religion in the world is Hinduism with approximately 900 million followers. Even though Christianity and Islam each have more followers, they are monotheistic religions. Shintoism and Animism are polytheistic religions but minor in number of followers compared to Hinduism.

16. D

Even though English is the world's primary lingua franca, in Eastern Africa, the lingua franca is Swahili. The language is spoken in trade and bartering transactions between people of different tribes. Over 40 million people speak Swahili as their primary language, but upward of 100 million people speak Swahili as a lingua franca in a region extending from Somalia to Tanzania. Zulu is an important language spoken in southern Africa. French is still a lingua franca in much of Western Africa.

17. A

Currently there are approximately 6,000 languages spoken in the world. Most of these languages are spoken by only a few hundred to a few thousand people. Within the next 100 years, over 90 percent of these languages will die out and be replaced by megalanguages, such as English, Mandarin Chinese, Hindi, and others. As remote villages encounter the global culture, the younger generations move away, learn languages that allow them to communicate with more people, and no longer speak their original languages. The result is the gradual dying out of languages.

18. E

The Tejano region has its own food, its own dialect (Spanglish), and its own style of music (Tex-Mex). The result is a culture within the boundaries of the United States that is neither American nor Mexican. Several years ago, *Time* magazine devoted an issue to this region and called it "Amexica." Even though the other groups in the answer choices are distinctive cultures, they do not border Mexico.

19. E

The blowfish is an example of a folk food that is part of the Japanese culture. Pizza and hamburgers are so common around the world today, they have moved from being folk food to the realm of popular culture. Likewise, KFC is extremely popular in China and has become a popular culture food.

20. C

The modern game of soccer originally diffused around the world because of British colonization. Many British people who relocated during the colonization process in the 1800s brought their games with them (relocation diffusion).

FREE-RESPONSE QUESTION

SAMPLE ESSAY

PART A

The English language is a product of relocation diffusion. Three Germanic tribes, the Jutes, the Angles, and the Saxons, invaded the British Isles and brought their linguistic traditions with them. These tribes intermingled with the indigenous Celts, blending various languages. In the ninth century, Vikings invaded parts of the British Isles, impacting language mainly on the eastern coastline. In 1066, the Normans conquered England, and French became the dominant language of England for nearly three hundred years. As result of these migrations and invasions, modern English did not become the dominant language until the 1500s.

PART B

With Britain colonizing many parts of the world from the 1600s to the 1800s, the English language diffused around the world. The British colonized South Asia, Australia, and New Zealand; most of North America; and parts of the Caribbean and Africa. As a result of British colonization, English was spoken around the world by the 1800s. Today English is the dominant language in the world largely because of American power and influence. American television shows, movies, and music are diffused via various forms of technology. Very few places on Earth seem to be off limits or not touched by American popular culture. The United States is also a leader in technology, so computer technological terminology is in English. The combination of American-driven computer technology and popular culture ensures that English will touch most places in the world.

PART C

As English diffused around the world, English-language speakers became isolated from one another, and over time the language diverged and a multitude of dialects emerged. One of the best examples of this is the difference between American English and British English. American colonists' isolation from England and each other in the 1600s and 1700s helped to create many distinctive American English dialects. In general, American English diverged in spelling, pronunciation, and vocabulary from British English. It didn't take long for American English itself to diverge into many dialects in the colonies. In general, on the East Coast there are three main dialects: northern, midlands, and southern. Each of these areas contains many subregions or dialects. In addition to the development of dialects in the United States, other areas of the British Empire developed their own distinct dialects too. Australia, for example, has a distinct dialect with unique vocabulary and pronunciation.

RUBRIC FOR FREE-RESPONSE QUESTION

Total point value for question 1 = 7

Part A—Two points possible:

- One point for discussing how English is a product of relocation diffusion.

  — English is a product of the Angles', Jutes', and Saxons' Germanic languages combined with linguistic influences from indigenous peoples, the French, and Vikings.

- One point for discussing the role cultural convergence played in shaping the English language.

  — The above mentioned groups converged to create the English language.

Part B—Two points possible:

- One point for describing how colonization diffused the English language to different parts of the world.

  — The British colonized North America, parts of Africa, South Asia, Australia, and New Zealand.

- One point for describing how globalization is diffusing English to most or all parts of the world.

  — The United States dominates internationally and diffuses the English language around the world.

Part C—Three points possible:

- One point for describing examples of where English is spoken differently in the world.

  — Difference between American English and British English or Australian English and British English.

- Two points for examining how geography contributes to dialects and language divergence.

  — Isolation (geographic separation) leads to differences in spelling, pronunciation, and word usage.

CHAPTER 6:   POLITICAL ORGANIZATION OF SPACE

IF YOU LEARN ONLY SEVEN THINGS IN THIS CHAPTER . . .

1. A nation is a group of people with common cultural characteristics, whereas a state is an area with defined boundaries that has sovereignty within its borders. A nation-state is a country whose political boundaries correspond with its cultural boundaries.

2. The heartland theory established by Halford MacKinder suggests that whoever owns the Heartland of Eastern Europe will control the world. The rimland theory developed by Nicholas Spykman suggests that sea power is more valuable and that alliances will keep the heartland in check. The domino theory, a response to the spread of communism, suggested that when one country falls, others around it will experience the same political instability.

3. Colonialism has had a profound impact on the world today. The major colonial powers were Great Britain, Portugal, Spain, and France.

4. Ethnicity is determined by race, skin color, language, religion, and other factors. Race is different from ethnicity and is determined by perceived inheritable biological characteristics.

5. There are five shapes to countries: compact, elongated, fragmented, perforated, and prorupted. Each of these has advantages and disadvantages.

6. Supranational organizations, such as the European Union and the United Nations, have a strong influence on the world's political climate.

7. Boundary disputes arise for various reasons. Some arise from the demarcation of the boundary, while others arise from the allocation of resources along the border. Inappropriate boundary lines in Africa led to wars from the moment they were drawn, because European countries used geometric and physical features to establish boundaries in Africa instead of cultural features, such as language and religion.

THE IMPACT OF POLITICAL GEOGRAPHY

Political geography, sometimes called geopolitics, is of vital importance in the understanding of the world around us. **Geopolitics** is the study of human systems, which are constantly in a state of spatially organizing the land to fit the needs of humans.

Political geography goes well beyond the scope of politics. Political geography includes the distribution of resources as well as gender and ethnicity. At its fundamental core, political geography is about how humans divide up the earth. Sometimes this is done effectively and efficiently, but often times the division of the surface of the earth with artificial boundaries creates conflicts among humans.

In this chapter, we will try to analyze the issues of geopolitics around the globe. Why are some areas more prone to war than others? Why are some countries larger than others? Who determines the boundaries of a state? Also included in this chapter is the study of ethnicity. Ethnicity is different from race: **ethnicity** deals with the cultural aspects of a group of people, while **race** deals with the biological heritage of a group.

UNDERSTANDING POLITICAL GEOGRAPHY

One is amazed at how often American media misuses the terms of political geography. For example, the differences between a state and a nation, as well as a nation-state, are profound. A **state** is an area with boundaries and sovereignty. A **nation** is a group of people with common cultural characteristics. A **nation-state** occurs when a state's boundaries coincide with the cultural boundaries of a particular group.

Iraq, for example, is a state divided among three nations. Somebody who uses the phrase "the nation of Iraq" is trying to describe the state of Iraq. The state of Iraq currently has three distinct nations within it: the Sunni Muslims, the Shiite Muslims, and the Kurds. These three nations within Iraq have disputes that are difficult to resolve within a single political system.

STATES

The Earth is divided among just under 200 countries. These countries are more correctly termed *states*. A **state** is any area with a defined territory that exercises its sovereign control over areas both inside and outside of its borders. In the 20th century, boundaries changed constantly. Many countries dissolved and became several countries. In the past 100 years, the number of states has increased by over 100.

In the United States, we have 50 subdivisions called "states," even though they are a part of one state, called the United States of America. The federal government of the United States holds the power over these 50 subdivisions.

TERRITORIAL OWNERSHIP

Some states are extended through colonialism or other forces. Great Britain, Australia, Denmark, and many other countries possess territories all over the world. The United States owns many territories, including American Samoa, Guam, the U.S. Virgin Islands, and the commonwealth territory of Puerto Rico. Puerto Rico is the largest territory in the world in terms of population. Another commonwealth owned by the United States is the Northern Mariana Islands in the western Pacific Ocean.

A **commonwealth** is a territory that has established a mutual agreement with another state for the benefit of both parties. In return for land for use as a military base by the United States, the citizens of the Northern Mariana Islands and Puerto Rico gain full U.S. citizenship rights except for representation in Congress.

Territorial disputes occur throughout the world. Even when territories are small, they may be sought after vigorously for their economic benefits, their raw materials, or the added prestige that comes with owning a new territory. A **territorial dispute** is defined as a conflict that arises when two or more countries vie for control over a territory.

In 1982, Great Britain took military action against Argentina over a small group of islands off the Argentinian coast, the Falkland Islands, which have a population of only about 2,500. The people of the islands primarily make their living from sheep ranching and fishing. Great Britain had owned the islands for over a century. However, Argentina claimed they were the rightful owners and invaded the islands in 1982. The war lasted for about two months, and Great Britain was victorious. After the war, the citizens of the islands voted that they wanted Great Britain to establish sovereign control over the islands and have since voted for English to be their official language.

During World War II, Pacific islands such as Guam and American Samoa were strategic points for both the Japanese and American militaries, which fought for control of them.

NATIONS

A **nation** is a group of people with common cultural characteristics. They may be linked by ethnicity, language, or religion. In many instances, the concept of nationhood is changing the world political system as we know it. Many people are becoming more loyal to their nation than to their state. For example, in the "war on terror," the United States is fighting an enemy that has no borders but is linked by its hatred of the United States and its radical Islamic views. Many members of Al-Qaeda have left behind their loyalty to the states of which they are citizens, instead pledging their allegiance to that organization, forming a nation.

Usually, nations are located within the borders of a country. Different nations in the world include the Koreans, Hmong, Kurds, Basques, Flemish, Walloons, and Zulus, just to name a few.

Many of these nations would like their own state, and conflict can arise from the clashing of two nations within one state.

NATION-STATES

The **nation-state** occurs when the cultural borders of a nation correspond with the state borders of a country. Two good examples of nation-states are Japan and Denmark. However, there is no perfect example of a nation-state. In a perfect nation-state, every person in the country would have to be the same ethnicity, speak the same language, and practice the same religion.

Japan consists of approximately 128 million people. About 129 million people worldwide speak Japanese as their primary language and claim to be ethnic Japanese. Within Japan, 99.5 percent of the people are ethnic Japanese. The remaining 0.5 percent are either Ainu or Ryukyuans. Probably at least in part because of its monolithic culture, Japan is very nationalistic, and its culture encourages loyalty to the state at the expense of individual gain.

Denmark is a small Scandinavian country located just north of Germany and has a population of about 5 million. Also, 5 million people in the entire world speak Danish as their primary language. The majority of the people in Denmark are Danish and speak Danish. Outside of the borders of the Denmark state, only a small section of northern Germany (the Schleswig-Holstein region) speaks Danish. The educational system in Denmark has realized that for its citizens to compete in a global economy, they will need to learn other languages. Thus, students are encouraged to learn English, German, and one other language in addition to Danish. Upon graduation, many Danish students are fluent in four languages.

SOVEREIGNTY

States regulate their own internal and external affairs. This power is called **sovereignty**. Once a country has sovereignty, it can determine its own tax structure, laws, and political structure.

A country cannot obtain sovereignty simply by declaring it. Once foreign countries begin to recognize the country and treat it like a state, then it becomes a state. Participating in international organizations such as the United Nations also goes a long way in achieving recognition of statehood and sovereignty.

Technically, Native Americans possess their own sovereignty when they are on reservations. Several Supreme Court rulings have concluded that the Native Americans on the reservation can abide by their own laws and customs separate and apart from the laws of the federal government. Different Native American tribes, such as the Navajo and the Ojibwa, have created their own constitutions on their reservations and have tribal councils to determine laws and government rulings. Because they do not have to abide by the laws of the U.S. government, some tribes have established casino gambling on their reservations. Casino income has greatly benefited some tribes, giving them resources unthinkable 100 years ago.

Native Americans' quasi-sovereignty has led to disputes over jurisdiction, intervention, and rights. In Minnesota, the Mille Lacs band of Ojibwa fish in Lake Mille Lacs with spears for cultural and sustenance purposes. However, resort owners were concerned that the fishing was hurting their revenue from tourism and got the State of Minnesota to sue the Mille Lacs band for not abiding by the hunting and fishing regulations of the state. The case went before the Supreme Court, which ruled in favor of the Native Americans, saying that the original treaty gave them permission to fish on that particular portion of the lake.

Sometimes, sovereignty is questioned within a state. In April 1997, a group called the Republic of Texas held the U.S. government at bay for almost a week. The Republic of Texas claimed that it had sovereign control over the western areas of Texas and lands extending northwards into Colorado. The standoff led to the deaths of several members of the Republic of Texas and the imprisonment of their leader, Richard McLaren. Threats to the sovereignty of a country are taken very seriously because they are threats to the very nature of the state itself.

When a state government is strong, it can usually quell such uprisings. However, when a government is weak, perhaps because of instability or a corrupt regime, a coup d'état may occur. A **coup d'état** is when a particular group leads a revolt against the current ruling power. A member of the military usually leads the coup. Coups d'états have occurred in the Philippines and Mauritania. One of the most recent coups d'état occurred in Egypt in 2013 when the military overthrew the regime led by President Mohamed Morsi.

THE STRUGGLE FOR SOVEREIGNTY

Some nations without a state have vowed to fight (some peacefully, others physically) against their home countries until they can get sovereignty of their own. Many of these nations have fought wars to try to establish their own nation-states. Six nationalities deserve particular mention: the Kurds, Basque, Flemish, Zulu, Palestinians, and Hmong.

THE KURDS

The **Kurds** are one of the largest nationalities in the world without their own state. The Kurds number approximately 30 million people worldwide, with most located in Turkey, northern Iran, and northern Iraq along with significant pockets in Armenia and Azerbaijan. The majority of the Kurds speak their own language (Kurdish) and practice Islam. For the most part, the Kurds have been persecuted within the states where they reside. Kurds who aspire to a nation-state would like it to be called Kurdistan.

THE BASQUES

Another nation without its own state are the **Basques**, who are a fiercely independent group living in the Pyrenees Mountains. The majority of Basques live in Spain, but small numbers live in Andorra and southwestern France. Basque separatists have resorted to **terrorism**, violence against a specific society to achieve political goals, to try to gain independence; they call their proposed nation-state Euskal Herria. The Basques have their own language, Euskara.

THE FLEMISH

The Flemish people live in the north of Belgium. The official language of the Flemish people is Flemish (also called Common Dutch). The Flemish are distinct from the Walloons of Belgium, who primarily reside around Brussels and whose official language is French. Religion also distinguishes the Flemish people: About three-fourths of all Flemish classify themselves as Roman Catholic. This separates them from many other northern Europeans, who tend to be Protestant. Flemish separatists would like their country to be called Flanders. The historical Flanders incorporated most of Belgium as well as parts of the southern Netherlands and northern France.

THE ZULU

About 10 million Zulus live in eastern South Africa. Shaka Zulu, leader in the fight against British invaders, has gained a cult-like status. Historically, the Zulu were a dominant nation in southern Africa with their own proud legacy of empire and conquest.

During the time of **apartheid**, when a white minority ruled South Africa, the Zulus were forced to occupy a low status, suffering discrimination in education, employment, and all other aspects of life. The Zulus have maintained their language, isiZulu, derived from Bantu. Most Zulus today are Christians as a result of colonial-era missionaries, but some Zulus practice their traditional religion, a form of animism. Zulu separatists would like their homeland to named KwaNdebele.

THE PALESTINIANS

The Palestinian population is estimated at 9.5 million people. The majority of Palestinians live in the West Bank, Gaza Strip, and the Golan Heights sections of Israel. However, in 1948 with the creation of the state of Israel, many Palestinians fled to neighboring countries, including Jordan, Syria, and Lebanon. The majority of Palestinians practice Islam, although some are Christians. The large majority of Palestinians speak Arabic, though many also learn Hebrew. Likewise, while the official language of Israel is Hebrew, Jewish students are required to learn Arabic.

The Palestine Liberation Organization (PLO), a separatist group, has defined a "Palestinian" as any person who was living in Palestine prior to 1947. This definition includes the entire male lineage of those people, including the Jewish citizens who "lived peacefully and loyally in Palestine," according to the Palestinian constitution. If a Palestinian state was created to ease tensions in the region, the state would be called Palestine.

THE HMONG

The Hmong are an indigenous group originally hailing from Mongolia thousands of years ago. Over the centuries, they moved south into China, where they were thought to be "barbarians" and persecuted. Many Hmong were killed and much of the population driven into the highlands of Southeast Asia. However, there are still considerable numbers of Hmong in southern China today. Most native Hmong live in Laos as well as in refugee camps in Thailand.

The Hmong allied with the United States during the Vietnam War. When the United States left the region in the early 1970s, it left the Hmong to deal with vindictive political regimes in Laos and Vietnam. Many fled to Thailand, where the Thai government set up refugee camps. Several Christian groups in the United States decided to adopt Hmong families. These Hmong immigrants brought over their next of kin, and now large settlements of Hmong are located in California, Minnesota, Wisconsin, and North Carolina. Hmong are also located in parts of Australia and France.

The Hmong speak the language of Hmong, which has different dialects, typically distinguished by color names: white, green, blue, and striped Hmong are just a few of the different dialects. The Hmong have an oral tradition of passing down stories from generation to generation. They have only had a written language for the past 60 or so years. The Hmong in the United States are primarily Christian, but in Asia, they retain their animist traditions, with the shaman being the spiritual leader of the village.

BOUNDARIES

Boundaries are a human made invention to separate areas on the earth. Natural features can be used as a natural break, but boundaries come in many different shapes and forms. Boundaries are used to delineate ownership on the earth. These arbitrary lines can be used on different scales. Boundaries establish the shape of countries, provinces, cities, towns, and even plots in urban areas. On the micro level, lawns are mowed based on property lines, a form of boundary.

When we look at a map of the world, that map is likely a political map that details the boundaries of states. Political boundaries have been fought over throughout history. Governments tend to want more and more space for economic gain or to have greater cultural influence in the region. The three primary factors that determine boundaries are latitude and longitude features or straight lines (**geometric boundaries**); natural features (**physical boundaries**); and cultural factors such as language, religion, or ethnicity (**ethnographic** or **cultural boundaries**).

GEOMETRIC BOUNDARIES

Geometric boundaries are created by using lines of latitude and longitude. These straight lines are easy to spot, because they are usually the only straight lines on the map. Many of the state boundaries in the western United States, such as those of Colorado, Wyoming, and Utah, are geometric boundaries. Much of the boundary between the United States and Canada is drawn according to latitude; from the state of Washington to Lake Superior, the border follows the 49th parallel. The only exception is the Northwest Angle, a peninsula in the Lake of the Woods, which borders Minnesota, Manitoba, and Ontario. Residents who leave this area must either travel by water or by entering Canada.

The 49th parallel is a good example of an antecedent boundary. An **antecedent boundary** is one that existed before human settlement of the area; that is, settlement followed the boundary. People who wanted to live in the United States settled south of the parallel; people who wanted to be Canadian settled north of it.

Other areas of the world are drawn with geometric boundaries. Iraq's borders with Saudi Arabia were drawn using geometric boundaries. The line is diagonal, but straight geometric boundary principles were used when drawing it.

Using latitude and longitude to set up boundaries has advantages. The lines are easy to determine with a global positioning system (GPS). Without a GPS or another way to tell latitude and longitude, however, you wouldn't know that you had crossed a border unless a sign was posted.

PHYSICAL BOUNDARIES

Using physical features is an easy way to determine where one area stops and another begins. For example, on one side of the Rio Grande is the United States, and on the other side is Mexico. Physical features can include rivers, lakes, mountains, deserts, peninsulas, and so on.

Many of the boundaries of the eastern United States were drawn using the physical features approach. The Ohio and the Mississippi Rivers separate dozens of states along their paths across the North American continent.

The Andes Mountains, sometimes called "the spine of South America," are used to determine boundaries between Chile and Argentina and between Ecuador and Brazil. The Himalayas, the highest mountains in the world, separated India from the rest of the world for centuries, causing India to be called "the subcontinent."

Using physical features to establish boundaries has some disadvantages. For example, if a river determines a boundary, then any project involving the river, such as building a bridge over it, involves working with two different governments and requires a lot of communication and cooperation. Another disadvantage of using physical features to create boundaries is that they can move. Rivers, for example, can change course. The boundary between Mississippi and Louisiana has been altered because the Mississippi River constantly shifts.

ETHNOGRAPHIC OR CULTURAL BOUNDARIES

Using ethnographic or cultural features, such as language, religion, or ethnicity, to establish boundaries is probably the best method, but such boundaries can be the hardest to enforce or establish. Lines between cultures can be ambiguous and fluid.

THE CREATION OF BOUNDARIES

Creating boundaries can resolve tensions—or incite hostilities. There are four main types of boundary origins that a geographer classifies on the landscape: antecedent boundaries, subsequent boundaries, superimposed boundaries, and relic boundaries.

ANTECEDENT BOUNDARIES

As previously mentioned, **antecedent boundaries** exist before the human settlement of an area.

SUBSEQUENT BOUNDARIES

Subsequent boundaries develop along with the development of the cultural landscape. A good example of a subsequent boundary is the border between Northern Ireland and Ireland. As the cultural landscape developed, the border was drawn to accommodate religious, cultural, and economic differences. Another example of a subsequent boundary is the boundary between China and Vietnam. This boundary has been in dispute on many occasions.

SUPERIMPOSED BOUNDARIES

A **superimposed boundary** is a political boundary that ignores the existing cultural organization on the landscape. It is usually placed by a higher authority, such as a superpower or a delegation of superpowers, to satisfy that authority's needs rather than the needs of the area. The boundary between North Korea and South Korea is a superimposed boundary. A demilitarized zone was placed along the 38th parallel to resolve conflict between the communists to the north and U.S. forces in the south. The irony is that the demilitarized zone is one of the most militarized zones in all of the world.

In 1884, 14 European countries that wanted to divide the continent of Africa into countries attended the **Conference of Berlin**. France, Great Britain, Portugal, and Germany were the major participants. Instead of drawing borders according to the different ethnicities in Africa, they superimposed boundaries that didn't fit the cultural boundaries. Ethnic groups that had been in conflict for centuries were now supposed to live together under the umbrella of one state. The result of the conference was a mishmash of countries that was doomed from the start.

RELIC BOUNDARIES

A **relic boundary** is, just as the term implies, a relic on the landscape. The boundary does not exist any longer, but its impact is still felt and seen on the landscape. The old boundary between East Germany and West Germany is a good example of a relic boundary. Economic development in West Germany was far greater than in East Germany. Upon **reunification** (the reuniting of two areas once apart as one state) of Germany in the early 1990s, the difference between the communist east and the capitalist west showed clearly on the landscape. For example, East Germans had built utilitarian concrete apartments, whereas West German residences were built to satisfy consumers' varied demands for attractive housing.

The actual process of drawing a boundary involves representatives of a minimum of two countries. Envoys or ambassadors of the two countries will usually meet in a neutral city to discuss the terms of the agreement. When the boundary is in dispute, a mediator from another country may be used to assist in determining where it should be located.

Boundary evolution is the technical wording of a treaty that legally defines where a boundary should be located. Once the boundary evolution becomes part of the official document, cartographers must accurately represent it. This transition or translation of the boundary evolution is called **delimitation**. After the process of delimitation has been established, the two countries place objects on the landscape, such as border crossings, fences, walls, and so on, that show where the boundary is located. This process of physically representing a boundary on the landscape is known as **demarcation**. The demarcation zone can be a tense area, where the hostilities of two countries come to a head. This entire process creates the **border landscape** of an area.

COLD WAR BOUNDARIES

The Cold War had a profound effect on the boundaries of Europe from the post-World War II era until the early 1990's. The Warsaw Pact countries were essentially puppet states of the former Soviet Union. These states were countered by a supranational organization known as the North Atlantic Treaty Organization (NATO). The borders between the these two halves of Europe were evident to the extreme in Berlin, where the Berlin Wall separated the Western section from the Soviet controlled section of the city.

BOUNDARY DISPUTES

Areas such as Rwanda, Uganda, and Sudan have experienced some of the greatest mass atrocities and refugee movements the world has ever seen. Millions of people have died as the result of violence arising from the inappropriate boundaries created at the Conference of Berlin. Ethnic conflicts involving the Hutus and Tutsis have created one of the largest refugee movements in the last 30 years. **Ethnic conflicts** are disagreements that usually result in military action or violence of one ethnic group against another. **Religious conflicts**, on the other hand, involve violence between members of different religious groups. This is currently occurring in Iraq between Sunni and Shiite Muslims. Also, violence has erupted from time to time in India and Pakistan as Hindus and Muslims have disagreed over where the boundary should be between the two countries, specifically in the Kashmir region.

The British established the boundaries between India and Pakistan, between Uganda and Rwanda in large part, around much of Yugoslavia, and between Israel and the neighboring Arab states. All of these areas have seen major political and military conflict in the past half-century.

In Yugoslavia, balkanization occurred. **Balkanization** is the breakup of an area into smaller independent units and usually involves some degree of hostility. After World War II, Yugoslavia was controlled by a dictator named Josip Broz Tito. When Tito died in the 1980s, the country began to unravel, and a civil war ended with the breakup of Yugoslavia into six different countries: Bosnia/Herzegovina, Macedonia, Serbia, Montenegro, Croatia, and Slovenia. A United Nations peacekeeping force led by the United States entered the area in the 1990s to end atrocities perpetrated by Serbian forces under leader Slobodan Miloŝević. Troops are still in the area—all because of poorly drawn boundaries over 50 years ago.

The opposite of balkanization is **annexation**, adding territory to an already existing state. For instance, when the United States purchased the Alaska territory from Russia in 1867, it annexed the land as a territory, even though Alaska didn't officially become a part of the United States until 1948.

Another boundary issue that many countries face today concerns the question of who owns what territories. Many of these cases, some of them involving the United States and Canada, are currently disputed around the globe. One example is the case of the Senkaku Islands/Diaoyudao Islands/Diaoyutai Islands located in the East China Sea. Japan, China and Taiwan all claim ownership to the small islands located several hundred miles southeast of Wenzhou, China and northeast of Taipei, Taiwan. Japan claims the islands are part of the same archipelago that includes Japanese territories such as Okinawa and Naha.

Another dispute involves the Dokdo/Takeshima Islands located in the East Sea/Sea of Japan. The small rocky outcrop is claimed by both South Korea and Japan. The islands occupy an important location for possible natural resource rights as well as fishing rights in the sea. Historical claims on the islands by both countries go back hundreds of years. The issue has become one of fierce national pride in South Korea where athletes have demonstrated at sporting events for control of the Dokdo Islands.

There are four types of boundary disputes: Definitional boundary disputes, locational boundary disputes, operational boundary disputes, and allocational boundary disputes.

DEFINITIONAL BOUNDARY DISPUTES

Definitional boundary disputes arise from the legal language of the treaty's definition of the boundary. One of the countries involved will usually sue another country in the International Court of Justice (the World Court), which will try to determine what was intended when the boundaries were initially described.

LOCATIONAL BOUNDARY DISPUTES

Locational boundary disputes arise when the definition of the border (e.g., "the Mississippi River") is not questioned but the interpretation of the border is. In these cases, the border has shifted, and the original intention of the boundary is called into question. Areas once in the state of Mississippi have found themselves in the state of Louisiana when the river shifted its course.

OPERATIONAL BOUNDARY DISPUTES

Operational boundary disputes occur when two countries next to each other disagree on a major issue involving the border. For example, the United States and Mexico disagree over the issue of illegal immigration into the United States. Both sides agree where the border is but cannot agree on how to handle border crossing.

ALLOCATIONAL BOUNDARY DISPUTES

Like operational boundary disputes, **allocational boundary disputes** do not question the boundary itself but rather the use of it. Allocational boundary disputes usually involve some type of natural resource, often in the open ocean and/or under the ground. For example, when an aquifer extends across a boundary, who has dominant rights to the water? Or who has the right to drill for oil out at sea?

The United Nations held a conference in 1958 to try to establish **UNCLOS**, which stands for the United Nations Convention on the Law of the Sea. When finally adopted as international law in 1983, the **International Law of the Sea** held two important points: Foreign countries could not have their military or other ships travel within 12 miles of the coast of any other country, and countries have **exclusive economic zones** (EEZs). EEZs mean that countries have the right to explore for resources up to 200 miles off their shores. For example, the United States can drill for oil and natural gas in the Gulf of Mexico out to 200 miles.

The International Law of the Sea doesn't always work. Sometimes the 200-mile barriers conflict with other countries. In these cases, sometimes the **median-line principle** is used. A line is drawn in the water equidistant from each competing party. However, the median-line principle does not necessarily give all parties equal access to the resources. In the Caspian Sea, Iran is contesting the median-line principle, because other countries, such as Turkmenistan, Azerbaijan, and Kazakhstan, would receive a greater percentage of the resources than Iran.

In some areas, called **global commons**, countries do not have the right to search for natural resources. One of the largest global commons areas is Antarctica (shown in Figure 6.1). No country may exploit Antarctica for natural resources, although several countries have claimed land on the continent. Australia claims the largest percentage of land, followed by Norway, France, Chile, Argentina, and the United Kingdom. However, it has been globally accepted that the land in Antarctica will be used solely for scientific research and not for military uses or resource exploration. Boundary disputes persist between the United Kingdom, Argentina, and Chile, which explains the overlap in Figure 6.1.

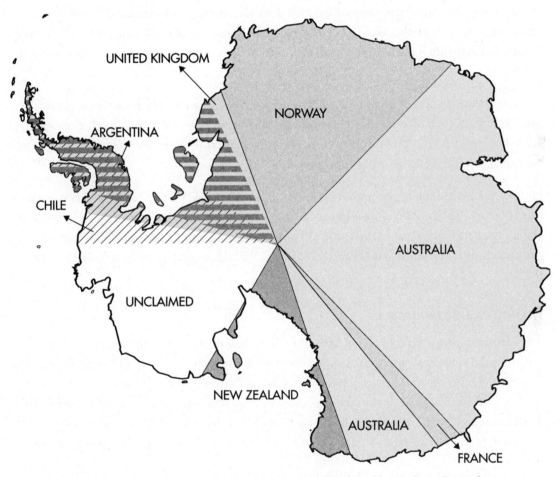

Figure 6.1: Map of Antarctica, Divided by Land Claimed by Various Countries.

COLONIALISM AND IMPERIALISM

GEOGRAPHIC COLONIALISM

Very few concepts have had as profound an impact on the world, as we know it, as colonialism. **Colonialism** is the practice of establishing political dominance over a people for economic, political, and territorial gain. **Imperialism** on the other hand is establishing control over an area that is already politically organized. There is a fine line between the two terms and sometimes controversy as to which definition applies for a given historical situation. It is widely accepted in most circles that Europeans colonized the Western Hemisphere and imperialized Africa. Colonialism began with the Ancient Greeks and their exploration of the Mediterranean Sea. Today, the era of colonialism has ended politically for the most part, but the issue of economic colonialism is still alive and well.

The political geographer Friedrich Ratzel, who coined the term *geopolitics*, based his **organic theory** on the growth of states. Ratzel argued that the state was like a living entity that constantly needed to grow to thrive. According to Ratzel's theory, states constantly need new territory to meet the demands of their ever-growing populations.

Europeans have had the largest impact on the world as colonizers. Europe colonized for four major reasons: to spread Christianity, to gain natural resources, for the prestige of owning more property, and for the benefits that more land could offer. James Rubenstein pointed out "God, gold, and glory" as the three reasons for European colonialism. We add geography, or land itself, to those reasons.

RELIGIOUS COLONIALISM

A fundamental tenet of the Christian faith is that one should seek to save the unsaved. All of the European colonizers participated in some form of conversion. The Spanish largely forced Christianity upon the indigenous peoples of South and Central America; if they did not convert, they were killed. The Spanish also set up missions in what is now the southwestern United States. The French and English set up missions in the New World, many of which still exist today. Montréal was first established as a mission and trading post on the St. Lawrence Seaway by the French.

Religion was also a push factor for persecuted religious minorities who emigrated to establish colonies. The Pilgrims came to the New World in hopes of religious freedom.

THE SEARCH FOR WEALTH IN THE NEW WORLD

Another reason for the spread of colonialism was the quest for wealth. Spanish explorers were always looking for the instant wealth that gold could bring. The myth of El Dorado, a city where the streets were made of gold, persisted up until the 19th century.

The French sought furs from the beaver and other animals to produce hats and coats that were adored by the upper classes in France. A fur hat cost the yearly wage of an average worker in Paris during the 17th and 18th centuries. The fur trade is memorialized by the Grand Portage National Monument in Minnesota. The **voyageurs** were the traders who went deep into the wilderness to trap the animals and bring back the furs in dugout canoes. The French established working relationships with the Native Americans along the borders of the present-day United States and Canada. These relationships were invaluable for trade and survival in the wilderness.

Colonies were expected to provide resources that the home country needed to sustain itself. For many years, the Spanish brought back ships filled with gold and jewels. The Spanish used this money to build vast castles and palaces. The British used its resources to modernize their military. Countries as small as Denmark and the Netherlands played an important role in the colonization of the Western Hemisphere and Africa. Denmark controlled Greenland and the Faroe Islands. The Netherlands was an important player in East Asia. The Dutch coveted the valuable spice trade in the East Indies. The cities of the Netherlands were some of the wealthiest in the world because of the spice trade. Until the mid-20th century, Indonesia was called Dutch Indonesia. (In 1650, Britain traded a small island in Asia called East Timor for a small island in the New World called Manhattan.)

Salt was another valuable commodity during the colonial times because it preserved food before refrigeration had been invented. Much of the salt that Europe used came from trade with Asia.

THE GLORY OF COLONIALISM

It was important for the prestige of the kings and queens of Europe to have colonies around the world. The saying "the sun never sets on the British Empire" was coined because the sun was always shining in a territory that the British owned somewhere in the world. Britain held the east coast of what is now the United States until the Revolutionary War in 1776, South Africa until the early 19th century, India until the mid-19th century, and Hong Kong until 1997. Canada and various points in Africa, including the Straits of Gibraltar and the areas around the present-day Suez Canal, were also under British control. The British also controlled all of Australia, which was originally established as a penal colony for offenders in Great Britain. New Zealand, Pakistan, Bangladesh, Egypt, Sudan, as well as ports in the Middle East, were all under the control of the British protectorate. The British provided them with military protection, and in return, the colonies provided Great Britain with valuable resources for its industrial base.

One of the most widely known stories of British colonialism is the story of the independence of India. Mahatma Gandhi started his independence movement through nonviolent protests. By controlling the salt trade and cotton manufacturing, rebel forces crippled British control in the region. The British were not able to control the combined countries of Pakistan, Bangladesh, and India and were forced to leave. A border clash soon followed between India and Pakistan.

Pakistan was separated into East Pakistan, later Bangladesh, and West Pakistan, which later became Pakistan.

SELF-DETERMINATION

Self-determination is the power of a people to establish their own government the way that they see fit. Many former colonies would rather see chaotic conditions ruled over by members of their own country than peaceful conditions ruled by a colonial power.

Many peoples want the right to **suffrage**, or the power to vote on issues regarding their welfare, as when American colonists spoke out against "taxation without representation."

To this day, in some countries men have the right to vote, but women do not. Even in the United States, **women's enfranchisement** (the right of women to vote) didn't come until 1920 with the passing of the 19th amendment to the U.S. Constitution.

PATTERNS AND IMPACTS OF COLONIALISM AND IMPERIALISM

When the British defeated the French in the French-Indian War, the French were forced to retreat to the Québec region. French is still spoken in Québec today. The Acadians migrated from the French-speaking regions of Canada to the southern Louisiana region, beginning the Cajun culture. The French dominated some islands in the Caribbean as well as French Guiana in South America. The French were integral players in Southeast Asia. A few elderly people in Vietnam today can still speak French as a result of the French control of Indochina.

The Spanish controlled the majority of the land to the south of the United States. This area extends through Central America down the west coast of South America.

Portugal controlled present-day Brazil. Because Spain and Portugal, two countries on the Iberian Peninsula, were both Roman Catholic countries, they decided to let the Pope make the call as to the ownership of the South American continent. The Pope declared that anything to the east of the 70th degree west longitude would be controlled by Portugal and any land to the west of the 70th degree west longitude would belong to Spain. Today, countries such as Colombia, Venezuela, Chile, and Ecuador all speak Spanish as their primary language. Brazil, the crown of the Portuguese empire, speaks Portuguese. Spain also controlled the Philippines for many years. The architecture and family surnames are Spanish in many areas of the country.

Denmark owned Greenland and still does to this day. However, Denmark has given Greenland more autonomy in making decisions concerning its own welfare.

The Netherlands owned Suriname, which still has Dutch as its official language. The Netherlands also owns several islands in the Caribbean, such as Aruba. The Netherlands owned the Netherland Indies until 1945, when the country of Indonesia became independent.

Belgium colonized much of central Africa, establishing the Belgian Congo. The Belgians were known for their ruthless King Leopold III, who more than half the native population in the Congo. World opinion quickly went against the king, and he gave control over the area to the Belgian parliament, which ruled it more benignly until the Congo gained its independence in 1960.

Italy took over sections of northeastern Africa. Italian East Africa, including present-day Ethiopia and part of Somalia, only existed from 1936 to 1941. Although the Italians use the word *colonized*, many consider their presence a brief occupation. In fact, the Ethiopians claim to be the only African nation not colonized by European forces. After World War II, the Allied powers established an ineffective boundary between Somalia and Ethiopia. Tension still exists today as both countries have mounted attacks on the other.

FACTORS OF SUCCESSFUL COLONIALISM AND IMPERIALISM

So why were some areas colonized while others were colonizers?

The Europeans, for the most part, had more advanced military technology—including horses, armor, and large, fast ships with cannons—than the people whom they conquered.

Another important factor was the impact of disease on native populations. Native populations had never been exposed to diseases that were common in Europe. Influenza, the plague, and even the common cold had devastating impacts on Native American populations. The natives had no immunity to the new diseases, and widespread contagious diffusion of these diseases wiped out as much as 95 percent of some tribes.

The lack of immunity proved a vital advantage for the Europeans in their control of the new territory. Supply lines would have been tested had they needed to reinforce armies.

European colonizers also established their dominance in the New World because of their strong industrial base, which allowed the production of military equipment, and their supply lines, which allowed constant refreshment of materials.

DEMOCRATIZATION

Democratization is the transition of an authoritarian regime (dictatorship) to a representative form of government. This has taken place in three different waves. The first wave of democratization took place in the 19th century in North America and Western Europe. The second wave occurred immediately after World War II when many former colonies gained independence. We are still experiencing the third wave of democratization, which started in 1974. There is a great deal of debate regarding the conditions that must be present for democratization to take hold and then ultimately become successful. Most importantly, some factors that are covered in the AP Human Geography course that are crucial for democratization include a country's level of wealth, educational system, reliance on one or a few natural resources, social equality, ethnic composition, culture, and age distribution. For instance, democratization is more likely to work if the country in question has a relatively high income, strong educational system, mobility between social classes, homogeneous population, long cultural history, and a stable older population. On the other hand, democratization will have little chance of success if the country relies on one or a few natural resources for its wealth. This is because the power elites are likely to be more concerned about controlling the resource(s) than gaining popular support. Lastly, a country with a classic population pyramid age distribution will have difficulty transitioning to democracy because of the overwhelming need to expand the economy and provide education and health care to a fast-growing population. Some experts speculate that globalization and the Internet will usher in a new era of democratization throughout the world. They believe that authoritarian regimes will find it more difficult to operate in a transparent and instant media environment.

THE FIVE SHAPES OF COUNTRIES

Countries come in different sizes and shapes. The bigger the country, the more potential resources the country possesses and the greater its industrial base. The downside for a large country is its difficulty in defending its borders. Larger countries generally, but not always, need a greater military. Conversely, small states usually have a relative lack of resources but also less area to defend. The smallest states are called **microstates** or **ministates**. Microstates are states that are small in area and population. City-states are microstates.

Countries take on five main shapes. A country can exhibit characteristics of one or more of these shapes. Sometimes these shapes are called **territorial morphology**. The five main shapes of countries are compact, elongated, fragmented, prorupted, and perforated. Figure 6.2 shows these shapes.

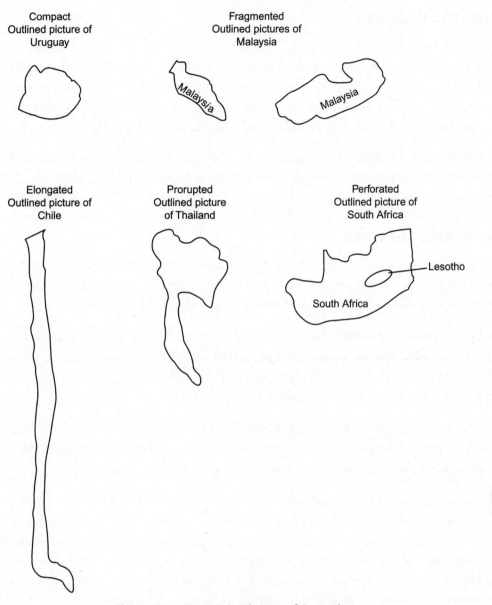

Figure 6.2: Five Main Shapes of Countries.

COMPACT COUNTRIES

The borders of a **compact country** are approximately equidistant from the center of the country. The country may be in the shape of a circle or a square. Uruguay in South America is a good example of a compact country, as is Poland in Europe.

Communications and transportation are relatively easy in a compact country, as is the mobilization of the military. A disadvantage for a compact country is a lack of resources, because compact countries tend to be rather small.

ELONGATED COUNTRIES

Elongated countries are at least twice as long as they are wide: they are long and skinny. There are many examples of elongated countries around the world, including Nepal, Italy, Gambia, and Chile. Chile stretches nearly 3,000 miles along the Pacific coast of South America while being only an average of 90 miles wide. Another example of an elongated country is Panama, which runs east/west across Central America. The Panama Canal primarily runs north and south.

Transporting raw materials to industrial centers can be relatively easy in an elongated state because it is so narrow. However, those living in the ends of the country can feel isolated, which can lead to separatist movements.

FRAGMENTED COUNTRIES

A **fragmented** country is in pieces that are not attached to each other. Fragmented countries are usually islands. The country that exhibits the most fragmentation is Indonesia. Indonesia comprises more than 13,000 islands that span a distance of over 3,000 miles.

When the United States added Alaska and Hawaii in 1959, it became a fragmented country. Alaska is an example of an **exclave**, an area separated from its state by another state. Canada separates Alaska from the United States. Kaliningrad is another example of an exclave. Lithuania, Latvia, and Belarus separate Kaliningrad from its home country of Russia.

Pakistan was a fragmented country after splitting from India, when it was two separate areas, East Pakistan and West Pakistan. East Pakistan eventually became the independent country of Bangladesh, whereas West Pakistan became simply Pakistan.

The advantage of being fragmented is that another country would have a hard time trying to occupy and control your country. For example, invading Indonesia would involve invading thousands of separate islands. However, communications and the transportation between the separated areas can be cumbersome, especially if another country is in the way. Relations between the United States and Canada are peaceful, so ties to Alaska are easy for the mainland to maintain. Other countries struggle to maintain the unity of the state.

PERFORATED COUNTRIES

A **perforated** country has an entire state completely inside of its borders. There are only two perforated states in the world: South Africa and Italy. South Africa contains the country of Lesotho completely inside of its borders. (The perforated country is South Africa, not Lesotho. Lesotho is an enclave.) Italy contains two countries completely inside of its borders, San Marino and the Vatican City.

A country that is inside another country is known as an enclave. An **enclave** is a country that is completely surrounded by another political state. Enclaves are always **landlocked countries** with no access to the sea. (Enclaves are always landlocked countries, but landlocked countries are not necessarily enclaves.) Any exports from an enclave must go through another country.

Landlocked countries are at a distinct political and economic disadvantage. Relations with neighboring countries must always be on good terms for fear of having access to oceanic trade cut off. Also, tariffs are usually associated with shipping products through another country, increasing the cost of the product and reducing its attractiveness in the world market.

Africa has the largest number of landlocked countries of any continent. Niger and Chad are landlocked countries in the middle of the Sahara desert. Lacking good agricultural land and lacking ports, these two countries are two of the economically poorest in the world. South America has two landlocked countries. Paraguay and Bolivia are dependent upon Peru, Chile, Argentina, and Brazil for access to the ocean. Also, Uzbekistan, Kyrgyzstan, Tajikistan, and Afghanistan in Central Asia are landlocked. Eastern Europe also possesses a large number of landlocked countries. These are some of the economically poorest countries in the region.

The advantage to having a country completely within your borders is that the ethnic group of the enclave has its own state. Usually, the enclave is ethnically different from the perforated country. If those people were part of the perforated country, there might be tension.

The disadvantage of having a country completely within your borders is that it may get in the way of transportation and communication. The shortest, least expensive route may run through the enclave country. Telephone lines, railroad tracks, and highways are all negatively impacted by having a country within your borders.

PRORUPTED COUNTRIES

A **prorupted** country has a protrusion extending out from its main base. Proruptions were often drawn by colonizers to ensure their access to raw materials or water transport.

One of the largest proruptions is in Namibia; the Caprivi Strip was created by the Germans to gain control of the Zambezi River. Two other countries with large proruptions are Thailand and Burma. These extensions go for hundreds of miles to the south along the Malay Peninsula. India has a proruption extending all the way around Bangladesh. The Baja region of Mexico is a proruption from the mainland of Mexico. Florida is a proruption from the United States. The Belgians separated Cabinda from the rest of Angola by extending the Congo borders to the Atlantic Ocean. The term *panhandle* designates a type of proruption.

One advantage of having a proruption is that it usually provides the country with access to a useful raw material. It may also provide trade opportunities. Having control of a river provides the opportunity to charge a tax, or tariff, on all goods passing through.

The disadvantage is that the proruptions are usually fiercely fought over. Proruptions are usually the doings of colonial powers and, therefore, hard to justify. Despite having stationed troops there for decades, Namibia continues to experience strife in the Caprivi Strip.

THE POLITICAL ORGANIZATION OF SPACE

Humans use space in different ways and have different methods of governing that space. These differences can cause harmony or dissention within and between countries. Governments usually create organizations to assist with their interactions with other countries. In the United States, the Department of State runs offices, called **embassies**, in most countries around the world. The embassies' job is to represent U.S. interests to the leadership of other countries. The lead officials representing the United States in other countries are called **ambassadors**. Embassies are usually located in the capital of a country. The Department of State also runs **consulates**, secondary offices that usually deal with economic issues as well as the granting of visas to enter their home countries. Consulates are usually located in large regional cities.

Other countries have embassies in Washington, D.C. Only the U.S. federal government has the right to establish U.S. embassies or consulates in other countries. The **federal government** is the central government of the United States. The U.S. federal government is based in the capital city of Washington, D.C. Individual states in the U.S. also have governments, called **state governments**. They may try to develop more trade opportunities for their particular state but do not have the authority to authorize treaties with foreign countries.

Many things lead to disagreements; disagreements can lead to military confrontation. Different organizations have been set up around the world to ease tensions between different states. The United Nations, the North Atlantic Treaty Organization (NATO), the Southeast Asian Treaty Organization (SEATO), and the Central Treaty Organization (CENTO) are just some of the international organizations that try to diffuse tensions around the globe. Some are more successful than others.

During the Cold War, world politics were dominated by two superpowers: the United States and the Soviet Union. American foreign policy was dominated by attempts to reduce the spread of communism and spread democracy. The U.S. fought wars in Korea and Vietnam and aided troops in Central America and Central Asia to oppose communism. Large military bases were established around the world, including in Korea, Taiwan, the Philippines, Turkey, Germany, and Iceland. When the Soviet Union started building missile bases on Cuba in 1962, sparking the Cuban missile crisis, the world came close to a nuclear war. Ultimately, the missile bases were removed.

The United States helped create the North Atlantic Treaty Organization (NATO) to enlist the assistance of other countries in opposing the Warsaw Pact, a bloc of Eastern European countries funded by the Soviet Union. Those countries that were **satellite states** of the Soviet Union and were under the control of that superpower created a cultural wall called the Iron Curtain. The **Iron Curtain** divided democratic, capitalist Western Europe from totalitarian, communist Eastern Europe. Figure 6.3 shows Europe during the Cold War.

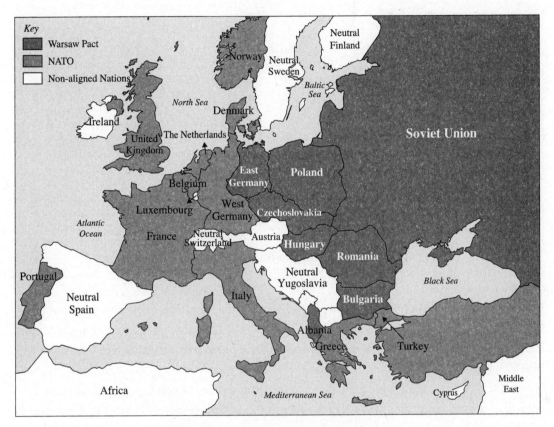

Figure 6.3: Europe During the Cold War.

For many years, the two superpowers battled indirectly by using other countries as pawns. Regions caught up in a conflict between two superpowers are called **shatterbelt regions**. Their boundaries are often changed as a result of the conflict. East Asia was a shatterbelt region during the Korean and Vietnam wars. The Middle East was a shatterbelt region as the superpowers vied for access to petroleum. During the 1980s, the shatterbelt region was in Central America with conflicts in Nicaragua and El Salvador. The United States gave resources and military equipment to the Contras, who were fighting against communism in the region. Many shatterbelt regions are areas that were politically and culturally splintered for most of their history. They are also often geographically splintered as well since many exist in mountainous regions. As this terrain is less easily accessed, these regions are difficult for government forces to control. Figure 6.4 shows the world's shatterbelts.

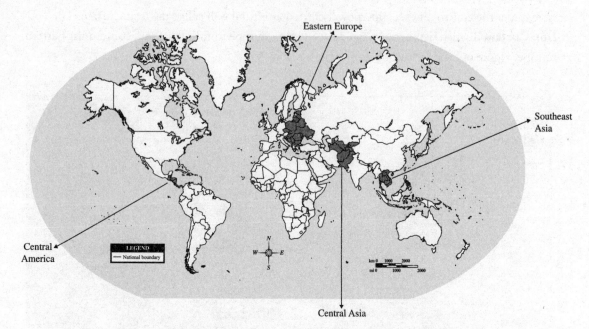

Figure 6.4: Shatterbelts around the World during the Cold War Era.

A **buffer state** is a country that lies between two other states but remains neutral in the conflict between them. One of the largest buffer states is Mongolia. Even though the former Soviet Union and China were both communist, their political philosophies were vastly different. Chairman Mao Zedong was much more idealistic than the leaders at the Kremlin in Moscow. Tensions rose between the two states, and Mongolia was caught in the middle. Armies are still placed on the borders of the two countries that abut each other in the western sections of China as well as the area around Manchuria in northeastern China.

THE HEARTLAND THEORY

In 1904, Sir Halford MacKinder, a British political geographer, wrote a thesis and presented it before the Royal Geographical Society in London. In his article titled "The Geographical Pivot of History," he outlined his heartland theory.

The **heartland theory** suggests that whoever owns Eastern Europe and Western Asia has the political power and capital to rule the world. Eastern Europe contained one of the richest agricultural regions in the world. The Ukraine region could produce enough wheat and other agricultural products to sustain a large population—and feed its armies. Also, abundant raw materials such as coal, essential to develop a military and industrial base, are available in this region.

Adolf Hitler believed in the heartland theory, which is why he invaded Eastern Europe. Hitler underestimated the Soviet citizens' resolve and the severity of the Russian winter and eventually had to retreat ignominiously. The Soviet Union lost 16 million citizens during World War II.

After World War II, the Soviet Union exerted control over Eastern Europe, greatly concerning Western Europe, the United States, and other noncommunist countries.

Prior to World War II, Eastern Europe was not as technologically advanced as Western Europe. However, after World War II, the Soviet Union began updating its technology base, posing a serious threat.

THE RIMLAND THEORY

Nicholas Spykman, another political geographer, used MacKinder's ideas when he wrote his own theory on world domination and politics. Spykman was originally from the Netherlands and came to the United States to teach at Yale University. He originated the rimland theory of containment and is known as the "godfather of containment."

The **rimland theory** believes that forming alliances is necessary to keep the Heartland in check. Because the heartland is so powerful, no individual country can contain it by itself. Hence the establishment of the North Atlantic Treaty Organization (NATO), the Southeast Asian Treaty Organization (SEATO), and the Central Treaty Organization (CENTO) in response to the spread of the communism around the world.

Spykman believed that the heartland may control the land but the rimland will control the sea. The heartland is trapped in a sense by its own geography. To the north of the heartland is an ocean that is icebound much of the year. To the east are the Ural Mountains and vast tracts of land with sparse populations. To the south is the Middle East with its immense deserts. The rimland would use the oceans to contain the heartland, engaging in a battle between land and sea.

Figure 6.5 shows the heartland and the rimland.

THE DOMINO THEORY

The **domino theory** was adopted by the United States in the 1960s and 1970s. The Central Intelligence Agency (CIA) developed this theory, which suggested that when one country experiences rebellion or political disunity, other countries around it will also experience turmoil as a result, leading to a domino effect of political instability in the region. Dwight D. Eisenhower first used the term *dominos* in the sense when he made a speech suggesting that the countries involved in a conflict would fall over like dominos.

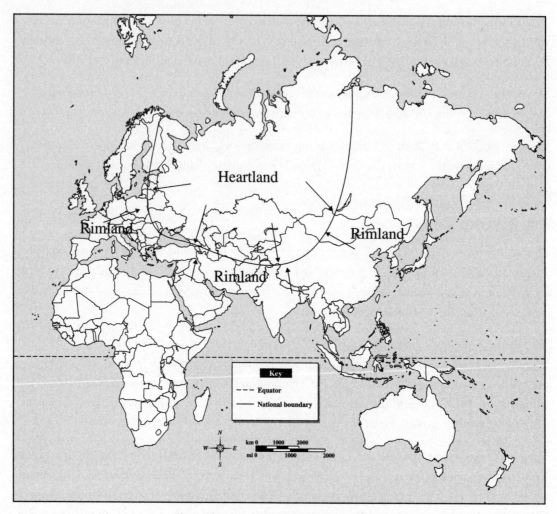

Figure 6.5: Heartland/Rimland Map.

The domino theory was established in response to the communist incursions that had been occurring around the world. It justified U.S. military involvement in Southeast Asia during the 1960s and 1970s and in Central America during the 1980s.

Opponents of the domino theory point to the political stability of the United States despite political instability in Mexico as an example of its invalidity. Proponents of the theory suggest that a lack of border security is causing political instability in the United States.

IRREDENTISM

Much of U.S. foreign policy has been aimed at irredentism. **Irredentism** is the attempt by one country to provoke coups or separatist movements in another country. For example, country A tries to spark a separatist movement from a nationality within country B. This can be done through literature, radio programs, or television ads.

The United States practices irredentism when it sends radio transmissions into another country to communicate the benefits of capitalism and democracy and relay truthful news about world events. The United States has sent transmissions from Florida into Cuba. The United States also sent radio transmissions into Eastern Europe during the Iron Curtain era. Often, the United States hopes that resistance movements will rise up, eventually overthrowing a leader unfriendly to the United States.

CENTRIPETAL AND CENTRIFUGAL FORCES

Forces that break up a state are called **centrifugal forces**. In contrast, forces that tend to unite a state are called **centripetal forces**. Centrifugal forces include anything that causes tension within the borders of a country. This could be religious, linguistic, or ethnic diversity. **Nationalism** focuses on a people's religion, language, or ethnicity rather than the state, potentially leading to the breakup of the state.

In the former country of Yugoslavia, ethnic and religious differences were so strong that the federal government of Yugoslavia could no longer control the different factions. The dissolution of Yugoslavia was inevitable after the federal government lost its authority.

The Soviet Union experienced strong centrifugal forces as well. Trying to rule a country as large and as diverse as the former Soviet Union was a difficult task. A poor economy contributed to the breakup of the Soviet Union. Shelves in grocery stores were empty or bare, causing unrest. As a result, Soviet leader Mikhail Gorbachev started *perestroika*, the restructuring of the economy.

Devolution is the giving up of power by the central or federal government to the different regions of the country. Latvia, Lithuania, Estonia, Belarus, and Ukraine in the west formed their own countries based on their different ethnicities and languages. In the Central Asian region, Kazakhstan, Uzbekistan, Kyrgyzstan, Turkmenistan, and Tajikistan seceded. The states around the Caspian Sea—Georgia, Armenia, and Azerbaijan—also broke off. The Russian state, under the leadership of Vladimir Putin and Dmitri Medvedev, has squelched further secession attempts.

Russia is still the largest country in the world and possesses vast natural resources and, recently, a growing economy. In the 1990s, however, the economy of Russia was in peril. The black market thrived, and the Russian federal government had very little control over pricing structures. Putin's leadership restabilized the country but at the expense of personal and political freedom, causing consternation among NATO countries, which fear another cold war.

Regionalism, the breaking up of an area into autonomous regions, has caused problems for some former Soviet states. Starting up a country is a big undertaking. Drawing up of a constitution, for example, can take several years. In the meantime, the country's economic structure must remain strong for the government to seem viable in the eyes of its citizens.

Centripetal forces might be symbolized through art, such as a flag or a painting. These symbols of nationalism are sometimes called **national iconography**. For most, their country's flag inspires patriotism, as does the national anthem. During the Olympics, national iconographies are very evident. Many people place a priority on the creation and protection of their state and are willing to die for independence. The Basques in Spain, in the name of independence, have felt justified in killing civilians through terrorism.

A religious or linguistic factor may be both a centrifugal and a centripetal factor at the same time. In countries that are **theocracies**, where one particular religion is intertwined with the political structure, religion is a unifying force. Many of the laws of the country are based on the principles of the official religion. Theocracies are common in the Muslim world. Countries like Saudi Arabia, Iran, and Afghanistan have many social laws that are based on Islam. The Vatican City is a Christian theocracy.

In recent years, the world has seen a rise in **supranationalism**, a method of extending state borders through the assistance and/or establishment of other organizations to further economic and/or political cooperation. One of the greatest examples of a supranational organization is the European Union (EU). Figure 6.6 lists the members of the European Union.

Austria	Germany	Poland
Belgium	Greece	Portugal
Bulgaria	Hungary	Romania
Croatia	Ireland	Slovaki
Cyprus	Italy	Slovenia
Czech Republic	Latvia	Spain
Denmark*	Lithuania	Sweden
Estonia	Luxembourg	United Kingdom*
Finland	Malta	
France	Netherlands	

* Even though the United Kingdom and Denmark have joined the EU, they are not bound by the currency of the euro. The UK has decided to stay with the pound and Denmark is staying with the krone. However, the uniting of the European countries has created a political and economic force to be reckoned with.

Figure 6.6: List of the European Union Countries.

Beginning as the European Economic Community (EEC) in 1957, the EU is 27 European states united into one organized unit for the purpose of increasing individual strength through collective effort. The European Union's headquarters is located in Brussels, Belgium. By converting most

European currencies to the euro, member countries have enjoyed a stronger position in international trade, and today the euro has surpassed the value of the United States dollar. Traveling in Europe used to mean exchanging currencies at every border. Now EU travelers need not exchange currency, and travelers from outside the EU only need to exchange money once. (Great Britain and Denmark have chosen not to convert to the euro. Great Britain still uses the pound, and Denmark still uses the krone.) Passport control, too, is no longer regulated at each border but rather at the entry point into a European Union country. Trade is much easier among the countries as well.

Another example of supranationalism is the establishment of the North American Free Trade Agreement (NAFTA). NAFTA eased trade restrictions among Canada, the United States, and Mexico. NAFTA keeps prices low by facilitating the importation of goods from Mexico, where they can be made at a relatively low cost. It also opens markets to companies in all three countries. NAFTA dismayed organized labor in the United States, which contested the agreement on the grounds that it would cost U.S. workers their jobs.

The North Atlantic Treaty Organization (NATO) is another example of a supranational organization. By combining their military might, the countries of NATO could effectively oppose their common enemy, the Soviet Union.

Other supranational organizations include the Organization of Petroleum Exporting Countries (OPEC), the Asia-Pacific Economic Cooperation (APEC), the Economic Community of West African States (ECOWAS), and the United Nations. Some of these alliances are more productive and profitable than others. Figure 6.7 lists the member countries of the United Nations and their date of acceptance.

Afghanistan (November 19,1946)	Barbados (December 9, 1966)	Cambodia (December 14, 1955)
Albania (December 14, 1955)	Belarus (October 24, 1945)	Cameroon (September 20, 1960)
Algeria (October 8, 1962)	Belgium (December 27, 1945)	Canada (November 9, 1945)
Andorra (July 28, 1993)	Belize (September 25, 1981)	Cape Verde (September 16, 1975)
Angola (December 1, 1976)	Benin (September 20, 1960)	
Antigua and Barbuda (November 11, 1981)	Bhutan (September 21, 1971)	Central African Republic (September 20, 1960)
Argentina (October 24, 1945)	Bolivia (November 14, 1945)	Chad (September 20, 1960)
Armenia (March 2, 1992)	Bosnia and Herzegovina (May 22, 1992)	Chile (October 24, 1945)
Australia (November 1, 1945)	Botswana (October 17, 1966)	China (October 24, 1945)
Austria (December 14, 1955)	Brazil (October 24, 1945)	Colombia (November 5, 1945)
Azerbaijan (March 2, 1992)	Brunei Darussalam (September 21, 1984)	Comoros (November 12, 1975)
		Congo, Republic of the (September 20, 1960)
Bahamas (September 18, 1973)	Bulgaria (December 14, 1955)	Costa Rica (November 2,1945)
Bahrain (September 21, 1971)	Burkina Faso (September 20, 1960)	Côte d'Ivoire (September 20, 1960)
Bangladesh (September 17, 1974)	Burundi (September 18, 1962)	

Figure 6.7: Member Countries of the United Nations.

Croatia (May 22, 1992)

Cuba (October 24, 1945)

Cyprus (September 20, 1960)

Czech Republic (January 19, 1993)

Democratic People's Republic of Korea (September 17, 1991)

Democratic Republic of the Congo (September 20, 1960)

Denmark (October 24, 1945)

Djibouti (September 20, 1977)

Dominica (December 18, 1978)

Dominican Republic (October 24, 1945)

Ecuador (December 21, 1945)

Egypt (October 24, 1945)

El Salvador (October 24, 1945)

Equatorial Guinea (November 12, 1968)

Eritrea (May 28, 1993)

Estonia (September 17, 1991)

Ethiopia (November 13, 1945)

Fiji (October 13, 1970)

Finland (December 14, 1955)

France (October 24, 1945)

Gabon (September 20, 1960)

Gambia (September 21, 1965)

Georgia (July 31, 1992)

Germany (September 18, 1973)

Ghana (March 8, 1957)

Greece (October 25, 1945)

Grenada (September 17, 1974)

Guatemala (November 21, 1945)

Guinea (December 12, 1958)

Guinea-Bissau (September 17, 1974)

Guyana (September 20, 1966)

Haiti (October 24, 1945)

Honduras (December 17, 1945)

Hungary (December 14, 1955)

Iceland (November 19, 1946)

India (October 30, 1945)

Indonesia (September 28, 1950)

Iran, Islamic Republic of (October 24, 1945)

Iraq (December 21, 1945)

Ireland (December 14, 1955)

Israel (May 11, 1949)

Italy (December 14, 1955)

Jamaica (September 18, 1962)

Japan (December 18, 1956)

Jordan (December 14, 1955)

Kazakhstan (March 2, 1992)

Kenya (December 16, 1963)

Kiribati (September 14, 1999)

Kuwait (May 14, 1963)

Kyrgyzstan (March 2, 1992)

Lao People's Democratic Republic (December 14, 1955)

Latvia (September 17, 1991)

Lebanon (October 24, 1945)

Lesotho (October 17, 1966)

Liberia (November 2, 1945)

Libyan Arab Jamahiriya (December 14, 1955)

Liechtenstein (September 18, 1990)

Lithuania (September 17, 1991)

Luxembourg (October 24, 1945)

The former Yugoslav Republic of Macedonia (April 8, 1993)

Madagascar (September 20, 1960)

Malawi (December 1, 1964)

Malaysia (September, 17 1957)

Maldives (September 21, 1965)

Mali (September 28, 1960)

Malta (December 1, 1964)

Marshall Islands (September 17, 1991)

Mauritania (October 27, 1961)

Mauritius (April 24, 1968)

Mexico (November 7, 1945)

Micronesia, Federated States of (September 17, 1991)

Monaco (May 28, 1993)

Mongolia (October 27, 1961)

Montenegro (June 28, 2006)

Morocco (November 12, 1956)

Mozambique (September 16, 1975)

Myanmar (April 19, 1948)

Namibia (April 23, 1990)

Nauru (September 14, 1999)

Nepal (December 14, 1955)

Netherlands (December 10, 1945)

New Zealand (October 24, 1945)

Nicaragua (October 24, 1945)

Niger (September 20, 1960)

Nigeria (October 7, 1960)

Norway (November 27, 1945)

Figure 6.7: Member Countries of the United Nations. *(continued)*

Oman (October 7, 1971)

Pakistan (September 30, 1947)

Palau (December 15, 1994)

Panama (November 13, 1945)

Papua New Guinea (October 10, 1975)

Paraguay (October 24, 1945)

Peru (October 31, 1945)

Philippines (October 24, 1945)

Poland (October 24, 1945)

Portugal (December 14, 1955)

Qatar (September 21, 1971)

Republic of Korea (September 17, 1991)

Republic of Moldova (March 2, 1992)

Romania (December 14, 1955)

Russian Federation (October 24, 1945)

Rwanda (September 18, 1962)

Saint Kitts and Nevis (September 23, 1983)

Saint Lucia (September 18, 1979)

Saint Vincent and the Grenadines (September 16, 1980)

Samoa (December 15, 1976)

San Marino (March 2, 1992)

Sáo Tomé and Principe (September 16, 1975)

Saudi Arabia (October 24, 1945)

Senegal (September 28, 1960)

Serbia (November 1, 2000)

Seychelles (September 21, 1976)

Sierra Leone (September 27, 1961)

Singapore (September 21, 1965)

Slovakia (January 19, 1993)

Slovenia (May 22, 1992)

Solomon Islands (September 19, 1978)

Somalia (September 20, 1960)

South Africa (November 7, 1945)

South Sudan (November 7, 1945)

Spain (December 14, 1955)

Sri Lanka (December 14, 1955)

Sudan (November 12, 1956)

Suriname (December 4, 1975)

Swaziland (September 24, 1968)

Sweden (November 19, 1946)

Switzerland (September 10, 2002)

Syrian Arab Republic (October 24, 1945)

Tajikistan (March 2, 1992)

Thailand (December 16, 1946)

Timor-Leste (September 27, 2002)

Togo (September 20, 1960)

Tonga (September 14, 1999)

Trinidad and Tobago (September 18, 1962)

Tunisia (November 12, 1956)

Turkey (October 24, 1945)

Turkmenistan (March 2, 1992)

Tuvalu (September 5, 2000)

Uganda (October 25, 1962)

Ukraine (October 24, 1945)

United Arab Emirates (December 9, 1971)

United Kingdom of Great Britain and Northern Ireland (October 24, 1945)

United Republic of Tanzania (December 14, 1961)

United States of America (October 24, 1945)

Uruguay (December 18, 1945)

Uzbekistan (March 2, 1992)

Vanuatu (September 15, 1981)

Venezuela, Bolivarian Republic of (November 15, 1945)

Viet Nam (September 20, 1977)

Yemen (September 30, 1947)

Zambia (December 1, 1964)

Zimbabwe (August 25, 1980)

Figure 6.7: Member Countries of the United Nations. *(continued)*

THE HISTORICAL GEOGRAPHY OF THE UNITED STATES

A subset of geography called **historical geography** analyzes geographical patterns through history. The United States has an interesting geographical pattern.

The United States is an immigrant state. An **immigrant state** is comprised primarily of immigrants and their descendants. Settlement of the United States began in the early 1600s and continues today, with people coming from around the world. The United States was a colony of Great Britain until the Revolutionary War in the late 1700s. After gaining independence, the first U.S. government was a **confederation**, or a loose grouping of states for a common purpose. Ultimately, the Articles of Confederation didn't work. The states had too much power, and the federal government didn't have enough; tax collection and national defense were insufficient. The federal government could not financially support itself.

A Constitutional Convention was convened in Philadelphia and the resulting Constitution granted more power to the federal government. The U.S. political system is considered a federal system, where the ultimate power rests in the hands of the national government. The state governments can establish laws but cannot supersede the authority of the national government. This form of government is in between a confederation, where power lies in the hands of the individual states, and a **unitary** style of government, where all decisions are made by the national government.

The U.S. government is a **representative** form of government. Leaders are elected from the individual states to be representatives and senators in two houses of Congress. Today, the United States has 100 senators and 435 representatives. A **senator** serves an entire state, while **representatives** serve their districts. These districts are **reapportioned** every ten years based on the results of the census so that each district has about the same number of people. Therefore, urban areas with a higher population density have smaller districts, while rural districts are larger. **Gerrymandering** is the redrawing of political boundaries for political gain by one of the major political powers. Gerrymandering is an illegal activity, but even as late as the 1990s, two congressional districts in the United States (one in North Carolina and one in California) were questioned on the basis of gerrymandering. In federal terms, gerrymandering only applies to Congressional districts and not to the senatorial level, since senators are elected on a state-wide basis.

After gaining its independence, the United States expanded steadily west. A **frontier** is an area that is not yet under the control of a state but where people from the state are migrating. The Louisiana Territory was one of the largest purchases of land by the U.S. government, encompassing land up the Mississippi river and westward to the Rocky Mountains. Lewis and Clark were sent out on expedition by President Thomas Jefferson to explore and bring back reports of what the new territory encompassed.

Westward expansion served the purpose of "manifest destiny." **Manifest destiny** was the belief that the U.S. government was meant to rule the land between the Atlantic Ocean and the Pacific Ocean. Manifest destiny was used to justify the acquisition of new lands by any means. Native American populations were often relocated. Reservations were set up for Native Americans, sometimes hundreds of miles from their original homelands. The Trail of Tears saw the Cherokees go on a forced migration from Georgia, their homeland, to a reservation in Oklahoma.

The United States filled its land between the coasts with migrants from different countries at different points in its history. It added a 49th and 50th state, Alaska and Hawaii, in 1959. A lingering question is whether or not the United States will ever have more states. Puerto Rico is a territory of the United States, and its citizens enjoy all of the privileges of being U.S. citizens except for representation in Congress and the right to vote for the president. However, they do not have to pay U.S. income tax, thus placing a financial burden on the United States. The majority of Puerto Rican citizens do not want their territory to become a state; they do not want to pay U.S. taxes.

In Canada, by contrast, the recently created province of Nunavut has been established as a homeland for Native Americans. This land, in the far northeastern and northern regions of Canada, is sparsely inhabited but contains numerous natural resources. Created in 1999, Nunavut was the first Canadian province added since 1949, when Newfoundland was established.

ISSUES OF GEOPOLITICS

There are many boundary disputes in the world today. Sometimes these disputes are decided diplomatically and sometimes by military action. The creation of boundaries is difficult. Self-interest and economic well-being often play a major role in the creation of boundaries instead of the population's ethnic and cultural characteristics.

Currently, land is in dispute in several areas. One is the Kashmir region of India, Pakistan, and China. In this remote territory, there are both ethnic and religious differences. Since Indian independence in 1947, India has fought four wars over the territory, three with Pakistan and one with China. Also crucial in this region are the rivers. Because Kashmir is high in the Himalayan Mountains, it is the source of many rivers, which flow into both India and Pakistan. The control of these rivers means the control of transportation and water resources.

Early in the settlement of Canada and the United States, there was some conflict over the interpretation of where the border lay. The Aroostook War was fought over the boundary between Maine and New Brunswick. An 1842 treaty permanently established the border between the United States and Canada.

If you look at a map of the Middle East today, you'll see a small region near the border of Iraq and Kuwait that some suggest is still in dispute today. The claim was settled by the United Nations in 1994, and the boundaries on current maps show that decision.

ETHNICITY AND CULTURE—CONCEPTS AND ISSUES

The concept of ethnicity is a difficult one for geographers to deal with because the definition of ethnicity is very difficult to establish definitively. **Ethnicity** is tied into the cultural traditions of a group of people. It is different from **race**, which is the biological characteristic of a group of people. Ethnicity tends to promote nationalism more than race and it tends to correspond with nationhood.

To many, ethnic groups are comprised of a number of different characteristics. Some suggest that religion and language determine ethnicity. Others suggest that country of origin or nationality determines origin. Others suggest that skin color and other racial characteristics indicate ethnicity. All of these characteristics can and are used to assist in defining ethnic groups.

GLOBALIZATION

Globalization is the movement toward one common culture across the world. Globalization can also refer to the interconnections of ideas, goods, and information around the Earth. As communication increases, globalization increases. Popular culture is spread quickly in today's world. Ethnic identities counter globalization, separating different groups of people and keeping individual differences alive.

A **cultural shatterbelt** is an area where people are caught between the globalization or modernization of their culture and their traditional cultural identity. This term can be applied to any area where different cultural elements come into contact and create instability. In Vietnam, for example, modernization is taking hold in the larger urban areas of Hanoi and Ho Chi Minh City, but the old culture persists in rural areas.

Lebanon, a Christian state surrounded by Islamic states and Israel, finds itself in a cultural shatterbelt. In 2006, the state was stuck in the middle of an ethnic conflict between the Israelis and the Muslim Arab Hamas military group. Such cultural battles are driving away much-needed tourism income and are dividing a country that is in need of centripetal forces.

Because of globalization, English has become the world's lingua franca. Most world business is done in English. All airline pilots in the world communicate in English. It can be argued that this process of **cultural adaptation**, the transition of a varied cultural environment into one culture, means that local traditions are dying out and new ones are emerging. For example, the use of cell phones and text messaging has created its own form of cultural communication among today's youth. Many schools are eliminating the teaching of cursive writing because it is not needed any longer.

However, cursive writing is distinctive to the English language. The greater usage of text messaging and less emphasis on cursive writing means a change in the culture of how we communicate.

IMMIGRATION

Because the United States is an immigrant state, the ethnicities or cultures in the United States are varied. One can find Americans with ancestors who are Italian, Swedish, Chinese, Vietnamese, and so on. Sometimes, the United States is called a "melting pot" of cultures.

Also because the United States is a country of immigrants, the process of acculturation has taken place. **Acculturation** involves the adaptation to a new culture from the old culture of the original location (**ethnic homeland**). Acculturation usually takes about three generations. In general, the first generation of immigrants in the United States primarily speaks the language of the country from which they came and speaks very little English. The second generation speaks both languages. The third generation speaks primarily English and often knows very little of the home country's language. Through the process of acculturation, immigrants have assimilated into the United States. The **assimilation** process gives immigrants a sense of belonging to their new country. Assimilation usually occurs within one individual's lifespan, whereas acculturation is spread out over several generations.

Many of today's U.S. immigrants are coming through the process of **chain migration**. Immigrants already here save money and send it to family members so they can come, too. For example, many of the Hmong in the United States are sending a large percentage of their incomes back to Laos and Thailand so family members can someday join them.

Most immigrants exercise **voluntary segregation** owing to the language barrier. Newly arrived immigrants who do not speak English often choose to live in an area where they can communicate and feel comfortable culturally. This voluntary segregation leads to the creation of ethnic neighborhoods. **Ethnic neighborhoods** share the same language and sometimes a dominant religion. Ethnic neighborhoods may have restaurants, clothing stores, music stores, and other retail shops that cater to that culture's needs.

New York City, a key immigrant entry point, is known for its ethnic neighborhoods. Little Italy in the lower east side of Manhattan was once known for its distinctive restaurants and shops catering to the Italian immigrants who lived there. Likewise, many recent immigrants from China have established commercial activities in Chinatown, and their cultural imprint has given this neighborhood a distinctive flair. A McDonald's located in Chinatown has its menu printed in Chinese. Tai chi classes are held at dawn in the parks there. A strong Puerto Rican community is concentrated in the Spanish Harlem area.

Brazilians, Poles, Jamaicans, and Greeks all have concentrated in different areas of New York City from Queens to the Bronx. These ethnic neighborhoods have left a distinct impression on the ethnic landscape. The **ethnic landscape** is the evidence of an ethnicity on the features of the landscape. This may include murals on public buildings and the nature of the commercial businesses in an area. In many large urban centers, a plural society has developed. A **plural society** is characterized by two or more ethnicities living in the same area but each keeping their own identity and characteristics.

The diversity of food, architecture, and culture is a positive characteristic of large urban areas in the United States, creating a wonderful cultural experience.

OPPRESSION OF MINORITIES

Forced segregation is the separation of a group of people by law. In the United States, the Jim Crow laws of the South, which, for example, designated separate drinking fountains for "colored" people (African Americans) and for white people, were an example of forced segregation. In addition, different bathrooms, schools, and legal status all were in effect for African Americans and whites based on the *Plessy v. Ferguson* court case. It allowed segregation on a "separate but equal" standing; however, the reality was that African American facilities were substandard to white facilities. In the *Brown v. Board of Education* case in the 1950s, the Supreme Court overruled *Plessy v. Ferguson* and outlawed all segregation based on race.

The world is full of stories of forced segregation. In South Africa, the policy of apartheid separated that country's ethnic groups through the 1980s. Under pressure from Nelson Mandela and from activists abroad, the policy of apartheid was abolished.

In one of the most severe cases of forced segregation, Germans during World War II segregated and executed millions of Jews, Romany (Gypsies), homosexuals, and disabled people during the Holocaust. Some Jewish people were rounded up and put into ghettos. **Ghettos** were essentially walled holding pens within cities where minorities were kept before eventually being taken to concentration camps. Ghettos are an example of an ethnic enclave. Just as a political enclave is a country that is entirely surrounded by another country, an **ethnic enclave** is an ethnic neighborhood that is surrounded by people of a different ethnicity; usually the surrounding ethnicity is hostile to the group in the enclave.

When two different ethnic groups vie for the same territory, the result is an **ethnic conflict**. In extreme cases, a dominant ethnicity will try to eliminate the less powerful group. This is called **ethnic cleansing**, a benign sounding term for **genocide**. Millions have been killed due to genocide around the globe. In another example, under Slobodan Milošević, Bosnian Serbs killed thousands of Bosnian Muslims. Also, Serbs tried to eliminate ethnic Albanians in the Kosovo region. Genocide has also occurred in Sudan and with the Hutu and Tutsi tribes in Rwanda.

ETHNIC DIVERSITY

The two largest minority ethnicities in the United States are Latinos and African Americans. Hispanics or Latinos account for almost 17 percent of the total population of the United States. African Americans comprise approximately 13 percent of the total population of the United States. Asian Americans account for just over 5 percent of the population. The evidence of an increasing Latino population is evident on the cultural landscape, especially in the Southwest and in large cities. Restaurants serving Latino food and bilingual street signs and advertisements are common in these areas.

Russia is the country with the greatest number of ethnicities located within its borders, including peoples of the Caucasus Mountains in the west to Asian ethnicities in the east, from the Eastern Orthodox religion in the west to Buddhism and Taoism in the east.

One reason so many new states broke away from the old Soviet Union was their various ethnicities and the nationalism they engendered. The Kyrgyz people established Kyrgyzstan; Armenians, Armenia. Uzbeks make up the largest percentage of the population in Uzbekistan. The Baltic Republics of Latvia, Lithuania, and Estonia also follow this trend.

If the government sees diversity as a strength, then it will enact measures to preserve the different ethnicities and cultures within society. When diversity is seen as a weakness, however, usually the less powerful ethnicity or culture will be suppressed or even eliminated, sometimes brutally.

REVIEW QUESTIONS

MULTIPLE-CHOICE QUESTIONS

1. Which of the following states is the best example of an enclave?

   (A) Lesotho

   (B) Gambia

   (C) Brazil

   (D) Belize

   (E) Papua New Guinea

2. The Berlin Wall is a good example of a(n)

   (A) demarcation line.

   (B) subsequent boundary drawn by European powers.

   (C) superimposed boundary created by communist Europe.

   (D) geometric boundary using latitude and longitude.

   (E) antecedent boundary located within an urban area.

3. Which of the following is the best example of a nation-state?

   (A) United States

   (B) China

   (C) Russia

   (D) Japan

   (E) Canada

4. Which of the following was a centrifugal force in the India/Pakistan relationship in the late 1940s?

   (A) Commonality of language

   (B) Commonality of religion

   (C) Differences in political border interpretation

   (D) Differences in religion

   (E) Commonality of climate

5. Which of the following is the best example of a perforated state?

   (A) France

   (B) Vietnam

   (C) Singapore

   (D) Ecuador

   (E) Italy

6. Which international organization could best be incorporated into Spykman's rimland theory?

   (A) United Nations

   (B) European Union

   (C) NATO (North Atlantic Treaty Organization)

   (D) NAFTA (North American Free Trade Agreement)

   (E) Warsaw Pact

7. The largest territory in the world in terms of population is

   (A) the Solomon Islands.

   (B) Puerto Rico.

   (C) the Falkland Islands.

   (D) India.

   (E) Taiwan.

8. Which of the following is the best example of city-state?

   (A) Malaysia

   (B) France

   (C) The Netherlands

   (D) Monaco

   (E) Israel

9. What is the best example of voluntary segregation?

   (A) Barrios in Spanish Harlem in New York City, United States

   (B) Ghettos during World War II in Munich, Germany

   (C) Refugee camps in Bangkok, Thailand

   (D) Ethnic neighborhoods in Tokyo, Japan

   (E) The ethnic landscape of Los Angeles, United States

10. The majority of African states entered the United Nations after 1960 because

    (A) they were not into the concept of the United Nations until then.

    (B) political differences with the United States didn't allow them to join until then.

    (C) the colonies in Africa were quasi-independent in the 1950s.

    (D) the creation of the African United Nations took precedence.

    (E) the majority of the states hadn't become independent until the 1960s.

11. Supranationalism has come at the expense of what other geopolitical concept?

    (A) Colonialism

    (B) Imperialism

    (C) Sovreignty

    (D) Theocratization

    (E) Settlement

12. What is the primary reason for establishing a proruption in a boundary?

    (A) To create hostility among the neighbors

    (B) To control different nationalities within the borders

    (C) To access more raw materials

    (D) To gain greater economic autonomy from colonizers

    (E) To establish communications in the country

13. The border between the United States and Canada along the 49th parallel is an example of what type of boundary?

    (A) Subsequent boundary

    (B) Antecedent boundary

    (C) Superimposed boundary

    (D) Relic boundary

    (E) Demarcation of a boundary

14. The civil war in Rwanda is most closely an example of

    (A) a religious conflict.

    (B) an ethnic conflict.

    (C) a pluralism conflict.

    (D) ethnocentrism.

    (E) an ethnic enclave.

15. Which of the following is a good example of an exclave?

    (A) Hawaii in the United States

    (B) The island of Sumatra in Indonesia

    (C) Alaska in the United States

    (D) Taiwan in relation to mainland China

    (E) Shikoku Island in Japan

16. Which type of boundary exists between the United States and Canada?

    (A) Geometric

    (B) Water

    (C) Cultural

    (D) Linguistic

    (E) All of the above

17. Fill in the blank: The German migration into the United States showed the process of _____, which meant that usually within three generations, all of the migrants' descendants spoke English.

    (A) assimilation

    (B) acculturation

    (C) barrio

    (D) pluralism

    (E) voluntary segregation

18. The redrawing of political districts for political gain is termed what?

    (A) Reapportionment

    (B) Core-periphery federalism

    (C) Gerrymandering

    (D) Immigrant statehood

    (E) Electoral regions

19. The United Nations' International Law of the Sea gave countries access to drill for mineral rights up to how many miles from shore?

    (A) 3 miles

    (B) 10 miles

    (C) 12 miles

    (D) 100 miles

    (E) 200 miles

20. Southeast Asia from the 1950s through the 1970s was considered a

    (A) theocracy.

    (B) nation-state.

    (C) shatterbelt.

    (D) regional conflict.

    (E) microstate.

FREE-RESPONSE QUESTION

Directions: While a formal essay is not required, it is not enough to answer the following question by merely listing facts. Your answer should be based upon your critical analysis of the question posed.

1. There are a number of high profile stateless nations in the world. Answer the following questions. When answering questions B and C, consider these three stateless nations: Palestine, the Basque Country, and Kurdistan.

    (A) What is a stateless nation?

    (B) Geographically and culturally, what makes each group a nation?

    (C) What role do boundaries play in maintaining each group as a stateless nation?

ANSWERS AND EXPLANATIONS

MULTIPLE-CHOICE QUESTIONS

1. A

An enclave is a territory that is completely surrounded by another country. The surrounding country is called a perforated country. The only two perforated countries today are South Africa and Italy. Italy contains both San Marino and Vatican City. South Africa contains Lesotho, making choice (A) the correct answer. Gambia comes close to being an enclave, but it borders the ocean, and an enclave is landlocked by definition.

2. A

The Berlin Wall was a demarcation line between capitalist West Germany and communist East Germany. The Berlin Wall partitioned the Russian-controlled section of the city from the sections controlled by Great Britain, France, and the United States after World War II.

3. D

While there are no perfect examples of a nation-state, where all people are homogeneous in ethnicity, religion, and language, Japan and Denmark come closest. The United States is an immigrant nation with a multiethnic society. Russia encompasses a variety of different ethnicities within its borders. Canada has both French- and English-speaking regions.

4. D

The question asks for centrifugal forces, not centripetal forces. Centrifugal forces tend to break up a state, whereas centripetal forces tend to unite a state. Therefore, any answer with "commonality" is incorrect. The main factor in the breakup of India was religious differences. Many Muslims who lived in India were forced to migrate to Pakistan, and many Hindus who lived in Pakistan had to migrate to India.

5. E

A perforated country has another state completely inside its boundaries. Italy possesses two enclaves, San Marino and Vatican City. Singapore is a city-state and an entrepot.

6. C

Spykman's rimland theory said that superior sea power established through alliances was required to control the power of the Heartland. NATO (North Atlantic Treaty Organization) is a military alliance set up among the Western European countries, Canada, and the United States. Opposing NATO was the Warsaw Pact, which said that the Soviet Union could occupy and rule the Heartland.

7. B

Puerto Rico is the largest territory in the world in terms of population with approximately 5 million people. The Falkland Islands only have a population of 2,500 people. India is a state and not a colony. Taiwan is in dispute. Mainland China maintains that Taiwan is a "renegade province." Most countries do not formally recognize Taiwan but do maintain de facto relations informally. The International Olympic Committee allows Taiwanese athletes to participate in the Olympic Games but under the name "Chinese Taipei."

8. D

City-states are small states made up primarily of one urban center. Malaysia is a large country at the tip of the Malay Peninsula. France is a state. The Netherlands, although small and mostly suburban, has many cities. Israel, like France, is a state. Monaco is a city-state abutting southern France and northern Italy. It is one of the wealthiest countries in the world.

9. A

Barrios are Spanish-speaking neighborhoods in large urban areas. Immigrants voluntarily segregate based on their limited English. Ghettos in Germany and refugee camps in Thailand are examples of involuntary segregation. Tokyo, Japan, has very few ethnic neighborhoods due to the homogeneity of its population. "Ethnic landscape" is not a location per se but the impact of an ethnicity on the landscape.

10. E

Colonialism was still prevalent in Africa up until the 1960s. From then until the 1980s, many African countries claimed their independence from colonial powers and gained statehood.

11. C

Sovereignty is the ability of a country to determine its own course of action. Supranationalism is the process of individual states giving up some of their own autonomy in order to achieve some other goal, usually economic or political. Colonialism, imperialism, theocratization, and settlement do not deal with the issue of supranationalism.

12. C

Proruptions are created to gain control of more resources and/or to gain access to some form of transportation.

13. B

The 49th parallel is an example of an antecedent boundary. An antecedent boundary is one that existed before settlement. Subsequent boundaries include the border between China and Vietnam, as well as between Ireland and Northern Ireland. Superimposed boundaries ignore cultural patterns, as in the case of the boundary between North Korea and South Korea. A relic boundary no longer exists but still impacts the landscape; the Berlin Wall's impact is still visible in Germany.

14. B

The civil war in Rwanda was fought between the Hutu and the Tutsi tribes. The battle stemmed from ethnic, not religious, differences. Millions were forced to flee the country.

15. C

An exclave is a region that is separated from a mainland by another country. Hawaii is not separated by another country but rather the Pacific Ocean. Taiwan, like Hawaii, is separated from mainland China by water. Shikoku is one of the four main islands of Japan. It is not separated from Japan by another land mass. Alaska is an example of an exclave; it is separated from the United States by Canada.

16. E

There are many types of boundaries that exist between the United States and Canada. A geometric boundary (line of latitude) exists at the 54th parallel. The most well-known water boundary between these two countries includes all of the Great Lakes except Lake Michigan. A cultural boundary exists between the two countries. Every country has its own unique culture. One of the most noticeable differences between the two countries is that Canada exhibits more ties to Great Britain than the United States. Finally, a linguistic boundary exists between Quebec, where French is the official language, and New York, Vermont, New Hampshire, and Maine, where English is the primary language.

17. B

The process of acculturation usually takes about three generations to complete. The first immigrants speak very little English; the second generation is bilingual in both English and the original language; the third generation speaks very little of the original language. Assimilation is a part of the process, but acculturation is the generational transfer of language and traditions.

18. C

Gerrymandering is an illegal activity that political parties use to try to reapportion districts in their favor. Reapportionment is not illegal; in fact, it is required of the legislative branch of government after each census.

19. E

The United Nations' International Law of the Sea allows countries to explore for and exploit resources up to 200 miles out to sea. The three-mile limit applies to foreign ships; if foreign ships enter a country's three-mile zone, the event could be interpreted as an aggressive military action.

20. C

From the 1950s to the 1970s, Southeast Asia was considered a shatterbelt between Western forces, led by the United States, and Eastern forces, led by the Soviet Union and China. A shatterbelt is a region that is in the middle of two superpowers fighting for control. The United States fought the Vietnam War to halt the spread of communism on the continent.

FREE-RESPONSE QUESTION

SAMPLE ESSAY

PART A

A stateless nation is a nation that has no state. In other words, it is a people who share a common culture (language, ethnicity, religion) and attachment to a place on Earth, but have little political power or sovereignty in their homeland.

PART B

The Kurds are an ethnic group of approximately 30 million people clustered in Southwest Asia, an area referred to as Kurdistan. They have a distinct culture, share a common language (Kurdish), and are predominately Muslim.

The European Basques are an ethnic group clustered in the Pyrenees mountain region of Spain and France, an area also known as Basque Country. They have a unique culture and speak a non-Indo-European language, one with different roots than those spoken in surrounding countries.

The Palestinians are Arabs originally from Palestine, a country that was dissolved with the creation of Israel in 1948. The region occupied by Palestinians is often referred to as Palestinian territories or the State of Palestine. This group primarily speaks Arabic and practices Islam.

PART C

The Kurds are divided among five countries: Turkey, Iran, Iraq, Syria, and Azerbaijan. As a result, Kurds are minorities in all five countries and are unable to acquire much political power. The region they inhabit is mountainous, which also makes it difficult for them to communicate and unite. The area also includes the headwaters of the Tigris and Euphrates Rivers. Since water is so valuable in this part of the world it is doubtful that Turkey or any other country will be willing to allow the Kurds more political power, let alone their own country.

The European Basques occupy an area near the Bay of Biscay in the western portion of the Pyrenees Mountains in both Spain and France. Since the Basques are spread across two countries, it makes it difficult for them to gain significant political power. The Basques are more numerous in Spain and have been fighting for autonomy from Spain for many decades. Basque separatists have resorted to terrorist methods to try to gain independence from Spain, but to no avail.

The Palestinians are mainly clustered in the West Bank, Gaza Strip, and Golan

Heights in portions of Israel. Significant populations live in refugee camps in Syria, Lebanon, and Jordon. The fact that they are dispersed in a number of areas makes it difficult for them to politically become a unified force. Additionally, often-violent protest tactics and failed diplomatic proceedings with Israel have made a stable Palestinian state untenable in the near future.

RUBRIC FOR FREE-RESPONSE QUESTION

Total points value for question 1 = 7

Part A—One point possible:

- Give an acceptable definition for stateless nation

Part B—Three points possible:

- Describe some basic cultural aspects of two of the stateless nations listed
    — Kurds (distinct ethnic group, shared language, practice Islam)
    — Palestinians (practice Islam, speak Arabic, and are Arab)
    — Basques (distinct ethnic group and speak a unique language)

Part C—Three points possible:

- Describe the basic geographical components that contribute to their statelessness
    — Kurds (spread among five countries, mountainous region); difficult to unite culture based on geography
    — Basques (live in the western Pyrenees Mountains spread between France and Spain); spread across two countries, makes negotiation to create a separate state more difficult
    — Palestinians (spread among the West Bank, Gaza Strip and Golan Heights in Israel and refugee camps in Syria, Jordan, and Lebanon); tactics and history of stalled peace talks with Israel make it difficult for a peaceful solution that includes a Palestinian state

CHAPTER 7: AGRICULTURE, FOOD PRODUCTION, AND RURAL LAND USE

IF YOU LEARN ONLY SEVEN THINGS IN THIS CHAPTER . . .

1. Many of the world's crop products are dictated by the climate of the regions where they are grown.

2. There were three agricultural revolutions that changed history. The First Agricultural Revolution was the transition from hunting and gathering to planting and sustaining. The Second Agricultural Revolution increased the productivity of farming through mechanization and access to market areas through better transportation. The Third Agricultural Revolution involves the genetic engineering of products as well as the increased use of fertilizers for crops and antibiotics in animal products.

3. Von Thunen's model focuses on transportation. The distance and the weight of crops as well as their distance to market affect which ones are grown.

4. There are two primary methods of farming in the world. Subsistence farming involves producing agricultural products for use by the farm family. Commercial farming involves the sale of agricultural products off the farm.

5. Many of the settlement patterns in the United States have been based on the agricultural possibilities of the areas.

6. Modern agriculture is becoming more industrialized and more specialized than ever. The loss of the family farm is a direct result of the rise of feedlots and mega-farms used to produce enormous quantities of agricultural commodities.

7. To compete with agribusiness in the United States, many family farms are turning to sustainable methods of production, organic agriculture, and catering to the local-food movement.

A HISTORICAL PERSPECTIVE

An old joke suggests that all farmers are "out standing" in their fields. In a way, this is more than accurate. Today's farmers grow more agricultural products on less land than ever before in human history. Farmers need to be masters of technology, transportation, and techniques of farming. They also need to be aware of crop prices and policies practiced not only in their own communities but also around the world. In a global market, farmers face increasing competition from down the street and from across the world.

In the United States, only 2 percent of the population is involved with farming as a full-time occupation. However, millions more are involved in the transportation, production, and distribution of agricultural products. In many Midwestern states, agriculture is a multibillion-dollar industry and the states' largest employer.

The concept of agriculture goes back as far as humans do. Humans have to eat to survive, and their food can come from either animals or crops. **Agriculture** is the raising of animals or the growing of crops to obtain food for primary consumption by the farm family or for sale off the farm.

The first way humans obtained food was by hunting and gathering. Nomadic tribes around the world depended on migratory animals for sustenance. These societies also depended on the existence of wild fruit and berries. However, during periods of drought, for example, the supply of fruits and berries was limited, causing starvation.

FIRST AGRICULTURAL REVOLUTION

Simultaneously, systems of agriculture began to develop around the world. The shift from being primarily hunting and gathering societies to ones that planted crops for food took many years. However, this transition changed human history. This **Neolithic Agricultural Revolution**, or First Agricultural Revolution, allowed humans to become more sedentary and avail themselves of a more reliable source of food.

Imagine that humans don't know how to grow crops—the idea of planting seeds and watering them to produce a plant has not yet been thought of. People depend on picking wild fruits and roots and hunting animals for food, a precarious existence. Eventually, however, people realize that some of the berries that were dropped the previous year left seeds on the ground, and that if given enough water and sunlight and the right temperature, they grow into plants and produce more berries.

This revelation came after hundreds, if not thousands, of years. Migrating people had to make the association of the dropped seed and new bush, and to have a chance to do that, they had to return to the same location year after year. When humans began to figure out how seeds worked, they started to plant and sustain those crops themselves. Many failed attempts preceded what we know as agriculture today.

The world practiced this form of agriculture for centuries. At first, humans could plant crops only on a relatively small scale. These societies could not support large urban areas. Agriculture was very labor intensive at this point, requiring many people to produce relatively small amounts of food.

Once people started to understand the process of planting crops, they began to get more successful at it, with dramatic effects. Now, instead of roaming the landscape in search of herd animals, they could wait for them until next year, in the meantime eating their crops. With a more stable food source, the population began to grow, more people needed more food, and growing more food required more labor in self-perpetuating cycles of population growth.

In addition to crop domestication, animal domestication became more common, changing the diets of people all around the world. **Animal domestication** is the process of taming wild animals for human benefit. Cows, pigs, and chickens were each domesticated in different parts of the world and today are staples of our diet.

WOMEN IN THE FIRST AGRICULTURAL REVOLUTION

Women played a key role in the First Agricultural Revolution. As men were off hunting prey for food, women oftentimes participated in the food gathering and reaping of the harvests. Women's roles were vital in maintaining a stable food source and keeping plants and animals healthy for consumption.

SECOND AGRICULTURAL REVOLUTION

Agriculture benefited from the Industrial Revolution, as did many other facets of society. During the Industrial Revolution, agriculture had its **Second Agricultural Revolution**. These two revolutions occurred from 1750 to around 1900 in the more developed world. The Second Agricultural Revolution used the technology provided by the Industrial Revolution as a means to increase production and distribution of products. Fields could double or even triple in size but still be worked by the same amount of labor. This increased productivity and allowed population to increase on both a local and a global scale. Many less developed countries are still in the Second Agricultural Revolution.

Eli Whitney invented the cotton gin in the United States in 1793. The cotton gin did the work of dozens of workers by removing the cotton fiber from the stalk and the pods of the cotton plant. This greatly increased agricultural production in the South, which had a climate conducive for growing cotton. In addition, wheat could now be harvested by machines instead of by hand. Corn farmers began using a technological forerunner to the combine, which is used today. During this time, dozens of inventions increased the productivity of agriculture. An individual worker could expand his or her production up to 10 times thanks to the cotton gin.

Increased productivity requires a market to handle the increased quantity of commodities, and advancements in transportation were vital to get goods to markets. Goods could now be shipped farther and faster to outlying regions, thereby increasing the market area for agricultural products. Ships had gained in speed, trains were becoming more reliable, and canals were being built to help get goods to markets faster. This was important because if the agricultural products couldn't make it to market in time, they would spoil.

As transportation continued to improve, productivity increased, which had a profound effect on agricultural methods and crops. This corresponded with the first wave of human population growth; the population began to climb the S-curve.

The Second Agricultural Revolution had a huge effect on farmers. More people left the farms, because less work was being done manually there. They moved to urban areas to fulfill industry's demands for more factory workers.

THIRD AGRICULTURAL REVOLUTION

During the latter half of the 20th century, the **Third Agricultural Revolution** began. This revolution corresponded with the exponential population growth occurring around the world, a direct result of the Second Agricultural Revolution and its profound effect on Europe's ability to feed itself. The Third Agricultural Revolution began in the early 1940s but took off on a massive scale in the 1960s. The Third Agricultural Revolution deals with the hybridization of crops (a separate issue from that of GMO's effect on agriculture, which emerged in the 1990s). Both plants and animals have been hybridized in the Third Agricultural Revolution, which has had a revolutionary impact on food production. Universities around the world now specialize in agricultural science as a result.

Many argue that the Third Agricultural Revolution started with Norman Borlaug, an agricultural specialist at the University of Minnesota. His work with wheat production in Mexico transformed that country from an importer of wheat to an exporter of the same crop within a few years. Borlaug's work expanded to other less developed areas around the world and to other crops.

The Third Agricultural Revolution, sometimes called the **Green Revolution**, involves the use of **biotechnology**, or **genetic engineering**. This involves altering the genetic material of plants and animals. Biotechnology takes place mainly in science laboratories and is then tested on farm fields around the world. Scientists have created many hybrids of plants and animals that grow in conditions where they normally wouldn't. The Green Revolution also involves the increased use of chemical fertilizers to enhance productivity and continues to benefit from mechanization, but it is much more than that. This revolution involves the rise of industrial farming, which is the mass production of agricultural products.

The Green Agricultural Revolution began on a massive scale in the 1960s in the United States. Genetic engineers modified wheat, corn, and other agricultural products to change their characteristics. For example, wheat traditionally needed to be grown in a dry climate; too much moisture meant that the crop would spoil in the fields. As a result of genetic hybridization, wheat can resist spoilage in the field. Corn, soybeans, cotton, and dozens of other products underwent similar modifications to their natural genetic properties.

THE GMO EFFECT?

The Green Revolution has not come without controversy. Many scientists and others argue against the use of what are known as **Genetically Modified Organisms**, or GMO's. GMO's are the result of the genetic engineering of any plant or animal. Genetic modification includes making a crop more drought resistant or developing chickens to produce more meat. The problem is the safety of the food itself, which some argue cause problems in humans, such as more allergies in children.

The third agricultural revolution primarily dealt with the hybridization of crops on a worldwide scale, as well increased use of erosion control and irrigation. The newest agricultural revolution deals primarily with the use of GMO's, which first entered the market in 1994. This modified revolution is still in effect today and is having a dramatic impact on the food quality in more developed countries. GMO modification of crops involves the genetic splicing of the DNA of the plant and replacing that with DNA that enhances its ability to resist drought and pests, or affects cosmetic features of the plant such as color. The future of GMO's may have profound effects on the productivity of agriculture as a whole.

One of the greatest feats in agricultural engineering took place with the genetic modification of rice. Rice was first modified in the Philippines and then diffused to other areas of Asia. Even today new hybrids are constantly being produced. Rice is now heartier and can be grown more quickly. This helps feed more people in some of the poorest regions of Asia. Also, **double-cropping**, the growing of two crops per year to double the harvest, and even **triple-cropping** can now be practiced in some areas of Asia, allowing even more people to be fed.

The Green Agricultural Revolution was also vital in the evolution of the modern supermarket. Agriculture has gone global with increased efficiency in transportation. Today, farmers in the Great Plains are checking the prices of wheat and corn in Asia and Europe, which directly affect their profits. Farmers in western North Dakota ship their wheat via train to Seattle, where it is then loaded onto ships and sent to Asia. Much of the Upper Midwest sends products down the Mississippi River to ports around New Orleans, where it is then sent to South America.

Because of the mechanization and mass production of farm products during the Green Agricultural Revolution, most food is now coming from highly industrialized, automated operations that produce millions of dollars in profit each year instead of small mom and pop farms in the Midwest. These industrialized farmers contract out with big processing facilities and manufacturers to generate profit for both the farmer and the manufacturer.

This has concerned some animal rights activists, who feel that the quality of an animal's life is adversely affected when it isn't living in natural conditions. For example, hundreds of thousands of chickens are forced to live literally on top of each other. Producers respond by saying that they're simply trying to meet the needs of a population that increasingly prefers white meat in its diet. Growth hormones and different antibiotics are given to chickens to increase breast size as well as reduce the spread of diseases, which can wipe out entire farms. Chicken has become a staple food in the Western diet, and the industrial-scale raising of chickens is an important aspect of the Green Agricultural Revolution.

For the most part, however, the Green Agricultural Revolution has worked extremely well. Farming productivity has never been higher in human history. The agricultural community is feeding more people around the world than ever. People are still starving in the world, but this is due to inadequate distribution systems to get products to hungry people, not to a lack of food production. Political systems and policies around the globe are more of an obstacle to feeding people than agricultural production.

Organic farming has grown tremendously over the past decade. Organic farming uses natural processes and seeds that are not genetically altered in any means. To be certified as organic in the United States, farmers must demonstrate organic methods on a number of different measures.

AGRICULTURAL HEARTHS

One of the preeminent cultural geographers in the history of the profession was **Carl Sauer**. Sauer was a professor of geography at the University of California–Berkeley and was one of the most vehement critics of the philosophy of environmental determinism. Sauer started the field of cultural ecology, and he believed that humans had power over their environment and weren't simply the product of their environment. Sauer mapped out the **agricultural origins** of both vegetative planting and seed agriculture.

HEARTHS OF VEGETATIVE AND SEED PLANTING AND ANIMAL DOMESTICATION

Sauer suggested that there were two distinct types of agriculture. **Vegetative planting** means removing part of a plant and putting it in the ground to grow a new plant. Hostas are a good example of a plant that can be spread through vegetative planting. A person can cut a hosta in half and replant both sides. The replanted halves will grow just like the original plant. **Seed agriculture** means taking seeds from existing plants and planting them to produce new plants. The vast majority of farmers use this method today.

It is generally believed that agriculture developed in three areas around the world: Central America and northwestern South America, Western Africa, and Southeast Asia (see Figure 7.1). All three areas were in tropical regions with climates conducive to growing agricultural products, and they had relatively large populations to provide the workforce to domesticate the plants and animals native to their regions.

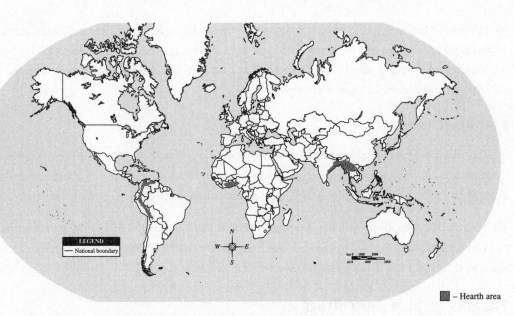

— Hearth area

Figure 7.1: Vegetative Planting Hearths.

CENTRAL AMERICA AND NORTHWESTERN SOUTH AMERICA

According to Sauer, the first agricultural region was in Central America and northwestern South America, two regions in proximity to each other that are considered one primary agricultural region. Although these two regions were independent of each other, they domesticated many of the same animals at the same time. The peoples of these areas were the Aztecs, Mayans, and Incas.

The first major hearth of vegetative planting was this area. Here, they grew manioc, sweet potato, and arrowroot. Manioc is a root crop that is still a staple food source in much of Brazil. It is poisonous if not fully cooked, but cooking the manioc releases its toxins, making it safe to eat.

The animals that were first domesticated in this area were turkeys, llamas, and alpacas. The llama and alpaca are indigenous to the Andes Mountains and are still very common along this "spine" of South America. Turkeys became famous as a meat source, and in the United States, many families cook them as a centerpiece of the traditional Thanksgiving meal. Llamas and alpacas were important for their wool, used in the production of clothing. Cotton, too, was used for clothing; the peoples of this region first domesticated cotton as well.

These products and animals later diffused from Central America and northwestern South America northward, into the present-day United States and Canada, and southward, to the tip of Patagonia in Argentina.

WESTERN AFRICA

The second major hearth of vegetative planting was Western Africa. The major agricultural products that were first domesticated in this region were yams and palm oil. The livestock that were first domesticated were cattle, sheep, and goats. These animals were later diffused into Europe, and from there, early explorers and settlers brought them to North America. Cattle became, and still is, a major agricultural industry in the United States. Our beef and dairy supply depends upon cattle, which were introduced by these early explorers.

SOUTHEAST ASIA

The third major vegetative planting hearth region was Southeast Asia. The crops that were first domesticated in this area were root crops, such as taro (now a staple in Pacific-island nations) and banana and palm trees. The animals first domesticated here were dogs, pigs, and chickens.

At first, the idea of eating a chicken was repulsive to many Europeans. As trading with Southeast Asia continued, however, Europeans became more interested in this food source. Today, chicken is a staple meat source in Europe and the Western Hemisphere.

HEARTHS OF SEED AGRICULTURE

In addition to the hearths of vegetative planting, there are also hearths of seed agriculture. **Seed agriculture** means taking seeds from existing plants and planting them to produce new plants. The vast majority of farmers use this method today. The four main hearths of seed agriculture are Central America, including the southern portions of Mexico; northeastern sections of Africa, including Ethiopia; northern China; and northeastern India (see Figure 7.2). These hearths were important because they diffused into areas that still predominantly practice this type of farming today.

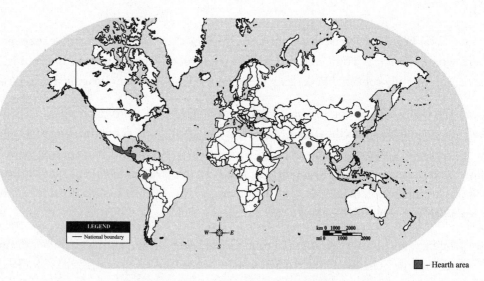

Figure 7.2: Seed Agriculture Hearths.

SOUTHERN MEXICO

The first major area of seed agriculture was southern Mexico. Squash, beans, and cotton were the major seed crops domesticated in this region. These products diffused into the United States, the rest of Central America, and South America over time.

Once European colonizers realized the importance of cotton, they sold it back to European markets for major profits. It is a very labor-intensive crop, and prior to the invention of the cotton gin, picking cotton had to be done by hand. Cotton fueled the slave trade, which supplied labor to harvest it in the southern United States.

NORTHEASTERN AFRICA

The second major hearth of seed agriculture was in northeastern Africa, around the present-day country of Ethiopia. One of the major crops domesticated was coffee. Coffee dates back approximately 1,200 years and is still a major source of national pride. Coffee then diffused to Western Africa and consequently to South America along with the slave trade. Northern countries in South America, such as Columbia and Venezuela, have prospered from the production of coffee.

NORTHERN CHINA

In the northern China region, millet was domesticated. Millet is a grain crop that possesses more calories than the average wheat plant. Millet is oftentimes used as a substitute in the diets of people who have allergies to wheat. The time between planting and harvesting is only between 45 and 70 days depending upon the climate where it is being grown.

NORTHEASTERN INDIA

Rice may have first been domesticated in northern India after arriving via trade routes from southwest Africa, but their precise origins are as yet unknown. Some geographers have given the nod to Southeast Asia as a forerunner in the development of rice because of its climatic conditions. Rice then spread throughout southern China and the remainder of South Asia and into the Pacific regions. Most geographers agree that wheat may have been domesticated in northern India. Today, wheat is one of the staple crops of the United States; as a main ingredient in bread and other food products, it is an essential part of the American daily diet.

THE IMPORTANCE OF TRADE ROUTES

Trade routes helped to diffuse many of the agricultural products that we use today. Colonialism brought many products to the Western Hemisphere. This movement was all part of the First Agricultural Revolution and initiated many of the vegetative and seed planting techniques still used today in the less developed world.

The diffusion of various products led to different styles of farming around the world. Climate dictates what crops can be grown where. Lemons and oranges do not grow well in New England. Wheat does not grow well in Florida. These differences led to a wide variety of styles of farming and types of farm products.

AGRICULTURAL REGIONS AND PATTERNS OF CHANGE

SUBSISTENCE FARMING

There are two predominant styles of farming in the world today. The first type of farming is subsistence farming. **Subsistence farmers** produce the food that they need to survive on a daily basis. They depend on the crops that they grow and the animal products they raise for their daily sustenance. Milk, not only from cows but from goats and camels, provides an important source of daily nutrition for millions around the world. Other animal products include wool for textiles and meat for protein.

SHIFTING CULTIVATION

One of the main types of subsistence farming is shifting cultivation. **Shifting cultivation** involves the moving of farm fields after several years in search of more productive soil after depleting the nutrients in the original field. Shifting cultivation takes place in tropical areas, which usually have a porous and shallow yet fertile soil, which many plants require for their survival. Because moisture and precipitation is plentiful, the soil erodes rather quickly.

Instead of using crop rotation techniques, the farmer practicing shifting cultivation doesn't mend the damage to the soil but instead leaves barren soil behind. The farmer moves on to the next area and clears the land of the vegetation, usually by burning it. This burning of the land is called **slash-and-burn agriculture**. This puts nitrogen into the soil, which is a nutrient needed by plants, until the farmer uses it up again after several years. This process continues, and the scars on the landscape indicate areas with little soil due to erosion. The dirt that is left behind is incapable of agricultural production. Soil that has been subjected to slash-and-burn agriculture can take decades to be replenished with nutrients. With farmers constantly moving on to clear more land for agriculture, they put rain forests and other native ecosystems at risk.

Shifting cultivation is seen in the tropical forested areas of Southeast Asia and Central Africa and the Amazonian rain forests in Brazil. Natural vegetation in this area keeps the soil from eroding because of its root structure. When the natural vegetation is removed, however, there is nothing to prevent the soil from eroding, sending thousands of tons of silt into rivers and eventually into the oceans.

CROP ROTATION

Crop rotation is the planting of different types of crops each year to replenish the soil with nutrients used up by the previous crop. An example of crop rotation would be a farmer planting corn in a field one year, soybeans the next, and then corn again.

Soybeans replace the nutrients that corn takes out of the soil and vice versa. This practice maintains the health of the soil for years. In addition, by planting other nitrogen-rich crops, such as clover, the farmer can further replenish the soil and improve agricultural productivity. Crop rotation is different than shifting agriculture. Crop rotation involves the use of the same field year after year but planting different crops on that same field. Shifting cultivation, primarily used in subsistence farming, involves the shifting of farming to different fields entirely to increase production.

PASTORAL NOMADISM

Another type of subsistence farming is pastoral nomadism. **Pastoral nomadism** is almost the opposite of shifting cultivation; it involves moving animals on a seasonal basis to areas that have the necessary resources to meet the needs of the herd. Nomads bring their herds to higher elevations in the summer to protect them from the lowland heat, and in the winter, they bring their animals back down to the valley floor. Pastoral nomadism is usually practiced in arid climates.

One of the best examples of pastoral nomadism is in the Saharan desert in northern Africa, which has some of the harshest environmental conditions in the world. Nomads have been taking their herds along trade routes in the region for thousands of years, and they not only survive but thrive. The Gobi desert region in Mongolia and northern China also has many nomadic tribes. The Mongols based their dominance of the region on the use of horses in war. The Middle East is also populated by a large number of nomads. The common characteristic of all of these regions is their arid climate and lack of precipitation.

The herds of pastoral nomads include camel, sheep, and goats. Cattle are not good nomadic animals, because they eat too much, are slow, and don't thrive on arid land. A typical family can survive with 10 camels and approximately 50 to 100 sheep and goats. These animals provide many useful products, including milk from the camels and meat from the sheep. Mutton (sheep meat) is a common item in the central Asian region. In much of central Asia, such as in Turkmenistan and Kyrgyzstan, the government keeps track of the number of sheep that each nomad possesses, and each sheep must be accounted for when it is killed. Even if the sheep is killed by a wolf or for a cultural celebration, it must be recorded. Pastoral nomads often trade their animal products for crops such as wheat, sorghum, or barley.

Both pastoral nomadism and shifting cultivation are a farming type known as **extensive subsistence agriculture**, which has been criticized for causing soil erosion, water degradation, and other environmental problems but is often more productive than other types of subsistence farming.

Extensive subsistence agriculture does not require a lot of labor, as opposed to Intensive subsistence agriculture, which does require a lot of labor.

INTENSIVE SUBSISTENCE AGRICULTURE

The third type of subsistence agriculture is called intensive subsistence agriculture. As its name suggests, **intensive subsistence agriculture** is a more intense style of subsistence farming. More work is needed to obtain the same level of production in this type of farming.

The number-one crop that geographers associate with intensive subsistence agriculture is wet rice. Wet rice is grown in **rice sawahs** (flooded fields where rice grows). Wet rice requires the planting and harvesting of each stalk by hand. Because the fields cannot be left alone, this type of farming is very time-consuming and labor intensive. Many of the rice paddies in Southeast Asia and southern China are built on the sides of hills. These hills are terraced so that water flows gently over the edges of each paddy into the next one below. This flow keeps the water from becoming stagnant. Carp often swim within the sawahs and both eat the insects, which could ruin the rice crop, and fertilize the crop itself. The rice grown this way is a crucial part of the daily diet of the fast-growing populations of Asia.

Other crops involved in intensive subsistence agriculture include wheat and barley. Like wet rice, they require a large amount of human and animal labor for production. The fields are tended on a daily basis. Oxen may pull the plows that break up the soil. Humans are aided by a few tools, including hoes and rakes, but the majority of the work is done by hand, consuming most of a farmer's time each day. Many farmers store their food over the winter and trade some of it. Farmers will save up for many years to earn enough money for an animal to assist with production. In many parts of Southeast Asia and Africa, intensive subsistence agriculture is the predominant method of farming.

INTERTILLAGE

Often, intertillage is used in subsistence agriculture. **Intertillage** is the clearing of rows in the field through the use of hoes, rakes, and other manual equipment. Because machinery is too expensive for subsistence farmers, they use manual labor to clear the fields of weeds and rocks.

Most of the world still practices subsistence agriculture in one form or another, depending upon the climate and the economic conditions of the country. In less developed countries, upward of 80 percent of the farming population may be involved in this type of farming. However, subsistence farming as a primary means of food attainment is decreasing even in less developed countries. In more developed countries, that percent age may be in the single digits.

COMMERCIAL FARMING

Commercial farming is the farming of products for sale off the farm. Commercial farming is usually done in more developed countries and requires the use of machinery.

Commercial farming is practiced in the United States and European countries, among others, and involves the mass production of specialty crops. These crops can often be produced at a reduced price and sold at an increased cost, depending on demand. This has made the United States one of the leaders in world crop production, especially in corn and soybeans, which are primarily used to feed livestock in the Midwest.

Farms involved with commercial agriculture tend to be large and may consist of tens of thousands of acres. Wheat fields in Kansas and the Dakotas are measured in thousands of acres, and ranches in the western United States are not measured by the acre but by the square mile. Machines and technology must be used to farm such large areas successfully. Ranchers may put radio collars on their cattle and fly in a helicopter to find them. The farmer can also track cattle on a computer to determine their location. Because of the size of ranches, fencing in the animals is not cost-effective. Cattle are allowed to roam free. There are even road signs that limit the liability of the farmer if drivers run into their cattle.

Although commercial farming is largely dependent upon climate, genetic engineering has led to increased production regardless of weather. For example, new hybrids may be more tolerant of drought, so farmers can experience the same productivity even if less rain falls than normal.

MEDITERRANEAN AGRICULTURE

There are many different types of commercial farming. One is Mediterranean agriculture. **Mediterranean agriculture** must be practiced in a climate that has a dry summer and a cool, moist winter. The crops associated with the Mediterranean Sea region consist of grapes, dates, and olives. Parts of California and some of the southern portions of Australia have a Mediterranean-type climate and are known for their wine production.

DAIRY FARMING

Another style of commercial farming is **dairy farming**, which has become highly mechanized in recent years. The old idea that the farmer milks the cows early in the morning and again in the afternoon is no longer the case. Most dairy farms in the Midwest are highly mechanized. Cows are brought into the milking barn and hooked up to mechanical milkers by their udders. The machines pump out the milk and store it in a large, cooled container. A milk truck picks up the milk, usually every other day.

The farmer has a contract with a milk or dairy company to provide a certain number of gallons of milk every month or year. Safety precautions tightly control the dairy industry to ensure that consumers and customers receive milk or other dairy products that are of high quality. For example, cows cannot be given certain antibiotics.

Dairy farming usually needs to be done relatively close to a major market. For years, Wisconsin, which is close to large urban areas such as Chicago, Detroit, Milwaukee, and Minneapolis/Saint Paul, held the title of "the dairy state." Milk is quickly sent to these urban areas and put on store shelves. If the milk takes too long to get to market, it spoils.

In the past decade, the title of "the dairy state" has become a matter of contention. With the increase in California's population, milk must be produced in the vicinity of the state's urban areas. As a result, California now produces more milk than Wisconsin. California's dairy farms are located in the valley in the center of the state, which is perfect for the cows. Milk has been a highly profitable industry in California. However, Wisconsin still holds the title of "the cheese state." Cheese, which has a longer shelf life than milk, can be produced in Wisconsin, sent to all areas of the country, and still have enough shelf life so as not to rot or spoil.

The region from New England through the Great Lakes, including a large section of the Midwest, still produces a large percentage of the milk and dairy products in the United States. Another large area of dairy production is in northern Europe, including Great Britain.

MIXED LIVESTOCK WITH CROP PRODUCTION

A third type of commercial farming is **mixed livestock with crop production**. In this type of farming, cows, grown for meat and other products, are fed with crops (including corn and soybeans) grown on the same farm. These animals require a large amount of food, and the majority of the corn and soybeans that are grown in the United States are not meant for human consumption but rather for livestock consumption. Cows are fed in the barn and led out to a pasture area, where they can eat grass and get fattened up before they are sold to the slaughterhouse. The cows are sold by the pound, so the more plump they are, the more money the farmer gets. Cows are not the only livestock raised in this fashion. Hogs are increasingly being raised, due to Americans' appetite for pork and other products from pigs.

This type of farming occurs in the Midwest region of America around Iowa and extends east into the Carolinas and south to Arkansas. In Europe, the mixed livestock and crop region lies in the center of the continent. The Manchurian region of China also has a large number of farms devoted to this method of farming.

LIVESTOCK RANCHING

Livestock ranching is another form of commercial farming. It almost always appears in more developed countries. **Livestock ranching** is done on land that is on the fringes of productive land. Because the feeding of livestock is done by allowing the animals to roam the fields without the assistance of the farmer, huge areas of land are needed. Much of the western portion of the

United States, west of the Great Plains and east of California, is dedicated to livestock ranching. Other areas with a large percentage of agriculture devoted to livestock ranching include the interior of southern Brazil, extending into Argentina; the interior of Australia; and the countries of Kyrgyzstan, Turkmenistan, and Kazakhstan in Asia.

Much of the livestock ranching in the United States and other more developed regions is done in remote, arid to semiarid regions, where the land is relatively inexpensive because of its remoteness from major urban areas.

SPECIALIZED FRUIT PRODUCTION

Another style of commercial farming is **specialized fruit production**. The orchards in the southwestern and southeastern portions of the United States, as well as all along the Atlantic coast, engage in this type of farming. In the dry regions of Arizona, **irrigation** provides crops with much-needed water. Around the world, specialized fruit production is found in scattered portions of southern South America and small portions of Eastern Europe. The climate is warm and humid in these areas, making it ideal for growing these crops. Large orchards produce most of the fruit crops in the United States, including oranges, lemons, limes, peaches, berries, and apples.

PLANTATION AGRICULTURE

Specialized fruit production is not to be confused with plantation agriculture. **Plantation agriculture** often occurs in less developed countries and usually involves the production of one crop, which is sold in more developed countries. Bananas, sugarcane, coffee, and cotton plantations are common in many tropical areas. Originally, these plantations were set up by colonial governments to provide agricultural products for their home countries, but they have persisted despite the end of colonialism because of their profitability. Many plantation owners are located in more developed countries, and their operations provide low-paying employment to hundreds of individuals who desperately need work.

Plantation agriculture involves interaction between **core countries** and **periphery countries**. Core countries often rely on periphery countries for their raw materials or agricultural products. For example, much of Europe depends upon Africa for citrus crops during the winter. Much of the U.S. fruit crop is flown in from Chile and other South American countries during the winter.

TRUCK FARMS

Truck farms are a key aspect of fruit farming. The term **truck farms** refers to a farm where farmers produce fruits for the market. Truck farms use mechanization to produce large quantities of fruits and vegetables, which are sold to processors. For example, many of the Jolly Green Giant plants in Minnesota receive their products from truck farms. These farms specialize in the production of beans or other vegetables and then sell them to the processor, who distributes them after either canning or freezing them. Many truck farms use migrant labor to keep costs low. This industrialization of farming has created a new source of wealth for farmers.

SUITCASE FARMS

Suitcase farms are farms on which no one resides permanently. Suitcase farms go against the grain of traditional farming in the United States. Migrant workers provide a cheap, abundant labor source; they work on the farm during the day and leave the farm at night. In some cases, work will be done during the evening, but there is no residence on the property. Many suitcase farms are in the business of market-gardening products.

This type of farming has led to the rise of agribusiness. **Agribusiness** is the mass production of agricultural products. A debate rages about the relative merits of family farms versus agribusiness. Mass producers of food, such as Cargill, are in the agribusiness industry, and they're constantly trying to find better ways to grow crops and improve their distribution systems to improve profits. Agribusiness is a form of **large-scale commercial agriculture** that has seen the expansion of cropland and production.

Mass production has led to the rise of agricultural industrialization. **Agricultural industrialization** is the increased mechanization of the farming process to increase productivity and profits. Farming is less and less an industry of individual proprietorships. Instead, farms are becoming larger and more geared toward the large-scale production of specific food products. Instead of 100 head of cattle, many farmers have 5,000 head. Instead of one farmer owning a farm, a group of people runs the operation like a business with a chain of command.

GRAIN FARMING

The last method of commercial farming is grain farming. **Grain farming** is the mass planting and harvesting of grain crops, such as wheat, barley, and millet. These fields take up an enormous amount of space because of the increasing demand for abundant production to meet the dietary preferences of more developed countries. Grain farming is often done in drier climates, where wheat is the predominant crop. The Great Plains is one of the largest regions in the world that specializes in the production of grain. Another is the Ukraine in Eastern Europe, one of the world leaders in the production of wheat. Also, some small pockets of grain are grown in South America and Australia.

The grains that are produced in commercial grain farming regions are sometimes known as staple grains. **Staple grains** include wheat, barley, millet, and other grain products that a large percentage of the world population depends on for survival. Check your kitchen cabinets for the food products that you own. You will find that many of the products in your kitchen have some type of grain in them. In the United States, much of it is wheat.

VON THUNEN'S MODEL OF AGRICULTURAL LAND USE

In 1826, **Johann Heinrich von Thunen** developed an agricultural land use model, shown in Figure 7.3, that suggests that certain crops are grown in direct relation to their distance from market. The products' weight determines where farmers must be in relation to the market to grow them. If a farmer grows products that don't fit the model, that farmer will go bankrupt from the increased costs of production and transportation.

Von Thunen's model revolves around specific agricultural markets and only applies to commercial agriculture. The model assumes that farmers sell all of their agricultural harvest. It describes six concentric rings around the market.

MARKET-GARDENING ACTIVITIES

The first zone in von Thunen's model is reserved for market-gardening activities. **Market-gardening activities** include various heavy and bulky products, such as melons and vegetables. These products need to be close to the market for two primary reasons: 1) If they are too far away, they will take too long to get to market and spoil, and 2) the cost of transporting these bulky items is relatively large because of their weight and mass. A truckload of watermelons is much more expensive to haul than a truckload of wheat.

To minimize transportation costs, these products are usually grown close to an urban market. Thus, the agricultural areas around urban areas are devoted to such items as fruits and vegetables. Because the cost of producing these products is usually high, owing to the high cost of land near the urban center, cheap transportation is needed to offset this expense.

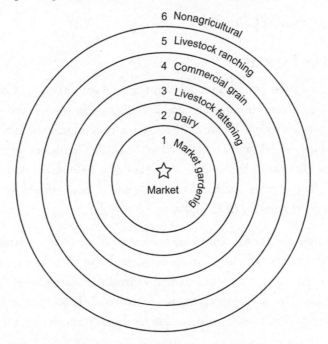

Figure 7.3: Von Thunen Model of Agricultural Land Use.

DAIRY FARMING

The second zone in von Thunen's model is devoted to dairy farming. Dairy, too, must be produced close to the market area. Dairy trucks must cool the milk, cheese, or other dairy product while in transit, adding to the cost of transportation. Also, because milk spoils more rapidly than the dairy products that are produced from it, milk production must be relatively close to large urban areas. This explains the rise of the California dairy industry in response to the population increases in many neighboring states.

LIVESTOCK FATTENING

The third zone in von Thunen's model is devoted to livestock fattening. **Livestock fattening** is the deliberate adding of weight to animals, such as cows and hogs, to increase their sale price. Cows and hogs are brought to the barn to be fed in a small space. Pastures are used, but they are small in comparison to livestock ranching pastureland. The cost of transporting livestock or poultry to urban areas for sale is high because of the weight of the animals. However, farmers don't need to do this on a daily basis. Farmers may only bring livestock to the slaughterhouse to sell several times per year.

Today, many livestock fattening areas are large feedlots. **Feedlots** are farms that specialize in cattle or hogs, and they may have thousands of head. One downside to feedlots is the runoff of waste products from them; these often infiltrate and contaminate local watersheds. Another downside to feedlots is the smell. The smell from a large feedlot can be overpowering for the surrounding countryside. The foul odor, along with potential groundwater contamination, has many people questioning the increased usage of feedlots.

Figure 7.4 shows the feedlots of Colorado.

COMMERCIAL GRAIN FARMING

The fourth major zone in von Thunen's model is commercial grain farming. **Commercial grain farming** is the selling of wheat, corn, millet, and other grains. The transfer process from ground to market area can be done rather quickly with the assistance of combines and semitrailers. Farmers simply need to combine the field and put the seed in the truck. **Combines** separate the seed from the shaft of the plant, eliminating the need to do so manually. Because combines are very expensive pieces of machinery, farmers often purchase one jointly and share the machine during harvest. One new combine can cost upward of $250,000.

After harvesting, commercial grain is sent to the market area, usually in semitrailers, where it is sold to a producer who makes a product, such as bread, with the grain. The product is then sold to a wholesaler, who sells it to a grocery store, where individual customers can buy it. This process is called the **food chain**. This is the process known as farm to fork. Sometimes this is called the **commodity chain**, which describes the process that food goes through to get from the primary

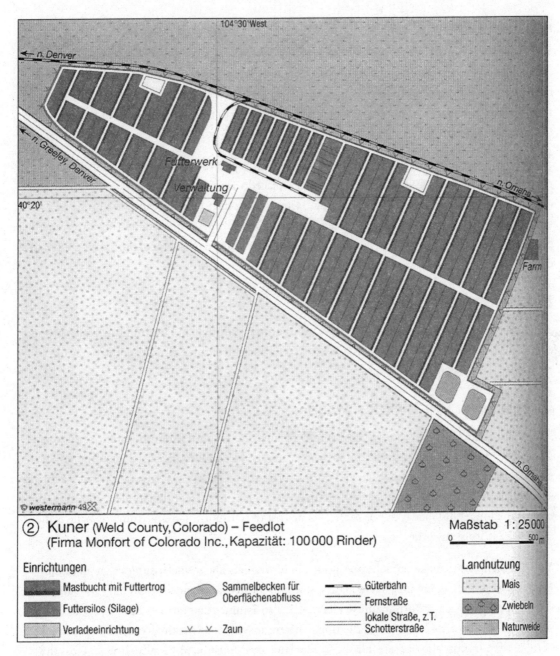

Figure 7.4: Colorado Feedlots. (Used with permission from Westermann Publishing)

sector (resource based) of the economy to the tertiary sector (service based). The in-between players include the transportation systems and two, three, or more different sellers before the consumer has the opportunity to purchase the item. Each time the commodity is sold, the transaction adds to the price of the product.

LIVESTOCK RANCHING

The fifth zone in von Thunen's model is devoted to livestock ranching. **Livestock ranching** uses the most land per farm of any of the zones in the model. Farmers can often afford the extra land because of their distance from the urban market area. Farmers let cattle graze freely, branding them so people know to whom they belong. Transportation to the market area occurs sporadically throughout the year.

The romantic vision of the cowboy on the range lingers as part of the image of U.S. livestock ranching, but the farmer on horseback has been replaced with high-end technology, ensuring the rancher's productivity and profit. Sometimes, farmers don't have fences around their property because their farms are so large, and cattle are often allowed to roam on neighboring government-controlled land. Although the cattle roam freely, they are tracked with global positioning units to ensure their safety and track their location.

NONAGRICULTURAL LAND USE

The last part of von Thunen's model is devoted to nonagricultural land use and isn't really a zone at all. In this instance, the distance to market is so far that the farmer cannot productively or profitably sell agricultural products.

DISCUSSION OF VON THUNEN'S MODEL

Within all zones, costs of products are carefully balanced to account for both distance and weight. Therefore, the cost of sending wheat to market would be identical to the cost of sending milk to market. Because milk needs to be cooled during its journey, the cost of refrigeration is offset by the shorter distance traveled, just as because grain is easy to take to market due to mechanization, the cost of the longer distance it travels is offset. The cost of transporting items from any zone is the same as that from any other zone.

Von Thunen had to make several assumptions in his model. The model assumes that all of the land has the same quality soil. Inadequate soil would mean that farmers would have to plant different crops to achieve profitability. The model also assumes that farmers have equal access to transportation across all zones of the ring. This means that if a trucking company operates in zone 1, then it must also operate in zone 5. The land areas must be physically similar across the model. Mountains, rivers, or other obstructions would mean an increase in transportation prices. Von Thunen's model also assumes an equal climate in all areas of the model and an equal political structure as well. An international boundary in the middle of the area could affect transportation routes because of tariffs on products as they crossed the border.

How well would von Thunen's model hold up today? Although models are representations of human behavior and activity on a mass scale, no model works perfectly in the real world. However, some patterns in real life support this model on a variety of scales.

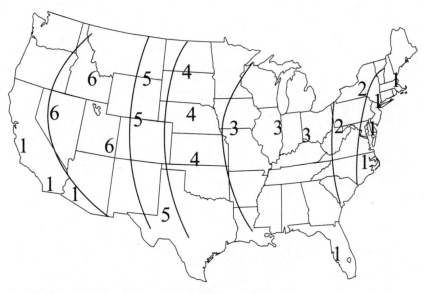

1. Market gardening
2. Dairy
3. Livestock fattening
4. Commercial grain
5. Livestock ranching
6. Nonagricultural

Figure 7.5: Von Thunen's United States Map.

Let's look at the United States in relation to the von Thunen model, as shown in Figure 7.5. Assuming that New York City, the largest city in the United States, is the market, would the model hold up? The answer is yes and no.

The area around New York City, including New England and upstate New York, is dotted with orchards and other farms that fit the bill for the market-gardening area. The next area is dairy farming. Dairy extends westward into Pennsylvania and upstate New York. The third area, a bit farther away than the dairy sections, is livestock fattening. By analyzing crop patterns in the United States, we see that corn and soybeans, intended mostly for livestock consumption, are grown in the Midwest.

The fourth area, commercial grain, extends out to the Great Plains. Wheat and barley fields cover the landscape in this region. The next area, livestock ranching, is in the Rocky Mountain states, mostly because of the relatively dry climate in the region.

The last area is that of nonagricultural land use. Vast sections of land in the western United States are unused, again an effect of the climate and mountainous terrain of the area. They serve no agricultural purpose and could be classified as nonagricultural.

Then we get to California, Oregon, and Washington, which confound the model. California is dominated by fruit farming and dairy products. Oregon and California are renowned for their wine production with their temperate Mediterranean climates. Washington is known for its apples. These products, along with the market-gardening areas in Arizona, tend to skew the model.

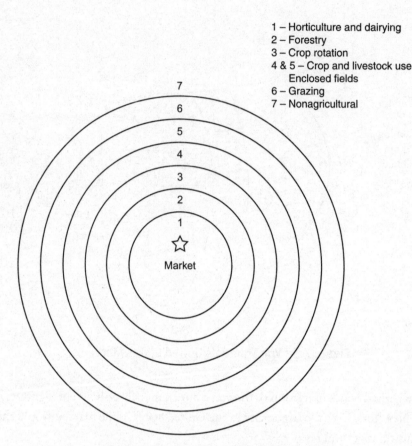

1 – Horticulture and dairying
2 – Forestry
3 – Crop rotation
4 & 5 – Crop and livestock use
        Enclosed fields
6 – Grazing
7 – Nonagricultural

Figure 7.6: Von Thunen Model—Modified.

Von Thunen's original model has also been shown to include horticulture and forestry, as seen in Figure 7.6. The center of the model is still the urban area where products are sold. All agriculture revolves around the market area. The next area consists of dairying and horticulture, or the growing of specified plants. The next ring includes forestry, followed by a ring of crop rotation, which includes the commercial grain crops outlined in the model. The last ring is used for cattle grazing, owing to the size of ranches needed for this type of farming.

ECONOMIC SYSTEMS AND ACTIVITIES

The type of economic system in which a farmer operates directly affects the degree of technology and mechanization of the farming system. Farmers in less developed countries are usually practicing some type of subsistence agriculture, which usually involves more manual labor and less mechanization. If plantation agriculture is practiced, the profits usually flow back to owners in a developed country.

There are different types of economic activities. **Primary economic activities** are subsistence farming using hunting and gathering techniques or pastoral nomadism. Some societies still practice hunting and gathering, including the Aborigines of Australia and the Bushmen of Namibia.

Secondary economic activities are the industrial sectors of the economy. Factories take raw materials, which may be natural resources, and produce some type of product for either trading or selling. Many people in the United States are still employed in secondary economic activities.

Tertiary economic activities involve the service sectors of the economy. People are involved in selling commodities rather than in producing them. For example, more people are involved in the selling and servicing of automobiles in the United States than in their manufacture. In addition, more people are selling, transporting, and servicing kitchen appliances than manufacturing them.

As technology continues to improve, economists and geographers have had to classify new levels of activities. **Quaternary activities** are those that one cannot hold or physically touch. They include the selling of Internet time or cell phone service. Tax services and other financial services also fall into this category.

Quinary activities involve the management decisions of a society. This sector may only employ 10 to 15 percent of the workforce, but these are the people who make decisions concerning the trade of commodities at the governmental level and the executive levels in businesses. Their decisions affect the lives of farmers throughout the world through commodity pricing and trade agreements, such as the North American Free Trade Agreement (NAFTA).

Farming today is much different than it was even 50 years ago. Traditionally, farmers would sell their products to the **elevator**, often a cooperative whose members were the farmers of that small town or village. The elevator company then sold the harvest to a processor, which transported it to a plant where the commodity was turned into some type of food product.

Today, advances in technology and mechanization allow farmers to grow more food than ever before in human history. The mass production of food products is hurting the small farmer, who must either conglomerate or face extinction. This has led to the **farm crisis**: Farmers are too productive, causing supply to exceed demand for many products, meaning lower prices and less revenue for farmers. Thousands of small farmers have been forced to leave the land that they have owned for generations. In addition, increased revenue has not kept up with rising operating costs, leaving many farmers bankrupt.

On the opposite end of the spectrum are the farmers who live or have lived close to urban areas. As urban areas expand and encroach on neighboring farmland, developers often pay premium sums to farmers for their land. Thus, land that might have been bought for dollars on the acre may be sold for tens of thousands of dollars per acre. This land is so valuable that many farmers feel they have no reasonable choice but to sell the land, and some farmers are walking away with millions of dollars.

What this leaves is an agricultural industry that continues to become more mechanized and industrialized. Farmers are quickly brokering deals with processing plants to produce a certain amount of product each year. Such contracts assure farmers a guaranteed income, usually more than what they would have earned had they continued to farm the land on their own.

Commercial farming is quite different from the subsistence farming in less developed countries, where the food is eaten in the rural villages that produce it. The majority of the world's population depends on subsistence agriculture. Such rural settlements are dispersed, making trade with other villages infrequent. Many of the villages in Southeast Asia employ intensive subsistence agriculture in the production of rice. Because rice is such a labor-intensive crop, villagers may all work together during the harvest season so that the whole crop can be brought into storage for the nongrowing season. Many societies that practice subsistence agriculture hold cultural festivals to celebrate the completion of the harvest.

AGRICULTURE IN THE UNITED STATES

The United States, like all other countries of the world, has relied on agriculture for the success of its society. Agriculture in the United States has changed considerably over the centuries that humans have been on the land.

THE EFFECTS OF EARLY EUROPEAN SETTLEMENTS AND WESTWARD MIGRATION ON AGRICULTURE

The first European settlers established Jamestown, Virginia, in 1607. This colony was doomed to fail from the start because of its poor agricultural practices. The colonists arrived in August and tried planting crops at this time, but the growing season was far too short, and the colonists didn't have enough food to eat. Starvation killed a large part of the population. What made things worse was that the colonists didn't befriend the Native Americans, who could have helped them; instead, they built forts as a defensive measure.

Another wave of settlers came to Plymouth, Massachusetts, in 1621. Instead of alienating themselves from the Native American population, these settlers befriended them. Native Americans assisted them with their agricultural practices, teaching them how to grow maize and other native vegetables. This assistance from Native Americans was vital to the success of the Massachusetts colony.

More Europeans began arriving in North America, and with them, they brought their cattle. Cattle were a source of milk and food for the growing populations. Horses also were used to assist in plowing the land. The soil in New England was very rocky so many people of European descent moved west, where the soil was richer and much more productive.

Europeans used traditional seed agriculture and began planting their crops in typical northern European style on the American landscape. The **metes and bounds** system, already used in Great Britain for many centuries, was used in many areas in New England during the 1700s. The metes and bounds system of measuring uses the land's physical features to describe ownership claims. The bounds system uses more generalized features, while the metes system uses traditional distance measurements.

The movement west in the United States was motivated largely by agricultural opportunities on some of the richest soil in the world. Railroads brought new immigrants to the Midwest and West; the U.S. government sold land to the railroads, which then gave the land to immigrants if they promised to farm it for five years. The railroads, in return for giving up land, earned profits from the farmers' transportation of agricultural products to markets in the East. The Homestead Act, passed by Congress in 1862, was one of the most successful laws to ensure settlement on the Great Plains. It allowed citizens to settle on up to 160 acres of surveyed but unclaimed public land and receive title to it after making improvements and residing there for five years.

As settlers continued to move west, they began using the **township and range** system. This broke up much of the Midwest into square-mile tracts known as **sections**, and settlements were often dispersed around the township. Farms were dispersed, but commercial enterprises needed larger residential areas as markets and to supply labor and so usually were located in the community center or town.

Evidence of the township and range land-use pattern can be seen when flying over the central portions of the United States, where you see patches of land of almost one square mile across sections of Missouri, Iowa, and Nebraska. This was done both for ease of settlement and so that the railroads, which owned most of this land, could bring in settlers and help export agricultural products to larger markets in the East. The township and range pattern seen in Oklahoma, as shown in Figure 7.7, is indicative of this settlement pattern.

Another type of survey pattern that is still evident on the landscape came from the French settlers, who used the **long lots** system along the rivers in Louisiana. Because the French used rivers as a primary form of transportation, the lots extended back from the river as far as one-half mile or more. The farmers would farm the land away from the river and use the river to haul their agricultural products to market, either up- or downstream.

Each system made its own imprint on the landscape, which is still evident today; the metes and bounds system is used today in New England, the township and range system in the Midwest and Great Plains, and the long lot system in and around New Orleans.

Early in the settlement process, the Erie Canal, connecting Lake Erie with the Hudson River, was built to bypass the formidable barrier of the Appalachian Mountains and link the fertile Midwest regions with the markets on the East Coast. Pennsylvania tried to construct something similar but was never as successful as the state of New York. This is one of the reasons why New York City is still the dominant urban center in the United States.

Farmers would receive huge profits from the productive use of the soil in the 1800s in the American West. Settlements began to fill in the central portions of the United States as well, inhabiting areas that had been labeled the "Great American Desert" by the early Spanish explorers. They had seen the Great Sand Dunes off the Platte River in Nebraska, and the name stuck until the mid-1800s. However, settlers found that the area was not a desert at all but rather a plain, and they used it to grow wheat and other commodities that require less moisture.

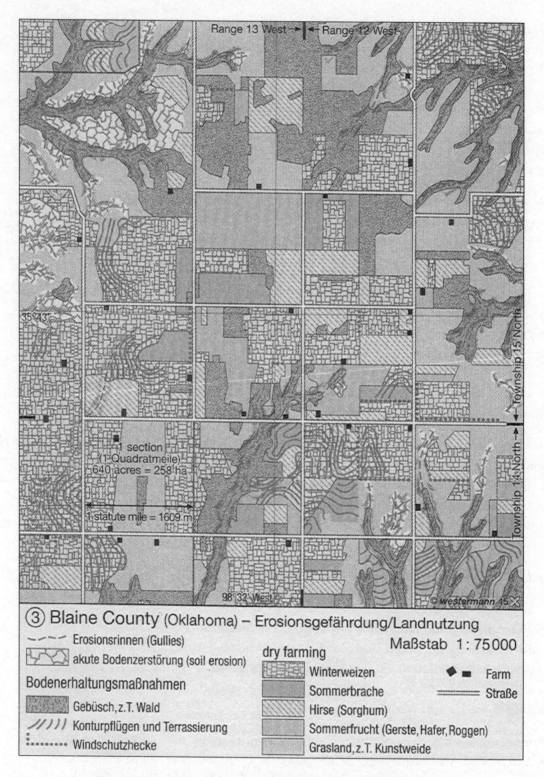

Figure 7.7: Oklahoma Township and Range Land-Use Pattern.

AMERICAN AGRICULTURE IN THE 20TH CENTURY

In 1910, a geographer at the American Association of Geographers (AAG) conference in Chicago by the name of Fredrick Jackson Turner wrote a paper declaring that the West was now closed. There were still spots of settlement to fill in, but he argued that the United States had reached its *Manifest Destiny*, to settle the land from the East Coast (Atlantic Ocean) to the West Coast (Pacific Ocean). Agriculture had provided a means and a reason for people to leave the East Coast in search of riches found in the dark, rich soil of the Midwest.

The idea that humans could influence nature was prevalent in the United States until the 1930s. There was a saying on the Great Plains that the "rain followed the plow," meaning that the more land was plowed and used for agriculture, the more rain would fall. Logically, it followed that more farmers were needed to plow the drier areas to increase precipitation and agricultural yields. During the 1920s, the Great Plains saw a time of abnormally high precipitation, seemingly verifying the theory.

This all changed in the 1930s, when the United States was flung into the Great Depression. While the stock market was teetering, the Great Plains region was suffering the effects of one of the greatest droughts in American history. The early 1930s marked the beginning of the Dust Bowl. Millions of settlers moved away or emigrated from the Great Plains. Thousands of head of cattle died in the drought. Storms on the Great Plains produced no rain, just clouds of dirt and dust that stretched as far as the Carolinas and other areas of the East Coast.

The "rain follows the plow" philosophy had largely been discredited. In fact, the direct opposite is known today. The more natural vegetation that a region possesses, the more likely precipitation will increase. Plowing the soil of the Great Plains had only fueled the dust storms that caused havoc for about a decade. Millions of tons of fertile, productive Great Plains soil literally vanished into the air as a result of wind erosion.

As the Great Plains were settled, people continued to move west but found the continent got drier the farther they went, until they reached the coast of California. California's climate was perfect for fruit production. Just as in Florida, river water could be channeled to orchards and fields to produce crops unlike those of any other area. Production of lemons, oranges, and pineapples boomed in these areas of California as well as in Arizona. Even today, market gardening or fruit farming produces the most cash crop receipts in the country, more than any other method of farming.

The West depends on irrigation for its water needs. The Ogallala Aquifer, a large body of water found under the surface of the Earth in the Great Plains, is being depleted at a rapid rate. Rainfall is not enough to replace the water that the farmers use to irrigate their crops.

Environmental modification is the introduction of manmade chemicals and practices to an area. At times, environmental modification has had drastic effects on the native soil and vegetation. The use of pesticides on farm products has led to decreases in crop losses from insects, but it also means more chemicals are present on food and in the natural environment. Organic farming has become more popular in direct response to the use of pesticides. This is one of the fundamental aspects of the Third Agricultural Revolution.

The effects of negative farming practices are being felt around the globe. Overgrazing has led to encroaching deserts within arid regions, a process known as **desertification**. When herds of animals graze on land that does not receive enough precipitation, the land becomes barren and desert-like, as is evident in the Saharan region. Southern Saharan regions have experienced a significant loss of farmland to the expanding desert. Desertification can only be reversed by not using such land for pastoral nomadism. However, the long-term goal of preserving inhabitable land is often in conflict with people's immediate need to feed themselves.

THE FUTURE OF AMERICAN AGRICULTURE

Agriculture is ever changing. New farms may hardly resemble the farms of the past. For example, new farms may be involved in **aquaculture**, the farming of fish for sale off the farm. Fish may be raised in pools and then sold for food or to stock lakes for the tourism industry.

Some don't consider forestry to be farming but rather the harvesting of a natural resource. Forestry will be discussed in more detail in the chapter on Industrialization and Economic Development. However, the issue remains that timber companies have replanted millions of trees to ensure a sustainable yield, that is, to produce a crop for many years to come.

This brings up the subject of **creative destruction**, the removal of what nature originally produced in a particular location to grow what is desired. With recent advances in genetic engineering, farmers can now grow crops where they previously could not owing to climatic conditions, earning more profits as a result.

In recent decades, the focus of U.S. agriculture has shifted away from small farmers selling their products or commodities to processors. The processors of livestock such as poultry and cattle have been complaining for many years that the quality and the quantity of the meat has been variable, because many different small producers or farmers have been providing the animals. Processors would rather buy from one mass producer or farmer, to achieve more uniform quality and also so that the processing plants do not have to shut down while waiting for another small batch of animals. One mass producer can ensure consistent quality and guaranteed quantity.

This preference has led to the rise of huge feedlot operations in the poultry, hog, and cattle industries. Huge feedlots can handle tens of thousands of chickens or turkeys at a time, feeding them in an industrial process that fattens them up before they are taken to plants for processing. Cattle were late arrivals to the feedlot game, but in recent decades, huge feedlots for cattle have been popping up, primarily in the western areas of the country. The poultry industry has been dominated by the South; North Carolina is one of the leading producers of turkeys in the United

States, and Arkansas is one of the leading producers of chickens, primarily because national brands have located their processing plants in these states.

What this method of farming has produced is a **"just-in-time"** method of delivery, where products arrive at the grocery store just before consumers purchase them. U.S. processors have become so efficient that they can process the commodity, usually in a plant very close to the farmers who raised the livestock, then ship the product directly to the grocery store just in time to fill an empty shelf so you can buy it. This keeps products fresh.

The development of mass production forces small farmers into a decision. Do they contract out with the processor or continue to go it alone? If they do contract out with the food processors, they will almost always receive a guaranteed income, but they must invest in new barns and holding areas for the hogs, chickens, turkeys, or cattle—a prohibitive cost for many farmers. The days when farmers produced all of their products for sale in the local grocery store have almost vanished. The raising of livestock in the Corn Belt has diminished greatly, and now those farmers who used to raise cattle as well as crops are being forced out of the cattle industry to focus on growing corn for sale to the huge feedlots.

Large corporate farms and feedlots have come under pressure from the public and press to clean up their operations because of environmental concerns. Large conventional farms use large quantities of pesticides and herbicides that impact wildlife and water systems. Massive feedlots have serious issues dealing with processing livestock waste, which can pollute local air and water.

Small family farmers have resorted to a number of methods to stay profitable and keep their businesses. First, many farmers have started to incorporate sustainable farming techniques such as ridge tillage, integrated pest management, limited use of pesticides and herbicides, and using a mixed crop and livestock operation. These methods help reduce costs for the farmer in an era of declining incomes. This type of agriculture is riskier, but once farmers have made the move to sustainable agriculture—eliminating all chemicals for weed, pest control, and fertilization—they can get more money per pound for their crops than if the same crop were grown conventionally. Farmers can earn even more if their crops are certified organically grown by the USDA, although this is often a lengthy and involved process.

Another strategy that small farmers have used is to take advantage of the "local food" movement. Many people feel that it is important to support local farmers because the food is fresher, does less harm to the environment (fewer "food miles" traveled), and helps the local economy. Grocery stores and restaurants have also used this angle to market their products and increase customer loyalty.

This idea of just-in-time production has produced a movement of consumers known as **locavores**, people who consume products grown or raised close to them. Locavore cafes have popped up around the United States and Europe serving locally produced items on their menus. Consumers like the idea of fast, fresh food that aids people in their local community rather than corporations located hundreds or thousands of miles away.

AGRICULTURE AND THE ENVIRONMENT

Agriculture, as a whole, has often been criticized in the past decades for not being environmentally friendly in its practices. Fertilizer runoff into streams, techniques that result in desertification, and other environmental practices adopted in the pursuit of profit have given agriculture a bad reputation. However, as the environment takes a larger role in public policy debates, practices of farmers are getting more attention.

In many places in the Midwest, runoff from animals and fertilizer from fields goes into rivers and streams where children swim only a few miles downstream. Efforts are now being made to protect these ecosystems from pollution by providing buffer zones between fields or pastures and the streams. These buffer zones may simply be an area of grass extending from both sides of the stream only 20-30 feet wide. However, during times of excessive water runoff from rains or snowmelt, the grassy area provides a buffer for the stream, keeping it cleaner.

Irrigation and other agricultural practices have often times come at the expense of the natural environment. New irrigation practices allow farmers to recycle water and use it over and over again while still providing nutrition and moisture to the crops. New technology in irrigation practices has meant a cleaner ecosystem for those living around rivers.

WORLD CROP REGIONS

When looking at world crop regions, the number one factor to examine in terms of productivity is climate. If one compares a world agriculture-regions map with a world climate-regions map it is obvious how climate determines what type of agriculture is practiced. For example, shifting cultivation dominates in the tropical rain forests, and pastoral nomadism is prevalent throughout most semi-arid regions of the developing world. Moving down the scale of analysis to the regional level, one can analyze the complexity of agricultural systems within a more developed country by considering the level of wealth and incorporation of technology within each system. A good example of an area where this kind of analysis is fruitful is California, where many different types of agriculture are practiced in a relatively small area. The second most important factor is the economic system of the country. If the country is a less developed one, its people are usually involved in subsistence agriculture, which means a dependence on animals in more arid climates and a dependence on crops in more moist climates.

The United States is the world leader in the production of corn, which is used to raise livestock and also as a food source for humans. The United States is also a large producer of soybeans, which are seen as a healthier alternative to many available meat products. Soy burgers and other natural food products are part of many Americans' diets. Many U.S. school districts have switched from providing meat to more of a soy-based diet in school lunches.

As the demand for fuel continues to rise in the United States, corn is increasingly being used to produce ethanol. Many states now require that a certain percentage of the gasoline sold within their state be made of ethanol. As the demand for ethanol increases, so does the demand for corn. As the demand for corn continues to climb, the price of corn continues to rise. This rise in price motivates more farmers to plant corn as their primary crop.

In South America, some ethanol is made from corn, but the majority is made from sugarcane. Brazil is one of the largest producers of ethanol. This ethanol is sold to more developed countries as well as being used in Brazil. Ethanol does not transport well.

In Eastern Europe, wheat is a major product, used to produce food for a large section of the population. Bread is a building block in most diets around the world, and Europe is no exception. The European Union has set strict policies regarding the growing of food in many portions of Europe today. Environmental regulations and soil conservation techniques have had a huge impact on European agriculture, as have regulations on the use of pesticides and the crops that can be grown in certain regions of the continent. As a result, almost half of the European supermarkets are filled with organic produce of some type. This market far exceeds that of the United States, where organic foods, although increasing rapidly in popularity, still make up a small percentage of the total food sold.

In Africa, the crop of choice is sorghum or millet. Both are high-calorie energy sources. As Africa's population continues to increase, the importance of agriculture to feed people continues to increase. Much of Africa is trying to gain the help of Western universities and research institutions to increase production and catch up with the modern technology used by the more developed world.

Rice is the staple food source in most of Asia. Areas from the Middle East to the Far East depend on rice for survival. Rice is often traded to people in drier climates for their animal products. Areas such as Southeast Asia, where rainfall is plentiful, can grow rice on terraced mountainsides. This terrain and the warm, moist climate there are ideal for the production of rice.

In a **planned economy**, or government-controlled economy such as China's, the government often dictates to farmers the quantity and type of agricultural products they can produce. As mentioned previously in China, there is a so-called "noodle line," which dictates the type of crops grown. To the north of the noodle line, where wheat is grown, the primary food is noodles. To the south of the noodle line, rice is grown and is the staple food. Dishes native to China can be distinguished based upon their noodle or rice accompaniment. American Chinese restaurants have intermingled the two based on American taste preferences, but original recipes are based on the climate of China.

REVIEW QUESTIONS

MULTIPLE-CHOICE QUESTIONS

1. In what zone of von Thunen's model would the fruit production method of farming best fit?

    (A) Market gardening

    (B) Dairy

    (C) Livestock fattening

    (D) Commercial grain

    (E) Livestock ranching

2. Which area of the world would most likely lead the others in the production of wheat?

    (A) Central Brazil

    (B) Interior Australia

    (C) Ukraine or Eastern Europe

    (D) Southeast Asia

    (E) Central Africa

3. What type of survey pattern of farming would be found in the Louisiana or Mississippi Delta region of the United States?

    (A) Township and range

    (B) Dispersed village

    (C) Metes and bounds

    (D) Nucleated format

    (E) Long lots

4. Which area of the world was the first to domesticate cattle, sheep, and goats?

    (A) Central America

    (B) Northeastern Africa

    (C) Northern China

    (D) Northeastern India

    (E) Northwestern South America

5. Which crop did Norman Borlaug use to initiate the Third Agricultural Revolution in Mexico?

    (A) Corn

    (B) Wheat

    (C) Rice

    (D) Sorghum

    (E) Manioc

6. Which of the following is NOT a form of commercial farming?

    (A) Grain farming

    (B) Fruit farming

    (C) Mediterranean agriculture

    (D) Livestock ranching

    (E) Slash-and-burn farming

7. Which was probably the first form of agriculture in human history?

    (A) Slash-and-burn farming

    (B) Seed agriculture

    (C) Hunting and gathering

    (D) Pastoral nomadism

    (E) Shifting cultivation

8. What is the primary difference between livestock ranching and livestock fattening?

    (A) Livestock fattening requires more human labor than livestock ranching.

    (B) Livestock ranching has more profit per head of cattle than livestock fattening.

    (C) Livestock fattening requires less feed per head of cattle than livestock ranching.

    (D) Livestock ranching requires more space than livestock fattening.

    (E) Livestock ranching requires more capital investment for feed products.

9. The majority of the world's population that is involved in agriculture is involved in what type of agriculture?

(A) Pastoral nomadism

(B) Mediterranean agriculture

(C) Shifting cultivation

(D) Subsistence farming

(E) Plantation agriculture

10. Von Thunen's model revolves around which of the following fundamental principles?

(A) The fertility of soil decreases as one moves away from the urban area or market.

(B) Access to transportation improves as one moves closer to the urban area.

(C) The climate in the area dictates the type of crops grown.

(D) In the village system, farmers are involved in subsistence agriculture with an urban area serving as a center point for culture.

(E) The farmers in the area are all involved in commercial agriculture, selling their products to a market located at the center.

11. Which of the following phrases would best fit the Second Agricultural Revolution?

(A) The Second Agricultural Revolution saw the beginning of seed agriculture.

(B) The Second Agricultural Revolution brought mechanization into the farming process.

(C) The Second Agricultural Revolution prompted farmers to develop new crops.

(D) The Second Agricultural Revolution allowed farmers to redesign crops to grow in nonnative climates.

(E) The Second Agricultural Revolution meant more profits for farmers due to less human capital being needed.

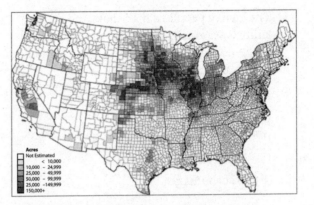

12. The map above shows corn for grain production for selected U.S. states. Which conclusion can be made based on the map?

(A) Corn is linked with the livestock-fattening region of the United States.

(B) Corn is a high-bulk food and therefore must be grown closer to urban centers.

(C) Corn is a staple food in the American diet.

(D) Corn is not grown much in the West due to dietary preferences.

(E) Corn is not that profitable a crop due to the influence of ethanol and other biofuels.

13. What is the process called of splitting existing plants into two and replanting both parts to propogate crops?

(A) Seed agriculture

(B) Aquaculture

(C) Vegetative planting

(D) Subsistence agriculture

(E) Plantation agriculture

14. The Tuareg people of the Sahara and their animals seasonally migrate to the higher lands in the summer and the valleys in the winter. This is an example of

    (A) pastoral nomadism.

    (B) livestock ranching.

    (C) livestock fattening.

    (D) dairy farming.

    (E) transhumance.

15. Which statement accurately describes the recent trend(s) in agriculture in the United States?

    (A) The average size of farms is decreasing.

    (B) The number of family-owned farms continues to increase.

    (C) The total revenue of agricultural sales is becoming more concentrated in fewer large corporate farms.

    (D) The cost of converting a conventional farm into a farm growing certified organic crops is relatively quick and easy.

    (E) Sustainable farms make up only a small percentage of total agricultural sales and their numbers are declining.

16. The process of growing crops in tropical areas for sale in more developed countries is what type of farming?

    (A) Slash-and-burn farming

    (B) Plantation agriculture

    (C) Intensive subsistence agriculture

    (D) Shifting cultivation

    (E) Commercial agriculture

17. The overgrazing of pasture areas in arid climates has caused which problem?

    (A) Global warming

    (B) Mass starvation

    (C) Desertification

    (D) Soil loss

    (E) Soil erosion

18. Farming in the United States, in particular, has experienced what pattern?

    (A) Movement to agricultural industrialization

    (B) Debt-for-nature swap

    (C) Tragedy of the commons

    (D) More sustainable yields

    (E) More work with intertillage practices

19. Why is double-cropping or even triple-cropping important?

    (A) It allows subsistence farmers to produce more income from selling their products.

    (B) It provides consumers with more choices of foods to eat.

    (C) It allows farmers the freedom to rotate crops without harming the soil.

    (D) It allows farmers to meet the demands of ever-increasing populations.

    (E) It gives producers the profit margins to meet demands of investors.

20. Three of the largest dairy regions in the United States are in the Northeast (New York and Pennsylvania), the Upper Midwest (Wisconsin and Minnesota), and California. What explains this phenomenon?

    (A) The transportation systems are much better in these areas.

    (B) The climates are more conducive to raising dairy cattle.

    (C) Large urban centers are located in each zone.

    (D) Industrial output is much greater due to the crops produced in these regions.

    (E) There are more milk drinkers in these parts of the country than in other parts.

FREE-RESPONSE QUESTION

Directions: While a formal essay is not required, it is not enough to answer the following question by merely listing facts. Your answer should be based upon your critical analysis of the question posed.

1. The Green Revolution, which was a part of the Third Agricultural Revolution, helped increase crop yields in the developing world after World War II.

   (A) Discuss three aspects of the Green Revolution that helped increase crop yields.

   (B) Discuss one example of the Green Revolution being successful, and one example of it not meeting expectations.

   (C) Given population trends in the developing world, why was the Green Revolution crucial in order to avert famine?

ANSWERS AND EXPLANATIONS

MULTIPLE-CHOICE QUESTIONS

1. A

Fruit production would best fit the market-gardening zone in von Thunen's model of agricultural land use. Fruits are bulky products that cost a lot to transport to the market, based on their weight and high spoilage rate. The rest of the answers would not fit fruit production in von Thunen's model. Dairy is milk or milk products, such as cheese and yogurt. Livestock is not mentioned in the question, and fruit is not a commercial grain.

2. C

The area of the Ukraine and Eastern Europe is the world leader in the production of wheat. Its arid climate and fertile soil allows wheat to grow at an exceptional pace. The former Soviet Union, with its planned economy, also instituted the practice of growing wheat. This was done to feed the people of the former Soviet Union. Today, much of this wheat is still eaten in the area, but much of it is exported to surrounding countries as well. Ukraine exported over 6.5 billion tons of wheat in 2005 and 2006. Central Brazil and Southeast Asia cannot be correct, because those areas are too moist, and the other answer choices have large areas of uninhabitable land due to their desert-like conditions, making agriculture unproductive.

3. E

The only three land patterns found in the United States are the metes and bounds, township and range, and the long lots systems. The long lots system was used by the French to section off land in areas such as present-day Louisiana. Narrow lots would abut a river and extend back for up to a mile. Farmers would send their products to market by means of the river. This is the correct answer. The metes and bounds system was started in Great Britain and is still in use in most parts of New England. The township and range system is predominant in much of the Midwest owing to the vast expanse of fairly flat land. The township and range system is an easy way to divide the land and allocate ownership.

4. B

Northeastern Africa was the first area to domesticate cattle, sheep, and goats. All three of these animals diffused into Europe, which then colonized North and South America. Central America domesticated the turkey, llama, and alpaca, whereas Southeast Asia domesticated the dog, pig, and chicken.

5. B

Norman Borlaug initiated wheat production in Mexico, transitioning that country from a net importer of wheat to an exporter. The hybridization of wheat became a central component of the work of Borlaug, who went on to work with wheat in many different regions of the world.

6. E

This is a type of question that you will see rarely on the AP exam, but you will see it. The *not* questions offer answer choices that are all correct except for one. In this case, all of the answers are correct except slash-and-burn farming. Slash-and-burn farming is a subsistence agricultural practice that involves burning the debris off the land and using the resulting phosphates as fertilizer for the new soil.

7. C

Hunting and gathering was the first form of agriculture in the world, although it is not "farming" as we tend to think of it today. It involved the hunting of game species, such as buffalo, and the gathering of natural plant products, such as berries and other fruits. Seed agriculture didn't develop until the First Agricultural Revolution. Pastoral nomadism involves the domestication of animals; before domestication, animals were used, but they traveled in their herd naturally instead of being herded.

8. D

The difference between livestock fattening and livestock ranching is the space involved. Livestock ranching requires much more space than livestock fattening. Livestock fattening is usually done in some type of feedlot or in a small pasture. Livestock ranching, on the other hand, is done in huge range areas, where technology is used to track the animals. Choice (C) is not correct because livestock fattening does not involve less feed. Livestock ranching and fattening both involve the same amount of food. In livestock fattening, the food is generally bought by the farmer and fed to the cattle, while in livestock ranching, the livestock forage for food in their grazing areas.

9. D

The majority of the world is involved in subsistence farming, using the land to sustain the population. A lot of labor is needed for subsistence farming, especially for intensive subsistence agriculture. Rice requires heavy, hard labor for the harvest to be successful. One of the choices, pastoral nomadism, takes place in arid areas where few people reside. Mediterranean agriculture is done in only a few areas of the world, where the climate is conducive for the growing of olives, dates, and grapes. Shifting cultivation is done in tropical areas, as is plantation agriculture; however, both of these forms of agriculture involve relatively few laborers. The only logical choice remaining is subsistence agriculture.

10. E

Von Thunen's model must be applied to commercial farming. If applied to subsistence farming, it would lose its characteristic concentric rings around the market area; they would be replaced by a system of small lot holdings around the village center. Von

Thunen made some assumptions in his model that everything in the rings of the circle would be consistent (i.e., transportation, climate, soil fertility would be the same as one moved from the market-gardening area out to the livestock ranching areas).

11. B

The Second Agricultural Revolution coincided with the Industrial Revolution. The Industrial Revolution mechanized industry and improved transportation for farmers, expanding the market area for their agricultural commodities. The First Agricultural Revolution introduced seed agriculture, meaning that choice A doesn't work. The Third Agricultural Revolution, which is still underway, has genetically altered crops.

12. A

This type of question will require you to read the map and then apply some prior knowledge to the map. Looking at the corn-growing regions, we see that they are primarily located in the central northern regions of the United States. Knowing that most of the corn in the United States is used for animal consumption of some sort, we can infer that this region is linked with the livestock-fattening region. The other answers do not fit with the question. Corn is not a high-bulk food but rather a commercial grain and, according to von Thunen, can be grown farther from large urban centers. Dietary preferences do play a role, but although Americans eat a large amount of corn in their daily diets, the majority of it goes toward livestock fattening. The production of corn for ethanol production has led to increased prices for corn bushels, increasing farmers' profits; the more demand for a product, the higher its price. This eliminates choice (E).

13. C

Vegetative planting involves splitting an existing plant and then replanting both halves to propogate the plant. Seed agriculture is the other main form of planting. Seed agriculture involves harvesting the seeds of the plant and planting them. The other choices are simply methods of farming that could use either vegetative planting or seed agriculture.

14. E

The Tuareg are a nomadic population that lives in the southern Saharan region of Africa and practices transhumance. They seasonally take their herds to the highlands during the hot, dry season and bring them down to the valley during the cool, moist season. Two of the answers (livestock fattening and livestock ranching) deal with commercial agricultural, which does not migrate herds at all. Ranching involves livestock roaming in the pastures, but their movement is not a seasonal migration. Pastoral nomadism is a close second choice for this question. However, pastoral nomads move their herds regardless of the time of year. Transhumance refers to seasonal migration based on temperature variation during the year.

15. C

There are a number of trends in modern agriculture in the United States. First, the average size of farms is getting larger because small farms are being bought out by larger corporate farms. Second, small family farms are having difficulty staying in business and thus are often absorbed by larger, more profitable operations. Third, a small number of large corporate farms account for an increasingly large majority of revenue of total agricultural sales. The process to convert a conventional farm into a sustainable or organic farm is a lengthly and involved one. Presently, sustainable farms make up less than 5 percent of total agricultural revenue, but they are growing in number at a rapid rate.

16. B

Plantation agriculture survived beyond colonialism because the plantations continue to provide employment to many of the workers in less developed countries. Plantation agriculture has created an export economy in many of these areas, which normally would be involved in subsistence farming. Slash-and-burn farming is more associated with subsistence farming than exporting crops to more developed countries. Choices (A), (C), and (D) are all forms of subsistence agriculture. Commercial agriculture involves the sale of products, as does plantation agriculture, but the more descriptive answer is plantation agriculture.

17. C

Desertification is a major problem in arid climates where poor farming practices have meant the loss of productive farmland to the ever-encroaching desert. Plants and trees naturally prevent erosion. Herders allow their animals to eat the vegetation that holds back the sand from encroaching on productive agricultural areas. Mass starvation can result from desertification. Soil loss is part of the problem, but mostly the good soil is covered up by sand. When windstorms arise, productive soil is often lost.

18. A

The trend for the previous 20 to 30 years in U.S. agriculture has been toward agricultural industrialization. Farmers are now using more technology. The food chain has been made much more productive and efficient through this process. As a result, the food that you buy in the supermarket is less expensive. Organic products, which take more human labor to be produced, cost more. A debt-for-nature swap is the forgiveness of debt by more developed countries in return for less developed countries promising to set aside land as a natural habitat or national park.

19. D

By double- or triple-cropping, farmers can double or triple their profits. Also, increased production from growing two or three crops per year can support more people in a given area. Because of increased agricultural production, the world will see less starvation.

20. C

Von Thunen suggested that dairy regions must be close to large urban areas. The three largest dairy-producing regions in the United States are all close to major urban centers that depend on dairy products as part of their daily diet. Transportation systems are the same in all of these areas, with road systems developed enough to provide adequate transportation.

FREE-RESPONSE QUESTION

SAMPLE ESSAY

PART A

The Green Revolution saw the adoption of machinery, pesticides, herbicides, and genetically engineered seeds in developing countries in order to produce more food. Machinery such as tractors and harvesters helped make various aspects of farming much more efficient, doing the work of many people. Pesticides cut down on the loss of crops due to insect devastation, and herbicides helped reduce weeds, which can out-compete plants for nutrients and sunlight. Genetically engineered seeds or high yield varieties (HYVs) germinate faster, thus allowing for two or even three harvests per year.

PART B

The Green Revolution was a success with respect to increasing yields, especially in Southeast Asia, parts of India, and Latin America. In some parts of India yields were consistently doubled, which helped these areas better deal with their growing populations.

The Green Revolution did not meet expectations in sub-Saharan Africa for a variety of reasons, such as widespread corruption, lack of cooperation and will from various governments, inadequate irrigation and infrastructure, and poor soils.

PART C

With the diffusion of modern medicines and medical practices to the developing world after World War II, these areas started to experience rapid population growth. Modern medicine and anti-malarial spraying campaigns brought down death rates in many countries, while birth rates remained high. The difference between these two rates led to rapid population growth. The agricultural yields in many of these areas produced by the Green Revolution helped to avert possible famine due to the growing populations in the developing world.

RUBRIC FOR FREE-RESPONSE QUESTION

Total point value of question 1 = 6

Part A—One point possible:

- One point for identification of high yield varieties, increased use of pesticides, herbicides, irrigations systems, and/or machinery.

Part B—Two points possible:

- One point for discussing where the Green Revolution was a success.

  — East Asia, South Asia (India), Southeast Asia (Indonesia and Philippines), South and Central America

- One point for discussing where the Green Revolution was not a success and the reasons why.

  — Sub-Saharan Africa

Part C—Three points possible:

- One point for examining why various parts of the world were experiencing massive population growth.

  — Diffusion of modern medicines and medical practices in LDCs

- One point for making the connection between population growth and a country's ability to feed its growing population with traditional forms of agriculture.

  — Connection between population growth and traditional agricultural methods of production

- One point for synthesizing why many countries needed to adopt the Green Revolution strategies given their circumstances and speculation on what might have happened if they had not taken this path.

CHAPTER 8: INDUSTRIALIZATION AND ECONOMIC DEVELOPMENT

IF YOU LEARN ONLY EIGHT THINGS IN THIS CHAPTER . . .

1. Industry is based on transportation and labor costs. Weber's least cost theory suggests that a production point must be located within a "triangle," with raw materials coming from at least two sources. Weight-gaining industries must have their production point closer to the market. Weight-reducing industries must have their production point closer to the source of raw materials.

2. The five main means of industrial transportation are truck, train, airplane, pipeline, and ship. Each has advantages and disadvantages for hauling raw materials or finished products to production points and markets around the globe.

3. Basic industries are city-forming industries, whereas nonbasic industries are city-serving industries. Basic industries are the main business for which a city is known. Detroit/automobiles, Pittsburgh/steel, San José/computer chips are just three examples of basic industries in major urban areas in the United States.

4. The main factor in determining an area's development is the Human Development Index, which measures life expectancy, literacy, education, and the overall standard of living for different countries around the world. It was developed by Pakistani economist Mahbub ul Haq in 1990, and has since been used by the United Nations as the primary indicator of countries' levels of development.

5. The core-periphery model describes regions as core, semi-periphery, and periphery areas. It also describes four areas, the industrial core, upward transition, downward transition, and resource frontier. The model can be used from a worldwide scale down to an urban scale to analyze city zones.

6. The latest development strategy, sustainable development, attempts to improve the lives of people without depleting resources for future generations. This approach is often successful on a small geographic scale.

7. Natural resources are either renewable or nonrenewable. The most important nonrenewable resources for industrial purposes are fossil fuels. The burning of fossil fuels and extraction of natural resources can have negative environmental consequences.

8. The United States is the leading consumer of fossil fuels in the world today. China, with its growing economy, is quickly increasing its energy consumption levels. There are alternative forms of energy such as hydroelectric, solar, nuclear, wind, and biomass, but it is debatable if these alternative sources of energy can seriously reduce carbon emissions from the industrialized countries of the world.

KEYS TO ECONOMIC AND INDUSTRIAL DEVELOPMENT

When discussing economic and industrial development, it's important to note that some countries develop faster than other countries. Some urban areas develop faster than other urban areas. Why is this the case, particularly when different areas seem to have the same natural resources? There are several reasons for the economic success and failure of certain countries and urban areas. Cultural factors often determine what wealth is.

Industrialization is one of the main components of economic success. Today, a country must make the leap to the industrial and tertiary sector to enjoy economic development. How countries do this is the real issue. Most societies want economic success and want to be modernized, to have the conveniences, including automobiles, cell phones, and refrigerators, that people in developed countries have become accustomed to.

One of the most important factors in why the United States, Europe, and some Asian countries possess these amenities, while many countries in Africa are struggling to free themselves from abject poverty, is the economic system of each country. There is a saying that suggests that capitalism is the uneven distribution of wealth, whereas communism or socialism is the even distribution of poverty. However, many Scandinavian countries, which profess to be socialist, enjoy some of the highest standards of living in the world. By allowing people the freedom to obtain their own wealth, societies can grow through the entrepreneurial spirit of the people themselves.

ECONOMIC SYSTEMS

There are three main types of economic systems in the world: capitalism, socialism, and communism. It is important to note that governmental systems, such as totalitarianism and monarchies, can have profound effects on economic systems, so no two countries are completely alike.

CAPITALISM

Capitalism, broadly, is the process of letting the competitive market determine the price of goods. By letting the market decide prices, people have the freedom to choose their own outcomes based on their ability and freedom to pay. For example, if one person wants to sell you your school lunch for $3 while another person will sell you your school lunch for $2, and the lunches are of equal size and nutritional value, you will choose the $2 lunch every time. Your money is valuable to you, and you want to keep as much of it as possible.

It has been suggested that capitalism, based on competition, inevitably means there are winners and losers and that those in poverty are largely ignored. Poverty is often a heavily debated issue in capitalistic countries.

SOCIALISM

Socialism is the government control of basic items in an economy. Government controls basic food prices as well as transportation and energy prices to ensure that everybody can pay for essential services. Individual tax rates are usually higher in socialist societies so the government can pay for the transportation and health care for its citizens. The return for paying higher taxes is that people enjoy services, such as health care, at no or little direct expense. The return for paying higher taxes is that people enjoy services, such as health care, at no or little direct expense, outside of income taxes.

It has been suggested that socialism provides no incentive for people to work, because the government provides social security for its citizens. Many young people in socialist countries refuse to work yet feel they are entitled to services and security.

COMMUNISM

Communism is the total government control of all prices in a society, ranging from bread to utilities. The former Soviet Union tried communism with some success, particularly in terms of military production, but the economic well-being of its citizens was in question. In the former Soviet Union, communism did not provide basic necessities to the population, ultimately leading to the economic system's downfall.

According to its detractors, communism offers no incentive to a person to succeed. Doctors, lawyers, and custodians all make the same salary. In addition, the government dictates your profession based on its assessment of your skills. Some people are made to train as athletes, others as scientists or doctors. These skills are sometimes determined early in life, and the government enforces mandatory training in that discipline.

ECONOMIC SUCCESS FACTORS

The following economic factors are vital in determining the success of companies on a local scale: environmentally friendly policies, political support, societal acceptance, and a strong economic support base, including trained, experienced workers as well as investment capital.

ENVIRONMENTALLY FRIENDLY ACTIVITIES

You simply cannot put a factory in the middle of a city and begin polluting the lakes, rivers, and air there. The citizens living near the factory will complain, and the local government will soon enforce regulations on your factory. You must show that your company treats the environment with respect. In many instances, severe fines can be levied against companies that pollute the air, soil, or water.

POLITICAL SUPPORT

The support of local politicians is important to a company's success. Local politicians set up zoning ordinances and approve construction plans. The local governments need to be in agreement with your plans for your business to start up and eventually succeed.

SOCIETAL ACCEPTANCE

Societal acceptance is also critical. You must be selling a product that the local citizens approve of. You cannot be selling something that violates cultural standards. For example, you will not find liquor stores located near schools.

ECONOMIC SUPPORT BASE

Another key factor for economic development is having an economic base of support, which involves worker training and experience. Training new employees often means that you're paying two workers to do the job of one. For example, a new cashier must be watched by somebody who is already trained in the job. Training and on-the-job experience minimize employee turnover and improve overall production.

The other part of the economic support base is capital investment in buildings and large equipment or vehicles. Sufficient credit is often needed to establish a business; most companies need loans to get started.

GEOGRAPHIC FACTORS

Two types of geographic factors, site and situation, contribute to the industrial development of some countries while keeping others reliant on their agriculture sectors. Some locations benefit from excellent site and situation factors. Others may have a good site but poor situation or vice versa.

SITE FACTORS

Site is a major geographic factor contributing to a country's economic success. **Site** is the internal characteristics of a place based on its physical features. Some places have excellent sites, while others struggle because of poor sites.

The physical characteristics of a particular location determine its site. For example, New Orleans has a poor site due to its location below sea level. When Hurricane Katrina hit, the city was flooded, although levees had been built to hold back water. Often, natural disadvantages are difficult to overcome.

SITUATION FACTORS

Situation is the relationship that a particular location has with the locations around it. Pittsburgh has an ideal situation for its production of steel. Iron ore, an essential component for the production of steel, comes from the Great Lakes region, including Minnesota, Wisconsin, and Michigan. High-quality anthracite coal, which can fuel blast furnaces, was found nearby in western Pennsylvania. Pittsburgh was also located on the confluence of two major rivers, the Allegheny and the Monongahela, which form the Ohio River. This river system gave the city a perfect means to ship its steel products all over the world.

Another city with an ideal situation is Detroit, which became famous for its production of cars. The city could export the cars by means of the Great Lakes and through the St. Lawrence Seaway with access to the Atlantic Ocean. Railroads could send the automobiles throughout the United States.

Both Pittsburgh and Detroit have established basic industries. **Basic industries** are the focal point of the economy for a city. For Pittsburgh, the basic industry is steel. For Detroit, the basic industry is automobiles. For Silicon Valley in California, it is the production of computer chips and equipment. For Minneapolis, it was the milling industry, which produced flour from the wheat grown on the Great Plains. There are dozens of different basic industries from which a city may grow. An urban area's site and situation determines which basic industry will work there.

Nonbasic industries are secondary businesses that sprout up after the city has already established its basic industry. An example of a nonbasic industry would be the construction industry needed to build homes for the workers in a city's basic industry.

All of these businesses together form the multiplier effect. The **multiplier effect** is the expansion of the economic base of a city as a result of the basic and nonbasic industries located there. For example, the steel industry in Pittsburgh led to the rise of a barge industry.

INDUSTRIAL FACTORS

A variety of factors contribute to a county's industrial success or failure, which impacts overall economic success. These factors could include anything from its economic system to its governmental systems. On a micro scale, the site and situation factors, including transportation systems, affect the success of a particular business involved with manufacturing. This industrial base is a prime factor in determining the overall success of a country's economy.

INDUSTRIAL COSTS

Industrial costs are either fixed or variable. **Variable costs** fluctuate based on the volume of the order. **Fixed costs** do not fluctuate based on the quantity ordered. Usually, the more of a product a customer orders, the less the price per individual item; the less the customer orders, the greater the cost per individual item. Businesses prefer to charge variable costs to encourage customers to buy more, clearing out their warehouse space and allowing them to replace old products with new ones. When businesses get buyers to purchase in greater bulk, they relieve themselves of inventory. This allows them to purchase newer materials, which most people prefer over older outdated materials.

TRANSPORTATION SYSTEMS

Transportation is one of the most important fixtures of industry. Industry needs to use a low-cost form of transportation yet ensure that products get to market relatively quickly. Transportation occurs throughout the industrial business process. Raw materials are transported to the production point. Finished products are transported to the wholesaler, perhaps traveling via several modes of transportation. Then the products are transported to the retailer, who sells them to you, and you take them home. Each of these steps in the industrial process may use different means of transportation.

When delivering products, time-space compression comes into play. **Time-space compression** is the effort to increase the efficiency of time in the delivery process by diminishing distance obstacles. One of the best ways to increase time efficiency is through the use of modern technologies, such as the Internet. This has greatly increased the speed at which industry can deliver its products.

A general rule in transportation is the greater the distance traveled and the weight of the products, the greater the cost to transport them. As distance and weight decrease, so does the transportation cost.

Prior to the Internet—think back farther, prior to the telephone!—commerce had to be done through face-to-face contact. Sometimes, one of the parties had to travel a long distance to conduct a transaction. Today, you can place orders within seconds online. By reducing the time used in the communication process, the overall process becomes more efficient. Distance is still a factor in the transportation cost of finished products. Even this is continually decreasing, though, with the increased speed and efficiency of the five primary means of industrial transportation: truck, train, airplane, pipeline, and ship. Each of these has advantages and disadvantages in terms of time and cost. Some are faster than others, some are more efficient that others, and some cost less than others.

TRUCKS

The first means of transportation is the use of a **truck** or highway carrier. Trucks are a highly mobile and efficient form of transportation that can go almost anywhere there are roads. Trucks are the most used method of industrial transportation. Companies order supplies, which are then hauled, usually by means of a semitrailer. Overland truck drivers can haul a fair amount of cargo for large distances relatively quickly. The efficiency of trucks means the products that you purchase in the store cost less. Most of the items that you purchase retail or even wholesale are delivered by truck.

There are some disadvantages to using trucks. One is delays due to weather. If a road is shut down, a truck cannot haul its payload over it. This loss of time means a loss of profits for the companies that depend upon truck delivery. Traffic delays can also diminish the efficiency of trucks. Many industrial areas are located in parts of town that experience high levels of traffic. Trucks themselves slow down traffic, because of their size and weight.

Another disadvantage of trucks is that they use fossil fuels. Most trucks run on diesel, which comes from the refining of petroleum products. Petroleum products cause environmental problems such as air pollution.

Trucks also have high maintenance costs. As their engines get older, they need more maintenance to keep running efficiently.

TRAINS

Trains are one the most efficient and most cost-effective forms of transportation available to industry. They can haul an immense amount of freight for long distances. In addition to their ability to haul huge loads, they are becoming increasingly fuel efficient.

Trains have some disadvantages. One is their lack of flexibility of routes. Train tracks don't go to every industrial location, and many trains must travel to a station, where the cargo must be unloaded from one form of transportation to another. These transfer points are called **break-of-bulk points**. Cargo is usually shifted from the train to a truck, which can then carry it the rest of the way. The bottom line is that almost all companies have roads leading to them, but not all businesses have train tracks leading to them.

Massive factories, like the huge automotive plants in Detroit, often have tracks built directly to their doorsteps to minimize transportation costs. Such factories do not have to use trucks to haul products to the train station, where the freight would have to be transferred.

An obvious disadvantage of trains is their inability to cross oceans. Trains are limited to land travel and cannot haul products to Asia from North America or vice versa. Also, the operating costs of a train can be high in relation to the land use of unused tracks compared to the other means of industrial transportation. In other words, the rails that the train companies built, at a considerable cost, are today used infrequently.

AIRPLANES

Airplanes are often the fastest way to get products to market. In many isolated areas, such as northern Alaska and the interior regions of Africa, planes are the only means of accessing the supplies needed for survival. Airplanes have a high degree of flexibility regarding their routes, but most freight hauled by airplane must go through a break-of-bulk point, usually to some type of truck.

Some of the produce consumed in the United States comes from Central and South American countries, and airplanes are used to haul fruit products to North America during the winter. Shipping the produce by other means would mean that the fruit would spoil; the only means of transport that is fast enough to do this is airplanes. Dozens of flights daily haul produce from tropical regions to other countries during the winter.

Although they are the fastest means of transportation, airplanes are also the most expensive to use. In addition, the fuel efficiency of airplanes is very low, and fuel costs can eat away at profits. Many airlines in the United States have suffered economically because of increases in fuel prices. Airlines have tried to offset this cost by charging passengers and shippers more.

Also, airplanes experience weather delays. In icy conditions, many planes are grounded for safety reasons. Just as passengers experience delays at the airport, industrial producers and consumers suffer from delays in the shipment of products. Such delays reduce or eliminate profitability.

PIPELINES

Pipelines are a highly efficient way of moving gas or liquid products from one region to another. Pipelines are also one of the safest means of hauling these products. However, pipelines are limited to gas and liquid products. Therefore, pipelines are generally limited to the transportation of natural resources from their extraction or mining points to production facilities, which may be hundreds or even thousands of miles away. The determining factor of whether pipeline transportation is feasible is the availability of pipelines between the point of extraction and the resource's destination.

One of the most famous pipelines in the world is the Alaskan Pipeline. The Alaskan Pipeline is an engineering marvel, extending over 800 miles through some of the highest mountains in North America. Its primary purpose is to get petroleum from the production point in the North Slope to the transportation point near Valdez, Alaska. This pipeline was built at an extreme cost with oil company money. These oil companies saw the building of the pipeline as an investment. The amount of oil in the North Slope of Alaska greatly eases the burden of importing foreign oil.

The safety record of pipelines in the United States is impeccable. There are very few incidents of pipeline failure. If maintained properly, a pipeline can last for many decades. However, as with all means of industrial transportation, pipelines have some drawbacks. As mentioned, pipelines can only haul gas or liquid products. Also, they're very expensive to build, and once a pipeline is built, moving any section of it is difficult. The line is usually built to cross the least distance possible to minimize construction costs.

As with the Alaskan Pipeline, environmental studies need to be done before construction can begin. These environmental studies are paid for by the primary user of the pipeline. The pipeline's environmental impact must be given a clean bill of health before any construction can take place.

SHIPS

Anything from small barges on inland waterways to supertankers that can haul tons of crude oil around the globe are used for industrial transportation. There are thousands of ships on the world's oceans at any given time. All different types of products are shipped by water. Many are hauled in cargo containers and shipped from massive ports, such as Hong Kong and Singapore.

The Panama Canal, a major shipping route for goods en route from the east coasts of North and South America to the west coasts of each continent, is due for a major renovation project because many of its locks are too small for the largest ocean-going vessels. The Panama Canal expansion is scheduled to be completed in 2015.

Ships are the most energy-efficient means of transportation, even more so than trains. The average cost per distance traveled is the lowest among the five means of transportation.

However, using ships is also the slowest method of delivering industrial products to either production points or markets, so it works best for products where speed is not a necessity. Athletic shoes coming from China to the United States can be shipped by ship, because they won't spoil on the way. Transporting products by ship keeps down costs.

Another downside to using ships is that many industrial plants lack access to waterways, so a break-of-bulk point is needed to get products from the warehouse or production facility to the port, where the cargo must be loaded. This break-of-bulk point adds to shipping costs. Also, there is a high terminal cost associated with using port facilities.

A final disadvantage of using ships is that they are weather dependent. Barge traffic on northern rivers in Europe and North America ceases during the winter months. On the open seas, storms have forced ships hundreds of miles off course.

LOCATION OF INDUSTRY

AGGLOMERATION

Agglomeration is the centralization of features of an industry for the mutual benefit of the industry as a whole. The best way to think about agglomeration is to think of your local shopping mall. You go to the mall to purchase a new pair of jeans. While walking to the store to buy jeans, you see a shirt that you just have to get to go with your jeans. While walking out of the mall, you also purchase a new pair of shoes to go with the outfit. Your intention was to only buy jeans, but you leave with an entire outfit. The entire mall benefited from your intention to purchase the jeans. The stores are in competition with each other to a point, but they also help each other by drawing in more people, thereby increasing one another's customer bases.

The agglomeration principle worked for Detroit by creating a competent workforce for automotive plants. General Motors, Ford, and Daimler-Chrysler all benefited from being near each other. Secondary industries, attracted by the industrial hub, provided products and services to all three. The unions provided the quality labor that was essential in the production of cars. Tires were made in nearby Ohio and sent to Detroit. When companies locate themselves around these major industrial centers, their production costs actually decrease, because raw materials don't have to be shipped as far to the assembly plants.

Much of **manufacturing** or **warehouse location** is based on the principle of agglomeration. Industrial parks can provide companies with tax breaks to locate their industrial plants at that particular location. Shared services, such as the construction of railroad tracks for train transportation, can greatly reduce costs.

Cumulative causation is continued growth due to the positive aspects of the principle itself. For example, if agglomeration is successful, more agglomeration occurs. Cumulative causation transpired in Detroit around the automotive industry. Cumulative causation can also lead to a disadvantage from the same agglomeration principle. The **deglomeration** of an economy can occur when the market has become saturated with a particular industry. This creates too much competition, forcing some of the businesses within that industry either to relocate or close down.

INDUSTRIAL REVOLUTION

The Industrial Revolution started in the mid-1700s and was an extension of the Enlightenment period in Europe. One major invention of the Industrial Revolution was the steam engine, which enabled farther and faster travel than ever before in human history. The steam engine could be used for trains as well as ships. As a result, both agricultural and industrial products had access to a bigger market, and more products needed to be manufactured to meet the demand. Mass production methods and technologies allowed industry to take advantage of the new business environment.

In contrast to today's mass production principles, much of industry was characterized by specialization prior to the Industrial Revolution. One person produced an entire product, using tedious methods and inefficient means. The Industrial Revolution, which began in England, allowed for more mechanization, speeding up the production process and allowing the quantity and sometimes the quality of the product to improve.

Prior to the Industrial Revolution, most industry was conducted in the form of **cottage industry**, or an industry where the process is done in an individual's home. After the Industrial Revolution, most industry transferred to the assembly line method of production where one person specializes in one facet of production. Henry Ford perfected this in his production of cars.

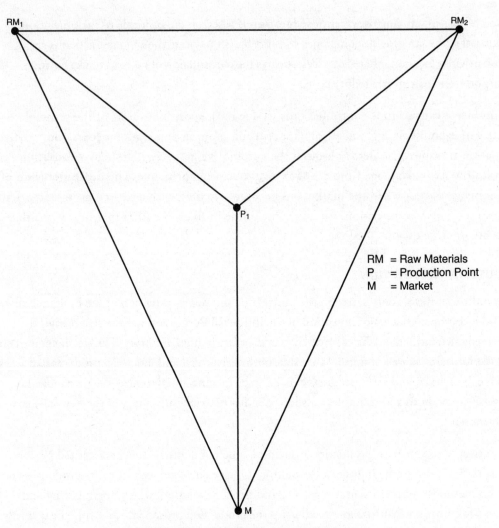

RM = Raw Materials
P = Production Point
M = Market

Figure 8.1: Weber's Least Cost Theory.

WEBER'S LEAST COST THEORY

One of the preeminent economic geographers is a man by the name of Alfred Weber. Weber was a German economist and socialist who in the 20th century developed a theory to try to describe the industrial location of certain industries.

Weber's theory, shown in Figure 8.1, became known as the least cost theory. His theory suggests that a company building an industrial plant needs to take into consideration the source of raw materials and the market for the product. Thus, the weight of the raw materials and the finished product will determine the location of the production facility for that company.

The fundamental principle is triangular. The base of the triangle consists of the two raw materials necessary for the production of the product. If the product being produced is a **weight-gaining**

industry (an industry where the finished product weighs more than the raw materials), then the industrial production point will need to be located closer to the market to minimize the transportation costs associated with a relatively heavy product (see Figure 8.2). If the industry is a **weight-reducing industry** (an industry where the raw materials weigh more than the finished product), the industrial production point will need to be located closer to the raw materials (see Figure 8.3).

Many of the resource-oriented industries are weight-reducing industries. The weight-reducing industries try to minimize the costs of hauling heavy materials, such as ore, long distances by placing their industrial production points closer to where the resources are located, such as mines.

The production of potato chips is an example of a weight-reducing industry. For our purposes here, let's assume that there are two primary raw materials, salt and potatoes, in the production of Geochips. Because the potatoes and the salt are heavier than the finished product, a bag of potato chips, the production point should be located closer to the potato farms and the salt plant.

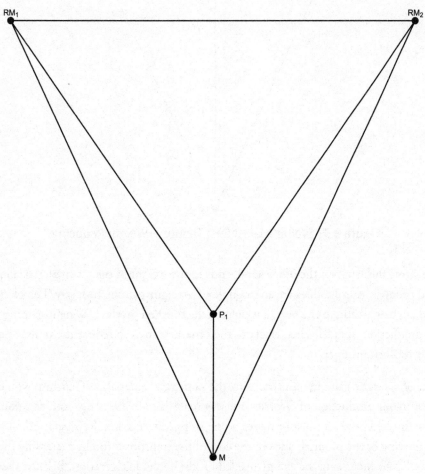

Figure 8.2: Weber's Least Cost Theory — Weight Gaining.

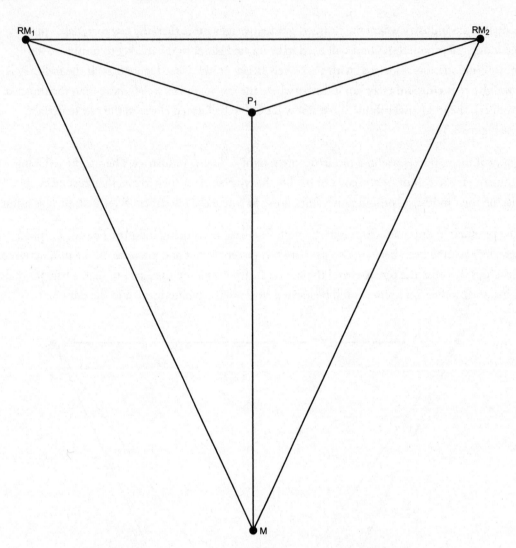

Figure 8.3: Weber's Least Cost Theory — Weight Reducing.

A weight-gaining industry, on the other hand, adds to the weight of the raw materials in making the finished product. Automobiles are an example of a weight-gaining industry. The plastic, rubber, and engines all add to the overall weight of the finished product. Weight-gaining industries want their production points located closer to their markets so as to reduce the transportation costs of the heavy finished product.

An example of a weight-gaining industry using the same raw materials as Geochips would be French fries. In our production of Geofries, the raw materials are the same—salt and potatoes— but now the finished product must be frozen when shipped to market. Refrigeration, or the cooling or freezing of the product, adds to the cost of the transportation by increasing the product's weight as well as by increasing the energy needed for the actual refrigeration. Because the Geofries are a weight-gaining product, the manufacturer will want to move the production point closer to the market.

Another example of Weber's least cost theory is the fictional "brick bunny." The brick bunny is built with two primary products: bricks and feathers. Because the bricks weigh more than the feathers, the producer puts the production point closer to the bricks to minimize their transport cost. The production point is skewed toward the side of the triangle where the raw material that is the heaviest (bricks) comes from. This is shown in Figure 8.4.

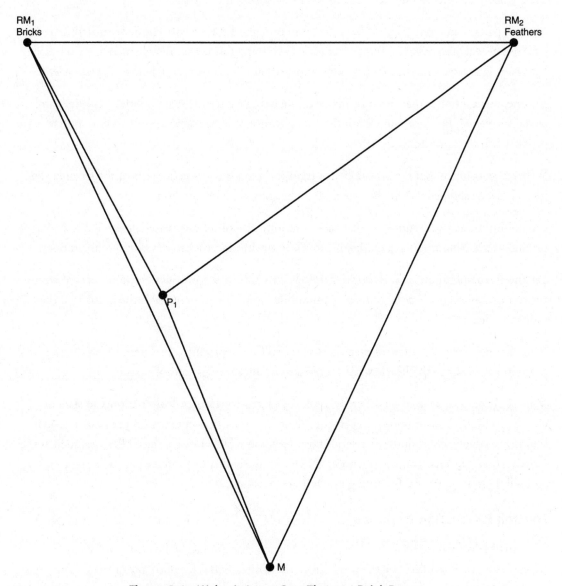

Figure 8.4: Weber's Least Cost Theory—Brick Bunny.

The three primary factors that Weber included in his model were raw materials, labor, and transportation. The most expensive is labor; however, transportation is the easiest item of the three to control through the location of the new industrial facility. Still, all three factors are vital in determining the success of a business or industry.

For Weber's theory to work, he had to make some assumptions. The industrial production point must be located somewhere within the triangle. Otherwise, excessive transportation costs will make the product too expensive, and the consumer will be able to purchase the same product more cheaply from another manufacturer who is located within the triangle.

Also, all parts of the triangle must be uniform in topography. Like von Thunen's agricultural land use model (also based on transportation), everything inside the triangle must have the same landscape characteristics so that transportation costs are the same everywhere in the triangle.

Another assumption is that the areas inside of the triangle have the same political, cultural, and economic values. Every person within the triangle must have the same opportunity to purchase the product and the same desire for it.

Weber also assumed that the availability of transportation is equal in all parts of the triangle. The items must be shipped via the shortest and/or cheapest available method.

Other important assumptions are that the minimum amount of raw materials needed to make the product is available and that a market is known to the producer when developing the product.

Yet another assumption is that labor is infinitely available to any production point located within the triangle. However, that labor force is immobile, unwilling to move with the industry if the industry relocates.

What happens when a variety of materials is needed for the production? Then the production point moves closer to the heaviest raw material to balance transportation costs.

Weber's theory can be used on different, typically macro-level scales, from national to state or city levels. Weber's assumptions suggest that all of the industry occurs within the same national boundaries. However, industrialization is becoming more global. With trade alliances, such as the **North American Free Trade Agreement (NAFTA)**, the ability to produce goods in one country and sell them in another is becoming much more common.

FOREIGN PRODUCTION OF GOODS

Maquiladoras are industrial plants located in Mexico that produce goods using relatively inexpensive labor and then sell the products in the United States for more profit than if the products were made in the United States. A debate rages over the **outsourcing** of jobs from the United States to less developed countries, where companies can pay employees pennies on the dollar. Unions and others are decrying the loss of American jobs to citizens in less developed countries. However, U.S. consumers benefit from buying products as cheaply as possible. This process is known as the **new international division of labor.** The new international division of labor, sometimes called the global division of labor, began in the 1960s and entails the outsourcing of jobs from more developed countries to less developed countries in order to take advantage of cheaper labor costs. The result has been a loss of manufacturing jobs in more developed countries and an increase of employment opportunities in less developed countries.

With the increased efficiency of transportation systems, companies can produce their goods around the world and ship them to the markets in the more developed countries with relative ease and lower cost expenses.

A **footloose industry** is a company with no allegiance or ties to a country or a location that, therefore, can move its primary locations at will. Many times, this is done for tax purposes. Companies will set up tax shelters in countries that have more favorable tax rates. Bermuda is a haven for international businesses because of its corporate tax advantages.

TRANSNATIONAL CORPORATIONS

Transnational corporations are large companies that have offices or divisions around the world. Many times, this is done to reduce travel costs or to enter different markets. These companies live in a global culture. Profits of these transnational corporations are measured in billions of U.S. dollars. Coca-Cola is an example of a transnational corporation with offices on every continent except Antarctica. The brand name *Coca-Cola* is recognized around the world and is one of the most recognizable brands on earth. Thousands of Coke products are sold every second. Another example is 3M (Minnesota, Mining, and Manufacturing), which has offices in Europe and Asia as well as North America. Many transnational corporations had their start in the United States, but other companies, such as the Union Bank of Switzerland (UBS), one of the largest financial institutions in the world, had their beginning in Europe.

The point of transnational corporations is to be ubiquitous. Being **ubiquitous** means that a product is available to consumers at any time and at any location around the world. McDonald's is a good example of a ubiquitous company. A person can go to almost any major city around the world and get a Big Mac.

Transnational corporations employ millions of well-educated people around the world. Employees who work for transnational corporations are often transferred from continent to continent as they move up the corporate ladder. Some people claim that the allegiances of transnational corporations and footloose industries are not to a particular country but rather solely to their profit margins and shareholders.

INTERNATIONAL DIVISION OF LABOR AND MASS PRODUCTION

The **international division of labor** says that when individuals can specialize in their individual production, their speed, efficiency, and quality increases, thereby reducing costs. Henry Ford applied this philosophy of labor to mass production, using the assembly line method to produce automobiles. Sometimes known as **Fordism**, this method involves each person on the assembly line doing a specific task to speed up the overall process of production. When workers specialized in individual areas of expertise, they were paid relatively well for their skill and could then afford to purchase the product that they were making. Prior to the assembly line method, most manufacturing was done by individuals making the entire product. This process was very slow and, therefore, relatively expensive.

The assembly line method became standard in almost every industry, increasing industrial profitability. The old way, of one person producing the entire product, is used today only for specialty products. People usually pay top dollar for this type of specialized product.

Some industries lend themselves better than others to mass production. In the automobile industry, new mechanization techniques have allowed many manual jobs to be taken over by machines. However, other industries, such as agriculture, are more labor intensive. Although items like grain can be mass-produced with the assistance of machines, like combines and tractors, other agricultural employment is very labor intensive.

Another example of a labor-intensive industry is the textile industry. Most of the clothes that you wear had to be handmade, often in a factory in a less developed country. Sometimes U.S. retail outlets have been accused of ordering clothes from factories called **sweatshops** owing to their poor working conditions.

The growth of **manufacturing exports** has led to a global economy of commerce. As production costs have continued to increase in the United States and Europe, more products are being imported from Asia and less developed countries around the world.

GLOBAL INDUSTRIAL ZONES

Where is industry located in the United States and the world today? Some areas have site and situation advantages that have contributed to various countries' economic success. All of these locations have found a large percentage of their employment sector involved in industry. There are four primary industrial zones in the world today: the northeastern portion of the United States and the southeastern portion of Canada; Western Russia and the Ukraine; Central and Western Europe; and East Asia, including China and Japan.

UNITED STATES AND SOUTHEASTERN CANADA

NEW ENGLAND

New England historically had some site and situation advantages that made it successful. New England benefited from the cheap labor provided by early immigrants who used Boston as their entry point into the United States. One of the largest industries in the Boston region was textiles. Much of this industry has moved to the South in recent decades because of the lack of unionized labor in the South, but New England used to be famous for its clothing manufacturing. Hydroelectric power from rivers provided much of the power needed to spin the belts and operate the machines to mass produce cloth. Much of the cloth was made from cotton, which was imported from the South.

Large factories were set up in towns such as Lowell, Massachusetts. Life for workers was difficult, but the pay was relatively good. Life in the factory was often strictly controlled by the owners. The owners of the factory set up bunks within the factory itself, and the workers stayed on the factory campus. Even religious worship was located in the factory, and the factory developed its own culture.

The large textile machines created a very loud, unhealthy working environment. Children were often used to clean the lint from the textile machines while they were still operating. Child labor laws in the United States arose from the textile operations in New England, along with the coal mining industry in West Virginia.

THE MIDDLE ATLANTIC

The Middle Atlantic region of the United States is known today as "the megalopolis." This area includes the large urban areas of New York City; Philadelphia, Pennsylvania; Wilmington, Delaware; and Baltimore, Maryland. This region had a large pool of available labor to work in factories. It also had a large market to purchase manufactured products. This area also was known for its major ports. Today, New York City is still one of the largest and busiest ports in the United States.

THE EASTERN GREAT LAKES

The Eastern Great Lakes region includes the southeastern portions of Canada, the city of Pittsburgh, and the upstate New York region. The majority of these areas received hydroelectric power from the Great Lakes and Niagara Falls. The situation of Pittsburgh was ideal for the production of steel. Barges and ships hauled iron ore from the Great Lakes to the port of Erie, Pennsylvania. From there, the ore was put on trains and hauled to Pittsburgh. Steel was then hauled to market via barges on the Ohio River and by train.

The southeastern portion of Canada, which extends along the St. Lawrence Seaway and includes Hamilton, Toronto, and Montréal, is some of the most valuable land in Canada in terms of industrial production. The majority of the Canadian population lives in this area. Canada's largest city is Toronto, with a little over 4 million people. This area has a large workforce and market ability to support industrialization. Since NAFTA was enacted, goods can be shipped across the U.S. border relatively easily. The St. Lawrence Seaway can export products to the Atlantic Ocean for transport to markets around the world.

THE WESTERN GREAT LAKES

The Western Great Lakes region includes the cities of Detroit, Chicago, and Milwaukee. Chicago is a hub of transportation in the United States because it is in the middle of the country. It contains O'Hare airport, one of the busiest airports in the world and a hub for two of the largest airlines in the United States, American Airlines and United Airlines. In addition, Midway airport is a hub for Southwest Airlines. Dozens of railroad lines converge in Chicago, as do many interstate highways. Engineers actually reversed the flow of the Chicago River to allow river traffic between the Great Lakes and the Mississippi River. Chicago is the largest city between the East Coast (New York) and the West Coast (Los Angeles), and it provides a major market for the resale of products, as well as a labor source for factories.

As aforementioned, Detroit has become a major automobile manufacturing region. All of the major automobile makers in the United States have huge factories there. However, new automotive plants have opened in the South, including a BMW plant in the Greenville/Spartanburg area of South Carolina, a Honda assembly plant in Lincoln, Alabama, and a Toyota plant in San Antonio, Texas. Many of these newer automotive factories have located in the South to take advantage of relatively inexpensive, nonunion labor.

The Rust Belt, shown in Figure 8.5, contains the greatest amount of industrial area in the United States. It is called the Rust Belt because of the huge factories that have shut down within the past two or three decades. The result is a crumbling infrastructure that cities in this region have been trying to clean up.

THE SOUTH

Today, there is a new industrial realm in the United States. Many Southern states are luring manufacturing industries to their cities to increase employment and tax revenues. Some cities even offer tax breaks or no taxes for several years to motivate companies to locate in their cities.

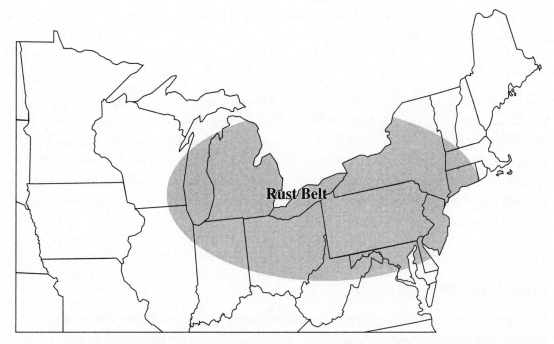

Figure 8.5: Rust Belt Area in the United States.

The changing face of industry in the United States is having a profound impact, both positive and negative, on different regions. Cities located in the Rust Belt have seen the loss of thousands of jobs in the manufacturing sectors of their economies, while other areas have seen an increase in the manufacturing sector. Many transnational corporations headquartered in foreign countries are building factories in the United States to minimize transportation costs. For example, the idea of a "foreign car" is becoming more and more foreign. Many "foreign" cars have parts that are produced and assembled in the United States. When these companies decide where to locate their factories, they often use Weber's theory to minimize transportation costs, thereby minimizing costs and maximizing profits for their shareholders.

THE UKRAINE AND RUSSIA

Russia and the Ukraine region have high levels of manufacturing due to the enormous amounts of natural resources located in the area.

THE UKRAINE

The Ukraine is one of the largest industrial areas in the former Soviet Union, because of its agricultural productivity and coal-mining activity. The Ukraine took away much of the Soviet Union's industry and natural resources when it became independent. It still provides Russia with many of its produced goods. This is also one of the major wheat producing regions of the world.

The agricultural portions of Ukraine provide it with a solid economic base, along with raw materials for energy production.

RUSSIA

Much of Russia's industrial base is in the west of the country, around Moscow and St. Petersburg. In addition to the major urban centers of Russia, the Siberian region contains a large amount of manufacturing due to its vast natural resources. In areas where forestry is practiced, the production of paper and packaging materials dominate the economy. The Siberian region has a very small population, and transportation, mostly by rail, is limited. The creation of the Trans-Siberian railroad, one of the great wonders of the transportation world, led to industrial cities growing up along its routes during the communist era.

Farther to the east, hydroelectric power on the Yenisei and Amur Rivers runs factories.

CENTRAL AND WESTERN EUROPE

The Central and Western Europe region includes the countries of Great Britain and extends eastward into northern France and Germany. This region initiated the Industrial Revolution and hasn't looked back since. The major coal-producing region of Europe is located around Belgium and northern France. Today, however, Europe uses much less coal and relies more on nuclear power. France uses nuclear power for upward of 70 percent of its energy needs.

GREAT BRITAIN

Large industrial areas in Great Britain include London, Manchester, Leeds, and Newcastle. These areas depend largely on the coal industry. Great Britain has been blessed with large deposits of coal within its borders, which have been instrumental in developing the industrial base for many of Great Britain's large urban centers.

GERMANY

In Germany, the steel industry depends on the coal that is mined within its borders. Germany has the other advantage of having two primary rivers to transport goods, the Rhine and the Ruhr. The area around Düsseldorf, even today, is considered heavily industrialized.

Because the population of Germany is spread out among many different cities, inland transportation via rivers and highways is very important. Today, Germany is the leader in industrial production in Europe. Abundant raw materials combined with an educated workforce and a close market with good transportation systems has enabled Germany to continue its industrial success.

FRANCE

Today, many other portions of Europe have become more industrialized. The production of automobiles in France and Germany, as well as airplanes in France, has provided many jobs. Airbus, with its headquarters located in Toulouse, France, is competing with Seattle-based Boeing to be the world's largest manufacturer of airplanes. With the aircraft market in Asia growing, both Boeing and Airbus have completed projects on new airliners, which can haul people farther, faster, and for less cost by using less fossil fuels.

IRELAND

Ireland has seen increasing economic prosperity due to industrial development. It has joined the European Union. Ireland has seen some of the highest economic growth rates in all of Europe.

EAST ASIA

China, Hong Kong (now a part of the People's Republic of China), South Korea, Taiwan, and Singapore have also entered the global marketplace. Many of the ports in China, Japan, and Korea are designated treaty ports. **Treaty ports** are international ports that must be kept open for international trade because of the signing of a treaty. China has more than 80 treaty ports as the result of treaties from different wars. Many of the ports in eastern China are **export processing zones**. These zones are designed to export goods made in China efficiently. Most of these products go to Japan, Europe, and the United States.

The new rising star in industry is China. The Chinese market, which includes more than 1 billion people and a growing middle class, has global industries clamoring to meet its needs.

China's gross domestic product has increased around 10 to 12 percent annually in recent years. China's population is increasingly gaining education and is more than willing and able to compete in a global marketplace. China has had some growing pains as it struggles to keep up with the infrastructure requirements of such a rapid growth rate. Figure 8.6 shows China's industrial regions.

CHINA: SHANGHAI

Probably no city represents the immense growth in industrialization and urban development in China better than Shanghai. Shanghai is the largest city in China in terms of population. Located at the mouth of the Yangtze River and on the Huangpu River, it has seen tremendous investment in its infrastructure and industrial zones in the past decade. The port of Shanghai, once a seldom-used facility, is now one of the busiest ports in the world. It has seen container volume increase by as much as 33 percent in one year. Goods made in China are produced relatively cheaply and then sent to more developed countries around the world. The textile industry in China employs tens of thousands of Chinese workers. WalMart receives many of its products from Chinese manufacturers, which keeps the cost of the products low.

Huge industrial parks are being established in and around the larger Chinese cities. Shanghai's industrial park is one of the largest in the world. The area known as Pudong has been one of the most successful economic initiatives in history. Pudong, which means "east of the river," has seen the development of a new international airport and a world-renowned convention center. The World Expo occurred in Shanghai in 2010, and China built extensive infrastructure for that event. The Maglev train, a new high-speed train, hauls passengers at speeds of over 300 miles per hour from the airport near the coast to the city center about 20 miles away.

The Chinese have set up **special economic zones (SEZs)**, designated specifically for foreign companies to locate their headquarters. Areas like Shanghai, also known as the Yangtze Delta region, have seen enormous investment from foreign companies trying to get into the Chinese market. Both Ford and General Motors have located plants near Shanghai, and Volkswagen just finished construction of a new plant aimed at producing more than 150,000 cars per year. Shanghai's population has grown as many rural farmers have moved into the area looking for work in manufacturing.

Government incentives have and continue to play a large role in the development of particular areas around the globe. Areas such as the Canary Wharf region in London and the Pudong region in Shanghai have seen billions of dollars invested into their infrastructure. The returns on this investment are new companies located within these regions, which increase the tax base for local and regional governments. Governments may also provide tax free time periods and other incentives for companies to located within these regions.

Driving around Shanghai, one notices the dominance of immense factories and industrial centers on the city's landscape. This industrial activity has come at a price. The air pollution in Shanghai and in other cities in China is some of the worst in the world. The skyline in Shanghai can rarely be seen owing to the smog and the amount of air pollution.

For the past half century, there has been competition in China between the government center in Beijing and the economic center in Shanghai. Historically, much investment was put into the government center, whereas Shanghai was viewed negatively. This has changed in the past decade as billions of U.S. dollars and euros have entered the economy. The Chinese government has invested in railroads, highways, and airports, as well as seaports. As a result, Shanghai is now one of the economic centers of East Asia and competes with areas like Hong Kong, Singapore, and even Tokyo for financial supremacy in all of Asia.

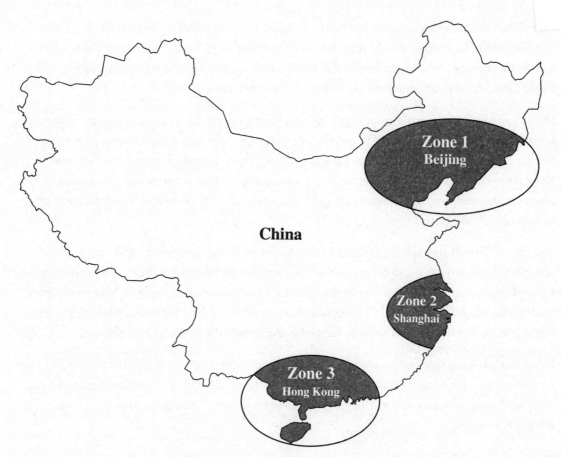

Figure 8.6: China's Major Economic Zones.

CHINA: NORTHEASTERN CHINA

Northeastern China, or Manchuria, includes the city of Beijing and includes the majority of China's natural resources. Coal manufacturing has dominated industrial activity in the region.

Because of the coal, steel is produced here. Much of the industrial activity in northeastern China has developed around the Huang He River. The Huang He River, sometimes called the Yellow River because of its color imparted by the soil in the area, is a major transportation route for manufactured materials. This region is akin to the northeastern United States. Steel, iron, agricultural equipment, and food processing have developed here. Like the U.S. Rust Belt, this area has experienced factories shutting down or leaving for other sections of the country.

CHINA: HONG KONG

In 1997, Great Britain relinquished its control of the port of Hong Kong, which it had gained in the Opium War in the late 1800s. For most of the century, capitalist Hong Kong was a beacon of economic success amid the squalid conditions just across the border in China. That has changed. Hong Kong is still a major trading post for all of Asia and is considered one of the "Four Asian

Tigers" (see the following section), but China is much more economically successful. Areas that neighbor Hong Kong have benefited from its reintegration into China. Cities along the border, such as Guangzhou, have begun to develop. Many of the factories in this region, including a Nike factory, specialize in textiles and other clothing and accessories.

Hong Kong has seen its economic growth continue despite being located in a communist country, in part because China has allowed free-market capitalism to take root. China also welcomes the foreign currencies Hong Kong pumps into its economy through trade. For many, in fact, Hong Kong represents what can be achieved with little to no government involvement in the economy. However, this means no safety net, and should a business fail, very few security systems are in place to help laid-off workers.

The port of Hong Kong is one of the busiest in the world. Hong Kong's main industry is the re-export of industrial products made primarily in mainland China. Its harbor is almost perfectly situated. Its site factors are questionable though. Rocky soil and mountainous or hilly terrain have made growth difficult. As a result, Hong Kong has one of the highest population densities in the world and has built up rather than out. High-rise apartments dominate its busy skyline.

Hong Kong is known as a major entrepot. **Entrepots** are areas where trade goods are brought to be reloaded onto other forms of transportation. Many of the textiles that are manufactured in China are loaded onto ships and sent to Hong Kong, where they are reloaded onto other ships to go elsewhere for resale.

THE FOUR ASIAN TIGERS

The **Four Asian Tigers**, sometimes called the Four Asian Dragons, are Hong Kong (see the previous section), South Korea, Taiwan, and Singapore (see Figure 8.7). Each is experiencing rapid economic growth due to its industrial base and the export of items to the United States and Europe. Each of the Four Asian Tigers has used the Asian model of economic success, namely trade. This model is based on the relatively inexpensive production of goods and their export to world markets. All of the Four Asian Tigers have access to a world-class port. They also have developed, educated workforces who are trained to do highly skilled labor. In almost all of the Four Tigers, manufacturing has consisted of low-quality textiles and toys. In recent years, however, the sector has shifted to include electronics and other higher-order goods.

Trade for the Four Asian Tigers is a **complementary** process, meaning that both sides benefit. The countries that manufacture products increase employment, and the countries that receive products satisfy their consumers. Thus, trade is a win-win situation.

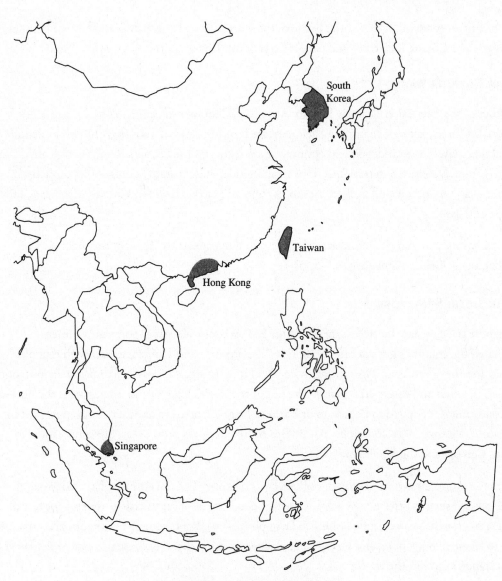

Figure 8.7: Four Asian Tigers Map.

ASIAN TIGER: SOUTH KOREA

South Korea is dominated by its capital city, Seoul. Seoul is the largest city in South Korea, with a population approaching 19 million people, a high-quality university and primary educational system, and a ready workforce. Seoul is truly a world-class city, even holding the summer Olympics in 1988 and hosting three World Cup soccer games in 2002.

South Korea exports automobiles and electronics. Port facilities are available in cities such as Pusan and Kwangju, allowing access to worldwide markets. The port of Incheon, west of Seoul, exports

South Korean goods all of the world. Some of the world's largest companies including Hyundai, Samsung and LG, are located in and export from South Korean ports.

ASIAN TIGER: TAIWAN

Another of the four Asian Tigers is Taiwan. After Mao Zedong took control of China in 1949, nationalist forces, led by Chiang Kai-shek, retreated to the island of Taiwan. A heated topic today is whether Taiwan is an independent country or a territory of the People's Republic of China. The United States has chosen to recognize Taiwan as an independent state because of its capitalistic economy and economic and military ties to the United States. However, China still believes Taiwan is part of China.

Taiwan has seen a rapid economic growth in response to exports. In Taiwan, the main port of Kaohsiung facilitates the majority of exports.

ASIAN TIGER: SINGAPORE

Singapore is a city-state located at the tip of the Malay Peninsula. Singapore's government estimated the country's growth rate in 2006 at 7.9 percent, comparing favorably with that of China and the other Asian Tigers. Singapore, like Hong Kong, is a classic example of an entrepot. It takes in goods and re-exports them to the rest of the world. The port in Singapore is the busiest **transshipment** (designed to be sent to one area to be re-exported to another—entrepot) port in the world. Massive cargo containers put dozens of freight boxes onto ocean liners for export to Japan, Europe, and the United States.

Singapore is also known for its tough policies against crime. The government has outlawed "bad habits," such as littering. As a result, many people are hesitant to visit as tourists for fear of punishment, which can include lashing. The opposite is true of business. International companies love to locate in Singapore, and businesspeople love working there, because it is one of the safest and cleanest places in the world.

There is a saying in Singapore that all of its citizens aspire to the five Cs: car, credit card, condominium, country club, and cash. Although the government is trying to sway people from an obsession with materialism, Western culture is exerting a strong influence. High-end automobiles and luxury clothing stores pervade the city.

THE "BABY TIGERS"

Areas like Kuala Lumpur in Malaysia, Vietnam, the Philippines, and Thailand are all growing their economies and following the model of the Four Asian Tigers. India is gaining status in the industrial sector. Many U.S. companies have located their call centers in India.

JAPAN

Japan's economic success can be traced back to World War II; the treaty that ended that war forbade Japan to build up its military. Without an army, Japan's government could invest in industrial development. Japan has very few natural resources yet is one of the world leaders in industry. Japan has used the world trade model to increase its share of world industry.

Japan's influence on the world has been especially pronounced in the automotive and electronics industries. Japan's workforce is extremely loyal to its companies, and workers equate personal and professional value with how the company performs. A highly skilled and educated workforce has been instrumental in the rise of Japanese industry. Areas around Tokyo, Yokohama, and Osaka have seen enormous increases in industrial productivity with major ports readily available. The transportation systems, including highways and rail transport, are world renowned, and Japan produced one of the highest-speed trains in the world—it moves at over 300 miles per hour. When taking the train from Tokyo to Osaka in southern Japan, one sees factory after factory on the way.

TRADE IMBALANCES

The United States has decried its trade imbalances with Japan and China and other Asian countries. Manufactured goods are coming into the United States at a greater rate than U.S. goods are entering Asian markets. Many Americans believe that this trade imbalance is hurting the American worker and the overall U.S. economy. However, some Asian companies have built manufacturing plants in the United States, and some U.S. companies have opened offices and set up manufacturing centers in Asia.

OTHER AREAS OF INDUSTRIALIZATION

Other areas of the world are experiencing rapid industrialization and, hence, rapid development in their economies. Mexico and Chile have greatly increased their exports in the past decade. In Africa and the Middle East region, Morocco, Turkey, and Saudi Arabia have increased their trade by a minimum of 5,000 percent since 1970. Much of this trade has been based on the exportation of natural resources.

A new area of industrialization is sometimes called an NIC or Newly Industrialized Country. An **NIC** is a country that exhibits rapid economic growth but has not yet reached the full level of developed countries by a variety of different measures. BRIC countries such as Brazil, Russia, India, and China contain vast segments of wealth and industrialization but, due to other factors, do not necessarily qualify as fully developed countries.

VIEWS OF ECONOMIC DEVELOPMENT

When discussing economic development, a primary issue is that of the haves and the have-nots. These issues, based on the unequal distribution of resources, continue to plague geographers, who classify these groups into two primary categories: the more developed countries (MDCs) and the less developed countries (LDCs), also labeled "third-world countries." LDCs continually lag in economic development, and the majority of their populations are mired in poverty.

OPTIMISTIC VIEWPOINT

The optimistic viewpoint of economic development is based on the principle that an abundance of resources is available in the form of both fossil fuels and alternative energy sources. Energy and other resources are distributed unevenly among countries. However, if humans work together, they can solve this problem of inequitable distribution. The **optimistic viewpoint** proposes allowing capitalistic forces the ability to enter countries and get resources to the areas that need them, at the same time profiting from their investment.

PESSIMISTIC VIEWPOINT

The **pessimistic viewpoint** views the inaccessibility of resources as a serious challenge and addresses three primary concerns vis-à-vis economic development.

The first of these concerns is that the distribution of resources does not correspond to demand for them. The demand for resources will continue to increase as the world's population grows, and their supply will decrease.

Another concern is that LDCs may not be able to achieve critical mass to start a cycle of economic growth. Usually, when there is a need for a product, the market fills that need. However, what happens when no market exists for a product? Going back to the discussion of Weber's least cost theory, the market may not be ready for the production of a particular product. In this case, industry trying to produce and sell products to LDCs may not be able to succeed because there is no demand.

The last concern is that investment is not allocated equally around the globe but rather is concentrated in only a few locations. A lack of investment seriously limits some areas' opportunities for growth. In some areas, such as in much of Africa, the potential gains are not worth the high risk of investing. African investment has been minimal. Aid from more developed countries has not been able to offset the environmental, population, medical, and political disasters in the continent. Africa is often deemed the poorest of all of the continents.

Foreign direct investment occurs when a company located in one country enters the economy of another country. The investor has a direct relationship with the product of the investment. In many Asian countries, foreigners invest by way of a stock market. In less developed countries, if there is any investment at all, it is usually in the form of direct ownership of a production facility or a plantation.

Much investment in recent years has been focused on Asia. The Four Asian Tigers have seen much investment in recent years, because such investments are usually safe and, of late, profitable. Although little investment has been made in certain areas in Africa and Latin America, development is better in some parts. For example, Americans looking for an idyllic location to retire have been purchasing land in Costa Rica and Panama.

Together, these three concerns of the pessimistic viewpoint mean that all sections of the globe will probably not see the same levels of progress in the upcoming decades.

MILLENNIUM DEVELOPMENT GOALS

The United Nations has set forth specific goals in the effort to eradicate poverty and disease, create more opportunities for women, and practice environmental stewardship on the land. These goals were first delineated in 2000—hence the name the **Millennium Development Goals**—with the aim of being met by the year 2015. These eight goals from the United Nations are:

1. Eradicate extreme poverty and hunger

2. Achieve universal primary education

3. Promote gender equality and empower women

4. Reduce child mortality

5. Improve maternal health

6. Combat HIV/AIDS, malaria, and other diseases

7. Ensure environmental sustainability

8. Develop a global partnership for development

How to meet these goals is a source of disagreement among many countries. Many developed countries suggest it is not their responsibility to fiscally support developing countries. However, most would agree that all of the above goals are problems in the developing countries.

WAYS TO DESCRIBE DEVELOPMENT

There are different ways to address development. Development does not necessarily mean wealth. In fact, it's much more than individual wealth. A society may even deem wealth as an adverse condition to development, where a few have gained personal wealth at the expense of general social welfare.

So what is development? **Development** is the continued progress of a society in all areas, ranging from demographics to economics to social factors.

HUMAN DEVELOPMENT INDEX

Economists and geographers agree that certain characteristics of development affect all members of the human race regardless of culture: life expectancy, literacy rate, average years of education, and GDP/capita. Together, these four characteristics comprise the **Human Development Index (HDI)**, developed by Pakistani economist Mahbub ul Haq in 1990. By applying a formula to these characteristics, one can determine the development of a country on a scale of zero to one. The HDI is the most often used measure of development and is utilized by the United Nations.

LIFE EXPECTANCY

Countries with a relatively high **life expectancy** can expect their citizens to live approximately 60 or 70 years. According to the Centers for Disease Control and Prevention (CDC), U.S. life expectancy averages 77.9 years. Women, on average, live longer than men. The average life expectancy for women in the United States is 80.4 years; for men, 75.2 years. There are two theories as to why this is the case.

One is that women are biologically stronger than men, because they must be able to give birth. Also, in many cultures, young men engage in high-risk behaviors, for example dangerous feats, which in some cases can lead to death.

Another theory, increasingly outdated in many cultures, is that men have to experience the stress of everyday work life, while women stay at home with the children. According to this theory, the stress of raising children does not compare with what the man experiences at work outside the home. Also, men are often involved in more dangerous professions, including fishing, drilling, and firefighting, which cause male death rates to be higher.

In more developed countries, people can expect to live longer thanks to better access to medical facilities and personnel. The sanitary conditions in more developed countries are much higher than in less developed countries. Life expectancy may only be as high as 50 years in some African countries.

LITERACY

Literacy is the percentage of a population that can fluently read and write. However, literacy goes beyond this. In essence, it's an ability to use a language to communicate. Literacy directly reflects the educational system of a country. The more people who can read and write, the greater a society's potential to succeed in the world economy. In more developed countries, the literacy rate may be as high as 99.9 percent. (The rate will never reach 100 percent, because in any society, some people will be unable to process language and writing.)

In many African countries, the literacy rate is below 30 percent, which means that over two-thirds of the country is unable to communicate effectively through writing and reading. The burden this puts on the governments of these countries is enormous. When more than 70 percent of a labor force cannot read or write, they can only perform low-skill labor, which inhibits economic growth.

The education system is the key to raising literacy rates. The problem stems from what the economic development pessimists claim is the lack of investment in these areas. The lack of investment means no money for schools, and a lack of employment means no tax base to fund schools. Many African countries are in a self-perpetuating cycle: They need education to get out of poverty, but poverty prevents them from funding education.

EDUCATION

Education itself is a measure of economic development. Being educated means that workers are more productive in their jobs, increasing the productivity of the society as a whole. In addition to having few educational facilities or teachers, many less developed countries are experiencing **brain drain**. Talented youth who receive scholarships to schools outside the country do not come back to initiate development in the area. Trained professionals, such as nurses and doctors, also leave for better living conditions in more developed countries. Brain drain is the opposite of **brain gain**, where less developed countries send their brightest students to colleges and universities in more developed countries, then see their investment return as former students return to their home countries and initiate development.

STANDARD OF LIVING

The **standard of living** is the measure of wealth or enjoyment that one experiences. Much of this is culturally determined. As in Singapore with its five Cs (cash, credit cards, condominiums, car, and country club), many people around the world seek such markers of well-being. To a nomadic tribe, however, standard of living may be measured by the number of animals someone owns. To someone in a developing country, it might be the ownership of a washer and dryer.

PHYSICAL QUALITY OF LIFE INDEX

David Morris developed the Physical Quality of Life Index (PQLI) as an alternative to using gross domestic product. The **Physical Quality of Life Index** puts the factors of the Human Development Index on a scale from 0 to 100. To calculate the PQLI, economic geographers use the following steps:

1. Determine the *literacy rate* for the country.

2. Subtract the infant mortality rate from 166 and multiply the result by 0.625. This is the *indexed infant mortality rate.*

3. Subtract 42 from the life expectancy and multiply the result by 2.7. This is the *indexed life expectancy rate.*

4. Add together the literacy rate, the indexed infant mortality rate, and the life expectancy rate and divide that sum by 3.

Let's examine the United States using the PQLI:

1. Literacy rate is about 99.5 percent.

2. Infant mortality rate is 6.7.

    $166 - 6.7 = 159.3$

    $159.3 \times 0.625 = 99.6$

3. Life expectancy is 78.

    $78 - 42 = 36$

    $36 \times 2.7 = 97.2$

4. Add together the results of steps 1–3, then divide by 3:

    $99.5 + 99.6 + 97.2 = 296.3$

    $296.3 \div 3 = 98.8$

The PQLI of the United States is 98.8, putting the United States at the high end of the development spectrum.

ECONOMIC DATA INDICATORS

Another way to measure the development of a society is by analyzing its economic data. Economic factors of development include a country's gross domestic product and gross national product, as well as the economic structure of the society as whole. Another measure of economic development is what people can afford to purchase with their expendable income. Finally, the availability of raw materials is an important economic measure of development.

GNP AND GDP

Gross national product (GNP) and gross domestic product (GDP) are two separate statistics. **Gross domestic product** is the selling value, or market price, of all the goods and services produced within a particular country's borders, typically in a given year. **Gross national product** is the value of the goods and services produced by that country's companies, usually within one year. This can include sales from transnational corporations in other countries.

For example, Coca-Cola has a production plant in Argentina. However, because Coca-Cola is an American company, its sales of Coke products from the plant in Argentina apply to the U.S. gross national product. In addition, because the Coke product was sold in an Argentinean grocery store, the transaction would count towards Argentina's gross domestic product.

GROSS DOMESTIC PRODUCT PER CAPITA

Gross domestic product per capita is the total amount of goods and services produced in a country divided by the total population of that country. The end result is the value of the average person's production in their country for a particular year.

As of 2005, the gross domestic product for the United States was over $12.4 trillion. The United States has just under three times the gross domestic product of the second-nearest competitor, Japan, which is followed by Germany and then China. Looking at the per capita statistics tells a much different story, however. In terms of gross domestic product per capita, the leading country in the world is Luxembourg, at almost $70,000. Luxembourg is followed by Norway and then the United States, at just over $41,000.

Countries on the lower end of the scale tend to be located in sub-Saharan Africa as well as parts of Asia. These countries' total gross domestic products may not even exceed $100 million. Looking at the gross domestic product per capita puts the inequity into further detail. More than a dozen countries produce less per capita than many U.S. high school students working part-time jobs.

ECONOMIC SECTORS

Another way to analyze economic factors of development is by looking at where the majority of people work in their economy. Going back to the demographic transition model, when the majority of the people in a society are employed in the agricultural sectors of an economy, it is less developed. As more people begin to be employed in the industrial sectors, the development of the society increases. As a society continues to progress into the tertiary and quatenary sectors of an economy, both its level of development and standard of living generally rise.

In a slight departure from the demographic transition model, economists classify the different **economic sectors** of an economy into primary, secondary, and tertiary activities.

- **Primary economic sectors** are involved in the basic activities, such as farming. Primary industries extract resources from the Earth, such as timber, fish, minerals, and soil.

- **Secondary economic sectors** use the materials from primary industries to manufacture a product for purchase. An example of a secondary industry would be furniture making. These companies use wood to produce furniture that a consumer then purchases.

- **Tertiary economic sectors** sell the products from the secondary economic sectors and provide services.

In the United States, many more people are employed selling and repairing automobiles than in their actual production, while less than 2 percent of the population is involved with agriculture. In less developed countries, most people are employed in the primary economic sectors.

EXPENDABLE INCOME

Another economic measure of development is **expendable income**. Expendable income is the amount of money left over after all of the bills have been paid. In the United States, the amount of expendable income is high. For example, some people spend thousands of dollars to purchase a cutting-edge television, and some households have more television sets than people to watch them. In many areas of the world, an automobile is considered a luxury item, but in many cities in the United States, it is considered a necessity.

TECHNOLOGY

The use of technology in a society is very indicative of its level of development. The **technology gap** describes the fact that some people have more technology than others, as well as the fact that some people know how to use it while others do not. For example, most students today know how to use technology better than their parents.

More developed countries have a faster technology transfer process. The **technology transfer process** is the amount of time that it takes a new technology to leave the laboratory and arrive on shelves for citizens to purchase. The ability of companies to move from the design phase to the production and distribution phase is important in determining their profits. Less developed countries have some research facilities but have great difficulty moving toward the production or marketing of a new technology.

RAW MATERIALS

The more raw materials that a country possesses the more developed that country is, right? Not necessarily. The answer to that question depends upon who owns the rights to and the profit from the raw materials.

For example, many Middle Eastern countries have immense wealth due to oil. However, this wealth is often concentrated in the hands of a small elite, hindering the overall development of these countries' economies. Other countries have access to raw materials but are still mired in poverty due to neocolonialism. Companies located in the more developed countries extract the natural resources and take the profits.

The majority of the more developed countries have adequate access to the raw materials needed for industrial production. However, countries can succeed without access to raw materials. Going back to the Four Asian Tigers, each of these countries has succeeded economically by using the trade model. They trade manufactured goods in exchange for many raw materials. Likewise, Japan has very few natural resources but has become one of the richest and most productive economies in the world.

DEMOGRAPHIC STATISTICS

Using demographic statistics and models, such as the demographic transition model, a geographer can determine whether a country is in the more developed or the less developed category.

Gender balance relates to both economic and demographic factors of development. Gender balance does not necessarily mean more of one sex than the other but rather the equal opportunity for women and men to succeed. For example, gender inequities are prevalent in many Middle Eastern countries, even today, where there are separate doors for entrances into public buildings for men and women. Women are discouraged from gaining education or participating in the workforce. During the First Gulf War, the U.S. military was faced with a quandary. Women are an essential part of the U.S. military. But upon arrival in Saudi Arabia, the women in the armed forces were not allowed to drive a motor vehicle. It was against the law.

Another key demographic factor of development is **birth rate**. Less developed countries tend to have much higher birth rates than more developed countries. This is due in part to the economic structure of a society (primary, secondary, tertiary, quaternary, and quinary). As a country moves from one economic structure to a higher level, more and more women participate in the workforce and fewer children are born. However, in less developed countries that are still involved in primary economic activities, children are seen as an economic asset, providing labor on the farm and providing security for the elderly.

Together, the crude birthrate and crude death rate make up the natural increase rate. A country with a higher natural increase rate is considered a less developed country; one with a lower natural increase rate is considered a more developed country.

ADDITIONAL DEVELOPMENT THEORIES

WORLD SYSTEMS THEORY

Geographers have tried to put world development into spatial terms. Immanuel Wallerstein did this with his **world systems analysis**. Wallerstein was the first person to coin the terms *core* and *periphery*. The **core areas** are the more developed countries, which use the resources of the periphery to continue their success. These are located primarily in North America and Europe and also include Japan and Australia. The **periphery areas** are the less developed countries. The lack of investment by the more developed countries continues to keep these countries in poverty. Also, the ownership of many of the natural resources, or at least the means of extracting them, benefits the more developed countries. Figure 8.8 shows the core and periphery countries. Wallerstein concluded that a line ran roughly at 30 degrees north latitude that separated the core from the periphery, with the exception of Australia and New Zealand.

In recent years, the **semi-periphery** has been added to the model. The semi-periphery are the countries, such as the Four Asian Tigers, that are gaining in development and have some of the benchmarks of success but are still lacking the political importance associated with the core countries.

Also, major urban centers serve the core area. New York, Tokyo, and London are considered **world cities** based upon their financial and cultural importance in their areas. In the semi-periphery are cities such as Chicago, Paris, and Shanghai. These cities serve as regional hubs for their respective regions but are not on a world scale. Other cities are in the periphery regions and serve the needs of the major core areas.

The **dependency theory** suggests that some countries are allowing themselves to remain in poverty as a whole to obtain some other type of economic power, usually for an elite class. In many cases, the less developed country's leadership is hoarding economic resources for itself, while the majority of the population is struggling to feed itself.

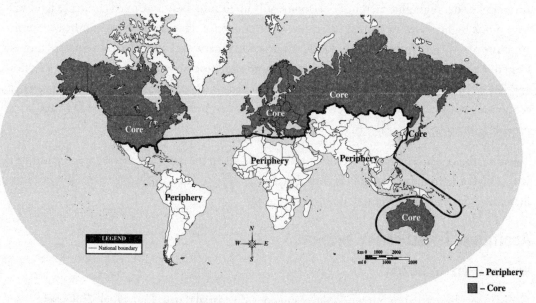

Figure 8.8: Core vs. Periphery Map.

The Core-Periphery Model

Another way to look at the **core-periphery model** of development is by looking at the concept through four primary factors: industrial core, upward transition, downward transition, and resource frontier. Each of these can be seen on a global scale down to a national or even urban scale.

The **industrial core** is where the majority of the manufacturing or industrial activities of a nation or a city are located. These areas usually contain large urban centers, which both provide the market for the products and the workforce to produce them. In the United States, the industrial core is the northeast, extending from New England to the western shores of Lake Michigan, including the cities of Milwaukee and Chicago. In Canada, the industrial core is located in the southeastern sections of Ontario and includes Hamilton, Toronto, Ottawa, and Montréal.

The next major area in the core-periphery model is the **upward transition** area. Upward transition means gaining jobs and attracting industry. Business incentives may include tax breaks and agglomeration. The tax base continues to expand in these areas, allowing more services (better schools, nicer parks, improved transportation) in a self-perpetuating cycle.

In the United States, the upward transition area is the South. This area is experiencing rapid population growth due to the relocation of industrial activities from the northeast. The Sun Belt extends from North Carolina to Georgia. Cities in this region, such as Charlotte, North Carolina, and Atlanta, Georgia, have experienced a renaissance of population and economic activities in the past decade. Another Sun Belt area is the central and coastal region of Texas, which includes the cities of San Antonio and Houston. The last major area of the Sun Belt is southern California and Arizona, including San Diego and Phoenix respectively.

In Canada, the upward transition area is in the western portion of the country around the Rocky Mountains. Cities such as Vancouver, Calgary, and Edmonton have all seen growth. The region is dominated by the crude petroleum coming from the western plains region. Tourism is also a major factor. The Vancouver area hosted the Winter Olympics in 2010, and Calgary held the Winter Olympics in 1988.

The third area in the core-periphery model is the **downward transition** area. Downward transition means that companies are leaving, and unemployment rates are high. As people leave an area, the tax base is reduced, and just as the upward transition area is in a self-perpetuating cycle upward, the downward transition area is in a downward cycle.

In the United States, the Great Plains region is experiencing a downward cycle, with the exception of Western North Dakota. At the beginning of the 20th century, the Great Plains area was in an upward transition due to the rich farmland and immigrants settling there. Today, companies are moving out of the Great Plains owing to the lack of population; because of the scarcity of good jobs, young people leave home to go to school and do not return, reducing the population further.

The downward transition area of Canada is the Atlantic Maritime Provinces. Nova Scotia and Newfoundland are struggling to find another means of economic success now that the fishing industry in the region has declined so much. Unemployment is at record levels in some areas, causing people to leave in increasing numbers.

The last section of the core-periphery model is the **resource frontier**. The resource frontier areas provide the majority of the resources for the industrial core. Many of these resources are used for energy production or are the base materials in manufacturing. Transportation systems need to be developed to get the materials from the resource frontier to the industrial core. The main forms of transportation used for this purpose are trains and pipelines. The incredible growth that occurs once a resource is found often ends once the resource has dried up, leaving rotting infrastructure and ghost towns behind.

In the early part of the 20th century, much of the western United States was a resource frontier section. Gold as well as other resources in the desert regions of Arizona, New Mexico, and California spurred growth. Today, the remote northern sections of Alaska, with crude oil resources, are the largest resource frontier in the United States. The Alaska Pipeline was built to get the crude petroleum from the northern part of the state to the transportation systems in the southern part of the state.

North Dakota's Bakken basin has seen incredible growth in the past half decade due to the oil industry. A newer method of oil extraction called fracking has enabled previously inaccessible oil to become available, creating thousands of new jobs in the upper Great Plains.

In Canada, the resource frontier is in the same region as the United States. The newly created territory of Nunavut has an abundance of raw materials that industries need. The Northwest Territories and the Yukon Territory are also rich in natural resources. However, the northern sections of Canada have the same problem as the northern sections of Alaska—transportation. Because of the incredibly cold temperatures, it is almost impossible to build roads and railroad tracks into the remote regions of Canada. Pipelines can be built. However, they are not flexible in their routes, needing to go directly from the source to the transportation hub, and they only work with liquids and gases.

On a city scale, different zones in the city may occupy different places in the core-periphery model. For example, certain areas of each large urban center are devoted to industrial output due to zoning provisions. Other areas, where people want to move, could be classified as upward transition areas. In contrast, certain neighborhoods experience higher unemployment rates and are less attractive; these are downward transition areas. The resource frontier is where natural resources are located. For example, sand and gravel, a base product used in many roads and driveways, is often found near large urban areas to reduce transportation costs (Weber's Theory).

GROWTH MODELS OF DEVELOPMENT

As societies move from the primary economic sectors to quaternary and quinary sectors, these countries go through different stages in their development.

ROSTOW'S MODEL OF DEVELOPMENT

Walt Whitman Rostow created a model of development (also known as the **take-off model**) to show the five stages that a country progresses through in its development. These are: 1) the traditional society, 2) the preconditions for takeoff, or the transitional stage, 3) the takeoff, 4) the drive to maturity, and 5) the age of mass consumption.

In the **traditional society**, the majority of the workforce is involved in the primary sector of the economy. Most people practice subsistence farming. Any trade involves farmers and their agricultural products. Mass production is not yet developed.

The second phase of Rostow's model is the **preconditions for takeoff**, sometimes called the **transitional phase**. In this phase, material conditions, such as transportation or other infrastructure, improve. Entrepreneurs are beginning to see money-making opportunities, and the economy shifts from primary to secondary activities. During this phase, expendable income begins to rise, and more people can invest in entrepreneurial activities.

During the **takeoff stage**, more companies become involved in the manufacturing sectors of the economy. The remaining farmers become less reliant on subsistence farming and sell more of their produce. Food is now largely being processed for resale. The primary regions where growth is taking place are usually around large urban centers. However, in this stage, growth is only taking place in a few industries.

During the **drive to maturity**, the technology that was available to only a few companies during the takeoff stage is now being diffused and integrated into all areas of the manufacturing sector.

The final phase of Rostow's model is the **age of mass consumption**. Workers have become highly skilled in their professions and are using their strengths for the overall benefit of the economy. Productivity, earnings, and savings are at all-time highs. The society as a whole has shifted from secondary sectors to more of a tertiary or service-based economy. Manufacturing is still occurring but has shifted from traditional sectors to consumer goods.

Rostow's model is based on the principle that consumers will save and invest personal wealth to improve their economic status. Industry needs this capital to grow and then generates a return on investment to shareholders.

Critics of Rostow with optimistic economic viewpoints cite the sub-Saharan countries' level of development as examples where his model does not apply. Critics with pessimistic viewpoints point to the inequities of resource distribution around the world and the lack of capital to invest in some areas.

Rostow's Model of Development has often times been compared to Wallerstein's World Systems Theory in terms of how each are measured. Both are measures of economic development in their own way, as each tries to place countries within a spectrum of development. Rostow saw growth as being initiated from within whereas Wallerstein saw growth determined by outside factors and suggested that core countries kept poor countries in the periphery in order to use their labor and resources.

RICHARD NOLAN'S STAGES OF GROWTH MODEL

Another model of development that has fused into economic geography is Richard Nolan's stages of growth model. This model describes individual companies' adaptation of technology to be competitive in the economy.

This model is similar to Rostow's but has six stages: 1) initiation, 2) contagion, 3) control, 4) integration, 5) data administration, and 6) maturity. Also, Nolan's model deals more with the integration of technology into a society, whereas Rostow's deals more with the fundamental principles of capitalism, such as investing and savings.

During the **initiation stage**, technology is used sparingly and primarily for data processing. The few users of technology do so to reduce the cost of human processing of data.

In the **contagion stage**, like a disease in a contagious diffusion pattern, technology begins to spread. There are more and more uses for technology, and often, the bugs need to be worked out of the system before people will purchase the product.

In the **control stage**, management is becoming more frustrated with the use of technology because employees don't necessarily have the training or the hardware to maximize their productivity with new software. People are confused and frustrated, but they also see the possibilities of technology. A micro example of this phase is a person buying a new computer and then, instead of using the computer for work or school, he or she simply uses it to play games all day.

During the **integration stage**, users have come to terms with technology and have found practical uses for it.

In the **data administration stage**, technology is used mostly in the collection and the storage of data. Less work is done by computer programs, while more use is made of computers' ability to store data.

The last phase is the **maturity stage**. During the maturity stage, new uses for technology are being integrated into the workplace. During this stage, the organization is looking for ways to use technology to advance beyond its competitors.

Nolan's model pertains more to individual organizations than to countries as a whole. But as companies begin to get more adept with technology, they are usually at the forefront of the infusion of technology into the daily lives of their workers. Companies usually initiate technological development because they possess the resources to purchase new technology when it is still relatively expensive. Cost decreases as the technology ages, or as competition arises.

Development is a difficult thing to quantify. In the past two decades, new means of measuring development, such as the Human Development Index and the Physical Quality of Life Index, have tried to quantify the different levels of development for countries around the world.

Many of the countries that are less developed are still in a colonial mentality. They depended upon their colonial powers for defense and in exchange gave up many of their economic raw materials. According to many economic geographers, **neocolonialism**, by which the less developed countries are still economically dependent upon the more developed countries, is still in effect today. Less developed countries depend on the more developed countries for investment.

SUSTAINABLE DEVELOPMENT

Sustainable development is a general term that means different things to different people. The most commonly accepted and used definition of sustainable development comes from the United Nations Brundtland Report in 1987, which defined sustainable development as "development which meets the needs of the present without compromising the ability of future generations to meet their own needs." Sustainable development takes into consideration economic development, social development, and the environment. It has been relatively successful on a small scale in a variety of settings throughout the world. Proponents of sustainable development have experimented with innovative projects that often focus on micro-loans, alternative energy projects, and women in development. **Micro-loan**s are loans usually under $500 that people can invest in to see a project get its start, usually in developing regions.

GENDER DEVELOPMENT INDEX (GDI)

The main drawback to the Human Development Index is the fact that it only takes into consideration four factors of development—longevity, health, education, and standard-of-living. There is so much more to understanding a society's level of wealth and well-being than four statistics. Most importantly, regional and gender differences exist within a country that do not show up in the HDI. The Gender Development Index (GDI) was created to give a clearer picture of what life is like for women throughout the world. The GDI uses the same statistics as the HDI but analyzes the data with an eye to gender differences. Its most significant finding is that women are not equal to men in any country in the world in terms of material wealth. Western European and North American women are the most nearly equal, whereas in sub-Saharan Africa women are the worst off, that is, that region has the lowest GDI.

THE GENDER INEQUALITY INDEX (GII)

The Gender Inequality Index (GII) is a relatively new measurement of economic development in a country. This quantitative data measures the disparity between males and females in a country's population. The GII analyzes three different measurements—labor market (women in employment), empowerment (political power), and reproductive health (fertility and mortality during birth process)—to show the level of a nation's disparity between men and women. GII is measured on a scale from 0-1.

LAND USE AND RESOURCES

LAND USE MODELS

Thinking about the land according to the different land use models helps us to determine how we use natural resources for the world's industrial activity and how to best use the land. There are four primary ways to think about land use to help us make decisions regarding these issues: economic, sustainability, environmental, and preservationist. Each has its advantages and disadvantages as well as variations on what area of the world is being analyzed. A balance of the four models is usually evident on the landscape.

ECONOMIC LAND USE MODEL

The economic land use model is used to develop and build on the landscape for profit. For example, a shopping mall development would use the economic land use model to analyze the construction of the mall.

The economic land use model looks at the present and addresses land use for development now. Thus, this model suggests that resources should be extracted from the environment now so that we can see an economic benefit within a short time. Urban areas are zoned using the economic land use model and assigned uses to land from gas stations to amusement parks to condominiums.

To some, using the land for economic reasons introduces the concept of **topocide**. Topocide is the killing off of a landscape to build a new one. The process is a deliberate one in which the intention of the development is to eliminate any aspects of the old landscape. While topocide often has its critics, in some cases it is a good thing. For example, topocide could be considered positive when urban areas are gentrified. Many blighted or run-down areas have been replaced with newer, more attractive buildings that can improve the overall economic condition of the neighborhood.

SUSTAINABILITY LAND USE MODEL

Another land use decision-making model is the sustainability land use model. This means taking something form the land and replacing it with something else. Renewable resources are an example of the sustainability land use model in action.

A good example of a sustainable industry would be the current U.S. forestry industry. A timber company, after cutting down old trees for logging, replants with new seedlings. In the next 50 to 100 years, those trees will mature and be ready for harvest. This sustainable approach ensures a future for the forestry industry well into the next century. This is an example of **sustainable development**, which ensures the use of resources for the future generations.

Farming also employs sustainable development when it uses the land. When farmers use crop rotation techniques, they are practicing sustainability. By planting soybeans one year and corn the next, the farmer replaces the nutrients that the other crop removed from the soil, thus ensuring the fertility of the soil for decades to come.

The sustainability land use model sees time in terms of several human generations. Resources should be available for one's grandchildren to use. If one generation uses up all of the resources, then it leaves future generations in a worse situation than today's generation. Resources can be used today but should not be depleted. Some Native American tribes, for example, use this philosophy when making decisions affecting the tribe. The impact of their decision is evaluated up to seven generations in the future.

ENVIRONMENTAL LAND USE MODEL

The next land use decision-making model is the environmental land use model. The environmental land use model suggests that we can use the land but must leave it in its natural state. Building can occur on the landscape. For example, shelters, walking paths, and camping structures can be built, but they must not be designed to overwhelm or alter the natural landscape.

The environmental land use model can be used for town parks as well. Any area that has kept its natural status yet allows humans to use the land would be classified as an environmental land use. Establishing the National Park Service was an example of the environmental land use model. The environmental land use model perceives time in terms of an ecosystem's life span. In some cases, this is thousands of years. Time is seen for as long as the natural ecosystem can remain viable without human alternation.

Conservation is a means of applying the environmental land use model. Conservation simply means holding onto something. This could mean resources such as in the sustainable model or the natural landscape as in the environmental model.

PRESERVATIONIST LAND USE MODEL

Preservationists see the landscape as sacred; therefore, it should not be touched by humans. The land is viewed as spiritual in nature.

Many Native Americans believe in the preservationist land use model for their spiritual heritage. There were and are spiritual sites that certain members of the tribe were not allowed to visit. In addition, Ayers Rock or Uluru in Australia has some properties of the preservationist land use model due to the Aborigines' view of the land there. Devil's Tower in Wyoming is another area of preservationist land use. Many of the local Native American tribes view this site as sacred and the National Park Service, which runs the park currently, asks climbers to not climb during the month of June to respect the Native American's view of the land.

Cemeteries are another example of the preservationist land use model. This brings in cultural aspects as well when looking at the spiritual use of the land. Folk stories have brought fear about cemeteries trying to assist people in respecting the dead.

In general, preservationists perceive time as infinite and immeasurable when discussing the environment. The environment has been around since the Earth began, and therefore must be protected at all costs.

LAND USE ISSUES

Each city, town, and hamlet must decide how it would like to use the land and resources of the area. Some areas have gained revenue through tourism. **Ecotourism** is using the natural beauty of an area as a selling point to promote tourism and generate funds to preserve the ecological community. The ecotourism industry tries to protect the areas that tourists are traveling to see, and the human community often becomes a focal point of preservation efforts. The ecotourism industry wants to preserve not only the natural landscape but also the local economy; when the local inhabitants are relatively prosperous, they will be more inclined to protect the natural landscape.

One dilemma that these communities face is the oversaturation of tourists. The more tourists that a town brings in, the more revenue comes in, but at a price; the more people that the town brings in, the less natural the area becomes. National parks are facing this dilemma. Yosemite National Park in California experiences traffic jams in the summer months. Parks located close to large urban centers on the East Coast of the United States face the same problems of overuse. Smokey Mountains National Park has faced such an increase in usage that pollution is now affecting the trees and animals. In addition, the experience of visiting these places is becoming less authentic because of the sheer numbers of people in the parks at any given time.

Less developed countries face a dilemma among the land use decision-making models. Many of the less developed countries labor under enormous debt, usually to more developed countries. As a result, there is pressure either to repay the debt or enact policies to protect the environment. A **debt-for-nature swap** is the forgiveness of debts in exchange for the setting aside of land for conservation or preservation.

Many African, Latin American, and South Asian countries are in a unique predicament. The choice for individual workers is either to farm the land and destroy the natural habitat or protect the land through conservation techniques. Usually, this is not a difficult decision; farmers will choose to feed their families at the expense of the land.

The governments of these less developed countries are in a tough position. Do they conserve the land, as more developed countries are pressuring them to do, or do they allow their citizens the freedom to farm or engage in other activities to develop their economies? Often, the governments are too weak to change or even enforce policies.

William Forster Lloyd conceived an idea in 1833 that Garrett Hardin then modernized, labeling this problem the **tragedy of the commons.** This theory suggests that humans will inevitably do what is best for them despite what is the best for the public good. When the best use of limited resources in a community comes up for debate, society must dictate the best uses of those natural resources. The political pressure on both sides of the spectrum makes choices difficult, and often one's position in the debate depends on which land use model one believes in.

TYPES OF RESOURCES

There are two distinct types of resources found in the world. **Renewable resources** can be used again. They grow or replenish themselves in nature relatively quickly, as with trees for lumber or corn or sugarcane for biofuel, or they are a constant asset, such as sunlight.

Nonrenewable resources are the opposite of renewable resources. These resources took tens of thousands of years to produce, and they do not replenish themselves within a human life span or even several human life spans. Once these resources are used up, they are gone forever.

When discussing fossil fuels, it is important to note that there are different kinds of reserves. A **proven reserve** is a reserve of a fossil fuel that has already been discovered. Proven reserves are generally very large and offer great energy potential. A **potential reserve** is a reserve that has yet to be discovered, but geology suggests it may exist in a particular location.

FOSSIL FUELS

Fossil fuels, including coal, oil, and natural gas, are examples of nonrenewable resources. These resources come from the breakdown of carbon-based sediment over long periods of time under great pressure. **Reserves** are the amount of the resource left in the ground yet to be used. **Production** is the removal of the resource.

Fossil fuels have been the subject of great debate in recent decades. The estimates of how long fossil fuels will last at current usage are anywhere from 10 to over 100 years. In any case, fossil fuels are finite and will eventually run out. Those who perceive the landscape in terms of environmental or preservationist viewpoints warn of the likelihood of fossil fuels running out fairly soon. They feel that we must invest in alternative fuel sources. Sustainability and economic land use believers have a more optimistic perspective on using fossil fuels into the next century. They perceive the landscape in terms of monetary gains. From their point of view, alternative fuels should be considered but, at least for today, they aren't efficient enough to replace fossil fuels.

The **resource crisis** is the eventual depletion of fossil fuels and a resulting collapse of energy-dependent societies. The world depends on these resources for its industrial base. Billions of people use fossil fuels. In addition, a multibillion-dollar industry has built the Alaska pipeline, supertankers, and other products necessary to extract and transport these resources around the globe. Fossil fuels provide hundreds of thousands of jobs in more developed countries, from drilling or mining to the transportation and sales.

The purpose of these **extractive industries** is to find the most efficient way to remove resources from the earth with minimal disruption to the natural environment. The need for money versus the need for space and place go head to head in this debate. **Space** is the actual location of the resource, and place is the description and the attributes that make the space valuable to some people.

As the debate continues, what is not in question is how dependent the world has become on fossil fuels. The developed countries around the world run on fossil fuels. The discovery of fossil fuels means more energy production. Also known as **mineral fuels**, they include gas, oil, coal, natural gas, and others. Fossil fuels are usually burned to produce electricity for communities. The locations of these resources are important to both local economies in terms of employment and national economies in terms of energy production.

The world is seeking alternatives to fossil fuels before they are completely depleted. During the energy crisis of the 1970s, the U.S. government formed the Department of Energy to assist in the development of alternative fuels to avoid future energy crises.

OIL

Many societies feel that the greatest of the world's natural resources is oil, or petroleum. Oil is the lifeline of modern industrialized societies and is fundamental to many Western countries' economies. Europe and North America both rely heavily on the production and consumption of oil. People in the United States use oil on a daily basis. If you have an automobile, you are not only using gasoline for your car, but you are also using motor oil to lubricate the engine, and much of the car's interior is probably made of plastic, also a petroleum-based product.

Today, the oil industry is alive and well. The majority of the oil in the United States comes from three major sources: states on the Gulf of Mexico, including Texas and Louisiana; the Northern Great Plains, including the Bakken basin in North Dakota; and California. Alaska and Oklahoma also produce a great deal of the nation's oil. Huge oil refineries located on the Gulf of Mexico produce the gasoline, motor oil, and other products that are necessary for U.S. industry and society to run.

Oil comes from deep inside the Earth. Many times, these oil reserves are located beneath the ocean, and oil rig platforms are used for their extraction. Miles of pipes tunnel deep under the Earth's surface to extract the oil located there. The different products that are made from oil come from the refining process. These include gasoline, methane, propane, butane, kerosene, diesel fuels, and jet fuel. Oil refineries produce these different products by extracting the resource at different points during the heating process.

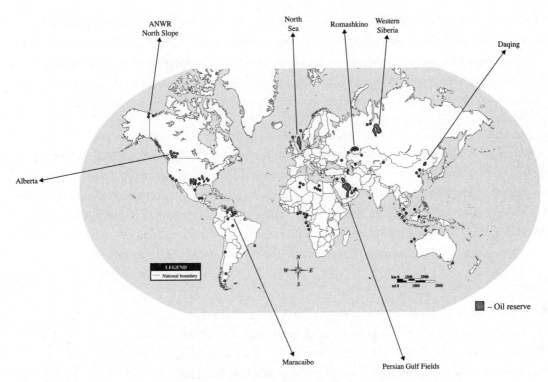

Figure 8.9: Oil Reserves of the World.

Most of the easily recoverable oil in the world has already been discovered. The increasing difficulty in finding and extracting the remaining deposits has increased the price of crude oil to some of its highest levels in history. Any break in the chain from extraction to production to delivery adds to the cost of the oil that we use in our daily lives.

Russia currently produces more barrels of oil per day than any other country, producing 10.9 million barrels per day. Saudi Arabia is next with 9.9 million barrels per day, while the United States is third with just over 8.4 million barrels per day. Figure 8.9 shows the distribution of oil around the world.

The United States uses 19.2 million barrels of oil per day as of 2010. The imbalance between U.S. production and consumption means the United States must import a large percentage of its oil. However, most U.S. oil comes from its domestic reserves as well as from other countries in the Western Hemisphere, including Canada, Mexico, and Venezuela. Another area that provides the United States with oil is the Middle East.

Huge oil companies have developed in the Gulf of Mexico. They are a large part of the economies of such cities as Houston, Texas. There is a saying that as the oil industry goes, so goes Houston. Houston has tried to diversify its economic base and reduce its reliance on the oil industry, but this industry still provides employment to a large percentage of the area's workforce.

Other countries in the world with large areas of proven oil reserves are Saudi Arabia, Venezuela, Mexico, Iran, and Iraq. Most of these countries have amassed great wealth from exporting oil to more developed countries whose production levels have not been meeting consumption levels. The majority of the world's oil reserves are located in the Middle East. Dubai, in the United Arab Emirates, is one of the wealthiest cities in the world owing to its oil reserves. Manual labor in this city is supplied by immigrants from Africa and India.

The up-and-coming giant of China is using more and more oil-based products, which further strains global supplies. As China continues to grow and its middle class continues to expand, so will its use of oil. Streets and highways are already clogged in China, and the desire to purchase and use automobiles is growing, particularly among the middle class. The higher the demand for a resource, the higher its price. Because oil is an essential component of manufacturing, this means that consumers will pay more for clothes, toys, and other products because the cost per barrel of oil is rising.

OPEC

The countries in the world that have large reserves of petroleum and export oil have organized themselves into a cartel, the **Organization of Petroleum Exporting Countries**, known as **OPEC**. This cartel was initiated in 1960, primarily with Middle East member countries. However, in recent years, countries from Africa and South America have been included. OPEC determines the price of crude petroleum by setting the numbers of barrels each member country will produce. The more barrels that are pumped, the lower the price and vice versa. Swings in oil prices are partially offset when the governments of consuming countries, like the United States, subsidize the cost of oil.

OPEC's relationship with the United States has sometimes been rocky. During the 1970s, OPEC decided to refuse to sell petroleum to the United States. Gasoline prices in the United States skyrocketed almost overnight. The price of gas more than doubled, and long gas lines were common. Many gas stations sold out within hours and then shut down until they could get more gasoline. The

OPEC COUNTRIES

Algeria	Libya
Angola	Nigeria
Ecuador	Qatar
Iran	Saudi Arabia
Iraq	United Arab Emirates
Kuwait	Venezuela

U.S. government determined the amount of gasoline that each station could sell. The price of a barrel of crude oil rose more than 1,000 percent in a matter of months. As a result of this crisis, the United States set up the U.S. Petroleum Reserve. This reserve can be tapped if the U.S. oil supply is at risk, ensuring the supply and keeping the price down, thus controlling price inflation.

Consensus has not always come easily for OPEC. Conflicts among its members have led some countries to "cheat," producing more than the allowed oil to gain more income at the expense of other OPEC countries. Sometimes, OPEC members have used oil revenues for military purposes, such as when Iran and Iraq were at war in the 1980s.

THE ARCTIC NATIONAL WILDLIFE REFUGE

Prices for a barrel of oil in recent years have ranged from around $40 per barrel to a high in July 2008 of almost $150 per barrel. Prices for a gallon of gasoline in the United States approached $5 a gallon in some parts of the country. The imbalance between supply and demand complicates U.S. foreign relations, and again, the land use debate arises. Should the United States develop a domestic supply of oil in the Arctic National Wildlife Refuge, or should we protect this wilderness area? As our consumption of oil increases and our desire for cheap gasoline continues, the debate will only intensify.

Most people agree that the United States needs to decrease its dependence upon foreign oil. The debate is over how to get the energy to drive the economy if not from foreign oil. Environmentalists and preservationists believe that the United States needs to increase its alternative energy capacity. Economic land use supporters suggest that the United States should further develop its natural oil reserves located in Alaska and the Gulf of Mexico. Most sources suggest that there is enough oil in the Arctic National Wildlife Refuge to supply the U.S. need for at least several decades. Opponents to drilling in the region suggest that the oil industry will disturb the natural ecosystem, threatening caribou, wolves, bears, birds, and other polar animals. Proponents of drilling suggest that only 1.5 million acres of the refuge's 19.2 million acres would be touched in exchange for significant recoverable oil deposits.

The Arctic National Wildlife Refuge encompasses over 19.2 million acres of land in northern Alaska. Oil abounds in the region. There are no roads within the Arctic National Wildlife Refuge. There is only one road on the edge of the refuge, and that is used to provide limited access to visitors, who can observe over 45 species of animals. The U.S. Fish and Wildlife Service runs the refuge. This is a different agency from either the National Park Service or the National Forest Service, which have different viewpoints on how the land should be used.

In the early 1900s, the area was already showing its promise as an oil reserve. It was labeled Naval Petroleum Reserve #4 in 1923, to ensure that oil would be available to the American consumer if needed. During the 1940s and 1950s, the American government sponsored oil exploration.

During the latter half of the 19th century, the environmental movement has been more politically active, and in 1953, the Sierra Club designated it a wilderness area.

Scenarios such as the one playing out around the Arctic National Wildlife Refuge can be found all around the world. For example, how much development should be allowed in the fragile ecosystem of Antarctica is debated. Africa and Asia are dealing with similar dilemmas. The less developed countries generally prefer to develop their land to ensure their economic security. The more developed countries tend to devote more land to conservation, because their economies are already developed and they can afford to sacrifice some potential resources.

Coal

The United States has abundant reserves of coal. For this reason, the United States burns coal more than any other resource to produce electricity. There are other uses for coal, including residential heating, but they are becoming more rare. Many states have coalfields within their boundaries.

Coal must be burned to produce energy. There are different forms of coal. The majority of the coal in the western states is lignite, which needs to be burned in greater quantities to produce the same amount of energy as the Appalachian coals, such as bituminous and anthracite. Because so much lignite needs to be burned to produce heat, it is not often used in blast furnaces to make steel; rather, the majority of this type of coal is used to produce electricity in power plants. Anthracite coal has the highest value of any coal because of its high heat output. This is the type of coal used most often to heat homes. Subbituminous and bituminous coal also generate high heat outputs. Each of these forms of coal is useful in creating electricity.

In 2005, the United States extracted more than 1.3 billion short tons of coal from its soil. As shown in Figure 8.10, this was the largest amount in history. The majority of this coal came from the western states; Montana, North Dakota, Wyoming, Colorado, New Mexico, and Utah all possess large amounts of coal. Most subbituminous coal is found in Alaska and some other western states. The majority of coal found in Texas, Montana, and North Dakota is the lignite form. The largest coal mine in the world by reserve is the North Antelope Rochelle Mine, located in Wyoming.

The next major source of coal in the United States is the Appalachian region, followed by the interior regions of the country, including Illinois, Iowa, Missouri, Oklahoma, and Texas. West Virginia, Kentucky, and parts of Pennsylvania have based their economies on the extraction of coal from the Appalachian Mountains. The majority of the coal found in the Appalachian region is bituminous coal. However, the purest form of coal, anthracite, is found in large quantities in Pennsylvania.

For most of the past 150 years, much of the coal found was shipped to Pittsburgh for the blast furnaces to produce steel. This steel provided the foundation for many of the buildings that still stand today. This transportation of coal has posed some problems. Much of it is shipped by means of truck and train. These transportation options use petroleum as their primary means of power. Using one fossil fuel to deliver another means the United States is using two separate power sources in the steel production chain.

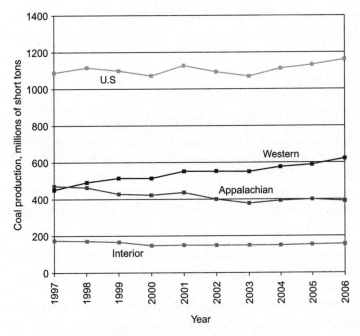

Figure 8.10: Coal Extraction Chart.

Coal is a vital aspect of overall energy production in the United States. Because the United States is loaded with coal reserves, it can produce large amounts of energy, and therefore it has been more reluctant to use alternative forms of energy than if coal were scarce. Transitioning to alternative energy would, at least temporarily, mean larger monthly energy bills.

As for worldwide coal production, China is the leader with the United States in second place. Other large producers of coal include Australia, Russia, and India. The safety records of Chinese coal mines have come under increased scrutiny. Recently, a number of coal mines have exploded or caved in due to poor safety standards. The industry will be subjected to even more pressure from safety watchdogs as the demand for coal continues to increase in China. China is also one of the leaders in coal consumption, which is causing air pollution in many urban areas.

In Europe, Great Britain has seen the greatest impact from coal. The coal industry is one of the reasons for the rise of the Industrial Revolution, which began in Great Britain. Europe has seen a downturn in its coal mining industry since the 1970s due to continued expansion of alternative energy uses, such as nuclear power. Europe gets much more of its power from alternative energy sources than the United States does.

Russia's coal mining industry has seen tremendous changes, which accompanied the political changes in the former Soviet Union. The privatization of the coal mining industry has brought about an improvement in safety standards. The majority of coal mining is taking place in Siberia.

In Africa, South Africa possesses a large amount of coal reserves. The area around the Vaal River is known for its industrial complexes and serves as a major consumer of the coal mined in the region.

NATURAL GAS

Another important fossil fuel is natural gas. Natural gas is an odorless, colorless gas from inside the Earth. When burned, it provides abundant heat to homes and businesses around the United States and the world. The majority of the homes in the United States are heated with natural gas.

The south central region of the United States produces the most natural gas. Texas produced over 5 billion cubic feet in 2005, and Oklahoma, Louisiana, Wyoming, New Mexico, and Colorado each produced over 1 million cubic feet that year. Natural gas is mined and distributed throughout the United States by means of underground pipelines.

In terms of world production, no other country comes close to Russia in regards to its reserves of natural gas. Russia contains one-third of all of the natural gas reserves in the world. Iran has the second-largest reserves, with about 16 percent of the total, and the United States has about 10 percent of the world's natural gas. These three countries together possess just under 60 percent of all of the natural gas in the world.

METALS

GOLD

Gold has always offered immediate wealth, so people have migrated to look for it. In the United States, gold reserves have been found in western states. Nevada is the largest gold-producing state, followed by Alaska and California. Various migrations have been initiated because people assumed gold could be found at their destination. The California gold rush of 1849 led thousands of settlers to the mountains of California in search of their dream. The Yukon region of Canada saw a gold rush in the late 1800s to early 1900s. Very few found the success that they were looking for, but some did find immediate wealth. Much of the gold that has been found in the United States was found by these pioneers during the late 1800s and early 1900s. Gold prospecting increased during the Great Depression, because of desperate economic conditions; people who had lost their jobs in the East traveled west as prospectors seeking instant wealth.

The majority of gold is mined, which involves either an **open pit mine**, where the land is removed and the resources are extracted in the open air, or a **shaft mine**, where tunnels are dug deep into the earth and extend for miles horizontally. Mines are also termed surface mines or underground mines. **Surface mines (strip mines)** are similar to open pit mines, because they dig up the earth and then replace the soil when the digging or drilling is completed. **Underground mines** use the shaft and tunnel systems. The majority of the gold in the United States is found through open pit mines.

California, Arizona, Colorado, South Dakota, and Oregon all have large areas devoted to gold mining. Gold mining today is done much differently than the pan mining of the past. Remote sensing devices search the earth for large deposits of gold. When a vein is found, much of the top layers of earth are removed in an open pit mining process.

In the past, gold was used for coins and as a backup to the U.S. monetary system. Gold is accepted worldwide as a measurement of wealth. It lasts for a long time and has traditionally been very stable in its value. The United States has since left the gold standard of monetary policy because of the continued fluctuation of gold prices. Much of the gold mined in the United States today is used for jewelry. Gold is also used in various industries.

South Africa leads the world in gold production, producing one-fifth of the world's total. In recent years, the United States has passed Australia, becoming the second-greatest producer with over 14 percent of the world's output. Australia produces another 14 percent. Together, these three countries produce almost half of the world's gold.

Recent discoveries of small amounts of gold in the Amazonian basin in central Brazil have led to a major migration into that country's interior regions. Poverty in the urban areas of São Paulo and Rio de Janeiro has inspired a massive surge of prospectors hoping for wealth.

Iron Ore

Another resource vital to the development of the United States and other developed countries is iron ore. Iron ore is a rock from which iron can be extracted. The most important use of iron ore is in the production of steel. The iron is used in huge blast furnaces that subject it to extreme heat.

The three main rocks that are used for iron production are hematite, magnetite, and taconite. Taconite is a hard ore. The taconite first must be crushed, and then operators must separate the magnetite to produce a pellet with a certain amount of iron in it. If the iron content is too low, it can't be used in the steel production process.

The largest iron ore mines in the United States are in the Upper Great Lakes region. Northern Minnesota, Wisconsin, and Michigan each have large areas devoted to the mining of iron ore. Northern Minnesota and northern Michigan have huge taconite mines. Figure 8.11 shows iron ore production in the United States and the world.

Towns such as Virginia and Hibbing in northern Minnesota saw their heydays in the early 1900s with the rise of the steel industry, which required coal for its furnaces and iron for production. Large ships hauled iron ore from the Great Lakes. Coal was sent by train northward from mines in West Virginia. Pittsburgh was perfectly sited to use iron ore and coal in the production of steel.

Iron ore production in the United States has been slipping in recent decades, as the United States depends less on steel. The United States now depends more on plastics, which are a product of the petroleum industry. As steel production continues to wane in the United States, so will the iron ore industry. As a result, the areas in northern Minnesota and northern Michigan have fallen upon hard economic times.

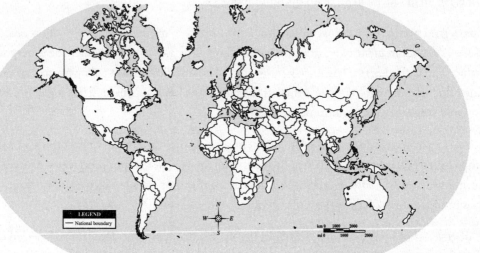

– Iron ore production center

Figure 8.11: World Iron Ore Production Centers.

The future of iron ore mines is in doubt. However, although the demand for steel has decreased in the United States, around the world steel is still a fundamental component in the construction of cities and transportation systems. A Chinese company recently purchased a mine in northern Minnesota. The Chinese dependence on steel is at an all-time high, and continued economic development in China ensures that steel will remain in high demand for a while. Iron ore can now be shipped from the Great Lakes through Canada and hauled by ship to China. Due to China's consumption of steel, there is a worldwide shortage of the metal. In fact, demand is so high that companies are sometimes forced to wait weeks for the steel they need to complete projects.

China's steel industry has grown exponentially during the previous two decades, now accounting for over 400 million metric tons of steel production. In comparison, Japan is second at 112 million metric tons, and the United States is third at 94 million metric tons. This demand for steel increases demand for coal and iron ore. As China's economy continues to grow at double-digit rates, its steel industry will only continue to grow.

China currently leads the world in iron ore production, with 280 million tons produced in 2004. Australia and Brazil were tied for second place with 220 million tons, followed by Brazil, India, Russia, Ukraine, and then the United States. The United States produced 54 million tons of iron ore in 2004. The company Companhia Vale do Rio Doce (CVRD), based in Brazil, is the world's largest producer of iron ore.

FORESTRY AND FISHING

FORESTRY

The forest industry in North America is a unique industry in relation to the land use models. The U.S. Forest Service is under the direction of the U.S. Department of Agriculture, which supports the harvesting of timber in national forests. The National Park Service, which is under the direction of the U.S. Department of the Interior, does not support chopping down trees. Sometimes Forest Service lands and Park Service lands abut each other, leading to a situation where on one side of the road you can harvest timber and on the other side you cannot, despite the fact that both sides of the road are owned by the federal government.

Forestry is a huge industry in North America. Forests are some of the most treasured national resources in the United States. The redwood forests in California are older than the first European settlements in the United States, and some trees have been alive for many centuries. Despite this, society needs the products that can be made from these trees. Products from the timber industry are used in everything from milkshakes to chewing gum to home construction. Furthermore, the efficiency of the timber industry has generated significant profits. According to the U.S. government, the number of forested acres is projected to increase 0.1 to 0.2 percent within the next two decades.

Often, a timber company owns a certain parcel of land, harvests the wood, and then replaces the trees that it cut down. Once the land has been replanted, it is left alone for several decades so that the trees can mature and then be cut down again. Sometimes, the timber companies contract out with local and state governments to harvest timber on government-controlled land. This may be done for profit for the local governments or to provide fire protection for human structures nearby.

North America, with its large areas of virgin forest, is the world leader in the production of timber. Billions of trees have been harvested on the continent since humans have lived there.

In the United States, the three major areas of timber production are the Pacific Northwest, the Great North Woods of the Upper Midwest, and the Southeast. Most of the wood harvested from these regions is used in the construction of homes. This includes anything from the framing of houses to furniture and cabinetry. In the Pacific Northwest, in states such as Oregon and Washington, land use management has become a major point of contention between the forest industry and forest service. Sustainable practices ensure the profitability and productivity of the industry for both the near and distant future.

An area with bright prospects for development is Brazil; but again, the debate over land use has arisen. Many environmentalists and preservationists feel that the virgin timberland of Brazil, much of it located in the interior of the country, should be preserved. However, Brazil needs resources and employment opportunities. A balance must be struck between the need for residential construction and jobs and the need to preserve the environment. The future of the forested areas in Brazil is in doubt, according to many environmentalists.

People who favor sustainability feel that Brazil is an example of effective sustainability programs, pointing out the amount of land that has already been replanted and is being used for tree plantations. This issue goes back to the debate over farming as well. Shifting agriculture means that settlers are cutting down forests or otherwise clearing areas, usually through burning, to plant crops. This bares the thin soil of the tropics, which washes away in the moist climate. Environmentalists fear that replanting trees may not happen quickly enough, if the soil has already eroded into the nearby streams and rivers.

Because of its location and climate, Brazil possesses many different species of trees. Some of the trees that grow in tropical areas are highly prized around the world. Key woods, such as mahogany and rubber, have their sources in Brazil. Other trees, with which Americans might be more familiar, grow in the more temperate southern regions of South America.

Other areas in the world, including many parts of Asia, must import their wood from North American countries like the United States and Canada, or from South America. China's demand for wood, for example, has been outpacing its ability to produce new trees.

Russia has a big forestry industry. Its large expanses of coniferous and deciduous forests allow Russia to produce 20 percent of all the world's forest resources. Upward of 40 percent of the land in the eastern sections of the country is covered with forests.

The future of forestry as a whole remains very strong owing to sustainable practices used to harvest this renewable resource.

THE FISHING INDUSTRY

The good news for the fishing industry is that there continues to be a high demand for fish products, including crustaceans. The opportunity for high profits exists, but only a few brave souls undertake what some consider to be one of the most dangerous jobs in the world.

Fishing, in terms of how it deals with a natural resource, is different from the aquaculture discussed in the chapter on Agriculture, Food Production, and Rural Land Use. Fishing entails the capture of fish from the wild, whereas aquaculture is the breeding and raising of fish and fish products, usually in fish ponds built by the farmer. Fishing is done in either large lakes, such as the Great Lakes, or in the ocean.

In the United States, one of the largest fished areas is off of the coast of New England. Cool waters from Canada and warm waters from the Gulf Stream produce ideal conditions for the capture of fish. However, the overfishing of these areas has contributed to what some now consider a biological crisis. The cod off the coast of New England and the maritime provinces of Canada have been severely depleted.

Fishing is one of the largest industries in Iceland. The icy waters are the perfect habitat for many species of fish, which congregate around the island country. The fish are kept on ice to retain their freshness, then sold in the nearby towns of Keflavik and Reykjavik.

Another area known for its fishing production is the Pacific Northwest region, including the coasts of Oregon and Washington. Unfortunately, the salmon for which the region is famous have been depleted. In addition, Alaska is one of the leading sources in the United States for crab and fish harvests.

Advances in technology have increased the fishing industry's yield, hence the large profits. Much of the industry, however, is at the mercy of the number of fish in the ocean. Fish, like trees, are a renewable resource. However, recent studies of world fish production have shown decreases in fish stocks. Environmentalists feel that the harvest of the fish has outpaced the ability of the fish to reproduce, leading to dramatic decreases in much of the world's fish population. Environmentalists predict that in the next half century, the world's fish production will cease owing to overharvesting. According to environmentalists, much of this overharvesting is being done by the more developed countries of the world. Others feel that such assertions are only scare tactics, pointing out the success of aquaculture in sustainably producing fish and seafood.

Figure 8.12 shows the fishing areas of the world.

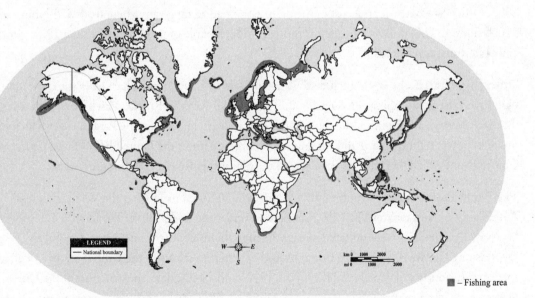

Figure 8.12: Key Fishing Areas of the World.

ALTERNATIVE ENERGY

Alternative energy sources are not as extensive as one would hope at this time. They cannot provide enough power to repay the work and money invested in them on a large scale. However, as technology advances, the industry attracts more investment. And, as the need for alternative energy increases, the reliability and the output of alternative energy sources will improve as well.

Currently, there are six primary forms of alternative energy: hydroelectric, solar, wind, nuclear, biomass, and geothermal energy sources. Each of these holds promise and poses challenges regarding future development.

HYDROELECTRIC POWER

Hydroelectric power is the use of water to create electricity. The power of falling water has been used in industry for thousands of years. People dug holes in the earth and diverted rivers into the holes; the falling water spun water wheels, which then spun turbines or belts in factories. Before electricity was distributed on a mass scale, factories had to rely on water as their primary source of power.

Huge dams have been built around the world to harness the power of moving water. The largest dam in the world is the Three Gorges Dam in China. At more than a mile wide, the Three Gorges Dam is the largest public works project that China, or the world, has ever attempted. It harnesses water from the Yangtze River to provide power for the population centers in the eastern portions of the country. The dam was finished in 2009, but all of the structural work was completed in 2006. Officials debate the true cost of the dam, estimated to range anywhere from $25 billion to $100 billion in U.S. dollars. The dam is thought to be capable of meeting more than 10 percent of China's future power needs.

Other large dams in the world include the Aswan Dam in Egypt, which harnesses the power of the Nile River; the Sayano-Shushenskaya Dam in the Yenisei River in Russia, which provides power for that country's aluminum industry; and the Itaipu Dam, located on the Paraná River which provides power to both Brazil and Paraguay. The largest dam in the United States is the Grand Coulee Dam, which produces its power from the Columbia River in Washington state.

The Works Project Administration (WPA) initially established in 1935 as the Works Progress Administration and renamed in 1939, was created under the leadership of President F. D. Roosevelt. His New Deal policies were initiated to ease the high unemployment rate due to the Great Depression. The WPA built dams throughout the western sections of the United States as well as roads in previously isolated areas. During the 1930s and 1940s, dam construction in the United States was at its apex; thousands of dams were built on little creeks and across great rivers. Most dams were built in the West, because the government owned a lot of land there.

There are some major downsides to hydroelectric power. Dams can create a lot of energy, but they are expensive to build and must be on a waterway that can provide the necessary power to produce large amounts of energy. Major rivers are prime sites for dams, but damming the river affects many people, both upstream and downstream. By blocking the river, a reservoir is created behind the dam, flooding that area. The Three Gorges Dam in China has flooded villages and forced the relocation of upward of 1 million Chinese citizens.

The United States uses many of these reservoirs as recreation areas. The Lake Mead area near Las Vegas was turned into a National Recreational Area when the Hoover Dam was completed. The damming of the Columbia River by the Grand Coulee Dam formed Franklin D. Roosevelt Lake.

Many dams are built on rivers that fish, such as salmon, use to migrate upstream. By blocking the rivers, dams create a barrier for the fish, halting their reproductive cycle. Newer dams are built with diversions that allow the fish to bypass the dam and complete their reproductive cycle.

Dams have also been known to break. The 1889 Johnstown flood, which killed over 2,200 people in Pennsylvania, was caused by the failure of the South Fork Dam. In Idaho, the Teton Dam broke in 1976, killing 14 people and causing over $1 billion in property damage. As recently as 1999 in Seville, Spain, the Los Frailes Tailings Dam flooded a large area with toxic waste, posing numerous environmental problems for fish and other wildlife.

SOLAR ENERGY

Another major source of alternative energy is solar energy. **Solar energy** uses the power of the sun to produce heat that can then be used to create electricity. Solar energy is one of the best renewable energy sources available. The sun will continue to exist for millions of years, and solar power is one of the cleanest sources of energy.

Passive solar energy systems use darker objects to absorb the heat of the sun and store it. Your latitude determines where your windows should be located in your home. In the Northern Hemisphere, the windows should face the south to receive direct sun exposure. In the Southern Hemisphere, the opposite is true. With the windows in your home, you can capture the sun's heat, minimizing the fossil fuels needed to heat your home. You will also need something to absorb the heat and store it. Once stored, the heat can be released to heat water and air.

What are the problems with solar energy? It cannot effectively power massive power plants or entire cities. Most people who have solar power in their homes use it just to heat water for their personal use. Solar or **photovoltaic cells**, panels that are used to convert light into electrical energy, are expensive to install, so not many people use them. Also, many people consider these panels outside their homes to be eyesores. The panels are relatively small, but when enough are placed together to create a significant amount of electricity, they can stand out.

Another potential downside is that in areas without direct sunlight during certain times of the year, solar panels cannot capture enough energy to heat a home. Higher latitudes do not receive as much direct sunlight as tropical areas. For example, in the winter, solar power is more productive in the Desert Southwest than in Alaska, simply because of the position of the sun in the sky.

However, newer technology has enabled solar panels to become smaller and more efficient. No longer do massive storage units need to be located on the outside of houses. New solar technology has enabled solar panels to be put directly on the roof. When people use these panels, they are using an active solar energy system. An active solar energy system soaks up light and converts it through photovoltaic cells to produce electricity. New technology has embedded photovoltaic cells in paint that can be applied to the sides of buildings.

Also, proponents of solar power feel that it will become more cost-effective in the future because of the absence of fossil fuels. Customers will pay more for fossil fuels as they become scarcer. Solar power, however, will not necessarily increase in price because of competition to create more efficient, more productive systems. Conversion costs for existing homes are somewhat prohibitive, but some new homes will have a solar energy system built in. Once the system is installed, the monthly costs of running it are minimal.

Even optimists about solar energy suggest that only 40 to 80 percent of a home's total heat can come from active solar energy. During extended periods of cloudy weather, the system cannot produce enough energy to heat a residence. Local government building codes are requiring that solar-powered buildings include a backup plan.

Wind Energy

One of the cleanest methods of producing energy is the use of wind. Huge wind turbines are located in windmill parks, also called **wind farms**. As air gets warmer, it rises, and as it cools, it falls. This movement turns the blades of large windmills, which then spin turbines that produce electricity. **Wind energy** is the movement of wind to create power.

Different areas heat up and cool down at different rates. Water heats up and cools down more slowly than land. Also, some land changes temperature faster than other land; deserts heat up and cool down faster than areas with darker, richer soil. As air gets warmer, it rises, and as it cools, it falls.

Wind energy is one of the alternative energy sources with the most promising future because it is one of the cleanest sources of energy. Wind energy is related to solar energy in the sense that most wind is a direct result of the sun's heating of the Earth. The Earth spins, and the rotation causes air to move from high-pressure to low-pressure areas.

Along with hydroelectric power, wind is one of the oldest sources of alternative power. Farmers have been using windmills for over a century. Prior to the electricity boom in the 1930s and 1940s, many rural areas in the United States did not have power. In fact, some areas were not connected to the country's power grid until the 1960s and 1970s. Such people had their own power sources, usually from the wind. They also used the wind to pump water for irrigation.

Wind farms are usually located in areas that experience more wind than other areas. All areas of the Earth experience the movement of air upon the surface of the Earth, but some are more windy than others. The Great Plains is a good example of an area that is windy because of a lack of natural windbreaks. Large areas of the Great Plains are being used to produce power from wind. Many farmers are building large windmills on their farms and selling their excess power to utility companies in larger urban areas, like Chicago. In fact, some farmers in the Great Plains have ceased to produce crops because of the low prices of agricultural commodities and instead have found a new source of wealth in producing wind energy.

The worldwide use of wind energy has seen exponential growth during the last decade. This growth is expected to continue, as many countries have mandated that larger percentages of total energy production come from wind energy in the coming decades. Currently, the United States is third in the world in using wind power. Only Germany and Spain produce more power from wind sources than the United States.

Wind power presents some challenges. Wind is not that productive yet. A lot of windmills are required to produce enough power to meet the electricity needs of cities. A nuclear power plant can generate more power while using a fraction of the space of a wind park.

Also, during overly windy conditions, windmills must be shut down. If the windmills are running in high winds, they may tip over. Wind speed needs to be an average of 6 to 20 miles per hour. Anything under that, and there is not enough wind to spin the turbines to create electricity. Anything over 20 miles per hour, and production drops because the windmills need to be turned off.

Critics of wind power also cite as an adverse effect that birds fly into the turbines and are killed. Another concern about wind energy is the blight on the landscape that wind farms create. Dozens of large wind turbines are needed to produce significant energy. Some people find them unattractive, and the noise can be a nuisance for those who live near them.

There are costs associated with wind power as well. A turbine that can generate one megawatt of power can cost upwards of $2 million. This investment may be prohibitive for many small farmers who would otherwise invest in wind power. Once established, though, wind power's costs are minimal and the profits high.

Nuclear Power

Another form of alternative energy comes from nuclear power. **Nuclear power** is one of the most controversial yet productive power sources in the world. Some people suggest that nuclear power shouldn't even be considered as an alternative energy source, because it needs uranium or plutonium (nonrenewable resources) for its production.

The power of nuclear energy cannot be overstated. The amount of energy produced from nuclear energy far outweighs the amount of energy from any other power source, including fossil fuels. Currently, the United States receives about 15 percent of its total power from nuclear energy. Some countries in Europe, such as France, receive over 70 percent of their power from nuclear energy.

There are two types of nuclear power: fission nuclear power and fusion nuclear power. When people are discussing nuclear power, they are describing fission power. **Fission nuclear power** involves the splitting of a uranium atom and harvesting the energy from the splitting process. This reaction is controlled through the use of water and supercontainers of concrete that can be upward of ten feet thick. Splitting a uranium atom produces heat, causing the water to boil. The steam is then used to generate electricity.

Fusion nuclear power is the joining of two hydrogen atoms to create a helium atom. This reaction takes place in the sun, a giant fusion reactor that produces an incredible amount of heat. Fusion occurs at millions of degrees Fahrenheit. Humans have not yet used fusion to generate power. The fusion process produces the power of a hydrogen bomb. It is an enormous source of power but one with serious consequences.

One of the biggest drawbacks to nuclear energy is plant safety and the potential for nuclear meltdowns. The largest accident in the history of nuclear power occurred in the Ukraine with the meltdown of Chernobyl in 1986. It was the result of inadequate safety measures and poor supervision of the nuclear fission process. Another nuclear meltdown occurred north of Tokyo in March of 2011, when the Fukushima Daiichi Nuclear Power Plant suffered a meltdown as a result of a tsunami hitting the power plant. The meltdown sent radiation into the atmosphere, contaminating the ground and water for dozens of kilometers around the nuclear site.

The Chernobyl accident sent clouds of radioactive dust throughout northern Ukraine. Exposure to a radioactive cloud can have severe health impacts. The Chernobyl incident exposed people to radiation at rates far higher than medically recommended. Following the disaster, rates of cancer and birth defects have been high. More than 20 years later, radioactivity is still high in the Chernobyl region.

The closest thing to a disaster in the United States occurred at the Three Mile Island nuclear power plant in Pennsylvania in 1979. A partial meltdown of one of the reactors started to happen. The reaction was brought under control within a few days, but the potential disaster has had a profound impact on the U.S. perception of nuclear power ever since.

The other major drawback to nuclear power is the storage of waste. The spent rods of uranium are radioactive. These radioactive rods must be disposed of somewhere. The question is where? Nobody wants to have radioactive waste near their homes. An acronym, NIMBY, has been coined; it stands for Not In My Back Yard. Currently, the United States sends its radioactive waste to a storage facility in Nevada. However, this is intended to be only a temporary solution.

Countries around the world could use nuclear technology to attack another country with great devastation. The United States used hydrogen bombs on Nagasaki and Hiroshima to end World War II. Those bombs caused incredible damage, yet they were small compared to nuclear bombs today.

By using breeder reactors, scientists can convert a nonrenewable resource (uranium) to a renewable resource (plutonium). The potential for this is both promising and problematic. Uranium is a very scarce resource and will run out within a few decades. Plutonium, while a renewable resource, is much more dangerous to humans than uranium.

BIOMASS

Another form of alternative energy in use today is biomass. The biomass industry is one of the fastest-growing industries in the United States. **Biomass** is the use of agricultural products, natural vegetation, or urban waste to produce a type of fuel that automobiles or other engines can use. The most common crops used to make fuel are sugarcane, as in Brazil, and corn, as in the United States. These agricultural products are used to make biodiesel and ethanol-blended fuels.

Many states provide subsidies for farmers to produce corn, which is then sold to produce ethanol. Ethanol can be added to gasoline to make it burn cleaner. Ethanol plants are dotted throughout the Midwest, corresponding to the Corn Belt. However, ethanol is too unstable to transport well, and it must be transported by train. Trucks cannot haul enough of it to supply refineries, and ethanol deteriorates if pumped through pipelines.

Responding to government mandates, many major automobile manufacturers have developed automobiles that will run on what is called E-85 gasoline, which is composed of 85 percent ethanol and 15 percent gasoline from petroleum. This fuel is much cleaner than pure gasoline. When ethanol is burned in the combustion engine, the by-product is carbon dioxide, which plants can use for photosynthesis. A by-product of the combustion of normal gasoline is carbon monoxide, which is dangerous to plants and humans.

Much of the gas that is currently used in automobiles may be as high as 10 to 15 percent ethanol. The new ethanol-based fuels will flip-flop the ratios, making the burning process cleaner in the cars that can use the new fuel. To use ethanol, a car must be fitted with an engine that can burn it. Putting an ethanol blend into an automobile that is not designed to burn it will cause serious engine problems. Ethanol-based engines can also burn regular gasoline. In addition to E-85, there are other ethanol-based fuels, such as E-70.

As the United States becomes more concerned with its environmental impact on the world, the use of ethanol-based automobiles will only increase. At least, the manufacturers of such cars hope that will be the case.

As with the other alternative energy sources, there are some problems with using biomass. Ethanol is acidic and rapidly corrodes fuel pumps. Also, gas mileage is much less for vehicles that run on ethanol fuels. Even though the cost of ethanol-based fuels is 50 to 70 cents less per gallon, mileage is almost cut in half. The initial cost of the vehicle and the cost of filling it up more often may come to more than purchasing and operating a vehicle that runs on regular gasoline.

In addition, ethanol-based fuels have a tendency to freeze in cold weather, an issue of particular concern in some states, where temperatures can get well below zero in the winter. This can make starting the vehicle nearly impossible. A way to heat the gas tank is required on all such vehicles to start them in subfreezing temperatures.

GEOTHERMAL ENERGY

Geothermal power uses the heat from the interior of the Earth to heat and cool buildings on the surface. There are two basic types of geothermal energy used today. Low temperature geothermal energy uses energy on a smaller scale for buildings by digging several feet below the surface of the earth. Under the surface of the Earth, even just ten feet down, the environment stays at a moderate temperature. This means that the interior of the Earth is warmer during the winter and cooler during the summer. This natural heating and cooling system can be harnessed to control temperatures in office buildings and homes.

High temperature geothermal energy digs deep into the surface of the earth, upwards of three miles, to capture steam from the Earth's magma. The steam is then used to spin a turbine, causing a generator to create electricity for an urban area. Large power plants need to drill deeper than residential heating and cooling systems. These high temperature systems are used to create electricity rather than cool or heat buildings.

Areas with high amounts of volcanic activity are most ripe for geothermal energy production. The Earth's magma is relatively close to the surface of the Earth in these areas. For example, magma is only two miles below the surface in Yellowstone National Park, located primarily in Wyoming. Most of the western United States has relatively large amounts of geothermal activity, allowing more power to be generated from this source. As much as 5 percent of the power in California comes from geothermal sources. Iceland uses geothermal power to heat buildings. There is even an outdoor pool called the Blue Lagoon where one can swim outside in geothermally heated water in the middle of winter. The water is kept at a steamy 100 to 110 degrees Fahrenheit.

Geothermal plants in Iceland use the Earth's internal heat and create electricity from the steam. These plants also use the steam to heat underground pipes in the capital city of Reykjavik to prevent city streets and sidewalks from icing up during the dark, cold winter months. Other countries that use geothermal power are Indonesia, Japan, Italy, and El Salvador. In some of these countries, as much as one-quarter of the total energy production comes from geothermal power.

Not all places can use geothermal energy. To use geothermal energy effectively, a location must have close proximity to the Earth's magma or interior heat. Otherwise, drilling down to capture the heat would be too expensive. However, many buildings are now installing heating and cooling systems that use low temperature geothermal energy. Digging doesn't have to be nearly as deep for low temperature geothermal energy, and the moderation of temperatures is a plus for many businesses. The savings in utility bills can outweigh the installation costs in many cases. In addition, the U.S. government has been giving tax incentives to businesses and residential areas that have converted or are converting to geothermally-based heating and cooling systems.

These alternative energy systems hold promise, but their ability to satisfy the majority of energy needs in the more developed countries still lies many years in the future. The current system is structured to depend on fossil fuels for energy and transportation. A huge investment in infrastructure will be needed to shift society from depending on fossil fuels to using alternative energy sources. Many businesses and governments do not yet feel they can make that commitment.

POLLUTION

Because fossil fuels must be burned to make energy, the result is a relatively large amount of air pollution. **Air pollution** is the occurrence of unnatural products in the atmosphere as a result of human activities. Some fossil fuels produce more air pollution than others when they are mined and/or burned to create energy.

There are different kinds of pollution. Carbon monoxide is one of the more common causes of air pollution. When the furnace in your house burns natural gas incorrectly, the by-product is carbon monoxide. When carbon monoxide levels get too high in your house, the gas reduces the amount of oxygen, causing sleepiness and ultimately death. Carbon monoxide is in the atmosphere as well. When too much carbon monoxide is introduced into the atmosphere, the same result occurs.

Another kind of air pollution is caused by hydrocarbons. In recent decades, hydrocarbons have been implicated in the depletion of the ozone layer over the polar regions. Hydrocarbons also contribute to the urban haze when prevailing winds can't diffuse the pollution in the atmosphere over a city. Hydrocarbons are released from aerosol cans, among other sources.

Mexico City is notorious for its air pollution. The haze surrounding Mexico City has caused numerous health issues for its citizens. The city itself has a poor site. Mountains on all sides do not allow adequate ventilation and diffusion of air pollution. If you drive a car in Mexico City, you have a certain color on your license plate, which indicates on which days you are allowed to drive. This regulation is designed to reduce the pollution from cars as well as to reduce some of the traffic congestion in the world's second-largest city.

Mexico City isn't the only city in the world with air pollution. Cities in China are also known for their air pollution. Shanghai is one of the world's great economic cities; however, if you go to the top of some of its highest buildings, you cannot see the horizon because of the amount of smog. Beijing is no different. In many cities, government standards have either not been enforced consistently or are nonexistent. Urban residents in the United States and Europe live in some of the cleanest cities in the world. The Environmental Protection Agency in the United States and government environmental agencies in European countries have set strict standards on the burning of fossil fuels to ensure clean air in large urban areas.

Coal is one of the biggest air polluters. In recent decades, however, the coal industry has greatly reduced the amount of air pollution caused by burning it. The Environmental Protection Agency has worked alongside the major coal producers to reduce the emissions of coal-burning plants. In the early 1900s, steel-producing cities, such as Pittsburgh, were covered in soot. Streetlights were turned on in the middle of the day to offset the dark conditions caused by air pollution.

Air pollution has also resulted in acid rain. **Acid rain** is the term used for any form of precipitation with an unusually low pH value. It is the result of pollutants, such as sulfur dioxide and nitrogen oxide, that chemically alter water droplets. The burning of fossil fuels into the atmosphere causes acid rain. The Rust Belt in the United States has a lot of heavy industry, with smokestacks billowing pollutants out into the air. Due to the prevailing winds of North America, which blow weather from west to east, the pollution formed acid rain in many sections of New England and southeastern Canada. High quantities of sulfur dioxide and nitrogen oxide have been found in lakes and buildings in these regions. Some of the regions with the highest amounts of acid rain have already been listed; other areas include the Great Plains, Rocky Mountains, and Pacific Northwest.

Acid rain has expedited the process of decay on buildings and other structures exposed to the rain. Forested areas have seen increases in soil acidity levels, creating unhealthy conditions for the native tree species. Acid levels have risen in lakes, destroying native fish species, sometimes to the economic detriment of people who depend on fishing tourism for their survival.

Ozone depletion is another result of pollution. A debate has risen over the emission of the pollutants that are causing the breakdown of the ozone layer. Ozone is a naturally occurring gas that is produced from a chemical reaction when sunlight hits the Earth's surface. Chlorofluorocarbons are released into the environment when an aerosol can is used. The chlorofluorocarbons break up the ozone layer, which is the Earth's main protection against the sun's ultraviolet rays. Ozone depletion has been especially severe over the polar regions. If the ozone layer breaks down further, many more cases of skin cancer will result from unprotected exposure to the sun's rays.

Critics of the theory that manmade pollutants are depleting the ozone layer suggest that the polar regions do not produce ozone because they are dark for several months of the year, resulting in ozone holes over the poles.

Debate continues over the use of chlorofluorocarbons, and the aerosol industry has changed many of their containers to meet environmental guidelines. Environmentalists ask: Is it too late? Has too much of the ozone layer already been depleted?

For consumers, picking a side in the debate often comes down to a choice of products. You may purchase a product that you have trusted and used for years. You know this product works and have depended on it for a long time. But one day, you learn that the product is not friendly to the environment. You now have a choice to make. You compare the benefits of the familiar product with a new, environmentally friendly product, and you may make a switch. This transition to a more environmentally friendly product is known as the **substitution principle**. Many aerosol cans no longer use chlorofluorocarbons in their products, but some still do. Switching from aerosol products that issue pollution to cans without chlorofluorocarbons is an example of the substitution principle.

Another major issue that has gained worldwide attention in recent years is the greenhouse effect. The **greenhouse effect** is the gradual warming of the Earth due to pollutants, which come primarily from more developed countries. Greenhouse gases, in effect, keep warm air closer to the surface of the Earth, causing a warming of the Earth's surface. A warming of the Earth's surface would have profound effects on life everywhere.

Scientists who support the concept of global climate change point out the retreating glaciers in both the Arctic and the Antarctic. Some glaciers that were once huge have been reduced to relatively small chunks of ice. The melting of the polar ice caps would result in massive flooding of coastal regions around the world.

Although many scientists recognize global climate change, some are critics of the global warming theory. Criticism primarily suggests that there is a lack of research supporting the concept that the Earth is heating. Global temperatures have only been recorded for the past 150 years. Doubters suggest that one cannot conclude that the Earth is heating up as a result of manmade pollutants, simply because of the lack of scientific study and data available. Scientists who are skeptical of the claims of global climate change also point out that the oceans have not been warming and, in some cases, have actually been cooling. To make a logical leap and suggest that the entire earth is warming would not be scientifically sound, according to the anti-global-warming scientists.

As stated, the warming and cooling of the oceans would have drastic effects on global weather patterns. Areas that were once prone to flooding may experience drought-like conditions, while arid areas may experience wetter conditions. The warming of the Pacific Ocean is called El Niño, and its cooling is called La Niña. Both of these phenomena can have profound impacts on weather throughout the United States.

Countries from around the world have gotten together and written protocols for the more developed countries to reduce the use of greenhouse gases. The process began in 1985 with the Vienna Convention for the Protection of the Ozone Layer. This conference, held in Austria, tried to establish a time frame to eliminate the use of some of these gases and halt the destruction of the ozone layer.

In 1987, the Montreal Protocol was signed by over 100 countries. Its primary target was to reduce the use of chlorofluorocarbons by one-half by the year 1999. Several other meetings, including conferences in Denmark, Brazil, and Japan in the 21st century, have further tried to curtail the use of fossil fuels, which put more carbon monoxide into the atmosphere.

Critics of these protocols suggest that this is simply a game of politics and political envy. Trying to curtail the use of greenhouse gases in the more developed countries is difficult. Hearing less developed countries tell more developed countries to curtail the use of these gases didn't make sense to countries like the United States. In negotiating many of these protocols, China was allowed not to participate in the decision and was excluded from the requirements. Excluding the country with one of the fastest-growing economies in the world and one of the worst pollution rates from the convention's requirements showed some of the political implications and hidden agendas of the meetings, according to the critics of these conferences.

REVIEW QUESTIONS

MULTIPLE-CHOICE QUESTIONS

1. Which form of transportation would most likely be used to haul fruit from Central America to markets in the United States?

    (A) Truck
    (B) Train
    (C) Plane
    (D) Pipeline
    (E) Ship

2. The most important cost in Weber's least cost theory is

    (A) transportation costs.
    (B) labor costs.
    (C) infrastructure costs.
    (D) energy production costs.
    (E) land plot costs.

3. What concept suggests that less developed countries are still economically dependent upon more developed countries for their economic livelihood?

    (A) Postcolonialism
    (B) Precolonialism
    (C) Neocolonialism
    (D) Natocolonialism
    (E) Market orientation

4. Which of the following factors would most likely increase the cost of transportation the most?

    (A) Refrigeration
    (B) Size
    (C) Weight
    (D) Finished products
    (E) Volume

5. Which of the following is used to determine the Human Development Index for economic development?

    (A) Contagion
    (B) Gender inequities
    (C) Literacy rate
    (D) Resource orientation
    (E) Natural increase rate

6. What region of the world has the lowest Gender Development Index (GDI)?

    (A) Latin America
    (B) Southeast Asia
    (C) South Asia
    (D) Sub-Saharan Africa
    (E) Southwest Asia

7. What major factor has led the Four Asian Tigers to economic success?

    (A) Raw materials
    (B) Trading goods
    (C) Cheap immigrant labor
    (D) Low transportation costs
    (E) Low land costs

8. The transfer of an automobile from a train to a truck at a distribution point is a good example of a(n)

    (A) gross national product.
    (B) growth pole.
    (C) outsourcing.
    (D) break-of-bulk point.
    (E) carrier efficiency.

9. Special economic zones (SEZs) are most common in which country?

   (A) Japan

   (B) China

   (C) Great Britain

   (D) Brazil

   (E) Russia

10. Company A orders 1,000 pounds of sugar at a cost of $1 per pound. Company B purchases 500 pounds of sugar at $2 per pound. This is an example of what concept?

    (A) Variable costs

    (B) Fixed costs

    (C) Carrier efficiency

    (D) Agglomeration

    (E) Substitution principle

11. The following map best shows what concept?

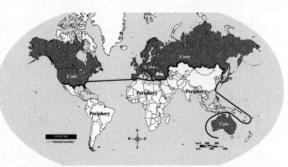

    (A) Technology gap

    (B) Agglomeration economies

    (C) Energy consumption

    (D) World systems theory

    (E) Neocolonialism

12. An industry such as potato chips, which uses potatoes and salt as raw materials, is a good example of what?

    (A) Variable costs

    (B) Fixed costs

    (C) Weight-gaining industry

    (D) Ubiquitous costs

    (E) Weight-reducing industry

13. Canada's northern region would be classified as what according to the core-periphery model?

    (A) Industrial core

    (B) Upward transition

    (C) Downward transition

    (D) Resource frontier

    (E) Semi-periphery

14. The country with the largest oil reserves in the world is

    (A) Saudi Arabia.

    (B) Kuwait.

    (C) Russia.

    (D) United States.

    (E) China.

15. The country with the largest coal reserves in the world is

    (A) China.

    (B) Russia.

    (C) Brazil.

    (D) United States.

    (E) Canada.

16. What is the major drawback to using wind power to supply energy?

    (A) The amount of space needed for each windmill or turbine

    (B) The lack of power produced from each turbine

    (C) The considerable installation costs

    (D) The noise and landscape pollution from the turbines

    (E) The lack of wind in most locations in the world

17. Which country possesses the greatest natural gas reserves?

    (A) United States

    (B) China

    (C) Russia

    (D) India

    (E) Brazil

18. This cartel, established in 1960, is the primary group in the world setting oil prices.

    (A) Oil Producing Exporting Countries

    (B) Organization of Petroleum Exporting Countries

    (C) Oil and Petroleum Exporting Countries

    (D) Organization of Phosphate Enhancing Countries

    (E) Oil and Petroleum Exporting Companies

19. Most of the ethanol (a form of biomass) produced in the United States comes from which biodegradable commodity?

    (A) Sugarcane

    (B) Urban waste

    (C) Wheat

    (D) Soybeans

    (E) Corn

20. What is the major drawback to burning lignite coal?

    (A) It produces a large amount of air pollution.

    (B) It cannot produce enough heat for many blast furnaces.

    (C) It costs too much to transport from its source in the Rocky Mountains to the industrial plants in the eastern United States.

    (D) Mining it is not profitable enough to justify the investment and effort.

    (E) The health of the coal miners is adversely affected by working in shaft mines.

FREE-RESPONSE QUESTION

> **Directions:** While a formal essay is not required, it is not enough to answer the following question by merely listing facts. Your answer should be based upon your critical analysis of the question posed.

1. The Human Development Index (HDI) is a measure of well-being that compares how countries are doing with respect to average years of education, literacy rate, life expectancy, and per capita gross domestic product (GDP).

   (A) Explain the significance for each term from an economic development perspective.

      (i)   average years education

      (ii) literacy rate

      (iii) life expectancy

      (iv) per capita GDP

   (B) Describe one advantage and one disadvantage of using the HDI as a measurement of development.

   (C) Describe the geographic distribution of the HDI from a north/south perspective and using a north polar projection. How does each view change one's perspective on the world's distribution of wealth?

ANSWERS AND EXPLANATIONS

MULTIPLE-CHOICE QUESTIONS

1. C

Because fruit is a perishable product, it needs to be hauled quickly to market. The fastest means of transportation is airplane. Most of the fruit hauled into the United States during the winter months comes from Central and South America by airplane. Other modes of transportation are too slow and could not get the produce to market before it begins to rot.

2. A

Although labor costs, infrastructure costs, energy production costs, and land plot costs are important to industry, the most important controllable cost is transportation. By reducing either the weight of a product or the distance it travels, companies can save money, which they can reinvest to grow the company.

3. C

The concept of neocolonialism says that less developed countries are economically dependent upon more developed countries.

4. C

The two most important factors in determining transportation costs are weight and distance. Although refrigeration can add greatly to the cost of transportation, products that require cool temperatures usually travel only a short distance from production to market. Size and volume are important, but weight is the main factor that adds to shipping costs.

5. C

Literacy rate determines the educational level of a society. The higher the literacy rate, the greater the development potential of a country. Contagion is a factor in Nolan's stages of growth. Gender inequity does determine development to an extent, but countries like Japan and Saudi Arabia would be considered somewhat developed even though gender inequities exist in those societies. Resource orientation is a factor in development but is not used in the Human Development Index. Natural increase rate is a demographic factor of development but is not included in the Human Development Index.

6. D

The GDI measures how women fare compared to men with respect to the same measurements in the Human Development Index (life expectancy, average years of education, literacy rate, and per capita GDP). In places with a high GDI, such as Western Europe and North America, women are more equal to men and have more opportunities for advancement; in places with a low GDI such as sub-Saharan Africa, the gender disparity is greater and women have fewer opportunities.

7. B

The Four Asian Tigers have based their success on the international trade model of development. Most of the areas in the Four Asian Tigers do not have access to raw materials. They do not use cheap immigrant labor, because many of the jobs are highly skilled positions requiring some form of higher education or training. Low transportation costs are a good answer based on the availability of ports in these countries. However, trading goods is a more correct answer than low transportation costs. Land costs are usually extremely high and have skyrocketed in the Four Asian Tiger countries based on their growing need for land.

8. D

A break-of-bulk point is any shift in the mode of transportation. Break-of-bulk points add to the cost of products because workers are required to move the products from one means of transportation to another. Carrier efficiency refers to the positive versus negative aspects of each form of transportation.

9. B

China has set up special economic zones specifically designed so that foreign or transnational companies can locate there as they seek footholds in Asian markets. Areas around Guangzhou and Shanghai have seen enormous growth in their special economic zones, where the factories produce goods using Chinese labor. The Chinese people benefit from these employment opportunities and have access to more material goods. The Chinese middle class is gaining more expendable income. The special economic zones are similar to Southeast Asian cities in terms of their drive for development.

10. A

Variable costs are passed on to the consumer or buyer, usually based on the volume of the order. The greater the volume, the less the cost per item. Fixed costs do not change based upon the volume of product ordered. Many times, you will incur shipping costs on items purchased online, but if you purchase a certain amount of the product, the shipping is free. Even though shipping costs are built into the products' prices, "free shipping" entices some people to purchase more of the product than they normally would.

11. D

World systems theory refers to the idea that there are three tiers of development (core, semi-periphery, and periphery countries). These tiers are based on a level of domination by the core countries and a theory of Marxism that suggests periphery countries are always at the mercy of the core countries.

12. E

The potato chip industry is an example of weight-reducing industry. The potatoes are cut up and sliced and then fried to produce the chips, which may be salted. The end product weighs less than its raw materials.

13. D

The resource frontier of Canada is located in the northern territories of Nunavut, Northwest Territories, and Yukon Territory. Exploiting the abundance of minerals in these areas is somewhat hampered by their inaccessibility. The lack of roads and railroad tracks means that the northern territories are remote from Canada's industrial zone in southeast Canada. The upward transition zone in Canada is the western section of the country. The downward transition zone is the Atlantic Maritime Provinces on the east coast.

14. A

Saudi Arabia contains the greatest oil reserves in the world today. Saudi Arabia possesses over one-quarter of the world's oil reserves. Iraq, Iran, and Kuwait each contain about 10 percent of the world's oil reserves. These four countries alone contain over half of the world's oil. The United States contains only 2 percent whereas Russia has about 5 percent of the total. China, like the United States, has a high petroleum consumption rate but only possesses 2 percent of the world's reserves.

15. D

The United States contains about one-quarter of the world's coal reserves. Reserves are different from production: reserves are what is in the ground ready to be extracted, while production is the amount taken from the earth for energy. The second-largest coal reserve nation in the world is Russia with about 16 percent. China has about 12 percent, while India has about 9 percent. Canada has less than 1 percent of the world's coal reserves.

16 C

Wind power is a very clean and, for the most part, efficient alternative energy source. The space needed for each windmill is not that great, but the total space needed for a wind farm can be considerable, and it can be a blight on the landscape. To some, this causes what is called "landscape pollution." Therefore, answer (D) does describe a drawback to wind energy. However, the number-one reason why more people are not getting involved in wind production on their property is the installation cost of putting up turbines.

17. C

Russia contains over one-third of all of the natural gas reserves in the world. Natural gas is a primary source of heat for homes and businesses in more developed countries. Those countries with the infrastructure to get natural gas from the earth to production facilities to people's homes by means of pipelines can heat homes for relatively little cost. Iran is second with about 15 percent of the world's natural gas reserves. The United States has one-tenth of the world's total.

18. B

OPEC stands for Organization of Petroleum Exporting Countries. This cartel was established in 1960 to bring consistent pricing and more money to oil-producing countries, especially in the Middle East. Later OPEC admitted other countries from around the world, including Nigeria and Venezuela. *Oil* and *petroleum* are synonyms.

19. E

The majority of the ethanol in the United States comes from corn. The majority of the ethanol in Brazil comes from sugarcane. This is more a matter of climate than anything else. The majority of the ethanol plants in the United States are located around the Midwest to reduce the transportation costs of both the corn to the production facilities and the ethanol itself to oil refineries to produce gasoline.

20. B

Lignite coal contains the least carbon of any form of coal. Because it contains the least carbon, blast furnaces need more of it to produce the heat to smelt steel or any other material. Burning lignite coal produces more air pollution than other forms of coal because more of it is needed. Although choice (A) is a reasonable answer, choice (B) is more accurate. Transportation costs the same no matter what type of coal it is. Choice (E) is a concern, but most of the mining for lignite is done in open pit mines, not shaft mines.

FREE-RESPONSE QUESTION

SAMPLE ESSAY

PART A

(i) Average years of education refers to the average number of years a person in a given country goes to school. This statistic is indicative of a country's level of wealth, because education is expensive, and the average years of education declines dramatically when parents have to pay large fees in order for their children to continue in school after the sixth grade.

(ii) The literacy rate is the percentage of the population that can read and write at a basic (grade 5) level. The literacy rate is indicative of the level of wealth in a country because of the expense involved in educating people. If the literacy rate is low that means that many students are unable to attend school after the third or fourth grade.

(iii) Life expectancy measures the average number of years a person can expect to live. This statistic ultimately measures the quality of health care and the access to it in a country, along with other resources such as clean water and food. Generally, the wealthier a country the longer people can expect to live.

(iv) Per capita GDP measures the total worth of goods and services produced in a country divided by the population. This figure reveals the average amount of wealth per person in a country.

PART B

One advantage of the HDI is that the UN can reliably get access to the data, so the index is an accurate measurement of how countries compare to one another in terms of development and standard of living. Since the data are easy to obtain, the HDI is a good starting point for analysis and comparison. One disadvantage of the HDI is that the measurement is simplistic. Four statistics are hardly a snapshot of how a country is doing economically. There are many more economic and cultural factors that should be taken into account to get a full picture of a country's development.

PART C

Analyzing HDI, or any other measurement of wealth, on a world map one notices there is a clear distinction between wealth above 30 degrees north latitude compared to the area south of this line. This observation was first made by Willie Brandt in the early 1960s and was referred to as the Brandt Line. Today most people refer to this division between the rich and poor as the north/south divide or north/south split.

If one looks at Earth using a north polar projection, the distribution of wealth resembles the Core-Periphery Model. Wealth is in the core countries surrounding the Arctic Ocean in the north (Europe, North America, and Japan), and the poor countries of the world are located in the periphery (Africa, southern Asia, and Latin America) or along the outside of the map.

RUBRIC FOR FREE-RESPONSE QUESTION

Total point value of question 1 = 10

Part A—Four points possible:

- One point for explaining the economic development significance for each term.

  — Role and cost of education (role average years and literacy rate play in helping a country economic develop)

  — Life expectancy is a function of a country's health care system, which is determined mainly by level of wealth

  — Per capita GDP is the average wealth per person based on a country's productivity

Part B—Two points possible:

- One point for describing one advantage of the HDI.

  — HDI statistics are relatively easy for the UN to gather and use as a basis for analysis

- One point for describing one disadvantage of the HDI.

  — Simplistic nature of four statistics cannot possibly summarize the economic welfare of a society or the a country's rich cultural heritage

Part C—Four points possible:

- Two points for describing the distribution of wealth in the world from a north/south divide perspective.

  — North/south divide is at 30 degrees north latitude and that there are a few exceptions in the south, such as Australia, New Zealand, Israel, and South Africa

- Two points for describing the distribution from a north polar projection perspective (core-periphery).

  — North polar perspective creates a Core-Periphery geographic distribution with Europe, North America, and Japan in the core

CHAPTER 9: CITIES AND URBAN LAND USE

IF YOU LEARN ONLY SEVEN THINGS IN THIS CHAPTER . . .

1. All cities fit within Christaller's central place theory. Some cities have greater ranges and need bigger thresholds. Range is the maximum distance people are willing to travel to get a product or service. Threshold is the minimum number of people needed for a business to operate.

2. There are three basic models of urban structure in the United States. The concentric zone theory, developed by Burgess, describes expansion in concentric rings around the central business district. The sector model, developed by Hoyt, suggests that growth extends along transportation routes. The multiple nuclei model, developed by Ullman and Harris, suggests that growth is independent of the central business district.

3. Different continents have cities with different characteristics. European cities are older and more historic. Asian cities are usually built on ports for trade. Latin American cities possess a spine of high-quality housing extending from the central business district. African cities have three separate central business districts, including a colonial central business district, contemporary central business district, and a market zone. Islamic cities are focused on the principles of the religion.

4. Cities have problems such as race relations, traffic, water delivery, pollution, and urban sprawl that can negatively affect their inhabitants unless handled appropriately by local government.

5. The three world cities are New York City, London, and Tokyo. Other cities are rated and ranked based on their economic, cultural, and political importance to the areas they serve.

6. The hierarchy of cities from smallest to largest is hamlet, village, town, city, metropolis, and megalopolis. The largest metropolis in the United States is New York City with over 18 million people in its metropolitan area.

7. Primate cities have at least twice the population of the next-largest city in the same country. London, Paris, and Buenos Aires are examples of primate cities.

People travel for different reasons. Many people travel for vacation, in search of rest and relaxation. They might go to a beach to bask in the rays of the sun. Others travel for excitement, to see something new and unexpected. Some go to cities, the epicenter of culture and the arts. Cities like New York, London, and Rio de Janeiro have a distinctive vibrancy. Major urban areas are a magnet for excitement and life itself.

People are moving to urban areas every day. In the United States, almost 98 percent of the population lives in an urban environment. Today, the world's **urbanized population**, the number of people living in cities, is higher than ever in human history. Cities serve and entertain. They harbor culture and keep history. Cities mold people as much as people mold them. Cities define their inhabitants. Urban areas can be as small as two families or huge megalopolises. For example, Tokyo, Japan, has close to 35 million people within its metropolitan area. The larger the city, the more purposes it fulfills and the more needs it serves. Large urban areas provide employment to millions, and their influence extends far beyond their borders.

This chapter discusses the definition of urbanization as well as the reasons for urbanization. Why do some cities grow more than others? What are the characteristics of different world cities, and are these characteristics beneficial or not? How do world cities change over time? What effect do transportation systems have on cities? How do American cities reflect their regions?

DEFINING URBANIZATION

Urbanization is the process by which people live and are employed in a city. People are drawn to urban areas for a variety of reasons. Cities provide products and services for their populations. Also, employment is usually very accessible, with more jobs available in larger cities than in smaller towns or rural areas; this attracts job seekers. The increased labor force then creates a larger consumer base that purchases goods and services. Thus, industries in cities have a ready market for their products and a ready labor force to produce them.

Urban areas have a **nucleated form of settlement**, which means that they have a center area of development, known as a **core area**. This is different from a **dispersed form of settlement**, which is usually found in rural areas where houses are far apart.

Site and situation factors determine where cities locate. Site factors are the physical location of where the city is. Some cities are built on swampland and others are built on highpoints for strategic locational advantage. Situation factors are the external characteristics of a place relating to the connections between cities. New Orleans has a great situation due to the city being located near the delta of the Mississippi River.

Cities offer many amenities, which may include professional sports teams, professional dance companies, and art museums. Large sports franchises, such as the National Football League (NFL),

Major League Baseball (MLB), National Basketball Association (NBA), and National Hockey League (NHL), have teams in major metropolitan areas. These teams have high thresholds. A **threshold** is the minimum number of people needed to meet the needs of the industry. Some cities, such as Chicago and New York City, are large enough for two professional teams playing the same sport.

URBAN ECONOMIES

Cities serve an economic function, which depends on what type of economy the country possesses. The chapter on Industrial and Economic Development discussed the different types of economies, ranging from primary services (agriculture, forestry, etc.) to secondary (manufacturing) to tertiary (selling goods and services). **Commercialization** is the selling of goods and services for profit. Cities begin as bartering or market centers, but they can grow to have global economic impact.

When one large industry moves into a city, it is known as a basic industry. A **basic industry** is a city-forming industry. Basic industries in the United States include steel in Pittsburgh, automobiles in Detroit, and computer chips in San Jose, California. After the establishment of a basic industry, **nonbasic industries** are established. These are the city-serving industries and may include anything from construction to industrial equipment. Together, basic and nonbasic industries form the economic base of cities, generating tax revenue and employment and spurring the development of infrastructure.

Cities move in their **employment structure** from industrial to tertiary to quaternary activities. First, most workers are employed in producing goods, then most become employed in selling and servicing goods manufactured elsewhere. Eventually, a city may become a **post-industrial city**, specializing in information-based work. This shift toward more specialized economic activities is called the **deindustrialization** of a city. When a city goes through deindustrialization, factories are shut down, but new jobs appear in customer service, professional services, and management.

Occasionally, a city will go through an underemployment situation. **Underemployment** occurs when too many employees are hired and there is not enough work for all of them to do. When this occurs, layoffs usually ensue. Cities with good educational systems can assist workers in developing new skills to meet an ever-changing job market.

URBAN HIERARCHIES

HIERARCHY BY SIZE

Urban areas are classified in a hierarchy depending on their population. **Unincorporated areas** were once considered urban areas, even though only two or three families live there today. Unincorporated areas are often found in the western United States. They once might have been a town or hamlet but have lost people over the years. Unincorporated areas also exist on the fringes of suburbs. They are rural areas that may someday incorporate once their population rises.

Hamlets may only include a few dozen people and offer very limited services. The people in the hamlet are clustered around an urban center, which may consist only of a gas station or a general store.

Villages are larger than hamlets and offer more services. Instead of just a general store, there may be stores specializing in the sale of food, clothing, furniture, and so on.

Towns may consist of 50 to a few thousand people. Towns are considered an urban area with a defined boundary but are smaller than a city in terms of population and area. Many towns dot the landscape of the Great Plains. The surrounding farms are the **hinterland** of the towns. The towns may serve area farmers, providing stores such as a supermarket. Towns typically have schools and libraries.

Cities are large, densely populated areas that may include tens of thousands of people.

Metropolises have large populations, incorporate large areas, and are usually focused around one large city. According to the U.S. government, a metropolitan area must have over 50,000 people. Metropolitan areas usually include suburbs from which people commute to their jobs in the urban core or in other suburbs. The central city and its suburbs usually border each other, and the suburbs are usually socially and economically dependent upon the urban core. Many of the larger cities around the world are centers of metropolitan areas.

The biggest urban area is called a **megalopolis** or **conurbation**, where several metropolitan areas are linked together to form one huge urban area. A good example of a megalopolis is the East Coast of the United States. The area that extends from Boston, Massachusetts, to Washington, D.C., along the Interstate 95 corridor is one large urban area. Besides Boston and Washington, it includes Providence, Rhode Island; Hartford, Connecticut; New York City; Newark, New Jersey; Philadelphia, Pennsylvania; Dover, Delaware; and Baltimore, Maryland. This area contains the largest concentration of population within the United States.

Another megalopolis is the southeastern region of Canada. The area extending from Hamilton through Toronto up to Ottawa in Ontario, and east to Montréal and Québec City in Québec is also considered a megalopolis. Even though these cities have far fewer people than the East Coast megalopolis of the United States, together they form the heart of Canada's population as well as its industrial core.

Megacities are cities that have a population over ten million people. Currently, there are 35 cities which could be placed in the megacity category, including New York City and Los Angeles. Tokyo is considered the largest megacity in the world with a population of over 37 million in its metropolitan area.

WORLD CITIES

Saskia Sassen wrote that certain cities possess more authority in terms of cultural outreach and political influence than others. These cities define not only their own countries but other countries in the region as well. Sassen gave New York City, London, and Tokyo each the title of "world city." (See Figure 9.1.) These three cities are the financial capitals of their regions, because they are the location of the major stock markets for their respective continents. Large financial institutions as well as large publishing companies and transnational corporations are located in these cities.

Also, these cities are characterized by their familiarity; they often appear on the news and as settings for films and literature. These cities have world-class international airports. Their infrastructure includes some form of mass transportation in addition to well-maintained freeways. New York and London have vibrant ethnic communities, and all three world cities have large expatriate communities—that is, many people from other countries live there for business or personal reasons. They have hosted global events, such as the Olympics or the World's Fair.

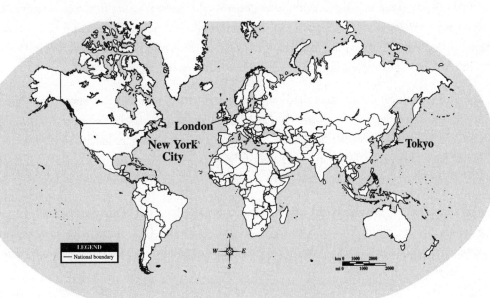

Figure 9.1: Three Key World Cities.

Sometimes, world cities have been called **great cities**, based on their economic importance. Whatever the term used, these world or great cities dominate their counterparts in terms of population and economic influence over an extended area.

HIERARCHY BY INFLUENCE

Cities are given rankings based on their amenities as well as their importance in global commerce. This **urban hierarchy** puts cities in ranks from small first-order cities upward to fourth-order cities, which are large, world-class cities. The higher the order of the city, the greater the sphere of influence that city possesses on a global scale. Fourth-order cities have a larger hinterland than first-order cities. On a regional scale, the terms for urban development are (in ascending order from smallest to largest): hamlet, village, town, city, metropolis, and megalopolis hierarchy.

One can also use the urban hierarchy on a smaller scale, such as at the individual U.S. state level. The state of New York would have New York City as its most important city owing to its financial and cultural importance. Albany would be in the next order along with Buffalo, Rochester, and possibly Syracuse. In 2004, Ithaca, New York, was voted the top emerging city in the United States according to *USA Today*. Smaller urban areas in the state would be ranked as category 1, those being the smallest, least influential urban areas.

Another way that geographers organize cities is by ranking them. Using the Greek alphabet, cities are sorted into alpha, beta, and gamma cities. The most important cities are the three **world cities**, which are New York City, London, and Tokyo. Some geographers also consider Paris part of this order. Other geographers insist that Shanghai should be included in this first tier of alpha cities because of the economic importance of China in the world market. Cities in the second tier of the **alpha world cities** are still impressive in their economic and political clout. These alpha cities include Los Angeles, Chicago, and Washington, D.C., in the United States; Frankfurt in Germany; Milan in Italy; Hong Kong in China; and Singapore (a city-state).

The next order of cities, sometimes called the **beta world cities**, includes San Francisco, United States; Sydney, Australia; Toronto, Canada; Zurich, Switzerland; Brussels, Belgium; Madrid, Spain; Mexico City, Mexico; and São Paulo, Brazil. Some geographers also include Moscow, Russia, and Seoul, South Korea, with this group. Each of the beta cities has a unique feature (e.g., it is a financial, fashion, or governmental center) that makes it important within its region.

The next order, called **gamma world cities**, includes Amsterdam, the Netherlands; Dallas, Houston, and Boston of the United States; Melbourne, Australia; Düsseldorf, Germany; Jakarta, Indonesia; Osaka, Japan; Caracas, Venezuela; Geneva, Switzerland; Johannesburg, South Africa; and Prague, the Czech Republic.

CITY TYPES

Emerging cities are experiencing population growth as well as increasing economic and political clout throughout their region. Shanghai, China, is quickly becoming one of the world's emerging cities. Shanghai is trying to compete for financial dominance in not only Asia but also around the world. Its exports of commodities along with its attraction of foreign investment has led to growth that could not have been imagined 30 years ago.

Other cities are gaining importance in the world economy. Many of these emerging cities are located in Asia. Hanoi in Vietnam, Bangkok in Thailand, and Dubai in the United Arab Emirates are all trying to establish their place as world cities. Dubai is considered the playground for the wealthy in the Middle East. Many flights from the United States and Europe to anywhere in the Middle East stop over in the Dubai airport. Dubai now has the tallest building in the world, the Burj Khalifa. Its influence in the region is growing yearly.

Many emerging cities are in less developed countries. Not only are many of these cities gaining more importance politically and economically, but they are also becoming extremely populated. In 1950 only seven of the world's twenty largest cities were in the developing world compared to sixteen by the year 2000.

Another type of city is a gateway city. **Gateway cities** connect two areas and serve as a gateway between them. Often, gateway cities connect two cultures and serve as a cultural point of entry. For example, Boston and New York City were the two primary entry points for European immigrants to the United States. Ellis Island, in New York Harbor, is a national park today, symbolizing its role as an entry point.

Likewise, San Francisco is considered a gateway city. Millions of Chinese have entered the United States through San Francisco since the mid-19th century. San Francisco's Chinatown is not only a tourist destination but also an important cultural center for thousands of Chinese and Chinese Americans.

Another gateway city in the United States is St. Louis, Missouri. St. Louis is so proud of its gateway heritage that it built a monument known as the Gateway Arch. The Gateway Arch symbolizes migration to the western United States, especially the important psychological step of crossing of the Mississippi River. To many pioneers, this river symbolized entry into the vast expanses of the plains.

Gateway cities are located around the world. In Australia, Sydney is considered a gateway city because it is where immigrants often enter Australia. One of the world's great gateway cities is Istanbul. Istanbul is the only city in the world located on two continents, with Europe on the west side of the Bosporus Strait and Asia on the east side. Istanbul, known formerly as Constantinople, has always been considered the gateway between West and East.

Many cities have what is known as a festival landscape. A **festival landscape** is a space within an urban environment that can accommodate a large number of people. It may be decorated and used for celebrations. One of the most famous festival landscapes is Central Park in New York City. Central Park was built specifically for the citizens of New York City to have a place to play within densely populated Manhattan. Central Park today holds concerts for tens of thousands of people on summer evenings. In Central Park, citizens can enjoy some semblance of nature within one of the most densely populated cities in the world.

Hyde Park in London is similar to Central Park. Hyde Park has a small lake where people can rent boats and ride trails on horseback. Shanghai has the People's Park, which can hold thousands of people. Flying kites is a popular activity in this park.

CHARACTERISTICS OF CITIES

U.S. CITIES

The **central business district** (CBD) is the commercial center of an urban area. It is the downtown region of a city. In the United States, many buildings in the CBDs are skyscrapers, which, because they are tall, maximize the occupancy on very expensive land. The **bid-rent theory** suggests that only commercial landlords can afford the land within the central business district. As a person moves farther from the central business district, the value of the land decreases. Therefore, the suburbs have more land per residence on average, because the land is cheaper than in the inner city. Homes in the inner city usually have smaller lots, because the land is more expensive. Residential properties in the central business district are usually apartment buildings.

U.S. shopping malls exemplify the principle of agglomeration. A **shopping mall** is a group of retail outlets that either share a roof or are connected by a set of walkways. Shopping malls attract more customers than a single store would. People shopping for one item may find themselves purchasing several items from several stores. Agglomeration is advantageous for every store in the mall. Sometimes shopping centers are located along a major transportation route, such as the Magnificent Mile on Michigan Avenue in Chicago. The agglomeration of retail outlets in this highly visible area, where thousands of tourists and customers walk by daily, presents an attractive business opportunity.

The United States is undergoing a revival in urban design and function. Edge cities are popping up around major metropolitan areas. One example is Crystal City in Arlington, Virginia, which is an edge city of Washington, D.C. These areas can see expansive growth and are sometimes called **boomburgs**. Other zones in the city are also seeing a revival. The area to the east of the United States Capital known as Eastern Market is becoming a high profile, chic place to reside. New restaurants, hotels, and shops are filling in areas that were previously abandoned. These areas, with entertainment options including restaurants, theaters, and commercial shopping, are known as **uptowns**. These uptown areas are usually within city limits yet a mile or more away from city centers.

Greenfields are zones where there is little development. Oftentimes the owner will simply donate the land to the city to avoid paying taxes. This land is then developed into some sort of commercial development in the hopes that the area will turn into another uptown region.

EASTERN U.S. CITIES

Eastern cities in the United States were built before the invention of the automobile, so their streets tend to be narrow and parking is usually done in the alleys. The residential areas are tightly packed, making for a dense population. Homes usually face the street with little or no yard in front; yards are in the back of the house.

Many eastern cities have some type of mass transportation, such as trains or subways. The density of the population on Manhattan Island would make travel by car difficult, if not impossible, without some form of train service. Subways run fairly regularly and are relatively easy to use. They provide a good way to get around the city without dealing with traffic-congested streets.

Traffic in eastern cities is heavy at most times of day but especially during **rush hours**. Rush hours are when people travel to work in the morning, usually between 6:00 AM and 9:00 AM and then home again between 3:30 PM and 6:30 PM. Commutes to work can often be measured in hours. Many suburban residents drive as far as the outskirts of the city and then take mass transportation into the core downtown where they work.

Washington, D.C., was built so that invading armies would have difficulty finding and taking over the city. This complex pattern has also made it a nightmare for people trying to drive in the city. Washington's subway system allows people to travel without dealing with its roads and traffic.

WESTERN U.S. CITIES

Cities in the western United States share some characteristics with eastern cities but are also profoundly different. As in East Coast cities, the central business districts contain skyscrapers. However, cities in the western United States are much more spread out, and the homes are often more widely spaced as well. Also, both front yards and backyards are common in western cities. These cities rely on the automobile, rather than mass transit, as the primary means of transportation.

Because these cities were built for the automobile and because many are built on relatively flat land, many use the **grid street system**. Streets run east/west and north/south, creating a grid pattern on the landscape. In many cases, these streets are named first, second, third, and so forth. North/south streets may be called avenues and may be numbered or given names that proceed alphabetically. This logical progression of street names is common in western cities because their grid layout allows it. Such street naming conventions allow for ease of navigation.

Many of these cities depend upon the interstate highway system for transportation, and interstates with eight lanes in each direction are not uncommon in the larger West Coast cities, such as Los Angeles and San Diego. In an effort to curb congestion of the interstates, some highway lanes are reserved for "multiple-occupancy vehicles" (MOVs) to encourage people to carpool. Others are being converted into toll roads, and people must pay to use them. Also, sometimes lanes will be open only one way, into the city, during the morning rush hour and again one way, out of the city, during the afternoon rush hour.

Another characteristic of western cities is the private residential garage. Garages, either attached to the houses or unattached, are common, because space is so plentiful. On the East Coast, cars are generally parked in the alley in back or in multilevel commercial parking garages for a monthly fee.

Suburbs are key to any western city. **Suburbs**, located on the outskirts of a central city, are usually residential but can possess numerous commercial and even industrial enterprises. Hundreds of thousands of people work in the suburbs in the western United States. The suburbs combined often have more people than the central city. The Minneapolis-Saint Paul metropolitan area is a good example of this. Minneapolis and Saint Paul combined have approximately 700,000 people, but the entire metropolitan area has close to 3 million people. Only one out of every four people in the metropolis live within the Minneapolis or Saint Paul city limits. In many eastern cities, the primary city still contains more people than the suburbs.

Seattle, Washington, is one of the few major cities in the northern United States with a high growth rate. Its port plays a vital role in the economy, making it one of the major ports of entry for Asian goods.

Utility infrastructure is becoming more important in city design and development. **Utility infrastructure** is the system set in place by the local government for delivery of electricity, sewer services, and even internet connectivity. Locations outside of the utility infrastructure may have to subcontract these services independent of city planning. Some cities do this intentionally to prevent urban sprawl.

FOUR STAGES OF U.S. CITIES

In 1967, John Borchert suggested that American cities went through four distinct stages.

1. *Stage 1: The sail-wagon period.* This period extended from around 1790 to 1830. The only means of international trade was sailing ships. Once goods were on land, they were hauled by wagon to their final destinations.

2. *Stage 2: The iron-horse period.* The railroad transported goods and people in this period, which lasted from 1830 to 1870.

3. *Stage 3: The steel-rail period.* From 1870 to 1920, steel was the primary building material in the United States. Mining its raw materials and manufacturing and transporting it provided many jobs.

4. *Stage 4: The auto-air-amenity period.* From 1920 through 1960, the engine transformed the American landscape via the automobile. People could commute farther to work and live farther outside the central urban area. The airplane meant that goods could be exported and imported much more quickly.

EUROPEAN CITIES

European cities are much different from American cities. European cities are much older and, therefore, have a different structure. Rome and Athens date as far back as 3,000 years; London and Paris date back 2,000 years; and even the newer cities in Europe had their beginnings before the Americas were settled by Europeans.

Europeans zone their cities differently than Americans. **Zoning laws** determine how land and buildings can be used. There are four different types of zoning: Residential, commercial, industrial, and institutional. **Residential zoning** is for housing, **commercial zoning** is for business or retail types of structures, **industrial zoning** is for manufacturing plants, and **institutional zoning** is for government structures such as schools, courtrooms, and government offices. In Europe, zones are often intermixed, allowing, for example, commercial establishments on the ground floor of a building and apartments on the upper floors. Structures in the United States are often zoned only for commercial use, and the entire building is an office complex.

In the United States, if something is old, it is often torn down and replaced. Europeans have a philosophy that what is old should be preserved. The preservation of historic buildings means that some districts in European cities are hundreds or even thousands of years old.

Many of the streets are in a **dendritic** pattern. This pattern looks like the root system of trees, with streets that curve and meander through the city. Unlike with the grid system, which is relatively easy to navigate, people traversing European cities can easily get lost if they don't know their way.

European cities were built when the automobile was still hundreds of years in the future. Designed primarily for foot traffic, city streets tend to be narrow. Some streets in Copenhagen, Paris, and London are only a few meters wide.

Copenhagen, Denmark, has the largest outdoor shopping mall in Europe. It was not always a mall but rather was used for transportation until recently. Such rezoning for commercial land use has revitalized many urban districts.

Like Copenhagen, Neuss in Germany contains an outdoor shopping mall. However, the narrow city streets show that this part of the urban area was built before the invention of the automobile. Trains move people around the densely populated interior.

The Industrial Revolution spurred major changes in European cities. Agricultural products could be sent farther, and markets grew with the increase in urban populations. Fewer people were needed on farms, and more people migrated to cities searching for employment. Cities began to feel crowded. Subways were built in London in the late 19th century, and these tracks are still in use today by the Tube, London's subway system. Despite the impact of the Industrial Revolution, cities in Europe are usually smaller than cities in the United States. London, Paris, Berlin, and Moscow are obviously very large cities. However, cities such as Copenhagen, which consist of only 1 million people, are considered a moderate size in the United States.

Another difference between the United States and Europe is in the distribution of people by social class. In the United States, the perception is that the lower classes live relatively close to the urban center in apartment complexes, while the upper classes live outside the city and commute to work. The opposite is true of European cities; the wealthy live in the central city and the lower classes live on the outskirts. Lower-income people can't afford to live in the inner neighborhoods of many European cities; housing costs are too prohibitive. Many of the wealthy escape to rural homes on weekends to enjoy fresh air and space not available in the core urban environment. City parks in European cities are very crowded on weekends, especially when the weather is nice.

Because European cities were built before the technology existed for skyscrapers, many of the structures within the central, older part of the city are only five or six stories tall. By the time skyscrapers could be built, many European cities had already established their downtown regions. Therefore, skyscrapers in European cities are built on the outskirts of town.

In London, the tallest buildings are located in the Canary Wharf area. The Docklands development is located just to the east of downtown London. What used to be desolate, low-income, industrial style housing has now become one of the most fashionable residential areas in all of Europe. The high-rises in the Canary Wharf area were built within the past decade. New development and investment in the area has meant more infrastructure and new buildings. In a neighborhood that used to be devoted to industrial activities around a port, expensive lofts and other apartment complexes are sprouting up.

In Europe, when the buildings of the central business districts were built, the wealthy lived in the bottom floors because elevators had not yet been invented. Less affluent people lived on upper floors and walked up and down stairs every time they left their apartments. Once elevators were invented, however, the upper classes wanted the views that the top floors provided, so upper-floor apartments became more valuable.

European cities may feel claustrophobic to people accustomed to the spaciousness of U.S. cities. The buildings in the inner city are all the same height and extend as far as the eye can see. There are no yards; instead, parks provide some open space. The density of these cities pose some problems for the residents, such as pollution. To prevent urban sprawl, urban planners established greenbelts. **Greenbelts** are rural areas that are set aside to prevent development from extending too far outwards. Greenbelts are prevalent in the United Kingdom. The metropolitan area of London has a greenbelt that is over 5,000 square kilometers. Another purpose of greenbelts is to prevent **in-filling**, the process of cities that are close to each other merging together. In-filling has occurred with U.S. cities such as Dallas-Fort Worth and Minneapolis-Saint Paul. The cities are politically separate and have distinctive cultures, but together, they form one giant metropolitan area.

When walking in European cities, one notices buildings that are hundreds of years old next to modern buildings erected within the past couple of decades. In World War II, urban areas in some countries were bombed. Bombs hit some buildings but spared others. The result is 500-year-old stone buildings next to 50-year-old glass-and-concrete buildings.

Eastern European cities are a little different from many of the cities in Western Europe owing to Soviet dominance during the Cold War. Communist planners built apartments of concrete.

For example, in Bucharest, Romania, rows of rectangular concrete apartment buildings were constructed. They were designed to be useful, not interesting or attractive. Eastern European cities have no high-rises in their central business districts. The money simply was not available, and commercial enterprises did not thrive under communism. Also, environmental damage caused by decades of Soviet rule will take decades to clean up.

Since the fall of communism, the urban dwellers of Eastern Europe as well as tourists are beginning to experience a reinvigorated urban lifestyle. Prague, with its historic districts, rivals the beauty of Paris. Berlin is now a shopper's paradise. Cities in the former Baltic republics of Latvia, Lithuania, and Estonia are attracting tourism dollars because of their beauty as well as the distinctive cultural experiences they offer.

LATIN AMERICAN CITIES

Cities in Latin American countries often integrate their native pasts into their design. This area is experiencing one of the world's fastest urban growth rates. **Urban growth rates** are the rates at which individual cities increase their populations. Cities are growing so rapidly owing to the poverty of the countryside. Many farmers are being forced off rented land for not producing enough profit, or they are leaving their own land because they cannot make a good enough living. The result is an influx of migrants looking for employment.

Latin American cities are distinctive in that their urban structure includes a "spine" of high-income residential areas. This spine extends outward from the central business district, while squatter settlements are located on the edges of the city. **Squatter settlements** are areas of squalor and extreme poverty.

The Latin American City Model (see Figure 9.2), developed by the late Dr. Larry Ford, a professor of geography at San Diego State University, shows the characteristics of many cities in Central and South America. Many of the high-income residences that extend out from the central business district are gated communities, designed to protect the residents from the crime bred by widespread urban poverty.

In Brazil, many of the squatter settlements are located in the large cities of Rio de Janeiro as well as São Paulo. Here, the squatter settlements are called *favelas*. In São Paulo, many of the *favelas* are located on the periphery of the city settlements. In Rio de Janeiro, the *favelas* are located throughout the city but are concentrated primarily in the northern sections. In many cases, anarchy rules within the *favelas*. Child gangs dominate the drug trade, and other crimes are rampant in these poverty-stricken areas. Police try to impose order, sometimes brutally, but the sheer number of people living in the *favelas* and their extreme poverty make control difficult.

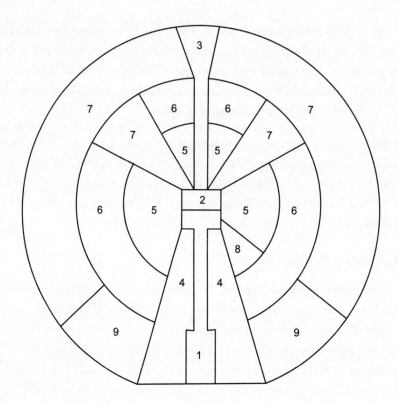

1 – Commercial business district
2 – Market district
3 – Industrial district
4 – Elite residential sector
5 – Zone of maturity
6 – Zone of in situ accession
7 – Zone of peripheral squatter settlements
8 – Gentrification
9 – Middle-class residential

Figure 9.2: Latin American City Model.

Another characteristic of Latin American cities is a focus on the central business district. Cities are laid out like the hub-and-spoke of a bicycle wheel. All roads lead to the center of the city, where commuters must hook up with another road or other transportation system to get to another section of town. Because of this hub-and-spoke pattern of transportation, the central business district is the focus of employment, entertainment, and economic activity. Roads, trains, and buses are fairly reliable in many of these cities.

Mexico City now has a population of over 20 million people. The constant influx of migrants is causing massive urban growth along with a high unemployment rate and an abundance of homeless, abandoned children. Much of the western section of the city is *barriadas*.

Mexico City was built on a former lake bed that has been filled in with dirt. As a result of urban structures resting on unstable soil, the city is sinking a few centimeters per year, posing a predicament that must be dealt with in the upcoming decades. Also, Mexico City is located on a fault line and suffers from many earthquakes. A 1985 earthquake had a magnitude of 7.4 on the Richter scale. Over 9,000 people lost their lives, over 30,000 people were injured, and over 100,000 people were left homeless. Another problem is that Mexico City is built in a mountain valley with mountains in all directions. Therefore, the city's pollution has little outlet. Warnings for air pollution are constantly being issued. To reduce emissions and improve public health, automobile license plates are color-coded so that certain colors may drive only on certain days.

ASIAN CITIES

Many Asian cities are some of the most prosperous cities on Earth. Their economic development of the past four decades has been extraordinary in terms of both infrastructure and economic importance. Asian cities for the most part are located on coasts and have been built for trade, with ports playing an important economic role. Much of their growth is due to trading goods to more developed countries, such as the United States and Japan. Investment of capital from more developed countries has also promoted growth.

Many of these cities have specific zones that have been established for Western companies to locate within their borders. These zones provide tens of thousands of jobs in cities such as Shanghai, China, and Mumbai (Bombay), India. The result is an infrastructure that is ultramodern in its appearance and financial capital measured in billions of U.S. dollars. Automobile companies, such as Volkswagen and Ford, have established production facilities in Shanghai, and Chinese demand for cars is increasing sharply as the middle class expands. Coca-Cola (the most recognized brand name in the world) and Pepsi have also seen opportunities in many Asian markets.

The model of the Southeast Asian city shown in Figure 9.3, developed by Terry McGee, shows the importance of the port zone; growth extends outward from the port. The specific areas designated as Western commercial zones are usually located near the port to easily export their products. Suburbs and squatter developments as well as market-gardening zones still exist.

Seoul, South Korea; Singapore, a city-state; and Hong Kong, China, have seen tremendous growth rates due to their ports. These **entrepots** reexport goods, sending them to all areas of the globe. Singapore and Hong Kong are magnets for foreign investment, which has generated much wealth in these cities. In Singapore, many foreign companies like its strict laws, which ensure low crime rates.

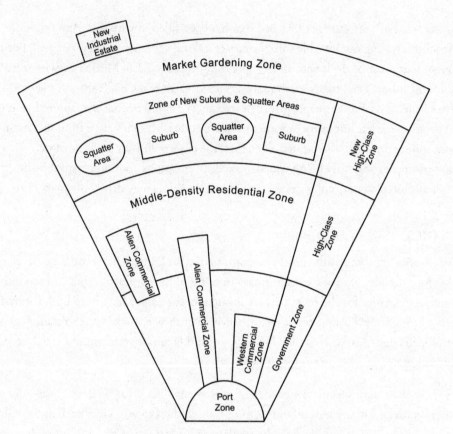

Figure 9.3: Southeast Asian City Model.

Shanghai has seen growth rates near 30 percent each year for the past decade, making it one of the world's largest ports. Huge industrial and office parks measure in the square miles. **Office parks** are agglomerations with shared phone and Internet services and transportation infrastructure. Office parks' **situation** advantages, such as freeway access and port facilities, allow companies to prosper. They also offer **site** advantages, such as low labor and infrastructure costs. One of these large office and industrial parks is located just outside of Shanghai in Suzhou. Suzhou was traditionally known for its imperial gardens and silk production. Today this area is becoming known as the "Silicon Valley" of China.

Asian cities have established many shopping malls of the kind that are familiar to Americans. For example, the Lotus Shopping Mall, located within Shanghai, has characteristics similar to those of the larger malls in the United States; it houses movie theaters, restaurants, and retail outlets. As Chinese consumers earn more expendable income, shopping malls will become more common across China and other Southeast Asian countries.

Because many Asian cities have grown within the past decade, their modernity is evident. Newly designed and architecturally creative skyscrapers grace many Asian cities. In Shanghai alone there are over 6,000 skyscrapers. The second tallest building in the world, the Taipei 101 building, constructed in 2004, reaches a height of nearly 1,700 feet and has 101 floors. The Petronas Towers in Kuala Lumpur, Malaysia, rise nearly 1,500 feet and are 88 stories high. The Jin Mao Tower in Shanghai is just under 1,400 feet and 88 stories. The Grand Hyatt Shanghai, which claims to be the tallest hotel in the world, is located on the upper stories of the tower and provides views of the city's skyline.

Asian cities have no formalized central business districts. Instead, growth occurs throughout the city, in part owing to few zoning laws and almost laissez-faire economics. The result is an incredible number of megacities. **Megacities** are cities with over 10 million people within their metropolitan areas. Tokyo and Osaka in Japan; Beijing and Shanghai in China; Delhi, Mumbai, and Calcutta in India; Karachi in Pakistan; Jakarta in Indonesia; Dhaka in Bangladesh; and Manila in the Philippines are all megacities and exercise a strong sphere of influence over their surrounding areas.

Asian cities usually include a market-gardening zone because of a cultural preference for fresh food. In some Asian cities, farmers grow vegetables next to skyscrapers. Many of the farmers are poor peasants, while the urban dwellers are middle and upper class. This inequity in wealth leads many rural people to migrate to urban areas looking for employment and dreaming of joining the middle and upper classes.

The workforce in many Asian cities is in high demand from transnational corporations, which can make a substantial profit from employing low-cost labor. Some profits are reinvested in the infrastructure of these cities, which will continue to grow and build skyscrapers. This is a prime example of the new international division of labor.

In Asian cities, along with cities around the world, high-tech corridors are also popping up. Like office and industrial parks, **high-tech corridors** use the principle of agglomeration to their benefit. These high-tech corridors are instrumental in providing the world with the computer equipment needed to run its operations on a daily basis. Computer chips are key components of computers, and computers facilitate much of the world's business and personal activity. In high-tech corridors, microchips can be produced cheaply.

ISLAMIC CITIES

Islamic cities are found in the Middle East as well as in parts of Indonesia, the country with the most Muslims in the world. Islamic cities are also located in North Africa. The largest Islamic cities in the world include Cairo, Tehran, Dubai, Istanbul, and Karachi. Islamic cities located in hot, desert regions have twisted streets, because the more twisted the street, the greater the opportunity for shade. Also, personal privacy as well as space for common gatherings are valued in many of these cities. Like many other large cities, large Muslim cities have squatter settlements.

What distinguishes Islamic cities from other cities is the religion itself. Much of the city layout is based on Islamic principles found in the Koran. The most important physical feature of an Islamic city is the mosque. The principle mosque, located in the center of the city, dominates the landscape and is usually the city's focal point. The primary mosque is often called a *jani*. The call to prayer is heard from mosques five times daily. Much of the traditional city is walled, just like many medieval European cities, for defense. The *jani* is often located within the walled portion of the city. The *jani* was to be protected above all else.

Because the purity of women is important in Muslim culture, structures are built to protect them. In residential areas windows are generally small, and doors or windows do not face each other on opposite sides of the street to ensure privacy. Although Islamic cities are densely compacted, they shelter the privacy of their citizens. Buildings are often connected, but homes are built so that it is impossible to view inside a neighbor's house. Cul-de-sacs are treasured in many Islamic cities because of the privacy they offer. While cul-de-sacs impede efficient travel across a city, they protect residents from quickly moving traffic.

Another commonality among many Islamic cities is the bazaar, particularly in North Africa. The **bazaar** is a street market sometimes called a *suq*. These *suqs* can be enormous, taking up several city blocks and selling anything from produce to carpets and clothing. Each alley is organized by what the market stalls are selling.

Modern Islamic cities, such as Dubai in the United Arab Emirates, are some of the most impressive cities on the planet. The tallest building in the world is in Dubai. The Burj Khalifa is over 2,700 feet tall. The building has 160 floors. The building is being promoted as the centerpiece of the Middle East's most prestigious development.

As the number of Muslims continues to grow, the importance of Islamic cities, such as Dubai, will grow as well.

African Cities

African cities are the fastest-growing urban areas in the world today. The economic conditions in most of Africa force people to migrate to urban areas to look for work. Unemployment rates in some countries are as high as 30 percent. Cities in Muslim-dominated northern Africa have high growth rates but not as high as cities south of the Sahara Desert (called the sub-Saharan region). Although urbanization is proceeding rapidly here, the region still has the lowest percentage in the world of urban population. More people are occupied by rural activities in Africa than on any other continent.

Because colonialism ended only as recently as four decades ago, a strong colonial imprint is still visible in the structures and functions of African cities. Many were trade centers for the exportation of resources to colonial powers. Because of colonialism, African cities have three distinct central business districts. The headquarters of the colonial government were found in the **colonial CBD**. The architecture in this area often resembles that of the colonizers' country. In much of West

Africa, the French style of architecture is evident in cities, such as Abidjan in Côte d'Ivoire. In other areas, such as in South Africa, Dutch architecture is prevalent.

The **traditional CBD** holds the distinction of being the current commercial center of these cities. Many of the financial institutions in the country are located in these sections of the city. They align closely in purpose with CBDs in U.S. cities.

The **market** or **bazaar CBD** plays a vital role in many African cities. The bazaar sells anything from rugs to vegetables to animals within a setting that can best be described as a farmers' market in the United States. Taxes are difficult to collect on transactions conducted in the bazaar because they are not easily monitored. Often these bazaars are huge, taking up city blocks, and people have been known to get lost in them. Thousands of people show up for the commerce and excitement that is associated with these CBDs. Cities such as Addis Ababa in Ethiopia and Mogadishu in Somalia possess large market areas.

The model of the African city in Figure 9.4 shows the three CBDs with ethnic neighborhoods extending outwards from them. Beyond the ethnic neighborhoods are the mining and manufacturing zones as well as informal towns (squatter settlements).

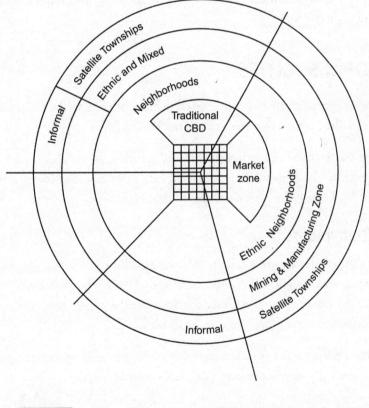

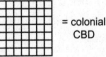 = colonial CBD

Figure 9.4: African City Model.

African cities, for the most part, lack the transportation systems that many cities in other parts of the world enjoy. Either the governments do not have the money to build transportation infrastructure, or the money has been misappropriated. Because of this, transportation is difficult in many sub-Saharan African cities. Many roads are unpaved. In addition, many African cities are afflicted by high rates of HIV infection and have large numbers of orphaned and homeless children.

There are exceptions to the picture of poor African urban areas. Most of the cities in South Africa, for example, are modern in their appearance and demonstrate characteristics common to many European, U.S., and Asian cities. Skyscrapers dominate the landscape, efficient transportation systems are in place, and suburbs are growing.

Cairo, Egypt, is quickly becoming a modern city. However, traffic is often at a standstill, and space is at such a premium that development is currently taking place on cemeteries. Cairo's long history on the banks of the Nile River has been important in determining its place in Egypt. The Nile is the life source of Egypt. The river provides the water for crops as well as for the urban population. The great pyramids were built in nearby Giza by ancient pharaohs. (Along with Kalyobia, the cities of Cairo and Giza compose the urban metropolitan area of Cairo.) The city is rich in history and contains one of the world's great museums, the Egyptian Museum, which has relics dating to the glory days of the Egyptian empire.

MODELS OF U.S. CITIES

Geographers have suggested many different models to describe cities in the United States. No one model accurately predicts or portrays every city in the United States.

All of these models deal with **social structure**, or class structure. Lower class, middle class, and upper class are the three classes most often associated with these models. However, these classes can be broken up further. **Class** is the basic demographic outcome of an economy.

CONCENTRIC ZONE MODEL

The **concentric zone model**, shown in Figure 9.5, was established by urban geographers Robert Park, Ernest Burgess, and Roderick McKenzie in the early 1920s. The model suggests that the lower classes live closest to the central business district while the upper classes live farther out because they can afford the commute into the city to work.

The central business district is the commercial center of the city and contains the **peak land value intersection**, the area with the greatest land value and commercial value.

Outside of the central business district is the **zone in transition**, which usually contains the slums. **Slums** are high-density areas of lower-class citizens who live in substandard housing. Many of the people living in this area are new immigrants to the city. Most residences are apartments; these are intermixed with industrial zones. Because very few people want to live next to industrial zones and their noise and pollution, the value of the housing is usually very low. Many of the apartments in these areas are tenements. **Tenements** are rundown apartment buildings that are minimally kept up by landlords because their value is so low. Landlords either barely comply with housing codes or don't comply at all.

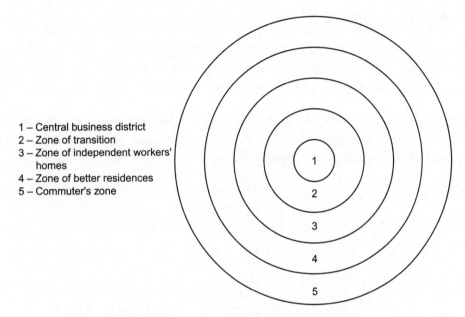

1 – Central business district
2 – Zone of transition
3 – Zone of independent workers' homes
4 – Zone of better residences
5 – Commuter's zone

Figure 9.5: Diagram of Concentric Zone Theory.

Next out from the CBD is lower-class housing. Typically these are older well-established neighborhoods. Working-class families and singles alike tend to purchase homes in this region.

The fourth zone is an area of middle-class housing. Homes get larger as the income of their inhabitants rises. The fifth zone is an upper-class residential area. The houses here are the largest in this area. In some cases, this zone is called a **commuter zone** because of the number of people who commute either into the city or to other suburbs for work.

Burgess elaborated on the concentric zone model to include the ideas of "invasion and succession." **Invasion and succession** refer to the continued expansion of the central business district and the continual push outwards of the zones. This pushing out process causes the zones to rebuild their infrastructures. Areas that were once low-income residences and older working-class neighborhoods are converted into apartment buildings. The upper class continually needs to commute farther and at a greater expense to maintain the lifestyle of the fifth zone. This is just the opposite of the situation in European cities, as mentioned earlier.

The concentric zone model was based on Chicago of the early 1900s. The problem with this model is that it reflects a perception about American cities but not the reality. The concentric zone model really does not exist in the United States today. Many upper- and upper-middle-class residents are moving back into the city, creating wealthy areas relatively close to the urban center. Stretches of upper-class residences usually follow transportation routes outwards from the central business district rather than occupying zones in concentric circles outward from the city center.

SECTOR MODEL

The sector model, shown in Figure 9.6, was established by Homer Hoyt in 1939. It is also based on class but describes social structure based on the transportation systems rather than on distance from the central business district. Zones extend along transportation routes.

The sector model is similar to the concentric zone model in that it uses social structure to determine neighborhoods. It should be noted that many other characteristics could be used to define zones, including ethnicity and physical features.

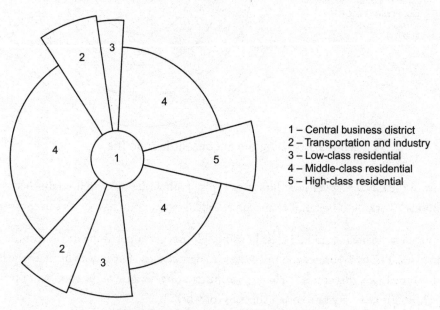

1 – Central business district
2 – Transportation and industry
3 – Low-class residential
4 – Middle-class residential
5 – High-class residential

Figure 9.6: Diagram of Sector Model.

Interestingly enough, Hoyt based his model on Chicago as well. He argued that Chicago showed growth extending outward, especially on the north side of the city where upper-income residences were being built. These residences were closer to the central business district than the concentric zone model would predict. Likewise, Hoyt argued that if the concentric zone model were true, high-income housing would be built on the outskirts of the south side of Chicago, as well as the north side, but it was not. Hoyt also showed that industrial zones in Chicago extended along the major transportation routes. At the time, trains were the primary means of industrial transportation, and industries extended outwards along the railroad tracks.

MULTIPLE NUCLEI MODEL

The multiple nuclei model, shown in Figure 9.7, was established by Chauncey Harris and Edward Ullman in 1945. It differed from the previous two models by suggesting that urban growth is independent of the central business district. Growth may begin in commercial, industrial, and even residential suburbs outside the central business district. Different industries spring up wherever there are opportunities for growth. According to the multiple nuclei model, growth may occur haphazardly and extend more in one direction than another. The different zones are still based on class, but more emphasis is placed on the extent and type of economic development.

One of the best examples of this model involves airports. Airports are usually located on the outskirts of the city for reasons of space and to limit noise and air pollution. However, around the airport is usually substantial development of hotels, restaurants, and entertainment facilities. This development does not arise from the central business district. Rather, an economic opportunity allows certain companies to prosper around the airport. Likewise, in this model, industrial development may occur around a port.

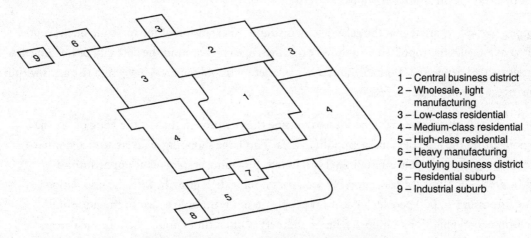

1 – Central business district
2 – Wholesale, light manufacturing
3 – Low-class residential
4 – Medium-class residential
5 – High-class residential
6 – Heavy manufacturing
7 – Outlying business district
8 – Residential suburb
9 – Industrial suburb

Figure 9.7: Diagram of Multiple Nuclei Model.

The multiple nuclei model also takes into account the economic effects of universities. Around college campuses, there are usually more fast-food restaurants, as well as coffee shops and bookstores. Again, development is independent of the central business district.

Although the central business district is still the commercial hub of the city and much development takes place there because of the economic activity, commercial and industrial enterprises may place a higher priority on being close to an airport or seaport. However, in these areas of growth, one would not likely find high-income housing. That tends to be built in its own area, based on the idea that the wealthy like to live next to the extremely wealthy and so on.

Many American cities follow the multiple nuclei model. Growth occurs where it is needed and where developers can maximize profits. Edge cities often result. **Edge cities** are large commercial centers that offer entertainment and shopping in the suburbs. Edge cities may approach 100,000 in population.

The **multiplier effect** is the principle that development spurs more development. When development occurs in a city, more services are needed to meet the needs of the growing population. When more infrastructure is needed, more tradespeople are needed. These people need more grocery stores, gas stations, and so forth, and more services attract more people. The city's tax base increases, supporting even more development through increased amenities such as parks, sports facilities, and better schools.

GALACTIC CITY MODEL

The **galactic city model** is a relatively new urban model developed in the late 20th century as a representation of a post-industrial city in North America. This model represents a city with growth independent of the Central Business District (CBD) that is traditionally connected to the central city by means of an arterial highway or interstate.

Some geographers argue that the galactic city is simply an extension of the multiple nuclei model. The Los Angeles metropolitan area shows extensive edge cities around the core city of Los Angeles. Cities such as Santa Ana, Burbank, and other smaller metropolitan areas have high rise areas within the urban core of the larger system.

Other cities have commercial areas located outside the city proper, such as the King of Prussia region within the Philadelphia metropolitan area. This large shopping area has attracted other amenities to the area such as restaurants and hotels, providing employment opportunities in the area. The King of Prussia area has seen near double digit growth, with the population now surpassing 20,000 people. Since most people do not want to live next to the noise and environmental pollution of industry, heavy industry is often times nonexistent in such areas.

Oftentimes, these larger areas of growth (edge cities) are located along major arteries of transportation routes. Interstates or rail lines will connect these areas to the core city but they are not solely dependent on the core city for their economic success. Many larger metropolitan areas have some type of growth outside of the downtown districts. Atlanta, Baltimore, and Minneapolis/ St. Paul all have large areas of growth in the suburbs.

KENO-CAPITALISM MODEL

Michael Dear and Steven Flusty, geographers from the University of California, Los Angeles (UCLA) and the University of Southern California (USC), created a somewhat controversial model in the 1990s. The Keno-Capitalism Model is based on Los Angeles and suggests that areas are zoned off or even gated off from other zones in the city.

The Keno-Capitalism city suggests that zones in the city are randomly placed in the city but are separated from each other by walls. Using the city of Los Angeles and not Chicago (as was often the case with traditional United States urban models), different areas of the city are described by such diverse features as street warfare and amusement parks. Other areas set aside for shopping malls are called "consumption opportunities." Yet other areas are designated as **ethnoburbs**, or neighborhoods dominated by a specific ethnic group, such as Chinatown or Little Saigon in Los Angeles.

Through a haphazard approach to management, these zones are adjacent yet may have little contact with each other. The city almost resembles a scrambled Rubik's cube.

CENTRAL PLACE THEORY

Walter Christaller established the **central place theory**, shown in Figure 9.8, in 1933 based on his study of Southern Germany. Like von Thunen, Christaller based his central place theory on assumptions of uniform topography, equal transportation systems, and that people will travel the least distance possible to meet their service needs.

The central place theory shows the relationships between urban areas, including their hinterlands, and the range that individual cities need to maintain their size. Larger cities need larger ranges and hinterlands. Urban businesses need a threshold to be profitable.

RANGE

Range is the maximum distance that people are willing to travel to purchase a product or partake in a service; it may vary depending upon the product. Let's say that you are craving a bottle of soda. You own a car and are willing to travel about a mile to a local convenience store to purchase your soda. The range for the soda is limited, because it is a low-cost item and commonly available. People go to the nearest store selling soda rather than travel to a store farther away if the price is about the same.

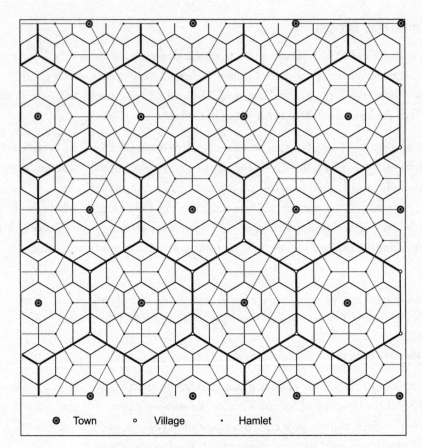

⊙ Town   ○ Village   · Hamlet

Figure 9.8: Map of Central Place Theory.

Now say you want to purchase a Rolls Royce. Rolls Royces are not sold in every metropolitan area. You must travel sometimes hundreds or even thousands of miles to purchase one. The range is greater for a Rolls Royce Phantom than for, say, a Ford Focus. In general, people are willing to travel farther to enjoy goods and services that are more rare.

People are willing to travel extended distances for concerts or sporting events. For example, the map of the Minnesota Twins radio stations, shown in Figure 9.9, extends all the way from Minneapolis-Saint Paul to western North and South Dakota. The market area of the Minnesota Twins even includes eastern Montana. The range does not go far to the east and south because of the Brewers in Milwaukee, Wisconsin, and the fan base of the White Sox and Cubs, both in Chicago, Illinois.

THRESHOLD

The **threshold** of a product is the minimum number of customers needed for it to succeed. The threshold for a bottle of soda is much lower than a threshold for a waterbed. Less range is needed to find customers for the bottle of soda than for a waterbed. However, more soda needs to be sold to make the same amount of profit as one waterbed. Usually, waterbed stores are located in larger urban areas, because they need more range to meet the customer base threshold to survive.

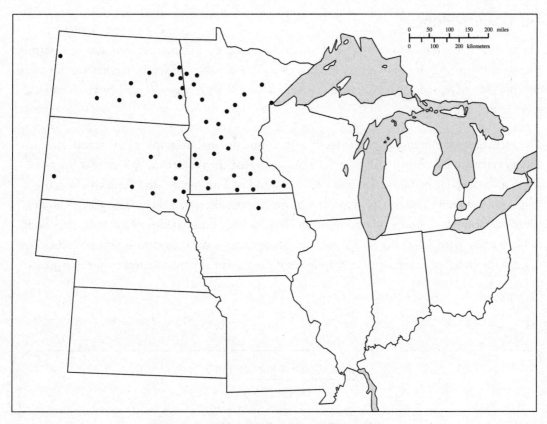

Figure 9.9: Minnesota Twins Radio Stations.

HINTERLAND

The **hinterland** is sometimes called the **market area** of the product. It is the area in which a product, urban area, or commercial outlet has influence. The hinterland is what makes the central place theory hexagonal in shape. It is equidistant along all edges from the product center or urban area. An entity's sphere of influence remains strongest near its source or center, but people in the hinterland may still be willing to travel some distance to purchase or enjoy it.

Smart new business owners find out the threshold for their business before they even open their doors. They must also try to find the range of their customers once the doors have opened. Finding the range can be done simply by asking customers where they are from. This is sometimes accomplished by collecting zip codes at the cash register.

To assist business people, census tracts are used to determine population. **Census tracts** are geographic areas with about 5,000 people on average, though they can vary from 2,500 up to approximately 8,000 inhabitants. From this, businesses can use geographic information system (GIS) technology and figure out the best location for their business.

THE GRAVITY MODEL

The gravity model relates to central place theory, because the mathematical formula can determine where the breaking point (BP) is between two cities. The BP determines the market area for each city. If a person lives somewhere between two cities the gravity model will predict which city has more retail pulling power.

The increasing dominance of cities ties in with a fundamental principle of urbanization. The **gravity model**, shown in Figure 9.10, suggests that the greater the sphere of influence a city has, the greater its impact on other cities around it. This means that there will be more migration between these points, regardless of the distance between them. The gravity model takes into account not only migration between cities but also travel between them, telephone calls between them, trade between them, etc. To determine the degree to which two cities are related, the populations must be multiplied and then divided by the square of the distance between the cities.

$$\frac{\text{Population 1} \times \text{Population 2}}{\text{Distance}^2}$$

Figure 9.10: The Gravity Model.

The Gravity Model is an effective way to determine the relationship between two urban areas. World-class cities such as New York City and Tokyo will have a high relationship even though the distance is far.

Let's assume that a city called Geograville, with a population of 10 million, and another city, Geotown, with a population of 8 million, are being analyzed for their relationship. The distance between Geograville and Geotown is 1,200 miles. Take the population of Geograville and multiply it by the population of Geotown. Ten million people multiplied by 8 million people gives us 80,000,000,000,000. This number must be divided by the distance between the cities squared: 1,200 squared is 1,440,000. By expressing all the numbers in millions, we get $10 \times 8 = 80$. Then $80 \div 1.44 = 55.5$, which means that Geograville and Geotown have a strong relationship with each other.

By looking at another example of smaller towns that are closer together, we can compare the results. Demograville has a population of 1,000, and Migrationton has a population of 500. The distance between these two cities is 500 miles. We calculate as follows: $1,000 \times 500 = 500,000$; $500^2 = 250,000$; and $500,000 \div 250,000 = 2$.

These results mean that the relationship between Geograville and Geotown is stronger than the relationship between Demograville and Migrationton. Thus, there would likely be more trade between Geograville and Geotown, even though they are farther apart. The cities of Migrationton and Demograville do not hold the same amount of sway over each other even though they are closer together. Instead, other trade areas or urban locations closer to them will dominate their migration, trade, and other patterns.

THE RANK-SIZE RULE

The **rank-size rule** states that the size of cities within a country will be in proportion to each other. The second-largest city should have half the population of the largest city, the third-largest city should have one-third the population of the largest city, and so on.

Primate cities have more than twice the population of any other urban area in that country. Primate cities are the most important urban areas economically, politically, and culturally in their countries. London is a good example of a primate city. London's population, depending upon how you measure it, exceeds 7 million. The next largest city in the United Kingdom is Birmingham, with 2.25 million people. Likewise in France, Paris's population approaches 10 million, while the next-largest city, Marseilles, has 1.5 million people. In Argentina, Buenos Aires is the largest city with a population approaching 14 million, while the second-largest city is Córdoba with a little over 3 million people. Thailand's largest city is Bangkok with a population of 7.5 million, while the next-largest city is Nanthaburi with just over 1 million.

Having a primate city does not make a country more developed or less developed. Great Britain and France, with London and Paris, respectively, are more developed countries. Thailand, with Bangkok, is considered less developed.

Many countries do not have a primate city. The United States does not have a primate city. New York City is the U.S.'s largest urban area with over 18 million people, and the next-largest is Los Angeles with about 13 million, more than half the population of New York City. Even though New York is considered the cultural and financial capital, it is not the primate city in the United States. China also does not have a primate city. Shanghai, Beijing, and Hong Kong are all large and function as financial centers for their respective areas, but they are not more than twice the size of the next-largest city. India also does not have a primate city.

Proponents of the rank-size rule suggest that if a country does have a primate city, it lacks an effective distribution of goods and services throughout the country. Therefore, less developed countries would tend to have primate cities, while more developed countries would not. For the most part, this is true, with the notable exceptions of London and Paris.

Opponents of the rank-size rule suggest that the United Kingdom and France and many other countries in Europe contain primate cities, even though they are developed, because most European cities simply do not tend to be very large.

BUILT ENVIRONMENT AND SOCIAL SPACE

All cities revolve around their central business districts. In the United States, CBDs are characterized by the tallest buildings of the urban landscape. In Europe, the CBDs don't contain the tallest buildings, because many of those areas were already fully developed before skyscrapers became technologically feasible. Building skyscrapers in cities such as Paris and parts of Rome is made even more difficult by the expanse of underground **catacombs**. For centuries, the dead were buried beneath the city, creating a labyrinth of pockmarks in the soil and making the ground too unstable to support the weight of skyscrapers. However, the core of European cities frequently contains beautiful old architecture, including churches and other landmarks, that is as distinctive as skyscrapers.

When cities are painted or imagined, usually their central business districts are pictured. Artwork that shows a city is called a **cityscape**. Many cityscapes are recognizable around the world. When people think of Paris, they picture the Eiffel Tower; London, the Parliament building with Big Ben watching over it; New York, the Manhattan skyline. Many cities around the world are trying to create a memorable cityscape. Seattle built the Space Needle, and Beijing has its Forbidden City.

A **symbolic landscape** is an urban landscape that reflects the city's history and that has become synonymous with the city. The symbolic landscape is not the economic foundation of a city but rather the imprint of its historical foundation. In Athens and Rome, for example, the ruins from the great Greek and Roman civilizations are still evident. The Seven Hills of Rome as well as the ancient temples of Athens have drawn millions of tourists to these urban areas. The symbolic landscape has become an icon for another cultural or political phenomenon.

One of the world's best-known symbolic landscapes was the World Trade Center Towers in New York City. They represented a particular aspect of Western culture in their grandiose splendor. This is why they were targeted for the 9/11 terrorist attack that destroyed them. The Pentagon, which symbolizes the U.S. military presence around the world, was also struck. Islamic fundamentalists were not only attacking these physical buildings but also the psyche of the citizens of the United States. A third potential target was the Capitol Building in Washington, D.C., which represents the U.S. government.

SUBURBANIZATION IN THE UNITED STATES

In many cities around the world, **suburbanization** is a source of growth. Suburbs are usually outside of the primary city, yet their economic and cultural focus lies within the city. Suburbs may have residential, commercial, and industrial zones. Often, commuters are not commuting from suburbs to the city but rather from suburbs to different suburbs. Some suburbs possess over 100,000 inhabitants. Outlying suburbs, which are newer, usually have modern buildings and bigger houses. First-ring suburbs usually have smaller, older homes.

Much suburbanization is centered around push and pull factors. American culture favors wanting something that is new. Therefore, many people prefer new houses, which are more abundant in the suburbs. At the same time, people are being pushed away from the core city by their negative perceptions of it. These perceptions may be based on reality, as described in the next section.

Suburbanization is changing the demographics of cities, resulting in a core city that is dominated by the elderly as well as younger couples with either no children or children of young age. As families leave the core city in the hopes of finding homes with more bedrooms and larger yards, better schools, and more amenities, they are often replaced by new immigrants from other countries and double-income no-kids (DINKS) couples, who like living close to the amenities that the core city offers. More nightclubs, theaters, and sports facilities are present in the core city than in the suburbs.

However, when suburban children move away to go to college or develop families of their own, many older couples move back into the city. They no longer want to keep up a large house and yard, and they are at a stage in life where they value the conveniences of the city. This move back can spark a gentrification initiative in many core city neighborhoods.

In many cities, an underclass has formed in these squalid outer areas. The **underclass** is made up of people who are excluded from the creation of wealth. In India, the "untouchables" are excluded. Even though the practice of the Hindu caste system has been outlawed, the cultural tradition persists. In Latin American cities, many of the *favelas* are located on the outskirts of the cities.

CHARACTERISTICS OF U.S. SUBURBS

The suburbs have more children per capita than urban areas. The suburbs also tend to have more parents between the ages of 30 and 50; on the other hand, the inner city has more 20- to 30-year-olds and elderly people. Both areas offer different amenities to different demographic segments.

The first ring of suburbs includes older neighborhoods that abut directly with the primary city. These suburbs saw their primary growth take place decades ago, and the result is a community with all of its available space filled with residential and commercial activities. The neighborhoods at one time may have been considered upper class or middle class but now may be considered lower class.

This is not to suggest that many of these first-ring suburbs are not nice communities. Many of these suburbs possess amenities that make them desirable places to live.

The second-ring suburbs are growing and infringing on the surrounding rural areas. This process of growth is called **urban sprawl**. Urban sprawl puts a strain on the resources of the core city. Sewer lines, utility hookups, water treatment plants, and transportation systems are often designed with a certain reach in mind. When the urban area continues to expand, they suffer strain. Second-ring suburbs may be two or three decades old.

Some communities even have third-ring suburbs. Third-ring suburbs abut and encroach on rural areas. In some states, real estate developers are offering farmers top-dollar for their land. Some farmers resist this easy money because they love the agricultural lifestyle, despite its difficulties, but many take the offer and retire comfortably for the remainder of their lives.

Many third-ring suburbs are adopting the trend of planned communities. A **planned community** is an area where the developer can plot out each house and can build the entire development from scratch. Many newer planned communities have multimillion dollar homes with community pools, golf courses, and parks and playgrounds. In some cases, these communities are gated to ensure that only the residents and their guests are allowed to enter; aptly, such communities are called **gated communities**.

This process of **New Urbanism** is evident in many of the newer suburban developments in the United States. New Urbanism is the movement to plan communities with a diversity of jobs, and that are more walkable rather than automobile dependent. By establishing diversity in economic structure, the community is less susceptible to economic downturns or recessions in the economy. The walkability factor ensures health in the society as well. Sidewalks and bike paths are built into the plans to ensure both recreational opportunities and transportation routes.

Many of the first ring suburbs—those bordering the central core city—are experiencing brownfields. **Brownfields** are former industrial sites that cities are now attempting to redevelop. The success of the development oftentimes is relative to the level of pollution left from the previous tenants. If there is little pollution, brownfields may even be converted to residential housing. If the soil has been contaminated and can be cleaned, large box stores such as a Walmart, Target, or Home Depot may convert the area into a store. These will be tied to railroad zones once used for hauling industrial products and may now even be used as passenger rail lines.

PROBLEMS IN URBAN AREAS

Cities suffer from the problems that arise when large numbers of people are concentrated together. These include crime, pollution, traffic congestion, housing costs, race relations, and many other problems. Some cities handle these issues better than others. When the problems of an urban area become so great that people leave, the process is called **counterurbanization**.

Different management structures can have either negative or positive effects on any urban problem. **Decentralization** is the distribution of authority from a central figure or point to other sectors in the city. **Centralization** is the opposite of decentralization; it is the focusing of power into one authority, usually the command of a mayor or city manager.

In terms of raw numbers, crime is higher in cities than in suburbs; there is more crime in larger urban areas. However, there are also more people in larger cities. On a per capita basis, urban areas may be no different than suburban or even rural areas in the incidence of crime.

Pollution is another difficulty plaguing larger urban areas. With the "greening" of cities, pollution has been curbed in the more developed countries. However, in the less developed countries, many of the larger urban areas are still health hazards for their residents. Rivers are polluted by industry, and local, state, or federal government agencies have few resources and little power to fight the polluting companies. Air pollution in many of these cities makes seeing the horizon a rarity. Waste management is another problem; indoor plumbing is nonexistent for many people in less developed countries.

Urban hydrology is how a city deals with getting clean water to its citizens and then removing dirty water and cleaning it before it is distributed back into the world's rivers and oceans. Many cities in less developed countries do not have the infrastructure or the resources to build water mains and sewage lines into every residence. In some cases, millions of structures need hook-ups. Improper sewage treatment leads to endemic disease and occasional epidemics. Sickness in large urban areas can kill hundreds quickly. Recently, Sudden Acute Respiratory Syndrome (SARS) and "bird flu" have become concerns in Asia. Many doctors fear a pandemic due to a lack of safe drinking water and inaccessible health care. Some argue that the cause of disease is not urban areas per se but rather poverty.

Another effect of pollution and congestion is that cities create their own heat. This process is known as the **urban heat island effect**. Usually cities are warmer by several degrees than their suburban areas. This can affect weather patterns around cities, even moving storms around a city. The urban heat island effect is due to **urban morphology**—that is, all of the street patterns, structures, and the physical form of the city. For example, all the blacktop and concentrated brick, stone, and metal in buildings hold the heat much longer than a natural landscape does.

Another problem often associated with cities is traffic congestion. Traffic can be a nightmare in many larger urban areas. There are simply not enough roads to meet the needs of the population. Cities have tried solving this problem in several ways. Mass transit moves tens of thousands of people around cities on a daily basis. Larger cities usually build trains or subways, which are expensive to construct, while smaller cities usually establish bus systems.

Another way to relieve traffic congestion is simply to build more roads, correct? It depends. Many traffic studies have suggested that the more roads that are built or lanes that are added to a freeway, the more traffic is created. More road space makes traveling by car appear more desirable, thus resulting in the congestion that the construction was intended to reduce. For example, thousands of people in the Dallas-Fort Worth area commute between the cities. Although the cities are connected by Interstate 30, many drivers do not use this road because it gets too crowded during rush hours. If developers added lanes to I-30, some commuters would leave the back roads and attempt to use the freeway. Now, instead of congestion on four lanes, there would be congestion on six lanes.

As cities continue to expand, the issue of how to move people around the city becomes more pressing. The issue of mass transportation versus more roads is constantly fought in the political arena.

Housing costs can be prohibitive in many larger urban areas. Gentrification is both a problem and an advantage in inner-city neighborhoods. **Gentrification** is the process of wealthy people moving into inner-city neighborhoods. These wealthy people make improvements to their homes, creating more demand for housing in the neighborhood. The result is a gradual increase of property value and then taxes. Eventually, the original inhabitants of the neighborhood can no longer afford the high property taxes and are forced to move. Also, landlords see an economic opportunity in converting shabby rented apartments to luxury condominiums, which their current occupants can't possibly afford. Many people who have lived in these neighborhoods for decades are being forced out.

On the positive side, the result of gentrification is a beautiful urban neighborhood with expensive homes. The wealthy urbanites who have moved in have made the neighborhood prosperous, and the city enjoys much higher tax revenue. Often, the city uses the expanded tax revenue to build parks, repair sidewalks, and provide amenities that make the area a very pleasant place to live.

Because gentrification can be a high-risk investment, it is often undertaken by a developer who razes old buildings to build high-end townhomes or condominiums in the hopes of attracting affluent residents. Much gentrification uses the postmodern architecture that is trendy today. **Postmodern architecture** blends historical foundations with modern touches. Postmodernism is a reaction to the modern architecture that prevailed in the 20th century in the United States. **Modern architecture** emphasized boxy structures, usually made from concrete and glass.

To prevent the economic decline of newly gentrified areas, **restrictive covenants** are enforced. For example, it may not be illegal to park your car outside at night, but your development may fine you for doing so. Garbage cans must be kept inside the garage, and in some cases, garage doors must be kept closed at all times.

In Portland, Oregon, the city council has restricted the expansion of the city limits. By restricting outward growth, the city has forced growth inward, creating a high demand for housing within the urban area. Outlined by mountains on many sides, Portland has a site advantage to limit growth. The downside to this urban planning approach is that housing costs have skyrocketed. First-time homebuyers are being forced either to buy outside of the city and face long commutes or make excessive mortgage payments on homes within the city limits. Many urban planners have praised

Portland's attempt at trying to halt urban sprawl. Opponents suggest that this strategy makes it nearly impossible for a lower-class or even middle-class resident to purchase a home within the city boundaries.

Yet another problem that cities around the world face is how to deal with race relations in the urban framework. Race riots have occurred in Los Angeles and other cities around the world. In some cases, illegal activities such as blockbusting have occurred. **Blockbusting** is when real estate agents try to induce people to sell their homes because of a perception that a different race is moving into the neighborhood. Real estate agents may claim that property values are about to fall, playing on the perception that the more minorities who move into a neighborhood, the lower property values will be. In fact, just the opposite may be true.

Racial steering also occurs in some areas today. **Racial steering** occurs when real estate agents show homes only in certain neighborhoods based on the race of the buyers.

Racial steering was often used in the South prior to the Civil Rights movement. Some, not all, Southern whites were afraid of racial integration. **Segregation**—the enforced separation of the races—was practiced in many urban areas in the South as well as in some northern cities. In some cases, the institutions of the city were involved in the segregation process. These institutions not only included the real estate agents but also financial institutions that lent money to homebuyers. **Redlining** is the refusal of lending institutions to give loans to minorities or even whites in high-risk areas. Redlining would be invoked in a neighborhood that had a high default rate on mortgages. It could be in an ethnic community or not.

Cities, like people, are constantly evolving. Sometimes this change is for the better, sometimes for the worse. Development brings in new buildings at the expense of older and sometimes historic buildings. The result is a new landscape that may be visually stimulating or aesthetically ugly. The one constant among cities is that they are vital to understanding human nature. Humans need cities for trade, services, and cultural amenities. As cities around the world have larger populations, their status will change. The city's responsibility to its citizens is to plan for the growth and develop according to need.

Another issue for many areas is the access to grocery or food stores, which poses particular problems for the poor. When there is a lack of fresh food available, less healthy options fill the gap. Though grocery stores have attempted to locate in cities and give people more options to fresher food, when a grocery store is more than a couple of miles away people are less likely to use the service. The **walkable city** has options such as grocery stores, bakeries, butchers, and other services within a walking distance of residences to reduce the need for automobiles.

THE ABANDONMENT OF CITIES

As the United States continues to deindustrialize, the old infrastructure of cities is often times left to rot or rust. Detroit, Michigan—once the bastion of industry and production—is experiencing a problem that other cities will begin to experience if adaption is not made. Detroit is facing **zones of abandonment**, or areas that no longer have police or fire protection because the city has decided the tax revenue cannot sustain public services to those areas. Large areas of Detroit have no buildings on city blocks, to the point where the idea of urban agriculture has even been discussed. As a result of these **disamenities**, people do not want to live in the city and oftentimes move away, exacerbating the problems of the inner city. In many cases these areas have a high rate of house foreclosures, resulting in abandoned neighborhoods that once thrived with children.

CHANGING EMPLOYMENT MIX

Because of the rapid suburbanization of many American metropolitan areas, the employment mix and opportunities have changed according to location. Prior to World War II, there were many industrial and manufacturing jobs located in cities. With the construction of the interstate highway system many industries moved to the suburbs and rural towns to take advantage of inexpensive land and good access to highways. Also, the central business district (CBD) of cities used to have the most retail and office space of anywhere in a metro area. So, prior to the 1950s there were plenty of service and secondary jobs in urban areas. Suburbanization over the last 50 years has been accompanied by the movement of retail business, office parks, and industry to the suburban fringe. As a result, many low paying service jobs in suburbia are difficult to fill. A larger percentage of low-wage workers live in the inner cities, and they often do not own automobiles or have access to mass transit systems that are convenient for places of work. Recent census data have revealed that American suburbs have become increasingly ethnically and economically diverse in the last decade. By analyzing the changing employment mix one could anticipate the demographic changes that have taken place.

REVIEW QUESTIONS

MULTIPLE-CHOICE QUESTIONS

1. Which of the following would be considered a primate city?

   (A) Berlin, Germany

   (B) New York City, United States

   (C) Beijing, China

   (D) Paris, France

   (E) São Paulo, Brazil

2. Which of the following best describes the urban hierarchy of settlements?

   (A) Town, hamlet, village, metropolis, megalopolis

   (B) Village, town, hamlet, metropolis, megalopolis

   (C) Megalopolis, metropolis, village, town, hamlet

   (D) Hamlet, town, city, metropolis, megalopolis

   (E) Hamlet, village, town, city, metropolis

3. The United Kingdom has established greenbelts around certain cities to prevent what?

   (A) Major traffic tie-ups

   (B) Urban sprawl

   (C) The spread of poverty

   (D) Unbearable pollution

   (E) Race relations from erupting into riots

4. According Ullman and Harris's multiple nuclei model, what develops at the outskirts of core cities?

   (A) Airports

   (B) Nucleated cities

   (C) Edge cities

   (D) World cities

   (E) First-ring suburbs

5. What city were the concentric zone model and the sector model based on when they were developed in the early 20th century?

   (A) Chicago

   (B) London

   (C) New York City

   (D) Philadelphia

   (E) Boston

6. What do most cities in the developing world have in common?

   (A) Urban areas are ringed by shantytowns.

   (B) The central business district suffers from a lack of resources.

   (C) The wealthy live in a commuter zone on the edge of the city.

   (D) Industry is located next to the central business district.

   (E) None of the above.

7. The Pentagon in Washington, D.C., is a good example of a(n)

   (A) festival landscape.

   (B) symbolic landscape.

   (C) military landscape.

   (D) urban landscape.

   (E) postmodern landscape.

8. What one characteristic links megacities?

   (A) Each city has an efficient form of mass transportation.

   (B) Each city has a population of more than 10 million people.

   (C) Each city has a world-class airport with connections to each continent.

   (D) Each city possesses financial wealth greater than its gross domestic product.

   (E) Each city follows a model that is focused around the central business district.

9. Medieval cities in Europe usually had what characteristic in common?

    (A) Moats

    (B) Protective walls

    (C) All roads leading to them

    (D) Well-developed urban hydrology plans

    (E) Sections devoted to specific social classes

10. Which statement would be the most accurate regarding the bid-rent theory?

    (A) Land value is the highest in the central business district, and land value decreases with distance from the CBD.

    (B) Land value is the highest in the suburbs, resulting in bigger houses.

    (C) More space is available in the urban core due to the plight of the inner city.

    (D) More space is available in the suburbs due to higher demand for land there.

    (E) Land value is constant throughout the urban area due to the high demand for residential space there.

11. Where is the Canadian megalopolis?

    (A) British Columbia, including Vancouver and Victoria

    (B) Canadian Rockies, including Calgary and Edmonton

    (C) Canadian Plains, including Regina and Winnipeg

    (D) Canadian St. Lawrence Seaway region, including Toronto and Montréal

    (E) Canadian Maritime Provinces, including St. John's and Halifax

12. Latin American cities have what common characteristic in the model developed by Dr. Larry Ford?

    (A) A spine of high-class housing extending from the city center

    (B) Dominance of the suburbs in urban growth

    (C) *Favelas* or squatter settlements in the interior of the central business districts

    (D) Three distinct central business districts: colonial, contemporary/traditional, and market zones

    (E) Transportation systems that ring the city and do not connect to the central business district

13. Range and threshold are important to commercial establishments because

    (A) without a range, there are not enough customers to support the establishment.

    (B) without a threshold, the distance is too far for people to go to partake in the goods or services offered.

    (C) the range determines the maximum distance that people are willing to travel to buy or enjoy something, while the threshold is the minimum number of customers needed for the business to survive.

    (D) the greater the range, the higher the cost of the item.

    (E) the greater the threshold, the less the cost of the item.

| City A—10 million |
| City B—5 million |
| City C—2.5 million |
| City D—1 million |

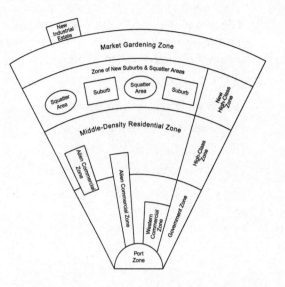

14. The cities in this chart, all located within the same country, represent what geographic factor?

   (A) Urban hierarchy

   (B) Rank-size rule

   (C) Dispersed settlement

   (D) Gentrification

   (E) Centralization

15. A business such as a high-end department store with a high threshold would most likely be located where in the urban framework?

   (A) Central business district

   (B) First-ring suburb

   (C) Third-ring suburb

   (D) Near a major interstate exit

   (E) Close to the airport

16. Homer Hoyt's sector model is based on what fundamental principle?

   (A) Development is based on the location of amenities.

   (B) Development is structured around the central business district.

   (C) Development is based around enterprises such as airports.

   (D) Development is centered around transportation routes.

   (E) Development is independent of the central business district.

17. The model above is best illustrated by which economic principle?

   (A) Core/periphery model

   (B) Trade alternative model

   (C) World systems theory

   (D) International division of labor

   (E) Physical quality of life index

18. What is the most noticeable geographic trend in the last 30 years with respect to the world's twenty most populated cities?

   (A) Most of the 20 most populated cities are now located in more developed countries.

   (B) Compared to 30 years ago, a much larger percentage of the cities are now located in Europe.

   (C) Most of the 20 cities are now located in less developed countries.

   (D) Most of the 20 cities are now located in Africa.

   (E) The specific cities have not changed in 30 years; they have only grown in population.

19. The area in the urban setting with the highest land value, usually located within the central business district, is called what?

    (A) Planned community

    (B) High lateral investment zone

    (C) Peak land value intersection

    (D) Third-ring suburb

    (E) Tertiary land value

20. Which world-class city is the best example of an entrepot?

    (A) Shanghai

    (B) Dubai

    (C) São Paulo

    (D) Madrid

    (E) Singapore

FREE-RESPONSE QUESTION

> **Directions:** While a formal essay is not required, it is not enough to answer the following question by merely listing facts. Your answer should be based upon your critical analysis of the question posed.

1. Sprawl is low-density suburban development that is characteristic of many cities in the United States.

    (A) Discuss in detail how one of the following contributes to sprawl.
       (i) transportation infrastructure
       (ii) edge cities

    (B) Discuss in detail how one of the following discourages sprawl.
       (i) transportation infrastructure
       (ii) New Urbanism developments

    (C) How does sprawl contribute to economic and age segregation in suburbia?

ANSWERS AND EXPLANATIONS

MULTIPLE-CHOICE QUESTIONS

1. D

A primate city is not only the largest city in a country but also has more than twice the population of the next-largest city. Paris, France, has around 10 million people, and the next most populated city in France is Marseilles, with about 1.5 million people. Berlin, Germany, would not count because Munich, Düsseldorf, and Frankfurt all have populations close to that of Berlin. In the United States, New York City is the largest city, but Los Angeles has more than half of New York City's population. Beijing, China, competes with Shanghai to be the most-populated city. São Paulo, Brazil, is closely followed by Rio de Janeiro in terms of population.

2. E

The correct order of urban hierarchy is hamlet, village, town, city, metropolis, and megalopolis. The urban hierarchy is determined by the population of the urban area. Hamlets may only have a dozen or so people, villages may contain up to about a hundred people, towns may consist of upward of several thousand people, cities have tens of thousands of people, metropolises have more than 50,000 people, and a megalopolis is made of several metropolises.

3. B

Greenbelts are areas around cities in the United Kingdom designed to prevent urban sprawl. Greenbelts are used to prevent different towns from blending together with their individual growth. Greenbelts also prevent the urban framework from extending farther beyond the city's borders than it can sustain. In other words, sewer, utility, and transportation systems are structured to extend a certain distance. When urban sprawl moves the city past the borders of these utility systems, the city loses money owing to the expense of providing those same services farther outwards. Greenbelts promote growth within the urban setting. Greenbelts also raise home prices within the urban setting by limiting the space available for building. Greenbelts do not prevent major traffic tie-ups. Lower-class homes are usually in the suburbs of European cities, but public transportation brings people into the city to work. Pollution is not increased by Greenbelts; in fact, pollution may be diminished by Greenbelts.

4. C

Edge cities are suburbs that develop around an amenity, such as an airport. This is the correct answer. First-ring suburbs are usually older suburbs where development occurred early in the city's history. Edge cities may have populations approaching 100,000 in some circumstances. Many edge cities are somewhat independent of the core city's central business district.

5. A

Both the concentric zone model and sector model of urban development were based on Chicago in the early 20th century. According to Burgess, the developer of the concentric zone model, development expands from the central business district in a series of rings in an "invasion and succession" process of development. The lower-class residential areas start relatively close to the industrial centers near the central business district but eventually move outwards. The sector model, according to Homer Hoyt, fit Chicago because upper-class citizens settled on the north side of the city along the major rail routes, which facilitated residents' commute into the central business district.

6. A

Quite often cities in the developing world are ringed by shantytowns, which are areas populated by recent migrants from rural areas. Shantytowns typically have no services, such as water, sewage, electricity, police protection, or schools. People have no title to the land they claim and use whatever materials they can find to build makeshift homes. Shantytowns have different names depending where they are in the world; for example, Brazil's shantytowns are known as *favelas*.

7. B

A symbolic landscape represents something else, usually some sort of political, economic, or cultural value. The Pentagon represents the military of the United States. A festival landscape is usually an open space where many people can congregate. An urban landscape is simply a city. Even though the Pentagon is a military building, a military landscape would most likely be a battlefield or military base.

8. B

Megacities are urban areas with over 10 million people. Megacities are growing as the rate of urbanization continues to climb around the world. Urban growth rates are especially high in less developed countries, where people move to cities looking for employment. India alone has three megacities, including Delhi, Mumbai (Bombay), and Calcutta. Many megacities have some form of mass transportation, but it is not necessarily efficient.

9. B

Many medieval cities built walls around to protect themselves against invading armies. Many of these walls are still evident today around the historic core of European cities, such as Paris and London.

10. A

The bid-rent theory is almost the opposite of the concentric zone theory. Whereas the concentric zone theory suggests that housing values increase as one moves farther from the central business district, the bid-rent theory suggests that land value is highest around the central business district because of competition for limited land. Because land here is so expensive, only commercial establishments can afford it; residential buildings are almost always apartments or condominiums. Therefore, inner city neighborhoods are not necessarily downtrodden. The suburbs have bigger homes and larger yards, because land is more available.

11. D

The Canadian megalopolis extends from Hamilton/ Burlington, Ontario, through Montréal, Québec, along the St. Lawrence Seaway. The majority of Canadians live here. Canada's largest city is Toronto with just over 4 million people. The interior portion of Canada is sparsely populated, much like the Great Plains of the United States. The Rocky Mountain region has beautiful cities, such as Vancouver and Victoria, but the land is rugged and cities are not very large. Calgary and Edmonton each have big cities but are still built on the Great Plains. Edmonton has benefited from the discovery of petroleum. The Atlantic Provinces are the poorest regions of Canada; people are leaving them because of the collapse of the Atlantic fishing industry.

12. A

Latin American cities possess a spine of high-quality housing extending outwards from the city center. Most transportation routes come into the central business district, ensuring its cultural and economic dominance. Many of the favelas or squatter settlements are located on the edges of the cities. Suburbs do not have nearly as much influence as the central business district.

13. C

Range determines the maximum distance that people are willing to travel for a product or service. The threshold is the minimum number of customers needed for an establishment to survive. Likewise, the more ordinary and inexpensive something is, the less the range of the product or service. Commercial establishments need to determine the best location to maximize the range and threshold for their product. Usually, the higher the price of the product, the greater the threshold and the farther the range needs to be. Professional sports are a good indicator of a threshold. Large cities, such as Los Angeles, Chicago, and New York, may be able to support two teams within the same sport because of their high populations. However, in other areas, a larger range is needed from which to draw the fan base (threshold) for their team to survive.

14. B

The rank-size rule states that the second-largest city should have half the population of the country's largest populated city. The third-largest city should contain one-third of the population of the largest city, and the fourth-largest city should have one-fourth of the population of the largest city. In this Country X, the rank-size rule applies. Urban hierarchy means categorizing urban areas based on population size.

15. A

A high-end department store would most likely need to be located near the central business district to enjoy the maximum range and threshold. Being located in a first-ring suburb would mean being surrounded by older residences, which are usually

inhabited by people with lower incomes than the store's target customers. Third-ring suburbs lack the dense population base needed for the threshold of the business. Access to transportation, such as an interstate highway, is important, but that usually is available in the central business district.

16. D

The sector model of urbanization is based on the principle that different zones within the urban area are dictated by transportation routes. Many areas of the same income class extend outward along transportation routes. Therefore, if a high-income zone extends outwards from the central business district in a particular direction, that zone will continue to move farther out in that direction.

17. B

The trade alternative model suggests that goods will be produced in a country for export. In the Southeast Asian City Model shown above, the port zone is used as an export zone to ship products to areas around the world after they have been produced nearby. The alien commercial zones demonstrate this impact on the multinational corporations that are oftentimes located within these large coastal Asian cities.

18. C

Most of the world's largest cities are now located in less developed countries (LDCs). This is a function primarily of the rapid population growth rates after World War II in LDCs. The excess population in rural areas often migrates to the largest city in the country to look for work and opportunities. This trend started in the 1950s and hasn't abated, leading to the massive growth in many LDC cities. Many of these mega-cities have more than 10 million people and some are growing so fast that government

officials are unable to accurately determine the
population.

19. C

The peak land value intersection is the location in an
urban setting with the highest land value, usually in
the central business district. A planned community
usually has a high property value but not the highest
in the city. The priciest land in almost every city is in
the downtown region. A third-ring suburb may have
high property values but not as high as the central
business district, because land is more available.

20. E

An entrepot is a port facility that takes in goods
from other areas and loads them onto other forms of
transportation for reexport. An entrepot is a break-
of-bulk point. Singapore and Hong Kong are the
world's largest entrepots. Shanghai produces many
products for export to Japan, Europe, and the United
States. Dubai is the commercial and economic center
of the Middle East, but it does not reexport goods
made elsewhere. Madrid is not even located on the
ocean, and while São Paulo is a world-class city in
terms of population, it exports goods primarily from
Brazil, not from elsewhere.

FREE-RESPONSE QUESTION

SAMPLE ESSAY

PART A

(i) The building of transportation infrastructure such as interstate highways significantly contributes to low-density development of suburbia. Starting in the 1950s, construction of interstate highways made it easier for people to commute longer distances into work and possibly spend less time in their cars. Before the construction of this infrastructure, it was impractical for people to live very far from work. Most office jobs were located in the central business district (CBD), so people would often live in city neighborhoods that were only a few miles away from their workplaces. Developers then bought up large tracts of land from farmers and ranchers far from the CBD and constructed hundreds or thousands of homes beyond the continuously built up urban area. As a result, the population density of the urban area declined (density gradient) as more prime agricultural land was converted to housing developments on the periphery.

(ii) Edge cities contribute to sprawl because these types of developments are dominated by a concentration of office buildings making it even easier for someone to live farther out from the urban area. Edge cities are usually situated at the intersection of an interstate highway and a beltway that circumnavigates the urban area. The intersection of these two highways is an attractive location at which to build office buildings, shopping malls, and other amenities that suburban residents desire. Now someone living in suburbia might not have to commute to the CBD for work and can move even farther away. Developers recognize this and respond by buying undeveloped land for housing developments contributing even more to the cycle of sprawl.

PART B

(i) Transportation infrastructure such as light rail helps to discourage suburban sprawl by making areas close to light rail stops more desirable and convenient places to live. These types of developments are referred to as Transit Orientated Development (TOD), which allows for mixed-use (commercial, residential, and office) higher density development around and near transit stops. TOD is convenient for commuting, and once home a person can walk to many amenities. In many suburban communities people have long commutes and have to use their automobiles for everything.

(ii) New Urbanism developments allow higher residential densities, and incorporate a variety of land uses in close proximity to each other, so people don't have to use their automobiles as much as in suburbia. The dense residential arrangement helps support retail and offices within walking distance. People like the convenience and community atmosphere that is often lacking in suburban housing developments.

PART C

Sprawl contributes to age and income segregation by separating land uses horizontally. As a result, housing developments are spread across the landscape with only a small range in cost between different models of homes. Therefore, only people with a certain level of income can afford to buy into a particular neighborhood. Since the housing developments are low density, it means that there are vast areas of suburbia that are unaffordable to lower income people. Since sprawl uses a great deal of land, it means that people have to drive long distances to go shopping or use any other service. Because of this, senior citizens are often underrepresented in many suburban areas. Other age cohorts that tend to be underrepresented in sprawling developments are people in their twenties and early thirties. There are few advantages to living in suburbia for this age bracket until they decide to start a family or can afford to purchase a large suburban home.

RUBRIC FOR FREE-RESPONSE QUESTION

Total point value for question 1 = 6

Part A—Two points possible:

- Two points for identifying how transportation infrastructure or edge cities contribute to sprawl.

  — Highways contribute to sprawl

  — Edge cities encourage leapfrog development and sprawl

Part B—Two points possible:

- Two points for discussing how transportation infrastructure (fixed rail) and New Urbanism discourages sprawl.

  — Light rail encourages denser development (Transit Oriented Development)

  — New Urbanism (mixed use, higher densities) reduces sprawl and automobile use

Part C—Two points possible:

- One point for discussing how suburbia contributes to economic segregation.

  — Housing developments usually have a limited range of house prices, which means only people of a certain income range can afford to live in certain suburban areas

- One point for discussing how suburbia contributes to age segregation (unique population pyramids) in suburbia.

  — Suburbia spreads horizontally, not vertically, which is not conducive for the elderly or other populations with limited means of transportation

  — Young single people don't find single-family homes and geographic isolation from services attractive or suitable to their needs

| Part Four |

PRACTICE TESTS

HOW TO TAKE THE PRACTICE TESTS

This section of the book contains two practice tests. Taking a practice test gives you an idea of what it's like to sit through a full AP Human Geography exam. You will find out which areas are your strengths and where additional review may be required. Any mistakes you make now, you will not make on the actual exam, as long as you take the time to learn where you went wrong.

The two tests here are both full length. They include 75 multiple-choice questions and 3 free-response questions. You will have 60 minutes to complete the multiple-choice section of the test and 75 minutes to complete the free-response portion of the exam.

Before taking the test, find a quiet place where you can work uninterrupted for just over two hours. The test will take you 2 hours and 15 minutes. Bring extra blank paper for your essays (you will get 16 pages for all three essays on the real exam). Time yourself according to the time limit at the beginning of each section. During the real AP Human Geography exam, you will have a break of approximately 10 minutes between the multiple-choice section and the free-response section. Feel free to take a short break in between the practice multiple-choice and free-response sections of these exams.

Remember to pace yourself. Train yourself to be aware of how much time you are spending on each problem. Take note of the general types of questions you encounter as well as what strategies work best for them.

When you are done, complete the "Assess Your Strengths" tables. These will assist you in identifying areas that could use additional review. You should also review the detailed answer explanations. Don't only focus on the questions you got wrong. For those you got right, as well as those you got wrong, you can benefit from reading the answer explanation. You might learn something that you didn't already know.

Before writing essays in response to the free-response questions, you may want to review the material on essay writing. Each essay is on a different unit, and each essay asks for a different instructional outline (explanation, analysis, evaluation, synthesis, etc.).

The sample free-response answers that follow in the Answers and Explanations section are intended to assist you in understanding how an informed student might approach the questions.

Good luck!

HOW TO COMPUTE YOUR SCORE

To determine your score on the multiple-choice section of the exam, first determine the total number you got correct out of the 75 total questions. Multiply that number by 0.8108 to determine your weighted score for the section.

Your score on the free-response section of the exam will be determined by the number of points that each free-response question is assigned. For example, for a question that is assigned 9 total points on the free-response section, the score you obtain out of 9 on the rubric is multiplied by 2.2222. When a question is assigned a possible score of 8 on the rubric, your score is multiplied by 2.5. When a question is assigned a possible score of 7, your score is multiplied by 2.7. When a question is assigned a possible score of 6, your score is multiplied by 3.3333.

To determine your composite score on the AP Human Geography exam, simply add your weighted score from the multiple-choice section to the weighted score from the free-response section. Your composite score should be rounded to the nearest whole number.

The following score chart will help you determine your final exam score. However, keep in mind that each year, the ranges differ slightly based on the statistical ranges found in the scores of the students taking the tests.

Composite Score Range	AP Score
74–120	5
59–73	4
45–58	3
35–44	2
0–34	1

Practice Test One Answer Grid

1. Ⓐ Ⓑ Ⓒ Ⓓ Ⓔ	26. Ⓐ Ⓑ Ⓒ Ⓓ Ⓔ	51. Ⓐ Ⓑ Ⓒ Ⓓ Ⓔ
2. Ⓐ Ⓑ Ⓒ Ⓓ Ⓔ	27. Ⓐ Ⓑ Ⓒ Ⓓ Ⓔ	52. Ⓐ Ⓑ Ⓒ Ⓓ Ⓔ
3. Ⓐ Ⓑ Ⓒ Ⓓ Ⓔ	28. Ⓐ Ⓑ Ⓒ Ⓓ Ⓔ	53. Ⓐ Ⓑ Ⓒ Ⓓ Ⓔ
4. Ⓐ Ⓑ Ⓒ Ⓓ Ⓔ	29. Ⓐ Ⓑ Ⓒ Ⓓ Ⓔ	54. Ⓐ Ⓑ Ⓒ Ⓓ Ⓔ
5. Ⓐ Ⓑ Ⓒ Ⓓ Ⓔ	30. Ⓐ Ⓑ Ⓒ Ⓓ Ⓔ	55. Ⓐ Ⓑ Ⓒ Ⓓ Ⓔ
6. Ⓐ Ⓑ Ⓒ Ⓓ Ⓔ	31. Ⓐ Ⓑ Ⓒ Ⓓ Ⓔ	56. Ⓐ Ⓑ Ⓒ Ⓓ Ⓔ
7. Ⓐ Ⓑ Ⓒ Ⓓ Ⓔ	32. Ⓐ Ⓑ Ⓒ Ⓓ Ⓔ	57. Ⓐ Ⓑ Ⓒ Ⓓ Ⓔ
8. Ⓐ Ⓑ Ⓒ Ⓓ Ⓔ	33. Ⓐ Ⓑ Ⓒ Ⓓ Ⓔ	58. Ⓐ Ⓑ Ⓒ Ⓓ Ⓔ
9. Ⓐ Ⓑ Ⓒ Ⓓ Ⓔ	34. Ⓐ Ⓑ Ⓒ Ⓓ Ⓔ	59. Ⓐ Ⓑ Ⓒ Ⓓ Ⓔ
10. Ⓐ Ⓑ Ⓒ Ⓓ Ⓔ	35. Ⓐ Ⓑ Ⓒ Ⓓ Ⓔ	60. Ⓐ Ⓑ Ⓒ Ⓓ Ⓔ
11. Ⓐ Ⓑ Ⓒ Ⓓ Ⓔ	36. Ⓐ Ⓑ Ⓒ Ⓓ Ⓔ	61. Ⓐ Ⓑ Ⓒ Ⓓ Ⓔ
12. Ⓐ Ⓑ Ⓒ Ⓓ Ⓔ	37. Ⓐ Ⓑ Ⓒ Ⓓ Ⓔ	62. Ⓐ Ⓑ Ⓒ Ⓓ Ⓔ
13. Ⓐ Ⓑ Ⓒ Ⓓ Ⓔ	38. Ⓐ Ⓑ Ⓒ Ⓓ Ⓔ	63. Ⓐ Ⓑ Ⓒ Ⓓ Ⓔ
14. Ⓐ Ⓑ Ⓒ Ⓓ Ⓔ	39. Ⓐ Ⓑ Ⓒ Ⓓ Ⓔ	64. Ⓐ Ⓑ Ⓒ Ⓓ Ⓔ
15. Ⓐ Ⓑ Ⓒ Ⓓ Ⓔ	40. Ⓐ Ⓑ Ⓒ Ⓓ Ⓔ	65. Ⓐ Ⓑ Ⓒ Ⓓ Ⓔ
16. Ⓐ Ⓑ Ⓒ Ⓓ Ⓔ	41. Ⓐ Ⓑ Ⓒ Ⓓ Ⓔ	66. Ⓐ Ⓑ Ⓒ Ⓓ Ⓔ
17. Ⓐ Ⓑ Ⓒ Ⓓ Ⓔ	42. Ⓐ Ⓑ Ⓒ Ⓓ Ⓔ	67. Ⓐ Ⓑ Ⓒ Ⓓ Ⓔ
18. Ⓐ Ⓑ Ⓒ Ⓓ Ⓔ	43. Ⓐ Ⓑ Ⓒ Ⓓ Ⓔ	68. Ⓐ Ⓑ Ⓒ Ⓓ Ⓔ
19. Ⓐ Ⓑ Ⓒ Ⓓ Ⓔ	44. Ⓐ Ⓑ Ⓒ Ⓓ Ⓔ	69. Ⓐ Ⓑ Ⓒ Ⓓ Ⓔ
20. Ⓐ Ⓑ Ⓒ Ⓓ Ⓔ	45. Ⓐ Ⓑ Ⓒ Ⓓ Ⓔ	70. Ⓐ Ⓑ Ⓒ Ⓓ Ⓔ
21. Ⓐ Ⓑ Ⓒ Ⓓ Ⓔ	46. Ⓐ Ⓑ Ⓒ Ⓓ Ⓔ	71. Ⓐ Ⓑ Ⓒ Ⓓ Ⓔ
22. Ⓐ Ⓑ Ⓒ Ⓓ Ⓔ	47. Ⓐ Ⓑ Ⓒ Ⓓ Ⓔ	72. Ⓐ Ⓑ Ⓒ Ⓓ Ⓔ
23. Ⓐ Ⓑ Ⓒ Ⓓ Ⓔ	48. Ⓐ Ⓑ Ⓒ Ⓓ Ⓔ	73. Ⓐ Ⓑ Ⓒ Ⓓ Ⓔ
24. Ⓐ Ⓑ Ⓒ Ⓓ Ⓔ	49. Ⓐ Ⓑ Ⓒ Ⓓ Ⓔ	74. Ⓐ Ⓑ Ⓒ Ⓓ Ⓔ
25. Ⓐ Ⓑ Ⓒ Ⓓ Ⓔ	50. Ⓐ Ⓑ Ⓒ Ⓓ Ⓔ	75. Ⓐ Ⓑ Ⓒ Ⓓ Ⓔ

PRACTICE TEST 1

SECTION I: MULTIPLE-CHOICE QUESTIONS
Time—60 minutes
75 Questions

> **Directions:** Each of the questions or incomplete statements below is followed by five suggested answers. Select the best answer to the question and then fill in the corresponding oval on the answer sheet.

1. The relationship between an object on the surface of the Earth and the same object on a map projection is known as what?

    (A) Map class
    (B) Map projection
    (C) Map scale
    (D) Map distortion
    (E) Map direction

2. Thomas Malthus predicted in the early 1800's that population was soon to be in what stage of growth?

    (A) Exponential
    (B) Negative
    (C) Static
    (D) Proportional
    (E) Linear

3. The hearth of contemporary country music is located around what city?

    (A) Houston, Texas
    (B) Dallas, Texas
    (C) Memphis, Tennessee
    (D) Nashville, Tennessee
    (E) Atlanta, Georgia

4. Which of the following countries is not one of the Four Asian Tigers?

    (A) Singapore
    (B) Taiwan
    (C) South Korea
    (D) Hong Kong
    (E) Vietnam

5. Johann Heinrich von Thunen's model of agricultural land use is centered on what basic concept?

    (A) The farmers sell all of their farm production to a market.
    (B) The higher-end commodities are located farther from the market.
    (C) The lighter commodities are closer to the market to ensure profitability.
    (D) The heavier commodities are around the market because they need irrigation.
    (E) The market is based on subsistence farming practices in less developed countries.

6. Weber's least cost theory is based on what primary cost?

    (A) Labor
    (B) Infrastructure
    (C) Transportation
    (D) Government taxes
    (E) Land costs

GO ON TO THE NEXT PAGE
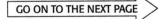

7. What model suggests that in an urban setting, the farther a neighborhood is from the central business district, the greater its wealth is?

(A) Sector model

(B) Keno capitalism model

(C) Multiple nuclei model

(D) Concentric zone model

(E) Urban periphery model

8. Which country has created special economic zones (SEZs) to attract investment?

(A) Japan

(B) Vietnam

(C) South Korea

(D) China

(E) Thailand

9. What stage in the demographic transition model has the highest growth rates?

(A) Stage 1

(B) Stage 2

(C) Stage 3

(D) Stage 4

(E) Stage 5

10. What type of survey pattern was initiated by the French in the United States and is still evident in the Louisiana region of the United States today?

(A) Long lots system

(B) Township and range system

(C) Metes and bounds system

(D) Nucleated town system

(E) Concentric urban framework

Algeria	Libya
Angola	Nigeria
Ecuador	Qatar
Iran	Saudi Arabia
Iraq	United Arab Emirates
Kuwait	Venezuela

11. Which organization, established in 1960, contains the members listed in the chart above?

(A) NAFTA (North American Free Trade Agreement)

(B) OPEC (Organization of Petroleum Exporting Countries)

(C) EU (European Union)

(D) PRA (Pacific Rim Alliances)

(E) CENTO (Central Treaty Organization)

12. Because of the signing of NAFTA (North American Free Trade Agreement), there has been an increase in

(A) transnational corporations.

(B) footloose industries.

(C) maquiladoras.

(D) sweatshop industries.

(E) international migration in North America.

13. Which religion is the largest universalizing religion in the world today?

(A) Christianity

(B) Islam

(C) Buddhism

(D) Judaism

(E) Hinduism

 GO ON TO THE NEXT PAGE

14. Which of the following is the best example of a nation-state?

    (A) Romania
    (B) Vietnam
    (C) Argentina
    (D) Zimbabwe
    (E) Denmark

15. Which of the following is the name for refusing to give loans to people living in specific areas of the city?

    (A) Blockbusting
    (B) White flight
    (C) Segregation
    (D) Ghettoization
    (E) Redlining

16. Edge cities would most likely be associated with which urban model?

    (A) Concentric zone model
    (B) Sector model
    (C) Peripheral model
    (D) Multiple nuclei model
    (E) Central business district model

17. What country has the largest coal reserves in the world?

    (A) China
    (B) United States
    (C) Russia
    (D) Canada
    (E) Mexico

18. Farming today in more developed countries is in a transition period. What transition is occurring?

    (A) The movement toward mechanization in the farming process
    (B) The movement toward industrial farming
    (C) The movement from hunting and gathering to planting and sustaining
    (D) The movement of population to rural areas
    (E) The use of less genetic engineering to modify plants and animals

19. A retired couple moves from Chicago to Arizona. This is most likely an example of what geographic factor?

    (A) Economic pull factor
    (B) Economic push factor
    (C) Environmental pull factor
    (D) Political pull factor
    (E) Political push factor

20. Which religion is the fastest growing of the world's five primary religions?

    (A) Christianity
    (B) Islam
    (C) Judaism
    (D) Hinduism
    (E) Buddhism

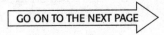
GO ON TO THE NEXT PAGE

21. What is the name of the theory that suggests that whoever owns the Eastern European region will or could control the world, based on the agricultural and industrial production of the region?

    (A) Rimland theory
    (B) Heartland theory
    (C) Domino theory
    (D) Transnational theory
    (E) Geopolitical theory

22. A family is moving from Los Angeles, California, to New Orleans, Louisiana, but stays in Albuquerque, New Mexico, because of the positive amenities. This is an example of what?

    (A) Distance decay
    (B) Environmental pull factor
    (C) Environmental push factor
    (D) Intervening opportunity
    (E) Intervening obstacle

23. According to acculturation, how many generations on average does it take for an immigrant family to lose its primary language?

    (A) One generation
    (B) Two generations
    (C) Three generations
    (D) Four generations
    (E) They never lose their primary language.

24. Prior to the First Agricultural Revolution, what were humans doing for food?

    (A) Fishing
    (B) Planting crops
    (C) Hunting and gathering
    (D) Genetically engineering food for mass production
    (E) Purchasing it in small, food-specific establishments

25. The delivery area of the Pittsburgh *Gazette* is an example of what type of region?

    (A) Functional region
    (B) Formal region
    (C) Vernacular region
    (D) Statistical region
    (E) Urban realm

26. The conflict in Rwanda and Uganda in the mid-1990s is an example of a(n)

    (A) religious conflict.
    (B) ethnic conflict.
    (C) transnational conflict.
    (D) ethnic enclave.
    (E) border conflict.

27. Which of the following cities is a primate city in its country?

    (A) London, United Kingdom
    (B) Venice, Italy
    (C) Frankfurt, Germany
    (D) Aarhus, Denmark
    (E) Medellin, Columbia

28. Which of the following demographic data has the greatest impact on growth rates?

    (A) Birth rates
    (B) Literacy rate
    (C) Per capita gross domestic product
    (D) Immigration rates
    (E) Life expectancy

GO ON TO THE NEXT PAGE

29. Islam is the fastest growing religion in the world today primarily because of

  (A) high birthrates.
  (B) contagious diffusion.
  (C) relocation diffusion.
  (D) cultural convergence.
  (E) assimilation in host countries.

30. Which of the following countries is an enclave?

  (A) United States
  (B) Indonesia
  (C) Lesotho
  (D) Egypt
  (E) Morocco

31. The Second Agricultural Revolution coincided with

  (A) increased genetic engineering of crops.
  (B) the Industrial Revolution.
  (C) the First Agricultural Revolution.
  (D) the Third Agricultural Revolution.
  (E) the Enlightenment in Europe.

32. In terms of today's global economy, which area would be considered the resource frontier of the world?

  (A) East Asia
  (B) Southwest Asia
  (C) Sub-Saharan Africa
  (D) Central and Western Europe
  (E) Eastern South America

33. Which of the following traits fits the definition of an Islamic city?

  (A) Twisted streets to maximize shade
  (B) Areas devoted to Western development
  (C) Squatter areas within the central business districts
  (D) Three separate, defined central business districts
  (E) Global cities without population problems due to religious values

34. Which of these five regions is not one of the most populated areas of the world?

  (A) East Asia
  (B) Southeast Asia
  (C) Central Europe
  (D) South America
  (E) Northeastern United States

35. What two areas are the hearths of the world's five primary religions?

  (A) Southern India and Eastern China
  (B) Southwest Asia and Northern Africa
  (C) Central Europe and Southwest Asia
  (D) Northern India and Southwest Asia
  (E) Eastern China and Southern Europe

36. The pessimistic viewpoint about a lack of economic development in certain locations on the globe can be attributed to their lack of

  (A) infrastructure.
  (B) physical features such as rivers.
  (C) labor availability.
  (D) foreign investment.
  (E) modern technology.

GO ON TO THE NEXT PAGE

37. Thailand is the best example of which type of political shape?

    (A) Compact
    (B) Perforated
    (C) Prorupted
    (D) Elongated
    (E) Fragmented

38. Which of the five means of transportation would fruit production in South America for market in the United States need to use?

    (A) Inland waterways
    (B) Overland trucks
    (C) Airplanes
    (D) Pipelines
    (E) Rail transport

39. The 12th Congressional District's boundaries in North Carolina were accused of using what tactic for political gain?

    (A) Gerrymandering
    (B) Reapportionment
    (C) Census stacking
    (D) Blockbusting
    (E) Redlining

40. What is the primary type of farming done in the tropical regions of Brazil?

    (A) Commercial agriculture
    (B) Slash-and-burn agriculture
    (C) Intensive subsistence agriculture
    (D) Truck farming
    (E) Irrigated fruit farming

41. Southeast Asian cities have promoted economic growth through what primary means?

    (A) Western transportation systems
    (B) Eastern religions
    (C) Western investment and trade
    (D) Eastern design layouts
    (E) Western cultural integration with Eastern theology

42. The area around the sub-Saharan agricultural regions is being adversely affected by what environmental problem?

    (A) Global warming
    (B) Desertification
    (C) El Niño
    (D) Increased earthquake activity
    (E) Transhumance

43. Eastern Europe during the 1940s through the early 1990s can be identified as a

    (A) region dominated by theocracies.
    (B) region with no political conflict.
    (C) core economic region.
    (D) homogeneous region.
    (E) shatterbelt.

44. Which of the following is the best example of folk culture?

    (A) Eating at McDonald's
    (B) Wearing blue jeans
    (C) Producing rocking chairs using traditional means
    (D) Listening to your MP3 player
    (E) Creating Web pages

GO ON TO THE NEXT PAGE

45. What city were the concentric zone and the sector model modeled after in the early 1900s?

   (A) New York City
   (B) Los Angeles
   (C) Philadelphia
   (D) Boston
   (E) Chicago

46. A country enters stage 3 of the demographic transition when

   (A) the death rate drops.
   (B) people decide to have considerably fewer children.
   (C) the birth rates remain high.
   (D) the birth and death rates are nearly equal.
   (E) family size stays the same.

47. Which region has the fewest languages that are under threat of extinction?

   (A) Europe
   (B) The Americas
   (C) The Pacific
   (D) Asia
   (E) Sub-Saharan Africa

48. The Gobi Desert in Mongolia uses what primary form of agriculture?

   (A) Truck farming
   (B) Slash-and-burn farming
   (C) Plantation agriculture
   (D) Commercial agriculture
   (E) Pastoral nomadism

49. Which continent uses nuclear power for a greater percentage of its total power output than any other continent?

   (A) North America
   (B) South America
   (C) Europe
   (D) Asia
   (E) Africa

50. Central Park in New York City is a good example of

   (A) a symbolic landscape.
   (B) a greenbelt.
   (C) a festival landscape.
   (D) urban development.
   (E) an ethnic landscape.

51. Around a local university, there are pizza restaurants, fast-food restaurants, and coffee shops. This type of development is best characterized by the

   (A) sector model.
   (B) multiple nuclei model.
   (C) peripheral model.
   (D) western U.S. city models.
   (E) concentric zone model.

52. The dominance of corn production in the United States correlates with what other agricultural practice?

   (A) Cattle production
   (B) Irrigated farmland
   (C) Dairy production
   (D) Market gardening activities
   (E) Pastoral nomadism

GO ON TO THE NEXT PAGE

53. The United States and many other more developed countries rely on what natural resources for the majority of their electricity production?

    (A) Petroleum

    (B) Coal

    (C) Natural gas

    (D) Uranium

    (E) Nuclear power

54. Which of the following religions is a monotheistic religion?

    (A) Hinduism

    (B) Shintoism

    (C) Animism

    (D) Judaism

    (E) Buddhism

55. The 38th parallel in Korea is an example of a(n)

    (A) demarcation line on the landscape.

    (B) antecedent boundary between two countries.

    (C) superimposed boundary created by outside forces.

    (D) geometric boundary dominated by the mountains in the area.

    (E) subsequent boundary established by China.

56. A population pyramid looks like an upside-down triangle. This area has a large percentage of

    (A) immigrants.

    (B) parents.

    (C) youth.

    (D) women.

    (E) elderly people.

57. Who first coined the term *geography*?

    (A) Plato

    (B) Aristotle

    (C) Zheng He

    (D) Socrates

    (E) Eratosthenes

58. A fad is started by a television personality of wearing shorts with a shirt and tie. The trend spreads throughout the United States. This is an example of what type of diffusion?

    (A) Expansion

    (B) Contagious

    (C) Stimulus

    (D) Relocation

    (E) Hierarchical

59. Which area of the world is currently experiencing the most rapid population growth?

    (A) Eastern North America

    (B) Central Europe

    (C) Sub-Saharan Africa

    (D) Central Asia

    (E) South America

60. Which region did not have a vegetative planting or seed agricultural hearth?

    (A) Southeast Asia

    (B) East Africa

    (C) South America

    (D) Europe

    (E) Middle America

GO ON TO THE NEXT PAGE ⇨

61. "The individual characteristics of a place that make it unique" defines which of the following terms most accurately?

    (A) Adaptive strategies

    (B) Built environments

    (C) Folk culture

    (D) Popular culture

    (E) Acculturation

62. Which of the following cities would be classified as a world city?

    (A) Shanghai

    (B) Madrid

    (C) London

    (D) Los Angeles

    (E) Buenos Aires

63. A city is located on a river that is prone to flooding yet provides trade advantages that bring measurable wealth to the city. Which statement would best fit that city?

    (A) The city has a good site yet a poor situation.

    (B) The city has a good situation yet a poor site.

    (C) The city has trade advantages that outweigh the disadvantages.

    (D) The city has flood disadvantages that outweigh the advantages.

    (E) The city should relocate because of the flooding problem.

64. The majority of the entrants into the United Nations, a supranational organization, came from where during the 1960s?

    (A) Europe

    (B) South America

    (C) Pacific Islands

    (D) Africa

    (E) Central Asia

65. Which statement would best fit a European city?

    (A) European cities have large areas of squatter settlements.

    (B) European cities have their skyscrapers located in the suburbs.

    (C) European cities have few forms of public transportation.

    (D) European cities have heavy pollution problems.

    (E) European cities have the poor living closest to their central business districts.

66. Potato chip production is a good example of what?

    (A) A variable-cost industry

    (B) A fixed-cost industry

    (C) A weight-gaining industry

    (D) A weight-reducing industry

    (E) A market-dependent industry

67. The largest territory in the world in terms of population is

    (A) the Solomon Islands.

    (B) the Falkland Islands.

    (C) Aruba.

    (D) Puerto Rico.

    (E) Greenland.

GO ON TO THE NEXT PAGE

68. Which is the world's primary lingua franca language?

(A) Mandarin Chinese
(B) Russian
(C) English
(D) Spanish
(E) Hindi

69. The S-curve is most often associated with what geographic factor?

(A) World population growth over time
(B) Immigration rates over time
(C) Economic development over time
(D) Cultural adaptation of ethnic groups over time
(E) The stability of countries' governments over time

70. Which crop has been credited with saving millions of people due to the hybridization of this crop in Asia?

(A) Corn
(B) Rice
(C) Wheat
(D) Sorghum
(E) Barley

71. The greatest percentage of people in the world participate in which type of agriculture?

(A) Subsistence agriculture
(B) Highly mechanized commercial farming
(C) Pastoral nomadism
(D) Hired help on plantation agricultural farms
(E) Slash-and-burn agriculture

72. Which of the following terms is NOT associated with the Hindu religion?

(A) Brahma
(B) Caste system
(C) Shiva
(D) Vishnu
(E) Mecca

73. Which of the following best describes the urban hierarchy of settlements?

(A) Hamlet, village, town, city, metropolis
(B) Hamlet, town, city, metropolis, megalopolis
(C) Megalopolis, metropolis, village, town, hamlet
(D) Village, town, hamlet, metropolis, megalopolis
(E) Town, hamlet, village, metropolis, megalopolis

74. Los Angeles receives goods from Asia via ships. In the ports, the goods are put on trains for distribution around the United States. Los Angeles is a(n)

(A) break-of-bulk point.
(B) variable-trading partner.
(C) entrepot.
(D) fixed-cost provider.
(E) trade alternative partner.

75. The border between the United States and Canada along the 49th parallel is a good example of what type of boundary?

(A) Subsequent boundary
(B) Antecedent boundary
(C) Superimposed boundary
(D) Relic boundary
(E) Demarcation boundary line

IF YOU FINISH BEFORE TIME IS CALLED, YOU MAY CHECK YOUR WORK ON THIS SECTION ONLY. DO NOT TURN TO ANY OTHER SECTION IN THE TEST.

STOP

SECTION II: FREE-RESPONSE QUESTIONS
Time—75 minutes

Directions: You have 75 minutes to answer ALL THREE of the following questions. While a formal essay is not required, it is not enough to answer a question by merely listing facts. Your answer should be based upon your critical analysis of the question posed.

1. Use the list of United Nations states added in the 1960s and 1990s to answer the following questions.

United Nations States Added in the 1960s

Algeria (62)	Barbados (66)	Benin (60)	Botswana (66)
Burkina Faso (60)	Burundi (62)	Cameroon (60)	Cen. Afr. Rep. (60)
Chad (60)	Congo, Rep. (60)	Cote d'Ivoire (60)	Cyprus (60)
Dem. Rep. Congo (60)	Gabon (60)	Gambia (65)	Guyana (66)
Jamaica (62)	Kenya (63)	Kuwait (63)	Lesotho (66)
Madagascar (60)	Malawi (64)	Maldives (65)	Mali (60)
Malta (64)	Mauritania (61)	Mauritius (68)	Mongolia (61)
Niger (60)	Nigeria (60)	Rwanda (62)	Senegal (60)
Sierra Leone (61)	Singapore (65)	Somalia (60)	Swaziland (68)
Togo (60)	Trinidad & Tob. (62)	Uganda (62)	Zambia (64)

United Nations States Added in the 1990s

Andorra (93)	Armenia (92)	Azerbaijan (92)	Bosnia & Herz. (92)
Croatia (92)	S. Korea (91)	Eritrea (93)	Estonia (91)
Georgia (92)	Kazakhstan (92)	Kiribati (99)	Kyrgyzstan (92)
Latvia (91)	Liechtenstein (90)	Lithuania (91)	Macedonia (93)
Micronesia (91)	Moldova (92)	Monaco (93)	Marshall Isl. (91)
Nauru (99)	Palau (94)	N. Korea (91)	Namibia (90)
Slovakia (93)	Slovenia (92)	Tajikistan (92)	San Marino (92)
Tonga (99)	Turkmenistan (92)	Uzbekistan (92)	

(A) What were the geopolitical circumstances that led to the majority of the states being created or added to the United Nations during the 1960s?

(B) What were the geopolitical circumstances that led to the majority of the states being created or added to the United Nations during the 1990s?

(C) What areas were most affected by the creation of new states during the 1960s and the 1990s?

GO ON TO THE NEXT PAGE ⟩

2. Compare cities between the United States and Europe by answering the following questions.

   (A) What are the demographic differences between the populations living in close proximity to a central business district on both continents?

   (B) What are the socioeconomic differences between the populations living in close proximity to the central business district on both continents?

   (C) What are the similarities in the central business districts in cities on the two continents?

3. Use the map of cattle production below to answer the following questions.

Cattle Map

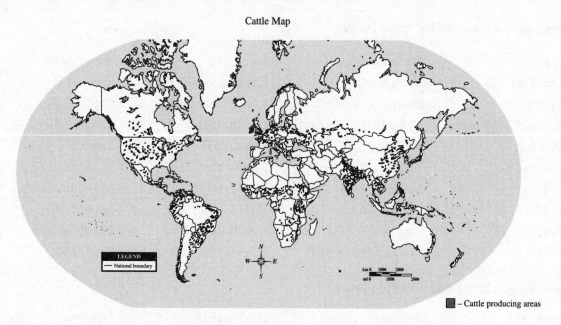

□ – Cattle producing areas

(A) Explain how climate affects the distribution of cattle around the world.

(B) Explain von Thunen's model of agriculture in relation to cattle production. Explain the cattle culture and how it affects the model.

(C) What would explain the lack of cattle production in certain areas of the world? Give two examples.

GO ON TO THE NEXT PAGE

GO ON TO THE NEXT PAGE

_____

_____

_____

_____

_____

_____

_____

_____

_____

_____

_____

_____

_____

_____

_____

_____

_____

_____

_____

GO ON TO THE NEXT PAGE ⟩

GO ON TO THE NEXT PAGE

GO ON TO THE NEXT PAGE

IF YOU FINISH BEFORE TIME IS CALLED, YOU MAY CHECK YOUR WORK ON
THIS SECTION ONLY. DO NOT TURN TO ANY OTHER SECTION IN THE TEST.

STOP

Practice Test 1 Answer Key

1. C	20. B	39. A	58. E
2. A	21. B	40. B	59. C
3. D	22. D	41. C	60. D
4. E	23. C	42. B	61. C
5. A	24. C	43. E	62. C
6. C	25. A	44. C	63. B
7. D	26. B	45. E	64. D
8. D	27. A	46. B	65. B
9. B	28. A	47. A	66. D
10. A	29. A	48. E	67. D
11. B	30. C	49. C	68. C
12. C	31. B	50. C	69. A
13. A	32. B	51. B	70. B
14. E	33. A	52. A	71. A
15. E	34. D	53. B	72. E
16. D	35. D	54. D	73. A
17. B	36. D	55. C	74. A
18. B	37. C	56. E	75. B
19. C	38. C	57. E	

PRACTICE TEST 1: ASSESS YOUR STRENGTHS

Use the following tables to determine which topics (chapters) you need to review most. If you need help with your essays, be sure to review Free-Response Essay Question Strategies.

Chapter and Topic	Question
Chapter 3: Geography: Its Nature and Perspectives	1, 25, 57, 58
Chapter 4: Population	2, 9, 19, 22, 28, 34, 46, 56, 59, 69
Chapter 5: Cultural Patterns and Processes	3, 13, 20, 23, 29, 35, 44, 47, 54, 61, 68, 72
Chapter 6: Political Organization of Space	11, 12, 14, 21, 26, 30, 37, 39, 43, 55, 64, 67, 75
Chapter 7: Agriculture, Food Production, and Rural Land Use	5, 10, 18, 24, 31, 38, 40, 42, 48, 52, 60, 70, 71
Chapter 8: Industrialization and Economic Development	4, 6, 8, 17, 32, 36, 41, 49, 53, 66, 74
Chapter 9: Cities and Urban Land Use	7, 15, 16, 27, 33, 45, 50, 51, 62, 63, 65, 73

Chapter and Topic	Number of Questions on Test	Number Correct
Chapter 3: Geography: Its Nature and Perspectives	4	
Chapter 4: Population	10	
Chapter 5: Cultural Patterns and Processes	12	
Chapter 6: Political Organization of Space	13	
Chapter 7: Agriculture, Food Production, and Rural Land Use	13	
Chapter 8: Industrialization and Economic Development	11	
Chapter 9: Cities and Urban Land Use	12	

ANSWERS AND EXPLANATIONS

SECTION I: MULTIPLE-CHOICE QUESTIONS

1. C

Map scale is the direct relationship of the actual size of the item in relation to the size of the item on a particular map. All items on the map should have the same scale for the map to be as accurate as possible. The different types of map projections, as well as the map classes, are used to minimize the distortion that occurs from the different map projections. Map direction refers to the cardinal and intermediate directions on the map orientation.

2. A

Thomas Malthus was the first person to use the term "overpopulation," which meant that population growth was growing exponentially while agricultural production was only growing linearly. This meant that the larger the gap between the population growth and food production, the greater the problem would be with starvation in the population.

3. D

Country music's hearth is located around Nashville, Tennessee. The Country Music Hall of Fame is located in Nashville, as is the Grand Ole Opry, considered the home of country music. However, Dallas, Texas, the center of north-central Texas cowboy music; the Ozark-Ouachita upland region in central and western Arkansas; and the middle-Tennessee and Kentucky-lowlands regions around Nashville and Knoxville are considered to be the three primary hearths of country music. Nashville has had a more profound impact on country music than the cowboy music started

around Dallas. Therefore, although Dallas is also correct, Nashville is the best answer.

4. E

Vietnam is not considered one of the Four Asian Tigers. The Four Asian Tigers consist of (1) South Korea, centered around the main city of Seoul; (2) Taiwan, centered around the capital city of Taipei; (3) Hong Kong, now owned by China; and (4) Singapore. All of these Tigers have modeled their economic development around the concept of trade. As a result of this trade, each of these four areas has seen economic growth skyrocket in relation to other areas in Asia.

5. A

Johann Heinrich von Thunen's agricultural land use model is focused on the basic concept of commercial farming. In commercial farming, all of the agricultural products produced by the farmer are sold to the market for sale off the farm. The other answers are incorrect. The higher-end commodities are usually products that must be grown closer to the market because of their weight and bulkiness, which adds to the cost of transporting them. The lighter commodities can be grown farther away from the market because it costs less to transport them.

6. C

Alfred Weber's least cost theory is based on the shape of a triangle. His theory suggests that the market must be located within the triangle to ensure the profitability of the products being produced. The location of the production point is dependent upon the weight-gaining or weight-reducing industries. If the industry is a weight-reducing industry, the production point should be located closer to the raw materials to reduce transportation costs. In weight-gaining industries, the production point should be located closer to the market to reduce the transportation costs for heavier products.

7. D

The concentric zone model suggests that economic structure is dependent upon an area's distance from the central business district. The lower classes live the closest to the central business district because that is the zone of transition. The working-class homes are the next stage outward, followed by middle-class homes and then by the commuter zone with high-end residences. According to the model, the wealthy can afford the commute into the city on a daily basis and, therefore, can afford the large homes in the suburbs. In many cases, the concentric zone model is a myth that most people believe to be reality. The inner city is filled with high-end residential areas with residents who want the amenities that the city has to offer.

8. D

China has created special economic zones (SEZs) in many of its larger urban centers. Shanghai, Hong Kong, and many other large cities have established specific areas within the urban framework where companies from more developed countries can establish their base of operations in China. The result is a greater tax base, increased employment in a country with over 1 billion people, and the positive experiences of companies trying to get into that market of over 1 billion people. Many office parks and industrial parks have been established as production centers for both export and resale in China itself.

9. B

The demographic transition model explains both population growth and economic development within a society. The highest growth rates are found in stage 2 of the model, the agricultural stage. Children are seen as an economic asset rather than a liability, as in stages 3 and 4. Children are workers on the farms as well as a source of social security in the society. The more children one has, the greater one's wealth, because one can afford more farmland. Children are fed from products available on the farm. The death rate decreases sharply in stage 2 because of a more reliable food source, as well as the increased availability and quality of health care.

10. A

The long lots system is the system that was initiated by the French in the United States. The long lots system is still in use in areas such as Louisiana. The long lots system is based on the river. The river is the transportation source for the agricultural products produced on the plantations and farms along it. The lots extend far back from the river, and many are rather narrow. The result is a land pattern system with rectangular plots of land extending backward from the river as far as half a mile or more. The metes and bounds system came from the United Kingdom and used stones and natural features to distinguish the ownership on the landscape. The township and range system was born from the relatively flat landscape in the Midwest and the ease of dividing the land and giving it away to settlers who promised to farm the land for several years. This ensured profitability to the railroad companies who were giving away the land, because they could earn money from transporting people to the farming areas and agricultural products back to markets in the East.

11. B

OPEC has a huge impact on the price of gasoline in the United States simply based on supply and demand principles. Demand is usually higher in summer and winter months. Geopolitical struggles also play a role, but drilling more barrels of oil per day means a reduction in the cost because of more supply. The reverse is also true: If production is cut, prices will rise due to a supply shortage (assuming an equal demand).

12. C

Maquiladoras are factories that produce goods in Mexico with relatively inexpensive labor and then sell the products in the United States. If the products were produced in the Untied States, higher labor costs would reduce profits. NAFTA (North American Free Trade Agreement) made the exportation and importation of products easier across country borders. Because the border became easier to cross, more companies chose to locate their factories in Mexico to take advantage of relatively inexpensive labor.

13. A

The largest universalizing religion in the world today is Christianity with just over 2 billion followers. Many of these are Roman Catholic, the largest denomination of Christianity; approximately 1 billion Christians around the world profess to be Roman Catholic. The second largest religion in the world is Islam. Islam is the fastest-growing religion in the world with close to 2 billion followers. Hinduism has approximately 800 million followers but is an ethnic religion confined primarily to India. Counting Buddhists is sometimes difficult, because many Buddhists practice other faiths at the same time. Judaism is the smallest of the world's five primary religions.

14. E

There is no perfect example of a nation-state. Many multinational corporations have people living within most countries, and many countries have at least one minority group that encompasses at least a small segment of their total population. However, some countries, such as Denmark, are close examples of nation-states. Denmark contains approximately 5 million people within its border. To be a nation-state, the entire population of the country must be the same ethnicity, practice the same religion, and speak the same language. Almost 99 percent of the people in Denmark are Danes. They follow the Lutheran religion and speak Danish. Japan is another country that is often associated most closely with being a nation-state.

15. E

Redlining is the refusal to give loans to people living in certain areas in a city regardless of race. Banks and other financial institutions know that default rates on loans are the highest in certain zones. The process of redlining is a protection measure for banks to keep loans from defaulting. The end product is an area where few people can get a loan to purchase a residential property. Banks are encouraged to use a person's lending history rather than geographic area in their decisions to grant mortgages and other loans.

16. D

Edge cities are associated with the multiple nuclei model. The multiple nuclei model suggests that growth is independent of the central business district. Because of that principle, economic development can occur around certain geographical phenomena, such as airports, universities, and other establishments. What is created is an area with development around it that is focused on the primary commercial activity in the area. Around airports, hotels and restaurants are located because the airport creates a demand for such establishments. Around universities, pizza places and fast-food restaurants are located because of the demographics of the area. Both the concentric zone model and the sector model are based on the rise of suburbs with extensions outward from the central business districts as opposed to edge cities, which are independent of the central business district.

17. B

The United States possesses the most coal reserves of any country in the world. Because the United States has more coal in the ground than any other country, the majority of its energy production comes from burning coal resources. The availability and the accessibility of coal means that power production can be done relatively cheaply. Like many European countries, France obtains more than 70 percent of its total energy production from sources such as nuclear power. The United States, owing to environmental restrictions and other policy regulations, has emphasized coal usage for its energy production.

18. B

Farming in more developed countries, such as the United States, for the past 100 years has seen the increased use of mechanization. The transition that is currently occurring on American farms is the increased use of industrial methods. Many farmers are subcontracting to producers of agricultural commodities. This process ensures a guaranteed profit for the farmers as well as a guaranteed stock that is consistent in terms of quality for the producer.

Average quality is good for the producer because it is better than poor quality. Poor-quality products mean a halt in the production process, hurting profits for the producer. More and more genetic engineering is being used to ensure and increase the quality of meat and other agricultural products for sale off the farm.

19. C

This retired couple is probably moving for environmental purposes to take advantage of the warm climate and amenities available to retired persons. When retirees move, the relocation is usually voluntary. Environmental conditions most likely involve a voluntary move. Many economic moves are also voluntary, but when the couple is retired, the move is primarily environmentally based. Almost all political push factors involve movement that was forced by the government in the home country. Political pull factors involve some type of positive perception of the new area.

20. B

Although Christianity is the largest of the five primary religions in the world, the fastest-growing religion in the world is Islam. Much of this has to do with where the religion is spreading. Northern Africa, the Middle East, and Southeast Asia, including Indonesia, are some of the fastest-growing areas in the world, based on their population growth and other demographic characteristics. Islam is also a universalizing or a proselytic religion, meaning that followers try to convert people to their faith.

21. B

The heartland theory was started by Halford MacKinder. MacKinder suggested that whoever owned the Eastern European region of the world would have the necessary food production and natural resources to rule the world. The Ukraine region is the world leader in the production of wheat; it produces enough to support a large population. The abundance of raw materials in the region supports Russia's and Ukraine's industrial activities, making it one of the top manufacturing regions in the world. The rimland theory, which was begun by Nicholas Spykman in reaction to the heartland theory, suggests that sea power is more important than the land power of the heartland.

22. D

An intervening opportunity is a positive experience along the migration route that induces a person to stop migrating and reside somewhere along the way instead. In the case of this family moving from California to New Orleans, they saw some amenities in the Albuquerque area that made them want to cease their migration and stay in the Albuquerque region.

23. C

The process of acculturation usually takes three generations to complete. The first generation to arrive in the new country speaks very little of the new language. The second generation is usually bilingual, speaking the new language at school and in the workforce yet speaking the original language at home. The third generation speaks very little of the original language and speaks the new language predominately in most situations.

24. C

Prior to the First Agricultural Revolution, which involved the process of planting and sustaining crops over an extended period of time, humans were involved in hunting and gathering. The hunting-and-gathering method produced unstable food

supplies, which often depended upon the availability of animals. When herds were scarce, mass starvation frequently ensued. The result was a world population that was slow to grow and remained relatively low in total population.

25. A

Newspaper delivery is an example of a functional region, because it can change based on the delivery habits of the subscribers to the newspaper. A formal region has defining characteristics, such as state or country borders. The demarcation line symbolizes the entrance or exit of the land. A functional region is used for market area or hinterlands and can shift over time. A radio station is another example of a functional region, because it can move; during the evening hours, the radio station can be heard farther away because solar radiation doesn't interfere with the signal, while during the daytime hours, the radio station's listening area shrinks.

26. B

The conflict in Rwanda and Uganda is a good example of an ethnic conflict. The Hutus and the Tutsis have been in conflict for the past two decades. However, during the 1990s, hundreds of thousands of Hutus and Tutsis were killed in clashes based on ethnocentrism. Both sides felt that they were superior to the other. The border was not in dispute between the authorities of the two countries. Rather, the conflict was between the peoples of the two ethnic groups.

27. A

London is a primate city. London has more than double the population of the next largest city in the United Kingdom, Birmingham, which has just over 2 million citizens. The others are not primate cities.

28. A

The number one factor in determining a population's growth rate is its birth rate. The birth rate is the number of births per 1,000 people. The higher the birth rate, the greater the population growth. Literacy rate does have a correlation to population growth. Generally, the higher the literacy rate, the lower the population growth rate. Per capita gross domestic product is an economic indicator, and generally the higher the wealth, the slower the population growth. Immigration rates do not affect world population data, because immigration is simply the movement of people on the surface of the Earth. Neither migration nor immigration add to the Earth's population. Life expectancy does affect total population growth. However, the countries with the highest life expectancies have some of the lowest birth rates.

29. A

Islam is the fastest growing major religion because of high total fertility rates among Muslim women. Although Islam is a universalizing religion, conversion is not the main reason for why the religion is growing so fast.

30. C

An enclave is an area completely surrounded by another state. Lesotho is completely surrounded by the country of South Africa. Other states that are landlocked completely within another country are San Marino and the Vatican City. Both of these small states are located within the borders of Italy yet have sovereign control over their foreign and internal affairs. The United States is not completely inside of another country. Indonesia is broken up into over 13,000 islands. Egypt borders several countries in northern Africa, and Morocco borders the ocean as well as other countries on the northwestern corner of Africa.

31. B

The link between the Industrial Revolution and the Second Agricultural Revolution cannot be underestimated. The Industrial Revolution provided the technology and the mechanization for agricultural practices to become much more efficient. The Industrial Revolution also increased transportation efficiency, allowing agricultural products to be sent farther and faster than ever before. This allowed farmers to till more land and increase profits. Farmers could now produce crops for export to other countries, whereas prior to the Industrial Revolution, agricultural products were consumed relatively close to their production points.

32. B

The resource that the world largely depends on today is petroleum. The area with the largest deposits of petroleum is the Middle East in southwest Asia. Other areas of the world depend on many different natural resources for their energy needs, but almost all of the more developed world, or the core countries, depend upon petroleum for their energy production.

33. A

Islamic cities are located in areas that are usually hot and arid. To keep homes cool and maximize shade, many of the streets are twisted or curved to provide relief from the heat of the midday sun. Asian cities have large areas devoted to Western development. Islamic cities do have squatter settlements, but they are usually located on the outskirts of the city. African cities have three separate central business districts. Many Islamic cities are gaining in population rapidly. Cairo, Istanbul, and Jakarta are all among the most populated cities in the world.

34. D

Generally, five main areas are included in the most densely populated areas in the world. Those five areas are northeastern North America, Central and Western Europe, East Asia, Southeast Asia, and northern and coastal India. These areas all have high population densities. The only choice that is not on this list is South America. Although Brazil contains the cities of São Paulo and Rio de Janeiro, the area is not considered by demographers to be among the top five locations in the world in terms of population density.

35. D

The two main hearths of the five world religions are southwest Asia, including Saudi Arabia and Israel, and northern India. Christianity, Islam, and Judaism all began in the Middle East area. Jerusalem is the holy city for all three of these world religions. Northern India is the heart for both Buddhism and Hinduism. Many anthropologists consider Hinduism to be the world's oldest religion. Other anthropologists consider Judaism to be the oldest world religion. Buddhism began when Siddhartha Gautama saw the poverty in India and Nepal and began his quest toward the easing of eternal suffering and the elimination of wanton desires. These two distinct areas are the hearths of all five of the world's main religions.

36. D

Foreign investment drives new technology and innovation in many areas of the world. Without foreign investment, the resources are simply not there to produce and develop into a global city or country for trade. Many countries are stuck in the self-sufficiency mode of trying to feed their populations instead of being able to develop. A lack of foreign investment does not give the much-needed boost to development. Labor is abundantly available in many of these locations. The unemployment rates are as high as 70 percent in some less developed countries. Although people crave employment, the resources and sometimes the political opportunities are not present for entrepreneurs to develop businesses and create wealth in these economies.

37. C

Thailand is a good example of a prorupted country. Prorupted countries have a main base with an extension of land that juts outward from the base. In many cases, the proruption of the border is motivated by political factors; Afghanistan has a proruption to prevent Russia and Pakistan from sharing a border. Proruption is also often motivated by economic factors, such as a desire to have access to a river or ocean or to keep resources in certain possession. Germany created the Caprivi Strip in Namibia, then its colony, to access the Zambezi River. Likewise, Belgium created Belgian Congo to have access to the South Atlantic.

38. C

Fruit is a highly perishable product. Because it is so highly perishable, it must be shipped quickly to the market for resale. The fastest means to ship any product is by air. Airplanes are also the costliest means to transport fruit. This is why U.S. consumers pay more for fruit during the winter than in the summer. Fruit must be imported from Central and South America during the winter, adding to the cost of fruit.

39. A

The 12th Congressional District of North Carolina, as well as another district in California, were accused of being gerrymandered. Gerrymandering is the establishment of congressional districts for political gain rather than to represent accurately the entire population. Every district in a state should have approximately the same number of people. This means some rural districts are very large and some urban districts small. However, when the boundaries of the district are stacked so that one political party will have control over the district, that is gerrymandering. The 12th Congressional District of North Carolina was found to be gerrymandered during reapportionment, the establishment of congressional district boundaries.

40. B

Slash-and-burn farming is a traditional method of clearing the land for agriculture. In tropical areas, the land is thick with native tropical vegetation, but the soil is generally thin. When the land is cleared of its vegetation, often soil erosion results. This forces farmers into new areas to feed their families within only a couple of years. The result is a large amount of wasted agricultural land in Brazil when the slash-and-burn method is used for subsistence agriculture. Plantation agriculture is practiced in tropical areas, but the land is usually owned by a company in a more developed country. The plantations in Brazil are generally owned by Brazilian companies.

41. C

Using the international trade alternative model, many Asian countries, including China, South Korea, and Japan, have gained immense wealth through trade with more developed countries. Developing countries can produce products with relatively inexpensive labor. Inexpensive toy products are generally the beginning of the process. When enough foreign investment and wealth gets accumulated, governments begin training the workforce for more highly skilled positions. The result is a shift in the manufactured products from inexpensive toys to luxury items, such as automobiles and electronic equipment. The end result is greater profits and a higher standard of living for the manufacturing workforce.

42. B

Sub-Saharan Africa is being invaded by the Sahara desert. The Sahara desert is constantly growing because of inefficient agricultural practices. Nomadic farmers allow their animals to eat the vegetation at the edges of the desert. Eliminating the vegetation allows for expansion of the desert, which often ruins previously agriculturally productive land for generations.

43. E

Eastern Europe during the 1940s to the early 1990s was considered a shatterbelt because it was an area sandwiched between the Soviet Union (communist) and Western Europe (democratic) during the Cold War. Additionally, Eastern Europe is fairly mountainous and ethnically diverse making it a region difficult to control and unite politically.

44. C

Producing rocking chairs would be an example of folk culture if they were produced the same way that they have been for generations within a family or a cultural group. If the rocking chair is mass produced, then the process moves from folk culture to popular culture. The rest of the choices in this question are all examples of popular culture. Each can be done anywhere the world regardless of the culture at the production site.

45. E

Chicago was the city on which both the concentric zone model and the sector model were based. Both Burgess, who developed the concentric zone model, and Hoyt, who developed the sector model, believed that Chicago exhibited traits of their models in the early 1900s. Burgess believed that Chicago saw its lower-class citizens living relatively close to the central business district. Burgess also saw the middle class living in the next ring, followed by the wealthy living away from the city because they could afford the daily commute into the city. Hoyt believed that his model was correct, based on the continued outward expansion of the wealthy areas as well as the outward expansion of the lower-class areas. Hoyt used the north side of Chicago to support his theory because of the high-income residences that continued to move outward from the central business district.

46. B

A country enters stage 3, characterized by moderate growth, when most people in a country decide to voluntarily reduce the size of their families. This is usually a result of a shift in the economy from agriculture to industry. In an agriculturally based economy having more children is an economic asset, whereas in an industrially based economy having more children is an economic liability. This decision to have smaller families brings down the birth rate so that it is more in line with the descending death rate, moving the country into stage 3 of the demographic transition. China is the exception to this trend, because they forced their population to limit their family size by adopting population-controling policies.

47. A

Europe has the fewest languages under threat of extinction. Languages that are in danger of going extinct are typically in isolated regions around the world. In these geographically isolated pockets the populations are aging and shrinking. Young people often migrate to cities and tend not to be interested in maintaining their language heritage.

48. E

Pastoral nomadism is used in desert areas with little rainfall. People practicing pastoral nomadism are largely dependent upon their animals for survival. To obtain crops, either they have to grow them or they must trade their animal products (milk, wool, meat, etc.) for grain products. The other choices involved hot, humid weather, which is effective for growing plants.

49. C

Europe has found itself using more nuclear power than ever before. This trend is mostly because Europe has the plants to produce enough power. The demand for coal as a means of power production has diminished over previous decades. Some countries, such as France, receive over 70 percent of their total energy output from nuclear power. Other areas of the world, including the United States, use nuclear power, but the United States receives most of its power from coal-burning power plants because of its large reserves.

50. C

A festival landscape is an area within an urban setting that is set aside for space and play. Many festivals, concerts, and holiday activities are held in these large open spaces within the urban framework. Festival landscapes are usually parks where parties and concerts are given. Central Park in New York City hosts dozens of concerts every year, so it is considered a festival landscape.

51. B

The multiple nuclei model suggests that development occurs within areas of need in the city independently of the central business district. Lots of restaurants and bookstores congregate around university campuses. Likewise, a lot of restaurants and hotels are built near airports because of travelers' high demand for them.

52. A

Cattle production correlates with corn production in the United States because the majority of corn in the United States is used for cattle feed. However, within the past decade, more corn has been used for ethanol production. Because of this demand for ethanol, the price of corn has continued to increase. This is good news for farmers who grow corn but bad news for farmers who must pay higher prices to feed their cattle. It is also bad news for people who are buying food made from corn. Dairy production uses corn feed, but the majority of corn feed is used in the livestock fattening regions of the United States, traditionally located in the Midwest.

53. B

The United States owns a large percentage of the world's coal reserves, which we use for the majority of our energy production. Because the United States has an abundance of coal within its borders, the cost of producing energy from coal is relatively inexpensive. Petroleum is used to feed our energy needs for automobiles as well as plastics, but very little petroleum is used for electricity production.

54. D

Monotheistic means "believing in one god." Judaism is the only religion of the choices that is a monotheistic religion. Yahweh is the God figure for the Jewish religion. Hinduism believes in millions of gods. Shintoism believes in nature gods. Animism believes in spirits that provide people with either good luck or bad luck. Buddhism is a polytheistic religion in the sense that one can practice Buddhism as well as other religions simultaneously.

55. C

A superimposed boundary is placed by outsiders on a landscape that has already been developed, and it ignores the cultural landscape imprinted on the land. In the case of the 38th parallel boundary in Korea, outside forces established the boundary, splitting up the Korean nation into two separate states. (The Korean people also extend northward into Russia as well as North and South Korea.) The line is also a demarcation line with guarded troops located on the borders of North and South Korea. However, the superimposed boundary is the best answer to this question. The answer cannot be a geometric boundary located in the mountains unless it follows straight lines of latitude and longitude. An antecedent boundary is one that existed before the establishment of countries on the landscape. An example of an antecedent boundary is the 49th parallel boundary between the United States and Canada. Settlement recognized the boundary between the United States and Canada, and settlers could choose which country they wanted to be citizens of. However, the line was there before settlement occurred.

56. E

Population pyramids are demographic tools to determine the sex and age ratios of a specific population. On the left of population pyramids are males, and on the right of population pyramids are females. The younger ages are at the bottom of the population pyramid, whereas the older people are located at the top of the population pyramid. Therefore, if a population pyramid has an upside-down triangle look, it has a high percentage of elderly people. Many of the retirement communities in Florida and Arizona have upside-down population pyramids. Population pyramids are useful for determining employment structures within a specific area. Also, areas with upside-down population pyramids will need a lot of medical care for their elderly populations. On the other hand, communities with a lot of children will need a lot of teachers. Educational institutions use population projections and pyramids to determine whether new schools are needed or if schools will need to be closed.

57. E

Eratosthenes was the first person to coin the term *geography*, which literally means "to write about the Earth." Socrates, Plato, and Aristotle all believed in geography as a discipline but did not coin the term *geography*. Zheng He was the dominant Chinese explorer and may have found the western coast of North America and the eastern coast of Africa in his journeys around the world.

58. E

Hierarchical diffusion occurs when information is spread by a member of the society's elite. The trait that is most often associated with hierarchical diffusion is the skipping of certain sections of the region, as not all areas receive the information at the same time. Usually, larger cities receive information first, and then it is disseminated to the rest of society.

59. C

The most rapid growth is occurring in the sub-Saharan Africa region. This is evidenced by the high crude birth rates in these countries. European countries, specifically in Eastern Europe, are experiencing population decline. More people are dying than are being born. East Asia and South Asia have the two largest countries in the world in terms of population (China and India), but the fastest growth rates are found in the African regions.

60. D

Europe is the correct answer because Europe did not have an agricultural hearth. Agriculture diffused into Europe from Southwest Asia. Seed agricultural hearths include East Asia, East Africa, the Indus River Valley, Meso-America, and the Peruvian Highlands. Vegetative planting hearths were located in the Peruvian Highlands, West Africa, and Southeast Asia and the Ganges River delta area.

61. C

The folk culture of a place is what differentiates that place from other places. Popular culture is what links that place with other cultures. Both of these terms can be used to define regions, and often culture is a good way to identify a characteristic of a region. Folk culture, such as storytelling or other craft procedures, can be a good way of defining the uniqueness of people. Adaptive strategies are the ways that people adapt to their environments. Built environments are the landscapes that humans build on the landscape and may be a reason for tourism. Acculturation is the process of adapting to a new country's culture.

62. C

According to Saskia Sassen, there are three world cities. London is the only world city among the answer choices. The other two world cities are New York City and Tokyo. World cities are defined by their importance to the areas surrounding them. However, these three world cities affect not only the areas around them but also the world with their financial dominance, as evident in their stock market activity. These world cities affect the culture and the political environment around their areas, as well with their importance to trade and commerce activity. There are also alpha cities, beta cities, and gamma cities. Cities are placed in these categories based on certain criteria, such as name recognition, economic activity, and other criteria that make them more or less important.

63. B

Site refers to the individual characteristics of a place in reference to its physical location. *Situation* refers to how easily connected the place is in relation to other places around it. New Orleans has an excellent situation because it is located near the delta of the Mississippi River. This brought immense trade wealth to the city of New Orleans, which during the early 1880s was one of the top cities in the United States in terms of population and economic wealth. However, the site of New Orleans is poor. Its central business district, or downtown region, is eight feet below sea level. When Hurricane Katrina hit the city in 2005, the city could not withstand the onslaught of water, and the result was a city that was underwater. Site and situation work together to grow cities or urban areas and provide unique advantages and disadvantages to industrial or manufacturing facilities.

64. D

During the 1960s, much of Africa gained independence from colonial powers, so many of the newly independent states that were admitted to the United Nations in the 1960s came from Africa. During the 1970s and 1980s, the newly created states that were added to the United Nations were Pacific Island countries. During the 1990s, many of the countries admitted to the United Nations were from Eastern Europe. Which countries enter the United Nations and why tells a lot about the world's political situation each decade.

65. B

European cities are older than U.S. cities, and the technology did not exist when they were built to build as high as current technology allows. The result is that the historical center of towns consist of buildings that are only five or six stories tall. Skyscrapers that are built today to meet the needs of large commercial establishments are built in the suburbs for two reasons. First, in many European cities, people historically buried their dead underneath the city in catacombs, which are located throughout the urban center. The result is a soil that is not stable enough to bear the weight of super skyscrapers. The second reason is that in European cities, the urban centers have already been built. Owing to cultural factors, Europeans do not tear down buildings as easily as Americans. History is treasured, and the result is a historic core that has not changed in centuries in many cases. Skyscrapers must be built on the outskirts of the city.

66. D

The production of potato chips is a good example of a weight-reducing industry. The primary products in the production of potato chips are potatoes, salt, and oil. The end product weighs less than the raw materials that were delivered to the production factory. If the end product weighs more than the raw materials, on the other hand, then the product is a weight-gaining industry. Automobile manufacturing is an example of a weight-gaining industry. Variable costs change based on the bulk of the order. Usually, the more ordered, the less the individual cost of an item. When costs do not vary by order size, they are fixed costs. All industries are market-dependent industries. If they were not market dependent, then they would not be in business. "A weight-reducing industry" is the best answer.

67. D

Puerto Rico is the largest territory in the world in terms of population. Puerto Rico, located on a tropical island in the Caribbean, has just over 5 million people. The island is owned by the United States, and there has been talk about adding Puerto Rico as the 51st state in the union. However, in the past citizens of Puerto Rico have voted against its becoming a state. Currently, citizens of Puerto Rico do not have to pay federal income tax yet are citizens of the United States. The downside is that they cannot vote in elections in the United States. The federal government of the United States has expressed interest in adding more revenue to its bottom line by bringing the territory into statehood. Instead of being an economic liability, Puerto Rico could be used for tax accumulation to recoup some of the resources entering the territory.

68. C

A lingua franca is a language that is mutually understood by two people and is usually used in some type of business transaction. The world's largest lingua franca is English. English is the global business language because of the dominance in economic activity of the United States as well as the United Kingdom. Many people in other countries are trying to learn English to compete in a world economy. Airline pilots and air traffic controllers around the world use English; for example, Indian pilots flying into an Ethiopian airport must communicate in English. However, there are other lingua francas. In eastern Africa, Swahili is quickly becoming the language used in most business transactions where the two parties speak different languages. Mandarin Chinese is quickly becoming a lingua franca in parts of Southeast Asia.

69. A

The S-curve is most closely associated with world population growth over the past two centuries. The S-curve suggests that population growth starts slowly but gains momentum, eventually growing exponentially. However, population growth eventually slows or ceases because the availability of resources does not match demand, and mass starvation is the result. Economic development would not be modeled with an S-curve. In many cases, economic growth goes up and down over an extended period.

70. B

The International Rice Research Institute, headquartered in the Philippines, has been conducting research on the hybridization of rice since the first uses of this method in the 1960s. Rice is still a staple crop in the daily diets of billions of Asians and the continued success of the crop in different regions of Asia has been credited in large part for the hybridization of the rice crop.

71. A

Most people in the world practice subsistence agriculture, farming to meet the food needs of the farmers' families. This type of farming is labor intensive and is the full-time occupation of many rural inhabitants of less developed countries. Subsistence crops vary depending upon location. Some of these crops are traded for animal products, and many subsistence farmers have both livestock and crop production to try to achieve adequate nutritional levels. Highly mechanized commercial farming is practiced in more developed countries, such as the United States and many places within Europe. Slash-and-burn agriculture is a form of subsistence agriculture that is primarily practiced in tropical regions. Pastoral nomadism is another form of subsistence agriculture; it is practiced in the drier regions of the world. Of the choices, subsistence farming is the best answer, encompassing both slash-and-burn farming as well as pastoral nomadism.

72. E

The Hindu religion is a polytheistic, ethnic religion that is practiced in India. There are three main deities—Shiva, Brahma, and Vishnu—and thousands of other deities in the religion. In India's caste system, a person is born into a particular caste and can never move out of the caste. If a person is born into the lowest caste, the untouchables, the result is often a life of poverty and discrimination. Although the caste system is dying, traditions are difficult to remove from culture. Mecca is the holiest city in the Islamic religion and the location or the end of the hajj. The hajj is the pilgrimage that all Muslims are supposed to make at least once in their lives to see the Kabah, a sacred structure located in the mosque at Mecca.

73. A

The correct urban hierarchy is: hamlet, village, town, city, and then metropolis, which is a large urban center. The rankings are based on the population of the urban area as well as their importance to the area surrounding them. This area that they support is known as their hinterland or their market area. Larger cities have larger hinterlands and affect more of the surrounding economic activities. World cities have the largest hinterlands and can affect areas extending hundreds, even thousands, of miles from their borders.

74. A

A break-of-bulk point is a location where goods are transferred from one mode of transportation to another mode of transportation. Los Angeles receives goods by ships from Asia and then transfers those products from the ships to the trains. The railroads then haul those products to all parts of the United States. This is a good example of a break-of-bulk point. Port facilities, airports, and rail yards are some examples of break-of-bulk locations within urban areas.

75. B

An antecedent boundary has remained intact despite settlement occurring at a later date. For the most part, citizens who settled in the northern portions of the United States realized that to stay in the United States, they needed to settle south of the 49th parallel. Likewise, Canadians stayed to the north of that boundary. The result is that when the boundary was put on the landscape, the 49th parallel was already a cultural icon, making the selection of the boundary's location an easy decision. Much of the boundary between the United States and Canada is unguarded, and it is the longest undefended border in the world. In many cases, people wouldn't know that they had crossed the border. Checkpoints do exist on several main roads, but for the most part, no fence delineates the border between the two countries.

SECTION II: SAMPLE FREE-RESPONSE ESSAYS AND RUBRICS

QUESTION 1

PART A

The geopolitical circumstance that led to the majority of the states being added to the United Nations in the 1960s was the end of colonialism in Africa. The majority of the states added during this period were the newly independent states of Africa. States were being formed in both the north and south of Africa after colonial powers allowed their colonies to achieve independence.

Belgium gave up the Congo region during this period. France gave up the Cote d'Ivoire region during this period as well. The European colonial era was ending on the continent of Africa. Many of the countries were newly created states based on the boundaries previously created by European powers.

PART B

The geopolitical circumstance that led to the majority of the states being added to the United Nations during the 1990s was the breakup of the former Soviet Union. The states that were added to the United Nations were the newly independent states in Eastern Europe, such as Latvia, Lithuania, and Estonia. Also, the newly created states in Central Asia, such as Kyrgyzstan, Kazakhstan, and Tajikistan, were created from the breakup of the former Soviet Union.

The breakup of the former Soviet Union was due mainly to economic reasons. The Soviet state could not compete in a world economy under the economic system of communism. The people were starving, and there was no incentive to succeed in the communist era. The result was separatist movements based on nationalistic forces. Many of the nationalities within the former Soviet Union wanted and eventually succeeded in creating their own states.

Other states were being added at this time in the Pacific Island regions, such as Kiribati, Nauru, Palau, and the Marshall Islands, but the majority of the countries being added to the United Nations during this period were from the breakup of the old Soviet Union.

PART C

The geographic area that was most affected by the establishment of the new states was the sub-Saharan African region. New states were being created, and colonialism was losing ground. New states were also being created in the Caribbean during this time. During the 1960s, the states of Jamaica as well Trinidad and

Tobago became members of the United Nations. However, the 1960s independence movement belonged to Africa.

During the 1990s, the creation of new states occurred in three distinct regions. Two of the regions, including Eastern Europe and Central Asia, were due to the breakup of the Soviet Union. The Baltic republics, the Central Asian states, and the states surrounding the Caspian Sea all became independent due in large part to the breakup of the Soviet Union. The Pacific Island countries also became more independent due in part to the decreasing importance of colonialism in the world.

In addition to these three areas, the microstates in Europe were being added to the United Nations. San Marino was added, and the breakup of the former Yugoslavian Republic caused the Aegean Sea region states to be added. Macedonia and Bosnia and Herzegovina were added as well.

RUBRIC FOR QUESTION 1

Total point value for question 1 = 6

Part A—Two points possible for any of the following answers:

- Colonialism ending in Africa
- Social pressure from European states toward independence

Part B—Two points possible for any of the following answers:

- The political breakup of the former Soviet Union
- The balkanization of Yugoslavia
- The Pacific Islands breaking away from colonial powers
- Islamic republics being formed in Central Asia

Part C—Two points possible for any of the following answers:

- Africa because of the end of colonialism
- Caribbean states such as Jamaica and Trinidad and Tobago
- Singapore, symbolizing a change in Asian statehood

QUESTION 2

PART A

The populations of European cities and U.S cities are demographically different, because in U.S. cities, primarily 20- to 30-year-olds and the elderly who live on fixed incomes live in close proximity to the central business district. In the United States, families mostly have moved out to the suburbs with their children. The highest percentage of people living in the inner city is young urban professionals who do not have any children. Frequently referred to as dinks (double income no kids), these people want to be located close to the entertainment district and the amenities that the central business district offers. The elderly have downsized their homes, preferring apartments or condos, and want to live close to the central business district so as not to have to drive the distances that living in the suburbs frequently involve.

In Europe, the central business district is often described as inhabited by young urban professionals who have children. The parks in many urban areas provide playgrounds for children to participate in recreational activities. The suburbs are for the wealthy, who do not need the amenities that the urban areas possess and who like the relatively quiet neighborhoods in the suburbs.

PART B

The primary differences between the populations living within close proximity to the central business districts include the socioeconomic status of the individuals living in these regions. In U.S. cities, the areas surrounding the central business district are primarily inhabited by lower-income citizens. One reason for this is the employment history of these people. Lower-income citizens usually hold manual skill positions. Factories tend to be located close to the central business district, and a lack of public transportation forces many of these citizens to live relatively close to their work. As American cities have developed, the wealthy have moved outside of the urban framework into the suburbs, because they can afford the longer commutes into the central business district where upper-income jobs are also located.

In Europe, mass transportation systems have allowed lower-income citizens to live in the suburbs. The mass transit system can transport them into and out of the city on a daily basis. The wealthy occupy the zones near the central business district because of the property value of these locations. The wealthy frequently leave the city on weekends and go to their estates or home in the countryside to escape the heat of the summer.

PART C

The similarities between the central business districts of cities in the United States and Europe involve the nature of the central business district itself—commercialization. The center for trade and commerce is often located within the central business district. In Europe, the interior of the central business district is often located in much older buildings, but shopping and other commercial activities frequently take place in these areas as well. In U.S. cities, the central business district is frequently populated by skyscrapers, but large areas are devoted to shopping and other tertiary activities, such as insurance and banking.

Other similarities include the traffic congestion in most commercial centers. Traffic is usually slower in the central business district, because the commercial establishments located there need the accessibility that the central location can offer. In Europe, the history of the city does not lend itself to the automobile. The streets are narrow, and traffic is usually slow as well, due to the dendritic pattern of the streets in many European cities.

RUBRIC FOR QUESTION 2

Total point value for question 2 = 6

Part A—Two points possible for any of the following answers:

- Large number of elderly living in central business districts within the United States
- Large number of young adults (ages 20–30) living in the central business districts of cities in the United States
- Large numbers of young adults (ages 20–30) living in the central business districts of European cities
- Large numbers of families living in the central business districts of European cities

Part B—Two points possible for any of the following answers:

- Lower-class citizens living within close proximity to the central business district in the United States
- Upper-class young people with no children living within close proximity to the central business district within the United States
- Upper-class professionals living within the central business districts of European cities

Part C—Two points possible for any of the following answers:

- Traffic congestion within the central business district
- Historical districts within the central business district
- Usually centered around some form of mass transportation
- Commercial center—shopping and other commercial activities agglomerated around the center for maximum exposure to products

QUESTION 3

PART A

Climate affects the cattle distribution around the world in many ways. The first would be applying von Thunen's principles of agriculture to modern agriculture in the world. Cattle ranching is done in areas that are far away from the market. Usually, cattle are allowed to roam over and eat on only poor-quality land. On land unsuited for farming, cattle can plump up to be sold to markets based on their weight. In some areas of the world, however, industrial agriculture is creating huge feedlots, such as in the Great Plains and Midwest regions of the United States. In feedlots, cattle are fed a prescribed diet to fatten them up and then they are hauled to market to be sold. This livestock fattening region is often situated near corn and other grain crops, which are used to feed the livestock. The climate in many cattle areas is dominated by a relative lack of precipitation. Even in the midwestern United States, many of the cattle are fed by the corn grown in the region, which may only need 30 inches of precipitation annually. Huge feedlots dominate the landscape in areas such as Nebraska and Colorado, which receive less than 20 inches of precipitation annually. In the western United States, where ranching is the primary form of agriculture, semiarid conditions persist in the ranching areas.

PART B

Culture affects cattle distribution around the world in profound ways. The first is the people's dietary preferences. People in European countries and those areas colonized by Europeans like to have beef in their diet. Also, beef is often eaten daily in many sections of the Great Plains region in the United States and the Argentinean plains regions. The abundance of cattle in this region due to the herding of the cattle encourages the dietary preference for beef.

In areas such as India, the cow is considered to be a sacred reincarnation of life. The cow brings forth life through its milk and manure. The dietary preference for beef is almost nonexistent due to Hinduism and the accompanying culture.

Because of this Hindu reverence for cows, the von Thunen market would be skewed in India. The model is a "relation to the principles," assuming a world without the influence of cultural factors. However, the commercial agriculture in von Thunen's model does hold up in the United States with the overlap of cattle production and the Corn Belt. Much of the corn in the United States is used to feed the livestock. Livestock farming in the United States today is based on feedlots. The feedlots breed the cattle, raise the cattle, and then haul the cattle to a processor, which is usually no more than a couple of miles away. The meat is then hauled to distributors to take the beef to market in as little time as possible, using the just-in-time principle.

PART C

The lack of cattle production around the world can be explained by two primary factors: climate and culture.

The first is climate. If the ground is too hilly or too dry, the cattle cannot get enough food and will starve. Areas around the Saharan desert and the Gobi desert are good examples of this. Pastoral nomadism should not involve cattle because they eat too much thus destroying vegetation and causing desertification. This process is occurring in many areas of Saharan Africa.

The second reason for the lack of cattle distribution is a prevalence of other crops. If farmers can make more profit on other items, such as cash crops of fruits and vegetables, they will likely use the crop method of farming. Much of this preference is determined by the selling price of the commodities. In many areas of the less developed world, specifically tropical regions, cash crops are the dominant form of agriculture rather than livestock and other animal farming. Cattle eat a lot and require lots of investment for relatively little return. Often in these less developed countries, cattle are seen as working parts of the farm; they are used to pull a plow or do other labor.

RUBRIC FOR QUESTION 3

Total point value of question 3 = 6

Part A—Two points possible for any of the following answers:

- Cattle in more developed countries are located in the drier areas using livestock ranching.

- Cattle in the less developed countries are located in the drier areas using pastoral nomadism.

- Cattle in the Midwest portion of the United States overlap with the Corn Belt, which supplies feed for the animals.

Part B—Two points possible for any of the following answers:

- Beef is essential in the Western diet, especially in areas of cattle production, such as the Great Plains and Midwest in the United States and Argentina in southern South America.

- Beef is taboo in India because of religious beliefs.

- Beef is not often eaten in subsistence farming locations, because cattle are seen as part of the workforce, not as a food source.

- Von Thunen's rings call for grain to be grown to feed the cattle in livestock-fattening regions.

- In livestock-ranching areas, the climate is relatively dry, requiring irrigation technology and large ranches to support huge cattle operations.

Part C—Two points possible for any of the following answers:

- In India, cattle are sacred in the Hindu religion.

- Some climates, such as deserts, do not provide enough vegetation for cattle to eat.

- Areas that are too cold cannot support cattle because of lack of food production.

- Areas of little development owing to lack of transportation systems, such as Mongolia, do not support cattle production.

Practice Test Two Answer Grid

1. Ⓐ Ⓑ Ⓒ Ⓓ Ⓔ
2. Ⓐ Ⓑ Ⓒ Ⓓ Ⓔ
3. Ⓐ Ⓑ Ⓒ Ⓓ Ⓔ
4. Ⓐ Ⓑ Ⓒ Ⓓ Ⓔ
5. Ⓐ Ⓑ Ⓒ Ⓓ Ⓔ
6. Ⓐ Ⓑ Ⓒ Ⓓ Ⓔ
7. Ⓐ Ⓑ Ⓒ Ⓓ Ⓔ
8. Ⓐ Ⓑ Ⓒ Ⓓ Ⓔ
9. Ⓐ Ⓑ Ⓒ Ⓓ Ⓔ
10. Ⓐ Ⓑ Ⓒ Ⓓ Ⓔ
11. Ⓐ Ⓑ Ⓒ Ⓓ Ⓔ
12. Ⓐ Ⓑ Ⓒ Ⓓ Ⓔ
13. Ⓐ Ⓑ Ⓒ Ⓓ Ⓔ
14. Ⓐ Ⓑ Ⓒ Ⓓ Ⓔ
15. Ⓐ Ⓑ Ⓒ Ⓓ Ⓔ
16. Ⓐ Ⓑ Ⓒ Ⓓ Ⓔ
17. Ⓐ Ⓑ Ⓒ Ⓓ Ⓔ
18. Ⓐ Ⓑ Ⓒ Ⓓ Ⓔ
19. Ⓐ Ⓑ Ⓒ Ⓓ Ⓔ
20. Ⓐ Ⓑ Ⓒ Ⓓ Ⓔ
21. Ⓐ Ⓑ Ⓒ Ⓓ Ⓔ
22. Ⓐ Ⓑ Ⓒ Ⓓ Ⓔ
23. Ⓐ Ⓑ Ⓒ Ⓓ Ⓔ
24. Ⓐ Ⓑ Ⓒ Ⓓ Ⓔ
25. Ⓐ Ⓑ Ⓒ Ⓓ Ⓔ

26. Ⓐ Ⓑ Ⓒ Ⓓ Ⓔ
27. Ⓐ Ⓑ Ⓒ Ⓓ Ⓔ
28. Ⓐ Ⓑ Ⓒ Ⓓ Ⓔ
29. Ⓐ Ⓑ Ⓒ Ⓓ Ⓔ
30. Ⓐ Ⓑ Ⓒ Ⓓ Ⓔ
31. Ⓐ Ⓑ Ⓒ Ⓓ Ⓔ
32. Ⓐ Ⓑ Ⓒ Ⓓ Ⓔ
33. Ⓐ Ⓑ Ⓒ Ⓓ Ⓔ
34. Ⓐ Ⓑ Ⓒ Ⓓ Ⓔ
35. Ⓐ Ⓑ Ⓒ Ⓓ Ⓔ
36. Ⓐ Ⓑ Ⓒ Ⓓ Ⓔ
37. Ⓐ Ⓑ Ⓒ Ⓓ Ⓔ
38. Ⓐ Ⓑ Ⓒ Ⓓ Ⓔ
39. Ⓐ Ⓑ Ⓒ Ⓓ Ⓔ
40. Ⓐ Ⓑ Ⓒ Ⓓ Ⓔ
41. Ⓐ Ⓑ Ⓒ Ⓓ Ⓔ
42. Ⓐ Ⓑ Ⓒ Ⓓ Ⓔ
43. Ⓐ Ⓑ Ⓒ Ⓓ Ⓔ
44. Ⓐ Ⓑ Ⓒ Ⓓ Ⓔ
45. Ⓐ Ⓑ Ⓒ Ⓓ Ⓔ
46. Ⓐ Ⓑ Ⓒ Ⓓ Ⓔ
47. Ⓐ Ⓑ Ⓒ Ⓓ Ⓔ
48. Ⓐ Ⓑ Ⓒ Ⓓ Ⓔ
49. Ⓐ Ⓑ Ⓒ Ⓓ Ⓔ
50. Ⓐ Ⓑ Ⓒ Ⓓ Ⓔ

51. Ⓐ Ⓑ Ⓒ Ⓓ Ⓔ
52. Ⓐ Ⓑ Ⓒ Ⓓ Ⓔ
53. Ⓐ Ⓑ Ⓒ Ⓓ Ⓔ
54. Ⓐ Ⓑ Ⓒ Ⓓ Ⓔ
55. Ⓐ Ⓑ Ⓒ Ⓓ Ⓔ
56. Ⓐ Ⓑ Ⓒ Ⓓ Ⓔ
57. Ⓐ Ⓑ Ⓒ Ⓓ Ⓔ
58. Ⓐ Ⓑ Ⓒ Ⓓ Ⓔ
59. Ⓐ Ⓑ Ⓒ Ⓓ Ⓔ
60. Ⓐ Ⓑ Ⓒ Ⓓ Ⓔ
61. Ⓐ Ⓑ Ⓒ Ⓓ Ⓔ
62. Ⓐ Ⓑ Ⓒ Ⓓ Ⓔ
63. Ⓐ Ⓑ Ⓒ Ⓓ Ⓔ
64. Ⓐ Ⓑ Ⓒ Ⓓ Ⓔ
65. Ⓐ Ⓑ Ⓒ Ⓓ Ⓔ
66. Ⓐ Ⓑ Ⓒ Ⓓ Ⓔ
67. Ⓐ Ⓑ Ⓒ Ⓓ Ⓔ
68. Ⓐ Ⓑ Ⓒ Ⓓ Ⓔ
69. Ⓐ Ⓑ Ⓒ Ⓓ Ⓔ
70. Ⓐ Ⓑ Ⓒ Ⓓ Ⓔ
71. Ⓐ Ⓑ Ⓒ Ⓓ Ⓔ
72. Ⓐ Ⓑ Ⓒ Ⓓ Ⓔ
73. Ⓐ Ⓑ Ⓒ Ⓓ Ⓔ
74. Ⓐ Ⓑ Ⓒ Ⓓ Ⓔ
75. Ⓐ Ⓑ Ⓒ Ⓓ Ⓔ

PRACTICE TEST 2

SECTION I: MULTIPLE-CHOICE QUESTIONS
Time—60 minutes

75 Questions

Directions: Each of the questions or incomplete statements below is followed by five suggested answers. Select the best answer to the question and then fill in the corresponding oval on the answer sheet.

1. Which map has the largest scale?

    (A) World map
    (B) Continent map
    (C) Country map
    (D) Regional map
    (E) City map

2. Areas in the Saharan desert region of Africa possess a low

    (A) carrying capacity.
    (B) birth rate.
    (C) death rate.
    (D) transhumance.
    (E) ecumene.

3. The Third Agricultural Revolution has coincided with the

    (A) Industrial Revolution.
    (B) Second Agricultural Revolution.
    (C) Green Revolution.
    (D) Enlightenment.
    (E) Protestant Reformation.

4. The United Nations developed which statistic as a measure of development in the 1970s to try to quantify economic development?

    (A) Physical Quality of Life Index
    (B) Purchasing power parity
    (C) Human Development Index
    (D) Technology gap
    (E) Dependency theory

5. The city of Istanbul would best be described as what type of city?

    (A) Federal capital
    (B) Gateway city
    (C) Frontier city
    (D) Edge city
    (E) Colonial city

6. In the early 1990s, Germany saw East and West Germany come together to form one country. This is the process of

    (A) regionalism.
    (B) gerrymandering.
    (C) reapportionment.
    (D) reunification.
    (E) supranationalism.

GO ON TO THE NEXT PAGE

7. Iran, Saudi Arabia, and the Vatican City are all examples of

(A) theocracies.

(B) barrios.

(C) ethnic homelands.

(D) monotheistic states.

(E) secularist states.

8. Mandarin Chinese is the most spoken language in the world. What language branch is it part of?

(A) Indo-European

(B) Sino-Tibetan

(C) Afro-Asiatic

(D) Austro-Asiatic

(E) Nilo-Saharan

9. What geographic theory suggests that the landscape and climate dominated human actions and behaviors?

(A) Possibilism

(B) Environmental determinism

(C) Global environmentalism

(D) Human/landscape analysis

(E) Cultural ecology

10. The commonly accepted definition of overpopulation is

(A) only a small amount of resources are available.

(B) too many people for the available resources.

(C) a high population density.

(D) a high total population.

(E) a place that experiences high growth rates.

11. What is the biggest downside to gentrification?

(A) Older neighborhoods are revitalized.

(B) Newer neighborhoods are added farther out, creating urban sprawl.

(C) Property taxes are increased, forcing people out of their homes.

(D) New transportation systems in older neighborhoods mean the razing of older homes.

(E) The crime rate increases substantially.

12. The language of the United Kingdom is broken down phonetically into Scottish, Irish, Cockney, and other

(A) languages.

(B) dialects.

(C) phonics.

(D) isoglosses.

(E) lingua francas.

13. Which two countries alone have close to 2,000 of the 6,000 languages spoken in the world today?

(A) China and India

(B) India and Nigeria

(C) Papua New Guinea and India

(D) Thailand and Papua New Guinea

(E) India and Thailand

14. The sub-Saharan and Saharan regions of Africa are suffering what environmental problem due to the overgrazing of animals?

(A) Climate change

(B) Acid rain

(C) Erosion of topsoil

(D) Carbon dioxide emission increases

(E) Desertification

GO ON TO THE NEXT PAGE

15. The peak land value intersection is usually located _____ for most North American and European cities.

    (A) in the central business district
    (B) on the suburban fringe
    (C) in edge cities
    (D) in the zone of better residences
    (E) adjacent to the main boulevard

16. The Tokyo-Yokohama-Kawasaki region is the world's largest

    (A) example of the sector model.
    (B) megalopolis.
    (C) minor city.
    (D) agglomeration.
    (E) deglomeration.

17. The most common crop grown using the practice of intensive subsistence farming in the world today is

    (A) corn.
    (B) wheat.
    (C) soybeans.
    (D) barley.
    (E) rice.

18. The domino theory was established in the 1970s by the Central Intelligence Agency in the United States. The domino theory was used to explain the spread of

    (A) religious fundamentalism.
    (B) linguistic diversity.
    (C) communism.
    (D) terrorism.
    (E) balkanization.

19. The world's largest frontier is located where?

    (A) Canada's northern territories
    (B) Russia's Siberian region
    (C) China's Manchurian region
    (D) Antarctica
    (E) Arctic regions

20. The Hmong tradition of bringing family members to the United States after some family members have migrated is an example of what?

    (A) Environmental pull factors
    (B) Intervening opportunity
    (C) Intervening obstacle
    (D) Chain migration
    (E) Brain drain

21. Which of the following lists Rostow's development model in order?

    (A) Traditional society, preconditions for takeoff, drive to maturity, takeoff, age of mass consumption
    (B) Traditional society, takeoff, preconditions for takeoff, age of mass consumption, drive to maturity
    (C) Preconditions for takeoff, takeoff, traditional society, drive to maturity, age of mass consumption
    (D) Drive to maturity, traditional society, takeoff, preconditions for takeoff, age of mass consumption
    (E) Traditional society, preconditions for takeoff, takeoff, drive to maturity, age of mass consumption

GO ON TO THE NEXT PAGE

22. Just-in-time delivery refers to what?

  (A) The process of getting food to the market before it spoils

  (B) The process of producing food in time to meet the demand for the food

  (C) The process of getting food to the market as people are willing to buy it

  (D) The process of moving materials to reduce cost

  (E) The process of reducing labor costs to control prices

23. The outsourcing or restructuring of labor from more developed countries to less developed countries to take advantage of cheaper labor costs is described by what term?

  (A) The new international division of labor

  (B) The core/periphery relationship

  (C) Economic factors of development

  (D) Standards of industrial development

  (E) Inadequate debt financing of employment

24. What was the basic industry of Pittsburgh during the early development of the city?

  (A) Steel

  (B) Glass

  (C) Automobiles

  (D) Leather products

  (E) Furniture

25. Which country is most likely to increase its percentage of the world's population the most in the next 20 years?

  (A) China

  (B) India

  (C) Nigeria

  (D) United Kingdom

  (E) United States

26. Which of the following is NOT a centripetal force?

  (A) National anthem

  (B) Homogeneous population

  (C) Monolingual society

  (D) National educational system

  (E) Religious diversity

27. Which supranational organization was established to prevent the Heartland from spreading after World War II?

  (A) European Union

  (B) North American Free Trade Agreement

  (C) Warsaw Pact

  (D) North Atlantic Treaty Organization

  (E) United Nations

28. A barrio is an example of a(n)

  (A) ethnic neighborhood.

  (B) ghetto.

  (C) blockbusted neighborhood.

  (D) redlined area.

  (E) adaptive strategy.

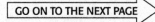
GO ON TO THE NEXT PAGE

29. What is the natural increase rate needed to maintain or grow a population?

   (A) 0.0 to 0.5

   (B) 0.5 to 1.0

   (C) 1.0 to 1.5

   (D) 1.5 to 2.0

   (E) 2.0 and above

30. Stage 4 of the demographic transition is characterized by

   (A) low birth rates.

   (B) low death rates.

   (C) low natural increase rate.

   (D) a stable population.

   (E) all of the above.

31. The movement of Mexicans from farmland to Mexico City is best described by which migration pattern?

   (A) Cyclical movement

   (B) Intercontinental

   (C) Interregional

   (D) Urban to rural

   (E) Transhumance

32. Tertiary economies are focused on what type of economic activity?

   (A) Primary industries

   (B) Secondary industries

   (C) Management industries

   (D) Farming

   (E) Service-based economies

33. Bananas, sugarcane, and coffee are what type of crops?

   (A) Plantation crops

   (B) Market-gardening crops

   (C) Slash-and-burn crops

   (D) Animal products

   (E) Subsistence crops

34. According to the core-periphery model of economic development, all of the following are peripheral areas of Europe EXCEPT

   (A) Portugal.

   (B) Greece.

   (C) southeastern England.

   (D) Ukraine.

   (E) southern Italy.

35. Immanuel Wallerstein developed the world systems analysis. He suggested there is a core and a periphery. Where is the world's core located?

   (A) Southern Hemisphere

   (B) Northern Hemisphere

   (C) Western Hemisphere

   (D) Eastern Hemisphere

   (E) Pacific Rim countries

36. Which of the following is NOT one of the primary industrial regions in the world economy?

   (A) Northeastern United States

   (B) Central Europe

   (C) Russia and Ukraine

   (D) Eastern South America

   (E) East Asia

GO ON TO THE NEXT PAGE

37. What is the process called when people move away from the central business district due to dissatisfaction with the urban policies and lifestyle?

    (A) Blockbusting

    (B) Redlining

    (C) Counterurbanization

    (D) Decentralization

    (E) Gentrification

38. Romanian, Spanish, Italian, French, and Portuguese are all part of the same

    (A) language family.

    (B) dialect.

    (C) toponym.

    (D) trade language.

    (E) isogloss.

39. Which of the following is the best example of a monolingual state?

    (A) Ethiopia

    (B) France

    (C) The Philippines

    (D) Papua New Guinea

    (E) Denmark

40. London, Paris, Buenos Aires, and Mexico City are all

    (A) world cities.

    (B) primate cities.

    (C) edge cities.

    (D) Spanish-speaking cities.

    (E) megalopolises.

41. What is the pattern in Von Thunen's model of land use?

    (A) Market gardening, dairy, livestock fattening, commercial grain, livestock ranching

    (B) Dairy, commercial grain, livestock ranching, livestock fattening, market gardening

    (C) Commercial grain, livestock fattening, livestock ranching, dairy, market gardening

    (D) Livestock fattening, livestock ranching, dairy, market gardening, commercial grain

    (E) Market gardening, livestock farming, livestock ranching, dairy, commercial grain

42. Iceland uses which alternative energy to heat many homes and businesses?

    (A) Nuclear

    (B) Natural gas

    (C) Coal

    (D) Wind

    (E) Geothermal

43. One of the world's largest shatterbelts from the 1950s to the 1970s was

    (A) Central America.

    (B) South America.

    (C) sub-Saharan Africa.

    (D) Southeast Asia.

    (E) Australia.

 GO ON TO THE NEXT PAGE

44. All of the following are nations without a state EXCEPT

    (A) Basques.
    (B) Hmong.
    (C) Zulus.
    (D) Kurds.
    (E) Thais.

45. Romania's relationship to the former Soviet Union could best be described as a

    (A) nation-state.
    (B) shatterbelt.
    (C) satellite state.
    (D) stateless nation.
    (E) unitary government.

46. Which religion allows its adherents to follow other religions simultaneously?

    (A) Buddhism
    (B) Hinduism
    (C) Islam
    (D) Judaism
    (E) Christianity

47. What Islamic city has best captured the idea of globalism with modern skyscrapers and trade advantages?

    (A) Istanbul
    (B) Cairo
    (C) Algiers
    (D) Tripoli
    (E) Dubai

48. Which land use system came from the British and is still used today in many parts of New England?

    (A) Metes and bounds
    (B) Long lots
    (C) Township and range
    (D) Agricultural ordinance system
    (E) Urbanization

49. Cities in the western United States have more of what characteristic as compared to cities in the eastern United States?

    (A) Mass transportation
    (B) Densely populated core areas
    (C) Urban blight
    (D) Population in the suburbs
    (E) Linguistic diversity

50. Which type of home would best represent traditional architecture?

    (A) Tudor style
    (B) Queen Anne style
    (C) Log home
    (D) Victorian
    (E) Postmodern

51. Thomas Malthus was correct about population increase but did not calculate what correctly?

    (A) Death rates
    (B) Birth rates
    (C) Population control policies
    (D) Agricultural productivity
    (E) Environmental disasters

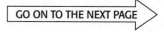
GO ON TO THE NEXT PAGE

52. The Wheat Belt in the United States corresponds with what region?

    (A) Pacific Northwest
    (B) Southeast
    (C) Midwest
    (D) Desert Southwest
    (E) Great Plains

53. Which area of the United States continues to gain the most in population relative to other regions?

    (A) New England
    (B) Southeast
    (C) Midwest
    (D) Mid-Atlantic states
    (E) Pacific Northwest

54. The central place theory posits which geographic principles are essential for the economic success of commercial establishments?

    (A) Threshold and range
    (B) Market area and economic structure
    (C) Threshold and globalization
    (D) Employment structure and range
    (E) Range and globalization

55. According to Carl Sauer, rice was probably first domesticated in which region?

    (A) Middle East
    (B) Northeastern Africa
    (C) Southeast Asia
    (D) Central America
    (E) Northwestern South America

56. A polar projection showing true distance in one direction is an example of which type of map?

    (A) Molleweide
    (B) Mercator
    (C) Goodes-Homsoline
    (D) Azimuthal
    (E) Robinson

57. What demographic equation is used to determine natural increase?

    (A) Births plus deaths minus immigration
    (B) Births plus deaths plus immigration
    (C) Births plus deaths minus emigration
    (D) Births plus deaths plus emigration
    (E) Births minus deaths

58. Which process has allowed much of Asia's population to be fed?

    (A) Plantation agriculture
    (B) Double cropping
    (C) Soil tilling
    (D) Desertification
    (E) Terraced irrigation

59. Buddhism's hearth was

    (A) China.
    (B) Japan.
    (C) India.
    (D) Israel.
    (E) Saudi Arabia.

GO ON TO THE NEXT PAGE

60. Olives, dates, and grapes are agricultural products practiced in what type of farming?

    (A) Plantation agriculture
    (B) Mediterranean agriculture
    (C) Subsistence agriculture
    (D) Pastoral nomadism
    (E) Slash-and-burn agriculture

61. What industry was the first to pay industrial workers high enough wages that they could afford the products that they were producing?

    (A) Steel
    (B) Airplanes
    (C) Automobiles
    (D) Food processing
    (E) Ammunition

62. Establishing settlements along the coast to use in trade best resembles which empire theme of colonization?

    (A) Sea empire
    (B) Settler empire
    (C) Colonial empire
    (D) Land empire
    (E) Postcolonialism

63. The largest religion in the world in terms of total numbers professing to follow the religion is

    (A) Christianity.
    (B) Islam.
    (C) Judaism.
    (D) Buddhism.
    (E) Hinduism.

64. Shopping malls, planned communities, and, in many cases, a popular landscape are representative of what geographic factor?

    (A) Suburbs
    (B) Office parks
    (C) Industrial parks
    (D) Positive situation factors
    (E) Tenements

65. Dividing a country's population by its total land area gives a geographer what statistic?

    (A) Physiologic density
    (B) Arithmetic density
    (C) Spatial density
    (D) Clustered density
    (E) Agglomerated density

66. The concept of the South means many things to many people, and many people draw the South using different boundaries. This is an example of a(n)

    (A) formal region.
    (B) functional region.
    (C) industrial region.
    (D) agricultural region.
    (E) vernacular/perceptual region.

GO ON TO THE NEXT PAGE

67. The following diagram best exhibits what model of urbanization?

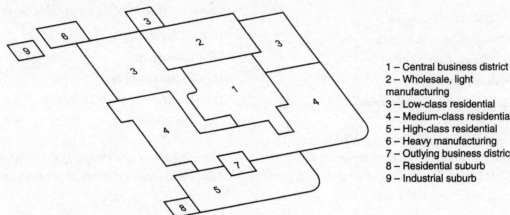

1 – Central business district
2 – Wholesale, light manufacturing
3 – Low-class residential
4 – Medium-class residential
5 – High-class residential
6 – Heavy manufacturing
7 – Outlying business district
8 – Residential suburb
9 – Industrial suburb

(A) Sector model

(B) Concentric zone model

(C) Central place theory

(D) Multiple nuclei model

(E) Peripheral model

68. The near secession of Québec from Canada in 1995 was based on what cultural factor?

(A) Religion

(B) Language

(C) Nationality

(D) Ethnicity

(E) Race

69. Which country possesses over 25 percent of the world's oil reserves and is a powerful member of OPEC?

(A) Iraq

(B) Iran

(C) Saudi Arabia

(D) United Arab Emirates

(E) Oman

70. The one-child policy in China has been relatively successful in controlling birth rates, natural increase rates, and doubling time. This is an example of what means to control population growth?

(A) Increasing death rates

(B) Decreasing birth rates

(C) Increasing birth rates

(D) Decreasing death rates

(E) Zero population growth

GO ON TO THE NEXT PAGE

71. The belief that one ethnic group is superior to others is an example of

    (A) genocide.

    (B) ethnocentrism.

    (C) ethnic conflicts.

    (D) ethnic homeland.

    (E) ethnic landscapes.

72. Which of the following areas is an exclave?

    (A) Hawaii, United States

    (B) Singapore

    (C) Kaliningrad, Russia

    (D) South Africa

    (E) Italy

73. Which is the first stage in Rostow's model of economic development?

    (A) The traditional society

    (B) The preconditions for takeoff

    (C) The takeoff

    (D) The age of mass consumption

    (E) The drive to maturity

74. Which crop is the most important grain for intensive subsistence farmers?

    (A) Corn

    (B) Wheat

    (C) Sorghum

    (D) Rice

    (E) Manioc

75. Pork production and hog raising are almost nonexistent in the Islamic world. What best explains this lack of pork production?

    (A) Ethnic taboos do not allow Muslims to eat pork.

    (B) Religious guidelines do not allow Muslims to eat pork.

    (C) The pork is not a customary food preference in the Islamic diet.

    (D) Muslim's dietary preferences tend more toward cattle production.

    (E) The Islamic religion exalts vegans as having religious purity.

IF YOU FINISH BEFORE TIME IS CALLED, YOU MAY CHECK YOUR WORK ON THIS SECTION ONLY. DO NOT TURN TO ANY OTHER SECTION IN THE TEST.

STOP

SECTION II: FREE-RESPONSE QUESTIONS
Time: 75 minutes

Directions: You have 75 minutes to answer ALL THREE of the following questions. While a formal essay is not required, it is not enough to answer a question by merely listing facts. Your answer should be based upon your critical analysis of the question posed.

1. Immanuel Wallerstein proposed the world systems analysis in 1987.

    (A) Define and briefly describe the world systems analysis.

    (B) Explain how the world systems analysis fits into the demographic transition of a country's development.

    (C) Describe the employment sectors of the economies in the world systems analysis using the demographic transition model.

2. Explain how the process of regionalism is constantly in opposition to globalism.

    (A) Define regionalism and globalism.

    (B) Give one example of regionalism and one example of globalism.

    (C) Explain the conflict between regionalism and globalism.

3. The European and North American populations, on the whole, are getting older. Asia, Latin America, and Africa's populations are getting younger. Explain the socioeconomic and demographic impacts of these population trends.

    (A) Explain the population decrease in the more developed world.

    (B) Explain the population increase in the less developed world.

    (C) Describe the socioeconomic and demographic impacts of this change on the population structure within each region.

GO ON TO THE NEXT PAGE ⟩

GO ON TO THE NEXT PAGE

_____

_____

_____

_____

_____

_____

_____

_____

_____

_____

_____

_____

_____

_____

_____

_____

_____

_____

_____

_____

GO ON TO THE NEXT PAGE ▷

GO ON TO THE NEXT PAGE

_____

_____

_____

_____

_____

_____

_____

_____

_____

_____

_____

_____

_____

_____

_____

_____

_____

_____

_____

_____

_____

_____

GO ON TO THE NEXT PAGE ▷

_____

_____

_____

_____

_____

_____

_____

_____

_____

_____

_____

_____

_____

_____

_____

_____

_____

_____

_____

_____

Practice Test 2 Answer Key

1. E	20. D	39. E	58. B
2. A	21. E	40. B	59. C
3. C	22. B	41. A	60. B
4. C	23. A	42. E	61. C
5. B	24. A	43. D	62. A
6. D	25. C	44. E	63. A
7. A	26. E	45. C	64. A
8. B	27. D	46. A	65. B
9. B	28. A	47. E	66. E
10. B	29. E	48. A	67. D
11. C	30. E	49. D	68. B
12. B	31. C	50. C	69. C
13. C	32. E	51. D	70. B
14. E	33. A	52. E	71. B
15. A	34. C	53. B	72. C
16. B	35. B	54. A	73. A
17. E	36. D	55. C	74. D
18. C	37. C	56. D	75. B
19. D	38. A	57. E	

PRACTICE TEST 2: ASSESS YOUR STRENGTHS

Use the following tables to determine which topics (chapters) you need to review most. If you need help with your essays, be sure to review Free-Response Essay Question Strategies.

Chapter and Topic	Question
Chapter 3: Geography: Its Nature and Perspectives	1, 56, 66
Chapter 4: Population	2, 10, 20, 25, 29, 30, 31, 51, 53, 57, 65, 70
Chapter 5: Cultural Patterns and Processes	8, 9, 12, 13, 38, 39, 46, 50, 59, 63, 68
Chapter 6: Political Organization of Space	6, 7, 18, 19, 26, 27, 43, 44, 45, 62, 71, 72
Chapter 7: Agriculture, Food Production, and Rural Land Use	3, 14, 17, 33, 36, 41, 48, 52, 55, 58, 60, 74, 75
Chapter 8: Industrialization and Economic Development	4, 21, 22, 23, 24, 32, 34, 35, 42, 61, 69, 73
Chapter 9: Cities and Urban Land Use	5, 11, 15, 16, 28, 37, 40, 47, 49, 54, 64, 67

Chapter and Topic	Number of Questions on Test	Number Correct
Chapter 3: Geography: Its Nature and Perspectives	3	
Chapter 4: Population	12	
Chapter 5: Cultural Patterns and Processes	11	
Chapter 6: Political Organization of Space	12	
Chapter 7: Agriculture, Food Production, and Rural Land Use	13	
Chapter 8: Industrialization and Economic Development	12	
Chapter 9: Cities and Urban Land Use	12	

ANSWERS AND EXPLANATIONS

SECTION I: MULTIPLE-CHOICE QUESTIONS

1. E

The best way to think of scale is to think of the size of your house on a map. The larger your house would appear on the map, the larger the scale of the map. Therefore, a global map would have the smallest scale. A map with the scale of 1:1 would have the largest scale possible and a life-size quality. A map of your desk with a 1:1 scale would be the size of your desk.

2. A

Areas in the Saharan desert have a low carrying capacity because the environment cannot support large populations owing to a lack of precipitation. People need food, water, and shelter to survive. When any one of these is not present on the landscape, the carrying capacity diminishes greatly, resulting in an area that is sparsely populated. Diminished carrying capacity is in large part due to either terrain or climate. Areas of the Saharan region in Africa possess a high birth rate and a high death rate as well, in part due to the conditions of the environment. An ecumene is an area where people live.

3. C

The Third Agricultural Revolution has also been called the Green Revolution. The Third Agricultural Revolution is characterized by genetic engineering of seed agriculture to produce heartier crops that are more resistant to pests and disease. The result has been a dramatic increase in the worldwide production of crops such as rice. The International Rice Institute in the Philippines developed a strain of rice that can grow in drier conditions than the rice paddies that are prevalent in many areas of Southeast Asia. The Third Agricultural Revolution has also coincided with the use of pesticides and fertilizers to increase the yields of agricultural commodities. This has meant much more availability of farm products, especially in the less developed world.

4. C

The problem that geographers and economists had for many years was how to quantify economic development. The United Nations established the Human Development Index in the 1970s to try to quantify the economic development of countries. The Human Development Index is a good measure because it looks at a variety of different demographic as well as economic indicators of development. The factors that make up the Human Development Index are the country's literacy rate, gross domestic product per capita, level of education of its citizens, and people's life expectancy. This is different from other measures of the economic development of countries, such as the Physical Quality of Life Index, because it uses different criteria to measure the outcomes of development.

5. B

Istanbul is one of the world's great cities. It has a population approaching 10 million and is considered the gateway to both Europe and Asia. Istanbul, formerly called Constantinople, has always been one of the largest cities in the Middle East region. It is separated from the European continent in terms of its Islamic culture, yet much of the city has European roots in terms of its architecture. Istanbul is the only city in the world that is located on two continents, Asia and Europe. Divided by the Bosporus Strait, the city serves as a link between the two continents. It is not located in a frontier region, such as the Amazonian jungle; therefore, it cannot be classified as a frontier city. Edge cities are cities that develop on the periphery of large urban centers. Colonial cities were dominated by colonial powers. Istanbul is truly one of the great cities of the world because of its situation between the two continents. Istanbul has a growth rate of over 3.5 percent. Rural-to-urban migration is making Istanbul one of the megacities of the world and one of the largest Islamic cities in the world.

6. D

When East and West Germany united in the early 1990s, the event was called the reunification of Germany. The economic differences between the two countries were profound. West Germany, which was capitalist, was modern and updated in terms of its technology base, industrial base, and infrastructure. East Germany, under the Warsaw Pact and controlled in large part by the former Soviet Union, was crumbling under the economic weight of communism. The result on the landscape was a decaying infrastructure and an economy in shambles. Germany has since regained its economic status and is considered by many to be the main economic power in terms of industrialization in Europe.

7. A

Theocracies are countries where religious rulers dominate the political rule of the country. In all of the examples, Iran, Saudi Arabia, and the Vatican City, the rulers of the state are also religious leaders in their areas. The Pope is not only the ruler of the Vatican City, but also the central figure in the Roman Catholic Church. Secularist states have no religion in their foundational principles, and the result is a separation of church and state.

8. B

The most-used language family in the world is Indo-European. However, the most spoken language in the world is Mandarin Chinese, which belongs to the Sino-Tibetan language family. The Sino-Tibetan language family is the second largest in the world, based on the number of speakers of the languages in the family. Other languages in the Sino-Tibetan language family include Cantonese, Thai, Burmese, and Hakka. These languages pale in comparison to Mandarin Chinese in terms of number of speakers. More than 800 million people speak Mandarin Chinese.

9. B

For the past several decades, geographers have accused environmental determinism of being racist in its origins. Environmental determinism suggests that the environment determines in large part the success of a particular race of people. Geographers, during the early years of the 1900s, claimed that location determined a people's motivation to succeed. According to this theory, races located in more temperate regions were more successful, while races in tropical regions were not as successful, being prone to laziness because the temperature was too hot. This theory has been counteracted by the possiblist approach to geography, which suggests that humans can dominate their environment and are not fated to success or failure depending upon their latitude and longitude.

10. B

The most commonly accepted definition of overpopulation is that there are too many people in a particular area for the available resources. On a small scale there are areas in the world that are overpopulated because the population is outstripping the available resources leading to a decline in the quality of life and possible famine.

11. C

Many would consider gentrification a negative; it forces those people who have lived in an area for an extended period of time out of their homes, because they can no longer afford to live in the area because of high property taxes. Gentrification involves wealthy people moving into a neighborhood and revitalizing it. The result is an aesthetically pleasing landscape of remodeled homes, which bring added revenue through higher property taxes, into cities that desperately need it. Many of the people who are forced out of their homes are either elderly and/or minorities and simply cannot afford the new tax burden put upon them. The result is that when they move out, the home is bought by a wealthy individual who remodels, and the process is self-perpetuating.

12. B

Dialects are varieties in language phonics, speed, and vocabulary. Some of the dialects in the United States include the Southern accent, which can be broken down further into the Carolina accent, the Texas accent, and numerous others. The northeastern portion of the United States around Boston has a specific dialect that makes it unique. In the United Kingdom, Scottish, Cockney, and Irish are just three of the dialects of English. Dialects can be difficult to understand, even for people speaking the same language. In the case of Chinese, many Mandarin Chinese speakers cannot understand the Shanghai dialect. Many people from the United States cannot understand the specific vocabulary associated with the British dialects.

13. C

The two countries with the greatest language diversity in the world are India and Papua New Guinea. Papua New Guinea is said to have over 1,000 languages. Many of these languages are only spoken by a few hundred people in the remote villages of the small island. Many of these languages will die out and be overtaken by the megalanguages that are becoming trade languages around the world. India has over 700 languages spoken within its borders. The attempt to unify a country with that many languages is a difficult task. A common language is one of the easiest ways to link a nation together.

14. E

Desertification is caused by livestock overgrazing in an area that is prone to drought and borders a desert region. In many areas of sub-Saharan Africa, the vegetation is being eaten down to the roots by goats, sheep, and camels belonging to nomadic herders. The loss of root systems prevents the vegetation from keeping the desert at bay, and the result is the erosion of topsoil and an ever-increasing area of desert-like conditions.

15. A

The peak land value intersection is usually located in the central business district at the 100 percent corner. This is the corner that has the most pedestrian and vehicular traffic in a metropolitan area. This is directly related to the bid-rent curve, where the value of land gradually decreases from the central business district to the edge of the metro area.

16. B

The Tokyo-Yokohama-Kawasaki region is the world's largest megalopolis. Tokyo by almost all measures is the world's largest city. Including its metropolitan area and suburbs, some geographers estimate that Tokyo has more than 35 million people. The next largest metropolitan area is Mexico City. Megalopolises are areas where the growth of metropolitan areas has expanded so much that they have merged to form one large metropolitan area.

17. E

The most common crop that intensive subsistence farming produces today is rice. Much of the rice crops in Southeast Asia are still planted manually and harvested through backbreaking labor. Other crops are planted and harvested through intensive subsistence agricultural practices, but rice is the largest of the crops and produces the most output.

18. C

The domino theory was established by the Central Intelligence Agency of the United States to explain the spread of communism. Since the end of World War II, until the beginning of the 1990s, one of the main missions of United States' foreign policy was to thwart the aggression of communists around the world. This meant fighting wars in Korea, Vietnam, Cuba, Central Asia, and Central America. The domino theory suggested that when one country fell, many other countries around the fallen country would experience political instability as well, resulting in more Soviet-backed communism.

19. D

The world's largest frontier area is located in Antarctica. The other choices, including Russia's Siberia region, Canada's northern territories, and China's Manchurian region, all belong under the sovereign control of those particular states. The North Pole region has no land and therefore cannot be claimed by any country. The International Law of the Sea applies to the frozen ocean at the North Pole.

20. D

The Hmong migration pattern of bringing family members to the United States is a good example of a chain migration into a country. First, some family members are usually sponsored and brought over, either on a work permit or via political asylum. These family members then send money to their families back in their homeland to save for the expensive migration. This process of chain migration may take decades to complete, and it usually means the separation of family members for that time. Environmental pull factors are not a factor in chain migration. An intervening opportunity is when positive amenities induce a person to stay in an area that is on the way to where he or she was originally migrating. An intervening obstacle is a negative factor that forces a person to halt migration. Brain drain is the emigration of a country's most educated citizens to areas where they can earn more income.

21. E

Rostowe's development model was created in the 1950s to help explain how a country can economically develop using the experience of many western societies. The model explains how an agriculturally based economy can move through logical stages of growth to become a country that produces and consumes a variety of goods.

22. B

The just-in-time principle refers to getting product to the market just as the demand for the product occurs. By using the just-in-time principle, stock and inventory are reduced. In terms of food, it helps to reduce some of the spoilage of crops, so choice (B) is a better answer than choice (A) because it broadens the horizons of the potential products. The just-in-time principle does not relate solely to food but also to many other products, including automobiles, brooms, and most other manufactured goods.

23. A

The new international division of labor means that jobs are outsourced from more developed countries, such as the United States and Europe, to less developed countries. This goes against the traditional division of labor, which suggests that labor unions dictate the wages of the workers, usually at a high level. The new international division of labor began in the 1960s as more transnational corporations were outsourcing their labor to less developed countries, which were competing to offer the lowest labor costs. Although the wages for these jobs were low by international standards, they were high in these countries. Outsourcing led to the rise of maquiladoras in Mexico and manufacturing centers around the world. They produced goods at very low cost to keep prices down for American and European consumers. The result has been a loss of American manufacturing jobs to less developed countries but increased purchasing power for the American consumer.

24. A

The basic industry is the largest industry in a given urban area that employs the most people. In Pittsburgh, the basic industry was steel. Pittsburgh possessed the perfect situation for the production of steel. Iron ore could be shipped via the Great Lakes to the port in Erie, Pennsylvania, and than hauled by railroad to manufacturing centers in Pittsburgh. The high-quality anthracite coal that was used in the blast furnaces was hauled up from West Virginia, near Pittsburgh in the Appalachian region. The Ohio River provided a route to ship the steel to the western states and the eastern urban centers, which were using steel to build the infrastructure of the United States. Steel wealth brought Pittsburgh fame and fortune, as well as numerous jobs for its citizens. The downside was the environmental impact of the air pollution that the steel factories spit out.

25. C

Nigeria's high birth rates and lack of family planning measures mean a large number of children are born. Nigeria is one of the top 15 countries in the world in terms of its total population. Nigeria also has an extremely high growth rate and doubling time. These two statistics together put Nigeria on a collision course with overpopulation within the next several decades. Nigeria will need either to increase its crop yields or import crops from other areas to feed its ever-growing population.

26. E

Centripetal forces unite a country. Traditional thinking is that ethnic, religious, and linguistic diversity make it more difficult to politically unite a country.

27. D

The North Atlantic Treaty Organization (NATO) was established soon after World War II to halt the spread of communism in Eastern Europe. The counterpart to NATO was the Warsaw Pact, which was the alliance of the Soviet-backed Eastern European countries. The rimland theory was a response to the heartland theory, which suggests that whoever controlled the land empire of Eastern Europe, including the Ukraine region, would and could control the world. The industrial and agricultural output in that region would be sufficient to support a large army and millions of people. The rimland theory, on the other hand, suggests that the land empire was not the greatest asset to possess; instead, controlling the oceans meant the heartland could be kept in check. Because the heartland was so large, many countries would have to band together in alliances for this to occur. In Europe, the alliance was NATO. In Central Asia, it was CENTO (Central Treaty Organization). In Southeast Asia, it was SEATO (Southeast Asian Treaty Organization). These all were set up to prevent the spread of communism during the Cold War era from the 1950s to the early 1990s.

28. A

A barrio is an example of an ethnic neighborhood. A barrio is a Latino neighborhood containing ethnic restaurants, shops, and other commercial establishments catering to Spanish-speaking residents of the neighborhood. Supermarkets carry goods catering to the Latino diet. Barrios can be blockbusted areas, but blockbusting is illegal.

29. E

The natural increase rate is the number of children needed to sustain a population given its death rate. A rate of 2.1 or higher is needed to increase the population. A rate of 2.0 will only maintain the population of a community or nation, by replacing the parents with their children when they die. In more developed countries, natural increase rates are dropping, and in many countries in Eastern Europe, the natural increase rate is below 2.0, resulting in population decrease.

30. E

In stage 4 of the demographic transition, both birth and death rates are low and not very far apart statistically. Therefore, the natural increase rate is low and the population is stable.

31. C

Rural-to-urban migration within a country is an example of an interregional migration pattern. When people move across continents, this activity is known as intercontinental migration. When citizens move within the same country, this activity is known as interregional migration. The migration that occurs in the United States from the Rust Belt to the Sunbelt is an example of an interregional migration pattern. The push and pull factors are irrelevant in describing the types of migration. What is more important is the starting and ending points of the migration.

32. E

Service-based economies are known as tertiary economies. Primary industries use the land to produce something. Farming and forestry are examples of primary industries. Secondary industries use the raw materials from primary industries to manufacture some type of product (e.g., a rocking chair is made from the wood from the timber industry, which sold it to the rocking chair company). Tertiary industries sell the rocking chair to the customer. In more developed countries, more people are employed in the tertiary industries as compared to people in less developed countries, who are largely employed in the primary and secondary industries.

33. A

Bananas, coffee, and sugarcane are all plantation crops. Plantations are large farms in tropical areas that grow one crop, usually for resale in a more developed country. Transnational corporations with headquarters in the more developed country may own the plantation. Plantation crops can be sold in bulk for high profit margins, because much plantation labor is cheap.

34. C

The economic core of Europe is in southeastern England/northern France/Belgium/Netherlands/Luxembourg/western Germany/Switzerland/northern Italy. The farther one gets from this core, the less wealth is present. Portugal, Greece, Ukraine, and southern Italy are geographically far from the core. Therefore they are located in the periphery with respect to geography and economic development.

35. B

Wallenstein's theory suggests that the core of the world is located in the Northern Hemisphere. The more developed countries of the world are located in the Northern Hemisphere, while the less developed countries are located in the Southern Hemisphere, with the exception of Australia. The core extends around the globe, including the United States; Europe, including Russia, and East Asia. The periphery, south of the core, depends on the core for foreign investment. The more developed countries depend upon the less developed countries for their cheap labor, according to the new international division of labor.

36. D

The only answer that is not one of the primary industrial areas of the world is eastern South America. The others, including the northeastern section of North America, Central and Western Europe, Russia and the Ukraine region, and East Asia are all top world manufacturing centers with primary industrial centers of the past located there.

37. C

Many people simply do not like living in the urban environment. The crime, noise pollution, high property taxes, and other problems associated with urban areas have caused many people to move to rural areas to escape these problems. This process is called counterurbanization. In other cases, many people like moving into the city, because they like the amenities that it offers. This centralization principle acts against counterurbanization.

38. A

Romanian, Italian, French, Portuguese, and Spanish are all have their origins within the Latin language, putting them in the same language family. Many of the words are similar across these languages due to their common ancestry. Dialects are different forms of the same language. Toponyms are simply place names. Trade languages are established by traders to communicate more effectively with each other and minimize having to learn several languages. Isoglosses are the boundary definitions for different languages spoken on the landscape.

39. E

Denmark is a monolingual state. This is one of the criteria that assists geographers in defining a nation-state. Language and religion are two of the biggest indicators of culture. When almost the entire population of a country speaks the same language, it is known as a monolingual country. The other countries listed have numerous languages spoken within their borders. Papua New Guinea has over 1,000 languages and is a good example of a multilingual country.

40. B

London, Paris, Mexico City, and Buenos Aires are examples of primate cities. Each of these cities has more than double the population of any other city within its country and, as a result, is a political, economic, and cultural capital on the landscape of the country.

41. A

Von Thunen's agricultural land use model is based on the cost of transportation to market, which is located in the center of concentric rings. Market gardening products must be grown closer to the market, because their cost to transport is greater based on their bulk and weight. The heavier the product, the more it costs to transport. Products that must be refrigerated throughout transportation, such as dairy, have a higher cost of transportation. Livestock fattening, followed by commercial grain and livestock ranching, round out the stages in von Thunen's model. Livestock fattening comes before livestock ranching, because more space is needed for livestock ranching and land is more expensive closer to the market or the urban center.

42. E

Iceland, because of its geographic location, uses geothermic power to heat many of its homes during the long, cold winter months. Iceland is located along a continental shelf, where the magma in the Earth's interior is closer to the surface of the Earth. Because of this geographic feature, Iceland can harvest some of the Earth's interior heat for a fraction of the cost of other locations, which would have to

drill down miles farther to receive the same energy. The heat or steam is captured and used to spin a turbine to create electricity as well. This geothermic energy system works well but is only feasible in certain locations.

43. D

A shatterbelt is an area that is located between two superpowers, which often fight for control over it. From the 1950s to the 1970s, Southeast Asia was where Western forces, led by the United States, fought against communist forces. In Southeast Asia, China played a large role in funding the communist movement in Vietnam. The Vietnam War, in large part, was a battle for the control of the shatterbelt known as Southeast Asia. Vietnam was the largest country in Southeast Asia, and control over it was important enough for both sides, communists and capitalists, to fight for almost a decade.

44. E

All of the answer choices are nations without a state except for Thai. The Thai nation has the country of Thailand belonging to it. The other nations live in other areas of the world and are often fighting for the independence of their nations within the context of another state. The Basques are a small nation located in northern Spain and southern France. The Basques speak their own language. The Hmong are a nation located in Southeast Asia, primarily in Laos, and many seek to create their own homeland in that particular region. The Zulu are fighting for independence in South Africa, while the Kurds are fighting for their own independence within northern Iran and Iraq, as well as eastern Turkey. Each of these groups has mounted a nationalist movement to fight for independence against other groups.

45. C

A satellite state receives financial help from a superpower and, in return, loses some of its autonomy in decision making. Although it still possesses sovereignty, it is in essence under the control of the superpower. For example, Romania during the Cold War was under the auspices of the Soviet Union, which initiated a communist economic system. Many of the states located within the Warsaw Pact during World War II became satellite states of the former Soviet Union.

46. A

Buddhism is a polytheistic religion and allows its adherents to follow different religions at the same time. A person can be a Buddhist and an animist or practice Buddhism and follow the principles of Shintoism. Buddhism encourages the elimination of earthly desires, and practitioners try to gain enlightenment through meditation.

47. E

Dubai has constructed the tallest building in the world. Dubai is trying to become the primary Islamic city with its oil wealth as well as its strategic location in the Persian Gulf. Dubai has also built a world-class airport, which is often a stopping point for travelers on their way to other cities in the Middle East. Dubai has increased its prominence on the world scene with its money and political clout. Although other Middle Eastern cities, such as Istanbul and Cairo, two of the world's largest cities, may have larger populations, they do not have the wealth of Dubai. Also, Algiers and Tripoli are important cities in northern Africa but lack the wealth of Dubai. Dubai has many immigrants from Africa as well as India doing the primary and

secondary jobs, while citizens of the United Arab Emirates do banking and other tertiary activities.

48. A

The metes and bounds system of land use came from Britain and has been used for over a thousand years in that island region. The metes and bounds system uses physical features on the surface of the Earth, such as trees and lakes, to define boundaries of property. The long lots system came from the French, whereas the township and range system began from necessity due to the vast spaces of the Midwest and Great Plains regions of the United States.

49. D

Western U.S. urban areas possess a lot of space. Because these cities have a lot of space, the majority of their population is located in the suburbs, whereas in cities in the eastern United States, most people live within the primary urban areas. Western cities are more spread out, making public transportation difficult due to the increased cost of establishing the light rail systems or subways.

50. C

Traditional architecture is the type of structures that were located in an area prior to European settlement or the mass settlement that occurred in many areas of the United States during the 1800s. Therefore, the log cabin home, built of readily available wood, is an example of traditional architecture.

51. D

Thomas Malthus coined the term *overpopulation*. Malthus believed that population was growing faster than agricultural productivity and mass starvation would result. Malthus made his predictions just as the Second Agricultural Revolution was beginning in Europe. He did not anticipate the agricultural productivity that would result from the increased mechanization of farming and the increased efficiency of transportation methods in getting agricultural products to market. Because of this, Malthus's ideas were correct, but he was about 150 years too early. Exponential population growth started in the early 1900s. During this period and shortly after, the Third Agricultural Revolution occurred, increasing farm yields through fertilization and genetic engineering.

52. E

The Wheat Belt in the United States is an extension of the Great Plains region. The Great Plains region is usually a relatively dry area suitable for the production of wheat, which traditionally does not require a lot of moisture for success. In fact, in many cases, the eastern sections of the United States would be too wet for growing wheat. With the advent of the Third Agricultural Revolution, however, wheat has been genetically engineered to grow in wetter areas than before. One of the largest cash crops in Tennessee today is wheat. Wheat is still the predominate crop in the Great Plains and many of the mountain states in the western United States. Wheat can be shipped easily by train or truck to all areas of the United States without spoiling, unless the crop has too much moisture in it.

53. B

The southeast (especially Virginia, North Carolina, South Carolina, Georgia, and Florida) has been gaining population for the past few decades relative to other regions of the country because of a variety of push and pull factors. The southeast exerts an economic and environmental pull, whereas the

northeast and Midwest are losing jobs and have cold winters, both push factors. Because the southeast is closer to these areas than the West Coast they receive more interregional migrants from the heavily populated Midwest and northeast.

54. A

Walter Christaller established the central place theory in the 1930s. The central place theory suggests that all urban areas have hinterlands or market areas that are serviced by the urban area's population base. The larger the population base, the larger the market area. Commercial establishments as well as manufacturing centers settle in these urban areas to take advantage of the labor and markets provided by larger cities. All commercial establishments have a range, which is the maximum distance that people are willing to travel to purchase their products. They must also know their threshold, which is the minimum number of customers they need to buy their products. Higher-end products usually need larger thresholds, which can be accomplished by increasing the range. This is why sports arenas have such large ranges. Attending a game is not a daily activity. Everyday items, however, such as soft drinks, water, and tissue, have a low range and threshold, because people are not willing to travel long distances to partake in services or purchase products that are used on a daily basis.

55. C

Carl Sauer, whom many believe to be the preeminent cultural geographer, came up with the agricultural hearths for both seed agriculture and vegetative planting agriculture. Sauer believed, based on his research, that rice was probably first domesticated in the Southeast Asian region. One reason is the area's favorable climate—hot and humid year-round—for growing rice. Rice has since become the dominant crop in much of Asia. The climate allows for the double-cropping of rice in many locations. Double-cropping is the harvesting of two crops per calendar year. In some cases, triple-cropping is possible due to the climate and irrigation techniques.

56. D

A polar map showing true distance in one direction is an azimuthal map projection taken from one of the poles. Usually, azimuthal projections are taken from the poles and are shown using either the North or the South Pole. However, during World War II, azimuthal maps were used to indicate targets for bombing raids by both Axis and Allied forces. Each direction on the map is the same direction. This means that an azimuthal projection from the North Pole shows each and all directions as being south. If one were to move left on the map, one would still be moving south. Conversely, if one moved right on the map, one would still be moving to the south. This creates an enormous amount of distortion on the opposite side of the globe. In fact, the opposite pole is shown circling the globe because of distortion.

57. E

The demographic equation relating to natural increase is simply births minus deaths. Immigration and emigration have nothing to do with natural increase. Immigration and emigration simply involve people moving on the surface of the Earth, not the creation or elimination of people on the Earth.

58. B

Double-cropping means growing more than one crop in a calendar year on the same plot of land. In some areas, triple-cropping can occur with certain agricultural commodities. Rice and other crops can be grown and then harvested within a six-month period. Double-cropping usually involves intensive subsistence agriculture and a climate type that is conducive to the growing of crops. The climate must be wet enough and warm enough year-round for these crops to flourish. In the United States, the growing season is relatively short in the northern regions of the country. Planting is usually done in April or May, and harvesting takes place in either September or October. This short season allows for only one crop to be grown throughout the yearly cycle.

59. C

Buddhism began in northern India. Siddhartha Gautama was a prince who lived in his palace in the north of the country. When he was a teenager, he wanted to know what was outside the palace gates. What he saw was mass poverty and starvation. Thus began his philosophy that life is eternal suffering and that eliminating earthly desires through meditation can help one reach enlightenment. Buddhism has since diffused into Eastern Asia, where it is still practiced today in China as well as most of Southeast Asia. Most of India practices Hinduism, the other major Eastern religion.

60. B

The Mediterranean climate and agriculture are conducive to growing such agricultural products as nuts, olives, dates, and grapes. The climate is characterized by warm, dry summers and cool, moist winters. This is the perfect climate for growing grapes for the production of wine. This Mediterranean climate type and these agricultural practices are also found in the northern sections of Africa. Plantation agriculture generally involves growing tropical fruits for resale in more developed countries.

61. C

The first industry to use the assembly line method was Henry Ford's automobile industry. His theory was to have individual workers specialize in a part of the production process. Prior to the Ford model of industrialization, individual workers each produced whole automobiles, which took a lot of time. Having workers specialize increased the volume and the quality in many cases of the cars. Henry Ford also wanted to pay his workers well. High salaries allowed workers to purchase the products that they were producing, thus increasing sales and increasing exposure of the automobiles. Ford's assembly line method was later adopted around the world to produce many products, because it decreased costs and increased productivity.

62. A

The sea empire theme used settlements along the coast as the primary means for establishing dominance in an area. These settlements were the bases for exploration of the interior of the frontier, which contained the wealth that was to be brought back to the home country. The Portuguese were the first people to use the sea empire theme, and this theme is still evident in the biggest colony that Portugal owned: Brazil. Here, large coastal cities are established with little settlement of the interior of the country. In the sea empire theme, the frontier was simply the location of resources. The resources needed to be protected, but the main base was located on the coast. São Paulo and Rio de Janeiro, two of the largest cities in the world, are located along the coast. The capital of Brazil, Brasilia, was

built in the interior of the country to try to ease some of the congestion of the coastal areas.

63. A

With approximately 2.1 billion followers, Christianity is the largest religion on Earth. The second largest religion is Islam. Islam is the fastest growing faith, but Christianity is still the most prevalent religion.

64. A

Suburbs are extensions of urban areas. Suburbs are residential communities where people live and often work. Many of these suburbs increase their tax base by including commercial and industrial activities within their borders. In some cases, suburbs encroach on the total population of the primary urban area they surround. Suburbs usually have well-developed transportation systems, because they have the space for wide roads, although they usually lack mass transit systems as compared to urban areas. Many suburbs may have outgrown their transportation systems and have traffic congestion as a result. Planned communities are newer communities where developers can break ground. Planned communities often include ponds, walking paths, and other amenities to draw more residents. Golf courses and swimming pools may also be provided to attract residents.

65. B

Arithmetic density involves dividing a country's total population by its total land area to determine the population density per square mile or kilometer. The problem with arithmetic density is that it is not a true measure of the population density of the area. Many areas are not used by humans because they are too hilly or the climate does not allow vegetation or agricultural productivity on the land. Physiologic density measures the land that people use (agriculturally productive land) and divides it into the total population to determine a country's population density more accurately. Many countries, such as Canada, have vast expanses of land that are not used by humans for any purpose, so only the range lands or natural resource production lands are included in the physiologic density.

66. E

Because the South means many different things to many different people, it is an example of a vernacular or perceptual region. Definitions of "the South" vary according to many different criteria. Climate, language dialects, and education levels can be used to determine the South.

67. D

The multiple nuclei model of urbanization relies least upon the central business district for its success. The multiple nuclei model suggests that the growth of the urban area is independent of the central business district and occurs where development is needed. Universities have development around them in the form of fast-food restaurants and bookstores. Airports have hotels and restaurants surrounding them to meet the needs of travelers. This model creates edge cities in which growth projects outside of the concentric ring model of development. Some cities extend their growth faster and farther in one direction than in other directions because of the multiple nuclei model.

68. B

Québec chose in the mid-1990s to remain with the state of Canada by a vote of 51 percent to 49 percent. The separation movement was focused on language. The French Canadians have always felt isolated from the rest of Canada, especially during times of British control. Cities such as Montréal and Québec are the hotbeds of separatist movements. Many separatist movements are based on the definition of nationalities by two primary characteristics, language and religion. In the case of the French-Canadian movement, separatism was spurred primarily by language.

69. C

Saudi Arabia possesses more than 25 percent of the oil reserves in the world. The world's increasing dependence on petroleum has fueled a surge in wealth for countries like Saudi Arabia.

70. B

China's one-child policy has dramatically decreased the birth rate, doubling time, and natural increase rate in China. Therefore, the correct answer is (B), decreasing birth rates.

71. B

Ethnocentrism is the belief that one group is superior to another group. Many wars have started due to this belief. The Hutu and Tutsi conflict is an example of an ethnic conflict based on ethnocentrism. Discrimination, which is the act of separation, is usually the result of ethnocentrism. Ethnocentrism is the opposite of acceptance of diversity.

72. C

Kaliningrad is a small area still belonging to the Russian state but which is located along the Baltic Sea. An exclave is an area of land belonging to a country yet not physically bordering the country. The exclave cannot be an island, so Hawaii is not an exclave. Singapore is a city-state and does not possess other land outside of its city borders. South Africa has an enclave within it, Lesotho, but the country is a perforated country and not an exclave. Italy also is an example of a perforated country, with San Marino and the Vatican City located within its borders, but the country itself is not an exclave.

73. A

Rostow's model of development begins with the traditional society and ends with the age of mass consumption. Rostow's model of economic development tries to explain the phases that a country goes through before it becomes modernized. In a traditional society, the majority of the country is involved in primary economic activities, such as farming and logging. As a country improves its economic status, the percentage of people in the secondary sectors, manufacturing and production, begins to increase. The tertiary, quaternary, and quinary sectors of an economy are the next to follow, bringing countries into the stage of mass consumption. During this last stage, the majority of people have moved out of heavy industrialized employment into the selling of products.

74. D

Rice is the most nutrient-dense grain; however it needs flat land, plenty of water, and a long growing season to thrive. Intensive subsistence farmers will plant rice if possible and often they are able to double-crop (get two harvests per year). As a result, intensive rice growing regions such as southern China, Southeast Asia, and parts of India can support dense and large populations.

75. B

The primary reason why pork is not eaten in the Islamic diet is for religious reasons. Hogs are seen as unclean animals and, therefore, must be avoided. Any type of food with pork in it is to be avoided by Muslims around the world.

SECTION II: SAMPLE FREE-RESPONSE ESSAYS AND RUBRICS

QUESTION 1

PART A

Wallerstein's world systems analysis divides the world into three primary categories: the core, semi-periphery, and periphery. Each of these three regions is defined based on its economic activities. The core has a more tertiary- or quaternary-based economy. The semi-periphery involves more secondary activities, such as manufacturing. The periphery country/region involves more primary activities, such as farming and mining. These types of activities involve using resources directly from the Earth.

In the world systems theory, the periphery depends on the core to fund employment. The core depends on the periphery for natural resources, which are then sent back to the core. In many cases, the manufacturing of goods and services is done in the semi-periphery due to its low-cost labor. This, in turn, produces low-cost products, which are cheaper for consumers, and provides much-needed employment in the periphery countries.

PART B

Usually, periphery countries have high growth rates. Much of the population in periphery countries is involved in agricultural production, possibly in the form of plantation agriculture or subsistence agriculture. Most agricultural societies have many children, because children are seen as economic assets. They are added help on the farm, as well as a form of social security when the parents age. This is stage 2 in the demographic transition model.

Many semi-periphery countries are in stage 3 of the demographic transition model. Women are more involved in the workforce, meaning that fewer children are being born. The economy is shifting from agricultural to manufacturing. The end result is fewer children being born and a continued decrease in the crude death rate and the crude birth rate.

Many core countries are in the waning stages of stage 3 or have already entered stage 4 of the demographic transition model. In these economies, the majority of the people are involved in the tertiary sectors of the economy, and many have moved into the quaternary sectors of the economy. Zero population growth occurs in stage 4, and many of the core countries in Europe are actually losing population, because their crude death rates have surpassed their crude birth rates.

PART C

The employment sectors of the economy for the periphery are based on its primary sectors. Many of the people work for themselves at subsistence farming. Some of the farming may even be intensive subsistence farming. Others will be involved in the direct extraction of raw materials from the Earth. Much of the employment is provided by companies located in the core countries.

In the semi-periphery, many people are employed in the manufacturing sector of the economy. These companies have outsourced their business away from the core countries into these semi-periphery countries to take advantage of relatively inexpensive labor and thus higher profits.

In the core countries, more people are employed in the tertiary sectors of the economy. People are selling items instead of producing them. Many are involved in the quinary sector, which is the management sector of an economy. Others are involved in the quaternary sector of the economy, which involves providing service of higher-order goods, such as the Internet and wireless services.

RUBRIC FOR QUESTION 1

Total point value for question 1 = 6

Part A—Two points possible:

- One point for a definition of world systems theory—the core, semi-periphery, and periphery

- One point for the discussion of the world systems theory using any of the following terms or phrases:

    — Core employs higher-end economic services, whereas periphery involves more agriculture.

    — Semi-periphery is the manufacturing center.

    — Core, semi-periphery, and periphery are all dependent upon each other.

Part B—Two points possible:

- Two points for using two of the following phrases or ideas:

    — Stage 2 countries are the primary agricultural regions.

    — Stage 3 countries are the industrial or manufacturing regions.

    — Stage 4 countries are the tertiary or quaternary economies.

    — Birth rates are high in primary countries.

    — Zero population growth in stage 4 countries.

    — Stage 3 countries are more involved in manufacturing, which means fewer births occur.

Part C—Two points possible:

- Two points for using two of the following phrases or ideas:

    — Primary sectors of the world systems theory are involved in agriculture or mining.

    — Semi-periphery countries are involved more in the manufacturing end of the economy.

    — Core countries are involved more in the service-based economy.

QUESTION 2

PART A

Regionalism can be defined as the individual characteristics or criteria of a place or region that make that area unique. Globalism is the homogeneity of a population or populations in many areas using any characteristics or cultural criteria.

PART B

An example of regionalism is Tex-Mex music. This style of music is very common along the U.S.-Mexico border. Singers sing in both Spanish and English in many of the songs. Spanglish is spoken in many areas. Although this style of music has diffused to other areas of the country, the primary region for Tex-Mex music remains along the Texas–Mexico border.

An example of globalization is *Pop Idol*. This show aired in the United Kingdom as a means for ordinary people to show their singing ability. This phenomenon diffused to North America. The result was *American Idol*, one of the most popular television shows of all time in the United States in terms of number of viewers. Today, many other countries around the world have used this idea and created their own programs.

PART C

Regionalism and globalism are constantly pushing against each other. Regionalism includes the characteristics that define the distinctiveness of a region, such as music, food, or language. These features are constantly in battle with globalism, which is the homogeneity of a population. In the United States, when everybody watches the same television shows, regional dialects start to fade away.

Many locations around the world market their distinctiveness through tourism. Tourism separates places based on their unique characteristics. However, many of the less developed countries want to be like the European countries and the United States, with people taking on cultural characteristics, such as clothing fads and language, thus making them global.

RUBRIC FOR QUESTION 2

Total point value for question 2 = 6

Part A—Two points possible:

- One point for defining regionalism as the individual characteristics of a place that make it unique using any criteria.

- One point for defining globalism as the characteristics of popular culture that make a place homogeneous with other places around it.

Part B—Two points possible:

- One example of regionalism—point could come from any of the following answers:
    - Regional food (grits in the South)
    - Regional dance (Irish dancing)
    - Regional languages (Welsh)
    - Regional religions (Shintoism)
    - Regional music (Tex-Mex music)
    - Regional architecture (log cabins)

- One example of globalism—point for any of the following answers:
    - Popular culture of food (McDonald's, KFC, Pizza Hut)
    - Popular culture of music (American music, European music)
    - Popular culture of language (lingua francas)
    - Popular culture of architecture (skyscrapers)
    - Popular culture of religions (Christianity/Islam/Buddhism in remote locations)

Part C—Two points possible:

- Discussion of the conflict between regionalism and globalism based on any of the following answers:
    - Tourism usually enforces regionalism.
    - Popular culture enforces globalization.
    - Regionalism maintains folk culture.
    - Globalism is the homogeneity of populations across regions.

QUESTION 3

PART A

The population decrease in more developed countries can be explained by the growing expense of having children. As a society becomes more modernized and developed, children are seen more as an economic liability than an economic asset. Women are more involved in the workforce, which means that they have less time to start families. Women are more career oriented.

PART B

The population increase in less developed countries can be explained by the economic situation in many of these countries. The total fertility rate in many of the less developed countries may be as high as six or even greater. Having a lot of children is logical, because children are seen as an economic asset. Also, in many of these countries, the culture gives a male greater status or standing in the society if he has more children. Children are also seen as sources of social security. Governments are not strong enough to ensure the economic well-being of the elderly, so people must provide for themselves. The result is many children.

PART C

The demographic trends mean that in more developed countries the population is getting older and there are fewer children in the society as a whole. The socioeconomic impact of the population trends in these countries is the prevalence of guest or migrant workers in Europe and the United States. The population is decreasing, leaving many jobs unfilled. Many of these jobs are the labor-intensive jobs that people in more developed countries refuse to do. In many cases, these labor-intensive jobs are in the construction, agriculture, and manufacturing sectors. These jobs are taken by immigrant workers looking for employment opportunities.

In less developed countries, a high dependency ratio places an even greater strain on already-limited resources. The number of children who are not of age to work is so high that many families are forced to sell children into slavery or other forms of forced labor. The child labor laws in many less developed countries are almost non-existent, meaning that these children can be exploited for their cheap labor. Also, the society will experience an increase in unemployment and all the problems of an overpopulated, undereducated society.

RUBRIC FOR QUESTION 3

Total point value for question 3 = 6

Part A—Two points possible:

- One point for any of the following explanations of population decrease in more developed countries for a maximum of two points:

  — Children are an economic liability.

  — A more service-based economy means less time for children.

  — Career-oriented women do not have time for families or delay childbirth.

Part B—Two points possible:

- One point for any of the following explanations of population increase in less developed countries for a maximum of two points:

  — Children are an economic asset in a farming-based society.

  — Children provide some social security for the elderly.

  — Children are integral for the economic success of the country.

  — Culture dictates having more children in many cases.

  — Lack of family planning measures means more births.

Part C—Two points possible:

- One point for the demographic and socioeconomic differences in more developed countries:

  — Having fewer children means society must have more guest workers.

  — The society gets older.

  — The society must place more emphasis on health care and less on youth activities, such as education (schools).

- One point for the demographic and socioeconomic differences in less developed countries:

  — Having more children means a greater dependency ratio.

  — Having more children means leaving a greater legacy in many cultures.

  — Having more children means placing a greater strain on the economic resources of the state.

  — Having more children means an increase in child labor in many countries.

GLOSSARY

INTRODUCTION TO GEOGRAPHY AND MAPS

Absolute location

Location based on latitude and longitude coordinates.

Aristotle and Plato

Greek philosophers who believed that the Earth was round.

Cartograms

Maps that assign space by the size of some datum. For example, world population by country is often illustrated in a cartogram, with countries with larger populations appearing larger on the map.

Cartographers

Map makers; they are very concerned with the problem of distortion.

Concentration

The density of particular phenomena over an area; in terms of concentration, objects can either be clustered or agglomerated.

Conformal maps

Maps that distort area but keep shapes intact.

Conic projection maps

Maps that put a cone over the Earth and keep distance intact but lose directional qualities.

Cultural landscape

Cultural attributes of an area often used to describe a place (e.g., buildings, theaters, places of worship).

Cylindrical maps

Maps that show true direction but lose distance (e.g., a Mercator map).

Dark Ages

A time when academic thought was not advancing in Europe but was very active across the rest of the world.

Density

Describes how often an object occurs within a given area or space; most often used in terms of population density.

Diffusion

Describes the spread or movement of a principle or idea.

Distribution

This term comes from the idea that everything on the Earth's surface must have a physical location. There are three different aspects of distribution: density, concentration, and pattern.

Environmental determinism

An important development in the field of geography in the early 20th century that stated that human behaviors are a direct result of their environment. This philosophy gave some people the justification to believe that Europeans were smarter than other peoples, because they live in a more temperate climate.

Equal-area projection maps

Maps that try to distribute distortion equally throughout the map; these maps distort shapes.

Expansion diffusion

The term used to describe the spread of a characteristic from a central node through various means. There are three different types of expansion diffusion: hierarchical, contagious, and stimulus diffusions.

Flow-line maps

Maps that are good for determining movement, such as migration trends.

Formal regions

Regions where anything and everything inside has the same characteristic or phenomena.

Functional regions

Regions that can be defined around a certain point or node; functional regions are most intense around the center but lose their characteristics as the distance from the focal point increases.

Geographic information systems (GIS)

A way for geographers to obtain new information, GIS layers geographic information into a new map, showing specific types of geographic data. Watershed, population density, highways, and agricultural data are geographic features that can be used as layers of data.

Geographical positioning systems (GPS)

A way for geographers to obtain new information, GPS technology is found in cars and cellphones; it uses the Earth's latitude and longitude coordinates to determine an exact location.

Geography

The description of the Earth's surface and the people and processes that shape those landscapes.

Hierarchical diffusion

The notion that a phenomenon spreads as a result of the social elite, such as political leaders, entertainment leaders, or famous athletes, spreading societal ideas or trends.

Human geography

The study of human characteristics on the landscape, including population, agriculture, urbanization, and culture.

Latitudes (parallels)

Parallel lines that run east/west on the surface of the Earth; the highest degree of latitude is 90 degrees.

Longitudes (meridians)

Parallel lines that run north/south on the surface of the Earth.

Maps

The basic tools used by geographers to convey information. Maps generally are a representation of the Earth's surface, although they do come in many forms.

Mental map

A map that contains what a person believes to exist; most people have mental maps, and they prove to be a useful tool in communication.

Mercator, Gerardus

One of the first people to produce a world map that showed, with relative accuracy, the general outline of the continents. His map exaggerated the landforms around the polar regions, because all lines of latitude and longitude meet at right angles.

Middle Ages

A time after the fall of the Roman Empire and before the Enlightenment.

Migration diffusion

The term used to describe the physical spread of people moving from one place to another.

Oval projection maps

Maps that combine the cylindrical and conic projections (e.g., the Molleweide projection).

Pattern

Describing how objects are organized in a space, patterns can be anything from triangular to linear or even three-dimensional.

Planar maps

Maps that show true direction and examine the Earth from one point, usually from a pole or a polar direction (e.g., any azimuthal map).

Possiblist

An approach to geography favored by contemporary geographers that suggests that humans are not a product of their environment but possess skills necessary to change their environment to satisfy human needs. With this approach, people can determine their own outcomes without regard to location.

Ptolemy

Wrote the series *Guide to Geography*, which gave very detailed descriptions of cities and people during the Greek period when the Roman Empire took hold of the Mediterranean region.

Region

A concept used to link different places together based on any parameter the geographer chooses.

Relative location

A location that is based on, or refers to, another feature on the Earth's surface.

Scale

The relationship between the size of a map to the amount of the planet it represents; the dimension into which one is trying to cast the real world.

Spatial interaction (movement)

Concerned with how linked a place is to the outside world, this theme of geography deals mainly with area, because how well an area is connected to the world determines its importance.

Thematic map

Used to determine some type of geographic phenomenon, thematic maps can be represented in various ways: area class maps, area symbol maps, cartograms, choropleth maps, digital images, dot maps, flow-line maps, isoline maps, point symbol maps, and proportional symbol maps.

Vernacular region (perceptual region)

A region that exists primarily in the individual's perception or feelings (e.g., the concept of "the South" differs depending on where someone lives in the United States).

Zheng He

In the mid 1400s, this famous Chinese explorer wrote in his journal of a coast with tall trees and mountains expanding as far as the eye could see. It is suspected that he may have come across the coast of Alaska or even the West Coast of the United States. His most famous explorations include those around the Indian Ocean.

POPULATION AND MIGRATION

Arithmetic density

Determined by dividing the population of a country by the total land area.

Coyote

A nickname given to person who is hired to assist illegal immigrants into the United States, often at a cost that does not depend upon success of entry.

Crude birth rate

The number of births in a society per 1,000 people.

Crude death rate

The number of deaths in a society per 1,000 people.

Cyclic movement

The seasonal migration of livestock to areas where food is more available.

Demographic equation

Determines the population growth rate for the world by subtracting global deaths from global births.

Demography

The scientific study of population characteristics that analyzes population trends and predicts future occurrences based on current statistics.

Dependency ratio

Determined by comparing the sum of persons age 0–14 and over 65 to those age 15–64; children and the elderly depend on the population's workforce for support.

Distance decay

The lessening of a phenomenon as the distance from the hearth increases.

Dowry death

This is the term used to describe a situation in certain countries where the bride is killed because of her inability to pay the promised dowry.

Emigrants

People who leave a country or region.

Gravity model

The greater the sphere of influence a city has, the greater its impact ("gravity") on other cities around it. This model is usually tested by measuring travel, phone calls, and overall trade between two or more cities.

Immigrant

A person who emigrates to another country.

Industrial Revolution

Starting in the mid-1700s, many European countries developed new technologies, spurring a more mechanized system of farming and eventually moving them to a stage 3 industrial economy. This transformation brought about many changes, including mass migration to cities and mass production in factories.

Infant mortality rate

The number of babies that die each year before their first birthday.

Intercontinental migration

The movement of people across an ocean or continent.

Intervening obstacle

A physical or mental factor that forces individuals to halt and often abort their migration plans.

Intervening opportunity

Favorable economic opportunity or environmental amenity that causes migrants to stop and stay at a location along their journey.

J-curve

Developed by Ian Bremme, this curve maps a country based on its "openness" and "stability." The movements of countries on both of these scales are largely dependent on their economic progress.

Malthus, Thomas

A British economist who, in the late 1700s, concluded that the rate of population was growing faster than agricultural productivity.

Net migration

The number of immigrants minus the number of emigrants.

Overpopulation

The lack of necessary resources to meet the needs of a population in a defined area determined by carrying capacity.

Physiologic density

Similar to arithmetic density but considered more accurate, this is determined by dividing the population of a country only by the land that is usable by humans.

Place utility

Incentives such as tax breaks and increased recreational opportunities that communities offer to entice people to move there.

Quotas

Limits put on immigration by certain countries.

Refugees

People who are forced to leave their country and seek refuge elsewhere, often because of religious or political persecution that may include death.

Sustainability

The saving of resources for future generations to allow them to live at the same standard of living or higher than the population is living at today.

Total fertility rate

The number of babies that an average woman delivers during her childbearing years.

Transhumance

The movement of livestock to higher elevations during the summer to escape the heat in the valleys and to lower elevations during the winter to escape the severe cold of the mountains.

Zero population growth

Describes a population in which the crude birth rate equals the crude death rate.

AGRICULTURE

Agriculture

The raising of animals or the growing of crops on tended land to obtain food for primary consumption by a farmer's family or for sale off the farm.

Biotechnology

A precise science that involves altering the genetic strands of agricultural products to increase productivity, biotechnology is developed mainly in science laboratories and is then tested on farm fields around the world, where it has been, for the most part, extremely successful.

Commercial farming

The farming of products for sale off the farm, commercial farming is usually a big business in developed countries and requires the use of heavy machinery.

Continentality

Describes the fact that an area's proximity to a body of water affects its temperature (e.g., because oceans have a moderating influence on temperature, areas near oceans experience less extreme temperature variation).

Creative destruction

Removing what nature originally produced in a location to grow what is desired.

Crop rotation

The planting of different crops each year to replenish the soil's nutrients that were lost to the previous crop.

Double-cropping

The growing of two crops per year to double agricultural output.

Environmental modification

The introduction of manmade chemicals and practices that, at times, have drastic effects on native soil and vegetation.

Farm crisis

Occurs when farmers are too productive, causing a surplus of crops and, therefore, lowering prices and producing less revenue for the farmers.

Feedlots

Farms that specialize in cattle or hogs and may have thousands of head of livestock, feedlots can create large amounts of waste runoff, air pollution, and groundwater contamination.

First Agricultural Revolution

The slow change from nonagriculturally-based societies to more agriculturally-based ones through the gradual understanding of seeds, watering, and plant care.

Food chain

After harvesting, commercial grain is sent to the market area, usually in semitrailers, where it is sold to a manufacturer who makes a product with the grain, such as bread. The product is then sold to a wholesaler, who sells it to a grocery store, where individual customers can purchase it.

Grain farming

The mass planting and harvesting of grain crops, such as wheat, barley, and millet.

Intertillage

The manual clearing of rows in the field through the use of hoes, rakes, and other manual equipment.

Long lots

A system of farming where lots up to a half mile or more extend back from a river, which farmers use as their primary means of hauling their agricultural products to the market.

Mixed livestock with crop production

A type of farming where cows raised on a farm are fed with crops that are grown on the same farm.

Planned economy (government-controlled economy)

An economy in which the government dictates the quantity and type of agricultural products that farmers can produce.

Plantation agriculture

Often occurring in less developed countries, plantation agriculture involves the cultivation of one crop to be sold in more developed countries (e.g., coffee plantations in Costa Rica).

Primary economic activities

Subsistence farming based on little mechanization. This is currently performed by aboriginal tribes in Australia.

Quartiary economic industries

Activities that produce nothing one can physically touch but are important in society (e.g., selling Internet time or providing satellite technologies, such as cell phone usage).

Quinary sectors

Usually involving only about 10–15 percent of the workforce in an economy, these sectors employ the people who make decisions concerning the trade of commodities at the governmental and business executive levels.

Sauer, Carl

Professor of geography at the University of California—Berkeley who started the field of cultural ecology, and began the hearths of seed agriculture and vegetative planting, Carl Sauer was one of the most vehement critics of the philosophy of environmental determinism. Instead, he believed that humans had power over their environments and weren't simply a product of them.

Second Agricultural Revolution

Coinciding with the Industrial Revolution, the Second Agricultural Revolution used the increased technology from the Industrial Revolution as a means to increase farm productivity. This revolution started exponential population increase.

Secondary economic activities

Industrial activities in which factories take raw materials, such as natural resources, and produce some type of product for either trade or sale. Many people in the United States are still employed in secondary economic activities.

Seed agriculture

The taking of seeds from existing plants and planting them to produce new plants.

Shifting cultivation

The moving of farm fields after several years in search of more productive soil after depleting the nutrients in the original field.

Slash-and-burn agriculture

The process of burning the physical landscape for both added space and additional nutrients put in the soil.

Subsistence farmers

Producing the food that their families need to survive, subsistence farmers depend on the crops that they grow and the animal products they raise for their daily sustenance.

Suitcase farms

These farms, where no one resides permanently and migrant workers provide the majority of manual labor cheaply, go against the grain of traditional farming in the United States.

Tertiary economic industries

Service activities in which an increasing number of people are involved in selling goods rather than producing them.

Third Agricultural Revolution (Green Revolution)

This transformation began in the latter half of the 20th century and corresponded with exponential population growth around the world.

von Thunen, Johann Heinrich

Developed an agricultural land use model that suggested that certain crops were grown in direct relation to their distance to market.

INDUSTRY AND ECONOMIC DEVELOPMENT

Acid rain

Describes any form of precipitation with an unusually low pH value. The low pH value is the result of pollutants, such as sulfur dioxide and nitrogen oxide, which chemically alter water droplets. The burning of fossil fuels increases the occurrence of acid rain.

Agglomeration

The centralization of parts of an industry for the mutual benefit of the industry as a whole.

Air pollution

The presence of unnatural human products in the atmosphere as a result of human activities (e.g., the presence in the air of the by-products of burning fossil fuels).

Basic industries

The industries that are the focal point of the economy for a city.

Biomass

The use of agricultural products or natural vegetation to produce a fuel that automobiles or other engines can use.

Capitalism

An economic system that lets the competitive market determine the price of goods in a society and in which people have the freedom to choose their outcomes based on their ability to pay for a product.

Communism

An economic system in which the government has total control over the prices of goods in a society, ranging from the price of bread to utility prices.

Core-periphery model

Model suggesting the core areas are more developed while periphery areas are less developed and often times the periphery is at the economic beckoning of the core through resources.

Cumulative causation (positive feedback)

Continued growth that feeds on itself.

Debt-for-nature swap

The forgiveness of debts in exchange for setting aside land for conservation or preservation; this swap is of interest to many less developed countries that have tallied up large debts to more developed countries and feel pressure to repay them.

Deglomeration

Occurs when the market becomes saturated with a particular industry, creating too much competition and forcing some businesses to shut down.

Dependence theory

Suggests that more developed countries exploit less developed countries to remain at the top of international trade.

Development

The continued progress of a society in all areas, including demographics, economics, and social factors.

Ecotourism

Using the natural beauty of the land as a selling point to promote tourism, which then provides the necessary funds to preserve that ecological area and, often, sustain the associated human community.

Fixed costs

Costs that do not fluctuate depending on the quantity ordered.

Footloose industry

A company with no allegiance or ties to a country or a location that, therefore, can move its primary location.

Fordism

Describes an assembly line on which each employee is doing a specific task to speed up the overall process of production.

Foreign direct investment

The direct investment by a company in the economy of a foreign country characterized by a direct relationship between the investor and the product of the investment.

Fossil fuels

Nonrenewable resources, including coal, oil, and natural gas, created by the breakdown of carbon-based sediment and, over time and under pressure, formed into the resources that we use today.

Four Asian Tigers (Asian Dragons)

Includes South Korea, Hong Kong, Taiwan, and Singapore, each of which is currently experiencing rapid economic growth as a result of its industrial base and the exporting of items to areas like the United States and Europe.

Geothermal power

An alternative energy source that uses the heat from the Earth's interior to heat homes and businesses on the surface of the Earth.

Greenhouse effect

The gradual warming of the Earth's atmosphere due to pollutants (greenhouse gases), primarily from more developed countries, which keep the warmer air closer to the Earth's surface.

Gross domestic product (GDP)

Determined by summing the selling value or market price of all the goods and services that are produced in a particular country in a given year.

Gross domestic product per capita

Determined by dividing the total amount of goods and services produced in a country by the total population of the country.

Gross national product (GNP)

Determined by summing the value of the goods and services produced by a country's factors of production within a given time period (usually one year).

Human Development Index

Includes the characteristics such as life expectancy, literacy, education, and standard of living that affect all people's lives regardless of culture.

Hydroelectric power

The use of water to create electricity.

Industrial Revolution

Starting in the mid-1600s, the Industrial Revolution was an extension of the Enlightenment period in Europe. The opening of thought and a movement away from the Catholic Church prompted many changes in thought, art, and technology, ultimately leading to major changes in the technology and transportation systems within industry.

International division of labor

The specialization of labor so that production becomes individualized, thereby increasing the speed, efficiency, and quality of the overall work process.

Labor-intensive industries

Businesses that require relatively more human effort in the production process (e.g., agriculture).

Multiplier effect

The expansion of the economic base of a city as a result of increased demand sparking increased production, which in turn employs more people who then demand even more goods and services.

Neocolonialism

A situation wherein the less developed countries of the world are still economically dependent upon the more developed countries.

New international division of labor

The outsourcing of jobs from more developed countries to lesser developed countries to produce goods more cheaply.

Newly industrialized countries (NIC's)

Countries that exhibit rapid economic growth but have not reached the full level of a developed country by a variety of different measures.

Nonbasic industries

Industries that serve as secondary businesses, established after the city has already established its basic industry.

Nonrenewable resources

These resources take thousands of years to be produced and cannot replenish themselves.

Nuclear power

A controversial form of alternative energy, nuclear power needs the nonrenewable resources such as uranium or plutonium for its production and creates long-lasting, dangerous waste products. It is, however, the most powerful energy source known. The two types of nuclear power are fission nuclear power and fusion nuclear power.

Open pit mine

A mine in which the land is removed and the resources are extracted in the open air.

Production

The removal of a resource from the Earth in order to obtain energy.

Renewable resources

Resources that have the ability to replenish themselves in nature relatively quickly, thereby being infinitely available to consumers.

Reserves

The amount of a resource that is left in the ground yet to be used.

Resource crisis

The eventual depletion of the fossil fuels on which energy-dependant economies rely heavily.

Shaft mine

A mine in which tunnels are dug horizontally under the surface of the Earth and shafts are placed deep into the Earth.

Site

The internal characteristics of a place based on its physical features.

Situation

The relationship that a particular location has with the locations around it.

Socialism

An economic system in which the government controls the basic elements of an economy, such as food prices, transportation costs, and energy prices.

Solar energy

The use of the sun's heat to create electricity, solar energy is one of the best renewable resources available because of its accessibility and cleanliness.

Time-space compression

The increase in the efficiency in the delivery process by diminishing distance obstacles, perhaps via email, fax machines, etc.

Topocide

The killing off of landscape to build a new one, topocide uses land for economic purposes in the sense that the intention is to destroy the previously existing landscape.

Tragedy of the Commons

Garrett Hardin's term for the idea that humans will inevitably do what is best for themselves despite what is the best for the public good.

Transnational corporations

Large companies with offices or divisions in countries around the world.

Treaty ports

Ports that must remain open for international trade because of the signing of various treaties.

Variable costs

Costs that fluctuate based upon the volume of the order.

Wind energy

Using the movement of wind to generate power by spinning the blades of windmills in wind parks, which then spin turbines, which then produce electricity, wind energy is one of the most promising types of renewable energy.

POLITICAL GEOGRAPHY

Allocational boundary disputes

Disputes that usually involve conflicting claims to the natural resources of a region and the drilling or mining of it.

Buffer state

A country that lies between two states in conflict but which remains neutral.

City-state

A state that is comprised of a large urban area or city (e.g., Singapore).

Colonialism

The practice of establishing political dominance over another people for economic, political, and territorial gain.

Commonwealth

Territories that have established a mutual agreement for the benefit of both parties.

Coup d'etat

A group revolt against a country's current ruling power.

Demarcation

The process of showing the physical representation of a boundary on the landscape.

Definitional boundary disputes

Disputes that arise from the legal language of the treaty definition of the boundary itself; one of the countries involved will usually sue another country in the International Court of Justice (World Court).

Devolution

The release of power by the central or federal government to the different regions of the country.

Ethnocentrism

The idea that one's own culture is the point of reference for everything else.

Ethnographic or cultural boundaries

Boundaries that are outlined by cultural factors such as language, religion, or ethic groups.

Exclave

A territory belonging to a state but separated from that state by another state.

Forward capital

A capital city that is put in a particular location to show that the home country intends to use that land in the future, although it is not currently in use.

Geometric boundaries

Boundaries created with latitude and longitude features or with other straight lines.

Geopolitics

A concept of political geography that is concerned with the study of human systems, which strive to organize land spatially to fit the needs of humans.

Gerrymandering

The illegal redrawing of political boundaries for political gain by a political power.

Global commons

Areas that no country is allowed to own or claim as its territory.

Immigrant state

A state that is comprised primarily of immigrants.

Iron Curtain

The division of the Western European states, which employed the traditions of democracy and capitalism, from the Eastern European states, which employed the traditions of totalitarian leadership and communism.

Irredentism

The attempt by one country to infuse ideas of coups or separatist movements into another country.

Locational boundary disputes

Disputes that arise when the definition of the border is not questioned but the intention of the border is, as when the border has shifted (e.g., a river shifts its course, changing the landscape).

Manifest destiny

The belief that the U.S. government, with divine intervention, was destined to rule the land extending from the Atlantic Ocean to the Pacific Ocean.

Operational boundary disputes

Disputes that arise from two abutting or adjacent countries disagreeing about a major functionality of the border, as when the United States and Mexico disagree over the issue of illegal immigration into the United States.

Physical boundaries

Boundaries created with naturally occurring features.

Plural society

A society characterized by two or more ethnicities living in the same area but each keeping its own identity and characteristics.

Prorupted country

A country that has a protrusion extending out from its main base.

Raison d'etre

Translated from the French "the reason for being." Many people feel nationalistic, placing great importance on the creation and protection of their state, and are willing to die for their state's independence.

Suffrage

The power to vote on issues regarding a person's or people's welfare.

Superimposed boundary

A political boundary that ignores the existing cultural organization of the landscape, a superimposed boundary is usually placed by a higher authority, such as a superpower or a delegation of superpowers, to ease tension and satisfy the demands of the superpower alliances rather than the needs of the country in which the boundary is dividing the population.

Theocracy

A country where one particular religion is intertwined with the political structure.

CULTURAL GEOGRAPHY

Acculturation
The cultural change of a people upon direct contact with a different culture.

Allah
The Islamic deity.

Animism
The belief in luck as well as in spirits.

Assimilation
The dying out of the old culture as it becomes replaced with the culture where a person or group of people currently reside.

Atheists
People who do not believe in any god or godlike figure.

Bahai
A universalizing religion that is practiced in parts of Africa and Asia, Bahai is similar to Sikhism in the sense that both advocate the elimination of religious differences.

Bible
The holy book of Christianity, the Bible is broken up into the Old Testament, which is based on the lives of the Israelites and follows the lives of Moses, Abraham, David, and other leaders prophesizing about the coming of the Savior, and the New Testament, which describes the life of Jesus Christ and the foundations of the new faith.

Buddhism
A polytheistic Eastern religion that focuses on the elimination of desires from the human soul through meditation.

Built environment
Produced by the physical material culture, the built environment is the tangible human creation on the landscape.

Christianity
The world's largest practiced religion has three main branches: the Roman Catholic branch, the Protestant branch, and the Orthodox branch.

Confucianism
Based on the teachings of Confucius, who lived in China at about the same time as Siddhartha Gautama lived in India, this religion focuses on the relationships within the world and is associated with the philosophy of feng shui.

Contagious diffusion
The process of spreading a culture from one place to another through direct contact, similar to the way disease spreads.

Culture
The way of life of a particular people that defines them as a people.

Denominations
Branches of a religion that differ on specific practices or principles of the religion.

Dialect
A form of a language that is different in sound, speed, syntax, and vocabulary from the language itself.

Ethnic religion
A religion into which followers are born and little attempt is made to convert others.

Folk culture

The practice of a particular custom of a relatively small group of people that increases the group's uniqueness.

Fundamentalism

A movement based on the literal interpretation of the faith's holy book that strictly enforces behavior to comply with the religion's basic principles.

Hajj

The fifth pillar of Islam, the Hajj is the Muslim pilgrimage to Mecca, the holiest city in the Islamic religion.

Hinduism

A polytheistic religion, thought to be the oldest religion on Earth, with three primary deities—Brahma, Shiva, and Vishnu—and many lesser deities.

Isoglosses

The definitional boundaries of a dialect.

Jainism

A religion that is based on nonmaterialism but at its core is considered an atheist philosophy.

Judaism

One of the oldest religions in the world, Judaism is based on the writings in the Torah and Talmud, the two holy books of the Jewish religion, and is an ethnic and a monotheist religion. The Jewish bible is called a Tanakh.

Koran (Quran)

The Islamic holy book.

Language

The ability to communicate with others in mutual comprehension in oral and written form.

Material culture

Anything that can physically be seen on the landscape.

Missionaries

People who spread a universalizing religion to other regions of the world.

Mohammad

The primary prophet of the Islamic religion, Mohammad lived in the sixth century CE and is said to have received the inspiration for the creation of the Koran.

Monotheistic religions

Religions that worship only one god.

Mormonism (Church of Jesus Christ of Latter Day Saints)

A universalizing religion centered in Utah, Mormonism's sacred books include the Book of Mormon in addition to the Old and New Testaments of the Bible.

Nonmaterial culture

Anything on the landscape that comprises culture that cannot be physically touched (e.g., language and religion).

Pidgin language

A mixed language that results from cultures coming into contact.

Polytheistic religions

Religions whose followers worship multiple gods.

Popular culture

The culture that is not tied to a specific location but rather a general location based on its widespread diffusion.

Ramadan

The fourth pillar of Islam in which fasting occurs for a whole month.

Reincarnation

The belief that one has lived a previous life and will continue to live another life after physical death.

Relocation diffusion

The spreading of a custom when people move; language tends to be spread through relocation diffusion.

Secularists

People who want to separate religion from all other aspects of society, including government and other social institutions such as marriage.

Sikhism

This religion, founded by Guru Nanak, holds a belief in one god, rejects the caste system of India, and believes that all people are created equal.

Stimulus diffusion

The spread of a particular concept that is then used in another product.

Taoism (Daoism)

Like Confucianism, this philosophy is based on the release of personal desires, but emphasizes mysticism.

Theocracy

A state that is ruled by religious leaders, where the church plays an integral part in the administration of the country (e.g., Iran and Saudi Arabia).

Universalizing religion

A religion whose members actively try to convert others.

Zoroastrianism

The belief that Zarathustra is the father of the religion.

URBANIZATION

Bid rent theory

Suggests that because the closer to the central business district, the higher the value of the land, that only commercial enterprises can afford the land within the central business district.

Blockbusting

The practice by real estate agents of inducing the sale of homes in specific areas by insinuating that a different race is moving into the neighborhood.

Central business district (CBD)

The commercial center or downtown region of an urban area.

Centralization

The concentration of power in one authority, usually under the command of a mayor or some other official.

Cities

Areas with a high population density that can include tens of thousands of people.

Colonial cities

Ancient cities that saw trade as imperative to their success; many of these cities became trading posts or major ports for colonizing countries.

Commercial zoning

The system of regulating land use for business or retail structures.

Commercialization

The process of selling goods and services for profit.

Concentric zone model

Developed by Robert Park, Ernest Burgess, and Roderick McKenzie in the 1920s, this model suggests that the social structure extends outwards from the central business district, meaning that the lower classes live closer to the city center, while the upper classes live farther from the city center because they can afford the commute.

Counterurbanization

The process of moving away from urban areas, usually when people want to get away from traffic, crime, and pollution.

Decentralization

The distribution of authority from a central figure or point to other sectors in the city.

Entrepots

Cities that reexport goods that are brought into their borders, sending items to all areas of the globe. Being entrepots has brought tremendous wealth to areas such as Hong Kong and Singapore.

Ethnic neighborhoods

Neighborhoods that are dominated by one ethnic group through its commercial establishments, community artwork, or other representations of ethnicity on the landscape.

Gentrification

The process of wealthy people moving into inner-city neighborhoods.

Greenbelts

Rural areas that are set aside to prevent cities from extending too far outwards. Greenbelts also prevent cities that are near each other from merging together.

Grid street system

The street pattern in cities, created for ease and convenience, characterized by an east-west pattern and a north-south pattern that create a gridlike visual.

Hamlets

The smallest of urban settlements with a counted population.

Hinterland

The market area where a product, urban area, or commercial outlet has influence.

Industrial zoning

The system of land-use regulation for the production of materials.

Infrastructure

All of the buildings and roads that make up a city.

Invasion and succession

The continued expansion of the central business district and the continual push outward of the zones, causing the zones to rebuild their infrastructures so that areas that were once low-income residences are converted into apartments.

Megacities

Cities with over 10 million people located within their metropolitan area and which have a huge sphere of influence over their surrounding areas.

Metropolitan areas

Areas with over 50,000 people.

Multiplier effect

The principle that development spurs more development.

Office parks

Agglomerations of office buildings with facilities established for the phones, Internet, and transportation that allow the successful conduct of business, office parks allow businesses of similar structure and production to locate near each other and, therefore, experience the benefits of the area's infrastructure.

Peak land value intersection

The area with the greatest land value and commercial trade, usually located in the CBD.

Planned community

An area where developers can plot out each house in the development and build the community from scratch.

Postindustrial cities

Cities that specialize in the technology of a specific, more-specialized economic industry through a process of deindustrialization.

Racial steering

The showing of houses only in certain neighborhoods by real estate agents based on the race of the buyer.

Range

The maximum distance that people are willing to travel to purchase a product or partake in a service, often depending on the particular product.

Rank-size rule

The principle that relates cities' relative population sizes to their rank within a country.

Redlining

The refusal of banks or other lending institutions to give loans in perceived high-risk areas.

Residential zoning

The system of land-use regulation for housing.

Social structure

The hierarchical classes that are evident within a society, such as the lower, middle, and upper class, which represent the basic structure of an economy.

Suburbs

Areas surrounding cities, generally consisting of residential districts but also possibly including numerous commercial and even industrial activities within their borders.

Threshold

The minimum number of people needed to meet the needs of the industry.

Town

An urban entity with a defined boundary but which is smaller than a city in terms of population and area.

Underemployment

The hiring of too many employees when there is not enough work for all of them to do, or the employment of overqualified persons in positions that do not utilize their skills.

Unincorporated areas

Areas that were once considered urban areas, even though only two or three families live there today.

Urban growth rates

The speed at which individual cities increase their population.

Urban heat island effect

The heat that cities generate as a result of having many buildings and few tress or other vegetation.

Urban hydrology

How a city deals with getting clean water to its citizens, removing dirty water and cleaning it, and then putting it back into the world's rivers and oceans.

Urban sprawl

The expansion of a city and its suburbs across surrounding rural lands.

Urbanization

The process by which people live and are employed in a city.

Urbanized population

The people living in the world's cities; currently, more people than ever live in cities, partially because of the increased efficiency of agriculture.

Villages

Areas that are larger than hamlets and offer more services.

White flight

The movement of white, middle-class citizens away from the inner city to the suburbs, which are perceived to be safer and more family friendly.

Zone in transition

This area, located outside of the central business district, usually contains the slums.

Zoning

A system of land-use regulation whereby cities determine where each type of economic enterprise—residential, commercial, and industrial—can be located.

NOTES

NOTES

NOTES

NOTES

NOTES

NOTES